The values of international organizations

Manchester University Press

Melland Schill Studies in International Law
General editors Iain Scobbie and Jean D'Aspremont

Founded as a memorial to Edward Melland Schill, a promising scholar killed during the First World War, the Melland Schill Lectures (1961–74) were established by the University of Manchester following a bequest by Edward's sister, Olive B. Schill, to promote the understanding of international law and implicitly lessen the possibilities for future conflict. Dedicated to promoting women's employment rights and access to education, Olive's work is commemorated in both the Melland Schill series and the Women in International Law Network at the University of Manchester.

The Melland Schill lecture series featured a distinguished series of speakers on a range of controversial topics, including Quincy Wright on the role of international law in the elimination of war, Robert Jennings on the acquisition of territory, and Sir Ian Sinclair on the Vienna Convention on the Law of Treaties.

In the 1970s, Gillian White, the first woman appointed as a Professor of Law in mainland Britain, transformed the lectures into a monograph series, published by Manchester University Press. Many of the works previously published under the name 'Melland Schill monographs' have become standard references in the field, including: A.P.V. Rogers' *Law on the battlefield*, which is currently in its third edition, and Hilary Charlesworth and Christine Chinkin's *The boundaries of international law*, which offered the first book-length treatment of the application of feminist theories to international law.

Closely linked to the Melland Schill Studies in International Law series and carefully supervised by the editors, these volumes have been updated and reissued in paperback with new material.

Principles of direct and superior responsibility in international humanitarian law Ilias Bantekas

The treatment and taxation of foreign investment under international law Fiona Beveridge

War crimes and crimes against humanity in the Rome Statute of the International Criminal Court Christine Byron

The boundaries of international law Hilary Charlesworth and Christine Chinkin

The law of the sea Robin Churchill and Vaughan Lowe

International law and policy of sustainable development Duncan French

The changing rules on the use of force on international law Tarcisio Gazzini

Contemporary law of armed conflict Leslie Green

Child soldiers in international law Matthew Happold

Human rights in Europe J.G. Merrills and A.H. Robertson

The rights and duties of neutrals Stephen Neff

Law on the battlefield A.P.V. Rogers

Indigenous peoples and human rights Patrick Thornberry

Jurisprudence of international law Nicholas Tsagourias

The law of international organisations Nigel D White

The values of international organizations

James D. Fry, Bryane Michael
and Natasha Pushkarna

MANCHESTER UNIVERSITY PRESS

Copyright © James D. Fry, Bryane Michael and
Natasha Pushkarna 2021

The right of James D. Fry, Bryane Michael and
Natasha Pushkarna to be identified as the authors of this
work has been asserted by them in accordance with the
Copyright, Designs and Patents Act 1988.

Published by Manchester University Press
Oxford Road, Manchester M13 9PL

www.manchesteruniversitypress.co.uk

British Library Cataloguing-in-Publication Data
A catalogue record for this book is available from the
British Library

ISBN 978 1 5261 5241 1 hardback
ISBN 978 1 5261 8242 5 paperback

First published 2021
Paperback published 2024

The publisher has no responsibility for the persistence or
accuracy of URLs for any external or third-party internet
websites referred to in this book, and does not guarantee that
any content on such websites is, or will remain, accurate or
appropriate.

Typeset by
Servis Filmsetting Ltd, Stockport, Cheshire

Eppur si muove

Contents

List of figures	page ix
List of organizations studied	xii
Acknowledgments	xvii
List of abbreviations	xviii

1 The principles guiding international organizations	1
Introduction	1
The problem and solution: strengthening the basis for the literature	4
Distilling principles from major international organizations law textbooks	7
Accounting for international organizations	19
Findings of the book	29
The meaning of constitutional language	38
The road ahead	57
2 The empirics of international organizational principles	60
Introduction	60
Understanding international organizational principles statistically	62
Searching for meaning in structures and networks of principles	85
Conclusion	104
3 Patterns of authority in international organizations' constitutions	106
Introduction	106
How constitutions refer to authority	110
Authority, from controlling member states to quasi-independence	123
Autonomy through authority	136
Communication as law, membership or operational act?	144
Recommendations: substantive and banal	150
Conclusion	155

4 The jurisprudence of organizations' aspirational values	158
Introduction	158
Determining which principles an international organization represents	159
Equality as an illustration of principles versus values	174
Mixing the principle of peace with other constitutional principles	187
The connection between representativeness and autonomy	197
Conclusion	210
5 Towards a new jurisprudence of international organizations law	212
Introduction	212
The similarity of constitutions as law in the making?	213
Jurisprudence against constitutional similarity creating law	217
The laws of international organizations	225
6 Conclusion	229
Bibliography	232
Index	253

Figures

1.1	Organizations with the most frequent mentions of each principle	page 21
1.2	Number of international organizations studied and the major values associated with those organizations	26
1.3	No apparent groups of constitutions mention communication and/or efficiency more than others	30
1.4	The start of principles "clustering" for different groups of organizations	30
1.5	Cluster analysis shows that different organizations promulgate different principles	31
1.6	The seven kinds of international organization (according to their principles)	33
1.7	An example of different "tracks" of authority by organizational size	34
1.8	A network representation of principles across organizational constitutions	35
1.9	A pure representation of principles in international organizations' constitutions (obvious patterns)	37
1.10	A diagrammatic illustration of why we measure words in international organizations' constitutions	47
1.11	What do our measurements actually mean?	54
1.12	The great diversity of principles mentioned among the international organizations' constitutions	56
2.1	Discussions about staffing and cooperation dominate the internal organization structure	62
2.2	Correlations between values show that the principles of staff communication and efficiency dominate the international system	63
2.3	Which principles correlate with the most other principles?	65
2.4	The "transivity" in these correlations means we can find long-linked clusters of principles living together in groups of constitutions	66

2.5	Difference in mentions of each legal principle between types of international organization	68
2.6	Regional organizations tend to mention almost all principles more frequently than do their universalist peers	69
2.7	Limited competence organizations refer to most principles more often than do their general competence peers	70
2.8A–E	The frequency of citation of most principles does not differ across types of organizations	71
2.9	Difference in mentions of each legal principle between characteristics of international organizations	81
2.10	Difference in mentions of each legal principle for location of the international organization	82
2.11	No theory can explain why organizations' size, age and membership would influence constitutional principles	84
2.12	Joining tree by values	86
2.13	Top dozen members of each cluster of organizations	87
2.14	Profiles of principles corresponding to different international organization types	89
2.15	Understanding long-linked "eigencentralities" in international organizations' constitution principles	93
2.16	Mapping the long-linkedness of constitution principles	95
2.17	Principles change in importance depending on the time period	96
2.18A	Principles coming into their own over the past 100 years: turn of the century (pre-1900 to 1917)	98
2.18B	Principles coming into their own over the past 100 years: interwar years (1918 to 1945)	98
2.18C	Principles coming into their own over the past 100 years: post-war years (1946 to 1972)	99
2.18D	Principles coming into their own over the past 100 years: oil shock years (1973 to 1980)	99
2.18E	Principles coming into their own over the past 100 years: information age (1980 to 1999)	100
2.18F	Principles coming into their own over the past 100 years: the new millennium (2000 to 2020)	100
2.19A	Different kinds of international organizations clearly have different constitutions that prioritize and "link" different principles: universal international organizations	102
2.19B	Different kinds of international organizations clearly have different constitutions that prioritize and "link" different principles: regional international organizations	102

2.20	All principles lead back to international organizations' executive staff	103
3.1	Most international organizations' founding constitutions refer to authority about 550 times per million words	116
3.2A	Authority a middle value among international organizations' constitutions	117
3.2B	Statistical analysis of values	118
3.3A	Few apparent differences in emphasis on authority between international organizations	119
3.3B	Difference in mentions of authority by various kinds of international organizations	119
3.4	Mention of authority most closely correlates with efficiency and recommendation	120
3.5	Legal provisions governing principles in universal and regional financial international organizations	121
3.6	The nexus of authority, communication and recommendation in international organizations law	122

Organizations studied

Advisory Centre on World Trade Organization Law
Africa Rice Centre
African and Malagasy Council for Higher Education
African Civil Aviation Commission
African Court of Human and People's Rights
African Development Bank
African Development Bank Administrative Tribunal
African Export Import Bank
African Intellectual Property Organization
African Regional Intellectual Property Organization
African Telecommunications Union
African Union
African-Asian Rural Development Organization
Agency for the Prohibition of Nuclear Weapons in Latin America and the Caribbean
Andean Community
Arab Bank for Economic Development in Africa
Arab League
Asia Pacific Association of Agricultural Research Institutions
Asian African Legal Consultative Organization
Asian Development Bank
Asian Infrastructure Investment Bank
Asian-Pacific Postal Union
Asian Productivity Organization
Association of African Central Banks
Association of Agricultural Research Institutions in the Near East and North Africa
Association of Caribbean States
Association of European Public Postal Operators
Association of Ibero-American States for the Development of National Libraries

Association of Natural Rubber Producing Countries
Association of Postal and Telecommunications Operators of the Portuguese Speaking Countries and Territories
Association of Supervisors of Banks of the Americas
Association of the Southeast Asian Nations
Banco del Alba
Bank for International Settlements
Bank of the Central African States
Benelux Court of Justice
Benelux Economic Union
Benelux Office for Intellectual Property
Black Sea Trade and Development Bank
Bureau of International Expositions
Caribbean Community
Caribbean Community Implementation Agency for Crime and Security
Caribbean Development Bank
Caribbean Meteorological Organization
Caribbean Postal Union
Caribbean Telecommunications Union
Central American Bank for Economic Integration
Central American Court of Justice
Central Bank of West African States
Centre for Agriculture and Biosciences International
Comite Intergubernamental Coordinador de los Paise de la Cuenca del Plata
Commonwealth Secretariat
Council of Europe
Council of Europe Development Bank
Court of Justice of the Andean Community
Desert Locust Control Organization for Eastern Africa
Development Bank of Latin America
East African Community
East African Development Bank
Eastern and Southern African Trade and Development Bank
Economic Community of Central African States
Economic Community of West African States
Economic Cooperation Organization
Economic Cooperation Organization Trade and Development Bank
Eurasian Development Bank
Eurasian Economic Commission
Eurasian Patent Organization
European Agency for Safety and Health at Work
European and Mediterranean Plant Protection Organization

European Aviation Safety Agency
European Bank for Reconstruction and Development
European Central Bank
European Chemicals Agency
European Court of Human Rights
European Investment Bank
European Organisation for Astronomical Research in the Southern Hemisphere
European Organization for Nuclear Research
European Organization for the Safety of Air Navigation
European Patent Office
European Space Agency
European Union
Food and Agriculture Organization
Gambia River Basin Development Organization
General Council for Islamic Banks and Financial Institutions
Gulf Cooperation Council
Ibero-American Social Security Organization
Indian Ocean Rim Association
Inter-African Coffee Organization
Inter-African Conference on Insurance Markets
Inter-American Development Bank
Inter-American Tropical Tuna Commission
Intergovernmental Organisation for International Carriage by Rail
International Association of Supreme Administrative Jurisdictions
International Atomic Energy Agency
International Bank for Economic Cooperation
International Bank for Reconstruction and Development [also known as World Bank]
International Bureau of Weights and Measures
International Centre for Settlement of Investment Disputes
International Civil Aviation Organization
International Civil Defense Organization
International Cocoa Organization
International Coffee Organization
International Commission for the Protection of the Rhine
International Commission on Civil Status
International Committee of Military Medicine
International Cotton Advisory Committee
International Council for the Exploration of the Sea
International Criminal Court
International Criminal Police Organization

International Development Association
International Development Law Organization
International Finance Corporation
International Fund for Agricultural Development
International Fusion Energy Organization
International Grains Council
International Institute for the Unification of Private Law
International Institute of Refrigeration
International Investment Bank
International Labour Organization
International Maritime Organization
International Monetary Fund
International Olive Oil Council
International Organization for Migration
International Organization of Legal Metrology
International Organization of Space Communications
International Organization of Vine and Wine
International Regional Organization for Plant and Animal Health
International Rubber Study Group
International Seabed Authority
International Sericultural Commission
International Sugar Organization
International Telecommunication Union
International Tribunal for the Law of the Sea
International Tropical Timber Organization
International Union for Protection of New Varieties of Plants
International Whaling Commission
Inter-Parliamentary Union
Interstate Bank
Iran–United States Claims Tribunal
Islamic Development Bank
Islamic Educational Scientific and Cultural Organization
Latin American Centre for Physics
Latin American Energy Organization
Latin American Fisheries Development Organization
Latin American Integration Association
League of Arab States
Mano River Union
Multilateral Investment Guarantee Agency
New Development Bank
Nordic Council of Ministers
Nordic Investment Bank

North Atlantic Salmon Conservation Organization
North Atlantic Treaty Organization
North East Atlantic Fisheries Commission
North Pacific Anadromous Fish Commission
North Pacific Marine Science Organization
Northwest Atlantic Fisheries Organization
OPEC Fund for International Development
Organisation for Security and Co-operation in Europe Conciliation and Arbitration Court
Organization for Economic Cooperation and Development
Organization for Joint Armament Cooperation
Organization for the Harmonization of Business Law in Africa
Organization for the Prohibition of Chemical Weapons
Organization of American States
Organization of Eastern Caribbean States
Organization of Ibero-American States
Organization of the Islamic Conference
Organization of the Petroleum Exporting Countries
Pan African Postal Union
Parliamentary Union of the OIC Member States
Permanent Court of Arbitration
Port Management Association of Eastern and Southern Africa
Secretariat of the Pacific Community
South Asian Association for Regional Cooperation
South Centre
South East Atlantic Fisheries Organization
Southeast Asian Ministers of Education Organization
Southern African Customs Union
Southern African Development Community
United Nations
United Nations Educational, Scientific and Cultural Organization
United Nations Industrial Development Organization
Universal Postal Union
West African Development Bank
World Bank Administrative Tribunal
World Customs Organization
World Health Organization
World Intellectual Property Organization
World Meteorological Organization
World Organization for Animal Health
World Tourism Organization
World Trade Organization

Acknowledgments

This publication has been made possible by a generous grant from the Research Grants Council of the Hong Kong Special Administrative Region, China (Project No 1740221). All of the raw data at the heart of this book can be found at www.law.hku.hk/academic_staff/dr-james-d-fry.

Abbreviations

ASEAN	Association of the South East Asian Nations
CERN	European Organization for Nuclear Research
EU	European Union
ICC	International Criminal Court
ICJ	International Court of Justice
ILO	International Labour Organization
IMF	International Monetary Fund
OECD	Organisation for Economic Co-operation and Development
OIC	Organization of the Islamic Conference
UN	United Nations
UNESCO	United Nations Educational, Scientific and Cultural Organization
UNIDO	United Nations Industrial Development Organization
WHO	World Health Organization
WTO	World Trade Organization

1

The principles guiding international organizations

Introduction

International organizations play a vital role in our daily lives. As U.S. Supreme Court Justice Stephen Breyer notes, international law and standards – as made and enforced by international organizations – affect even the most domestic aspects of our lives.[1] However, media attention focuses heavily on international organizations and their organs like the International Criminal Court, the International Court of Justice and the UN Security Council during times like the Afghanistan, Iraq, Serbia and Syria conflicts, to name only a few.[2] The World Trade Organization (WTO) gets paraded out when politicians want to garner political capital by appealing to written and unwritten principles of reciprocity and fair dealing.[3] Some developing states may disagree so much with the values and principles of particular international organizations that they decide to splinter off, as happened with the World Olive Oil Trade Group splintering off from the International Olive Council.[4] Staff members of international organizations may even go on strike when an international organization diverges from its principles and values, as observed with the International Telecommunication Union in 1964.[5] These principles and values enter into

---

1 *See* Stephen Breyer, *The Court and the World: American Law and the New Global Realities* 196–99 (2015).
2 *See, e.g.*, Ian Hurd, *International Organizations: Politics, Law, Practice* 7 (2013).
3 *See, e.g.*, Montek Singh Ahluwalia, "The WTO: Is It All Over or Can Something Be Done?," *LiveMint*, Oct. 29, 2018, *at* www.livemint.com (last visited Mar. 25, 2020).
4 *See* Wendy Logano, "New World's Producers Set to Announce Trade Group to Rival International Olive Council," *Olive Oil Times*, 2016, *at* www.oilolivetimes.com (last visited Mar. 25, 2020).
5 *See, e.g.*, Henry G. Schermers & Niels M. Blokker, *International Institutional Law* 326 (5th rev. ed. 2011).

the vast array of international standards that the states of the world adopt.[6] Even though broad principles like peace are enshrined in the United Nations (UN) Charter, technical standards also reflect and help promulgate these deeper principles and values.[7] Indeed, measurement standards from the International Bureau of Weights and Measures affect even the most seemingly non-value-laden aspects of our daily lives.

The principles these organizations live by, advocate, promulgate and otherwise serve to promote affect our lives. Do the UN, European Union (EU), North Atlantic Treaty Organization or Economic Community of West African States, among others, have a "responsibility to protect"?[8] Must international judicial organizations act according to fundamental principles?[9] The international community clearly sees international organizations as being able to be held responsible for their actions, as evidenced by the 2011 Articles on the Responsibility of International Organizations (ARIO). Such rules would thus make them responsible for doing an act to someone for something.[10] What are these indefinable somethings?

These "somethings" represent these organizations' principles and values. The Organisation for Economic Co-operation and Development's (OECD) constitution provides an obvious example.[11] The nine recitals found at the beginning of the OECD's constitution present the principles guiding the Organisation. These include "the purposes of the United Nations" (which are discussed at length throughout this book), "individual liberty," "general

---

6 These standards either reflect existing principles (usually not universally shared) or help mold them. For a deeper discussion, *see* Carol Harlow, "Global Administrative Law: The Quest for Principles and Values," 17 *Eur. J. Int'l L.* 187 (2006).
7 *See* Charter of the United Nations art. 2(3), Jan. 26, 1945, 1 UNTS XVI [hereinafter UN Charter].
8 *See generally International Organizations and the Implementation of the Responsibility to Protect* (Daniel Silander & Don Wallace eds. 2015).
9 *See* C.F. Amerasinghe, *Principles of the Institutional Law of International Organizations* 227 (2d ed. 2005).
10 Almost all of the literature focuses on such responsibility in the context of wrongs, torts and other obligations incurred by these organizations. However, the principles impelling these organizations' policies, actions and discourse, as well as the results of these activities, necessarily promote certain principles and values. For a discussion about the link between responsibility (as a principle in itself) and the principles the international organizations uphold, *see generally* Moshe Hirsch, *The Responsibility of International Organizations Toward Third Parties: Some Basic Principles* (1995). The ARIO represent a framework that makes this relationship clearer. *See* Mirka Möldner, "Responsibility of International Organizations – Introducing the ILC's DARIO," 16 *Max Planck* YB UN L. 281 (2012).
11 *See* Convention on the Organisation for Economic Co-operation and Development, Dec. 14, 1960, 12 U.S.T. 1728, 888 UNTS 141.

well-being," "strengthening the tradition of co-operation," "peaceful and harmonious relations," "highest sustainable growth of their economies" and the "improvement of international economic relations."[12] These principles affect all of our daily lives. However, they do not come with an instruction manual or even a legal definition, which can be problematic.

Which items mentioned in the OECD's constitution represent actual, useable legal principles? While individual liberty represents a goal, such a statement itself represents an aspiration.[13] Cooperation represents a value (as something cherished or literally valued) as well as a guiding principle. The improvement of harmonious international economic relations probably represents a restatement of the broader principle and value of cooperation. However, neither the OECD's constitution itself nor any law underlying the constitution, such as the Vienna Convention on the Law of Treaties, defines these terms.[14] Other cooperative arrangements have promulgated similar values, from the Organisation of Islamic Cooperation to the Association of South-East Asian Nations (ASEAN) to the Central American Integration System.[15] Despite over a century of writing and interpreting of treaties, the international legal principles driving international organizations remain as hazy now as ever.[16] This book aims to remedy that situation with an empirical exploration of the constitutions that form our international organizations.

---

12 *Id.*, preamb. ¶ 2.
13 Despite judicial attempts to clarify these principles and the line between principles and values, such work remains as stunted as when it began in the 1890s. For further background on this more-than-century-long-effort, *see* Cherif Bassioni, "A Functional Approach to General Principles of International Law," 11 *Mich. J. Int'l L.* 768 (1990).
14 The Vienna Convention on the Law of Treaties, as the blackletter statement of customary law, provides the best venue for trying to tackle these issues. Unfortunately, the Convention remains as silent on the issue of international organizations' principles as on most important topics impacting on international law. *See generally* Vienna Convention on the Law of Treaties, May 23, 1969, 1155 UNTS 331, 8 ILM 679.
15 As the book shows, regional associations in particular reference many grandiose principles. However, they completely avoid defining them. *See* Carlos Iván Fuentes, "The Interpretative Principles of the Vienna Convention on the Law of Treaties and the Pact of San Jose in the Jurisprudence of Inter-American Court of Human Rights," Oct. 1, 2008, *available at* https://ssrn.com/abstract=1276479 (last visited Mar. 25, 2020) (providing a discussion in the Latin American context).
16 For a further discussion, *see* Lucas Lixinski, "Treaty Interpretation by the Inter-American Court of Human Rights: Expansionism at the Service of the Unity of International Law," 21 *Eur. J. of Int'l L.* 585 (2010).

The problem and solution: strengthening the basis for the literature

Do the agreements and rules governing international organizations like the UN even represent their own, distinct branch of law? Many researchers traditionally have argued that such law merely represents the norms and conventions of states that interact on the world stage.[17] Since the Second World War, authors like Rudolf Schlesinger have noted that the development of principles guiding these organizations has arisen concomitant with the development of the broader principles governing international law.[18] From the embodiment of intergovernmental relations to entities with limited self-autonomy in their own right, international organizations take actions and decisions which, over the years, have led many to argue that they represent founts of international law in their own right.[19] Such a confluence of actions and principles has led some authors to argue for a common law of international organizations that is developed from the ground up.[20]

International organizations law clearly comes from somewhere. Perhaps such law represents a haphazard group of practices and agreements – the coalescence of states' self-interested decisions as they seek to cooperate while preserving their own interests.[21] Perhaps such law comes from deeper

---

17 States have the power, by tradition and right, to create bodies with their own (though highly contested) legal personality. This book does not have the space to discuss such personality or the way that the evolution of international organization personhood has contributed to the development of the principles governing these entities. For a further discussion, *see* Amerasinghe, *supra* note 9, ch. 3; Marie-Clotilde Runavot, "The Intergovernmental Organization and the Institutionalization of International Relations: The Modelling of International Organization at Stake," *in Evolutions in the Law of International Organizations* 17 (Roberto Virzo & Ivan Ingravallo eds. 2015) (providing an explanation of the way that such traditions and rights have coalesced into institutions).
18 *See* Rudolf Schlesinger, "Research on the General Principles of Law Recognized by Civilized Nations," 51 *Am. J. Int'l L.* 734 (1957).
19 This chapter singles out White, who does not represent a lone voice in this area, but best illustrates the kind of primer used to teach new generations of lawyers about the institutional lawmaking of international law. *See* Nigel D. White, *The Law of International Organisations* ch. 6 (2005).
20 *See* Jan Klabbers, "On Seyersted and His Common Law of International Organizations," 5 *Int'l Org. L. Rev.* 381 (2008) (providing one of the clearest statements of such a position).
21 *See* Catherine Brölmann, *The Institutional Veil in Public International Law: International Organisations and The Law of Treaties* ch. 11 (2007) (providing a recent, challenging and invigorating perspective on such a common law, as the evolution of treaty agreements over the decades has turned into something more than the sum of their parts).

principles driving peoples of all nations towards a universal *jus gentium* or *jus cogens*.[22] Regardless of the position any particular scholar or international civil servant takes on these principles, steady patterns of principles and values do exist across international organizations.[23] Perhaps such law does not represent something as coherent as a system of global governance.[24] Nevertheless, the fact that so many researchers even accept the existence of the legal underpinnings of such global governance shows that international organizations law exists "out there in the real world."[25] Despite the decades of pontificating about the principles and values driving such international organizations, no one has taken the time or exerted the energy to carry out a careful census of these international organizations' rules. Indeed, none of these researchers can back up their observations with more than a few examples, hand-selected by the same authors, to illustrate their case.

Few authors have tried to use data and statistics to test whether the generalizations about international organizations law stand the test of falsification.[26] Many papers look at the way members' preferences of

---

22 Many have written on this subject. However, many tend to treat universal principles as distinct and separate from the way that treaties like the UN Charter have affected the evolution of these principles in international law. *See* Kamrul Hossain, "The Concept of *Jus Cogens* and the Obligation Under The U.N. Charter," 3 *St. Clara J. Int'l L.* 372 (2005) (providing an analysis of interplay between the development of these supposed universal principles and the way treaty law reifies them).

23 For Klabbers, the fact that a faculty member dedicated to the study of the law of international organizations suffices to show that such a law exists in its own right and not as part of another field. *See* Jan Klabbers, "The Paradox of International Institutional Law," 5 *Int'l Org. L. Rev.* 151 (2008). As the only means by which formal agreements may arise between nations, White sees international organizations as necessary to the rational planning of international relations and broader international law. *See* Nigel D. White, "Separate but Connected: Inter-Governmental Organizations and International Law," 5 *Int'l Org. L. Rev.* 175 (2008).

24 *See* Eyal Benvenisti, *The Law of Global Governance* (2014).

25 *See* Klabbers, *supra* note 23, at 151. Benvenisti does not represent a lone voice among researchers. Heupel and Theresa as well as Baber represent recent attempts to think through the principles driving the law, which, in turn, drives a possible global governance. If anything, he has called for more regulation of such governance. *See* Benvenisti, *supra* note 24, ch. 2; *The Rule of Law in Global Governance* (Monika Heupel & Theresa Reinold eds. 2016); Walter F. Baber & Robert V. Bartlett, "The Role of International Law in Global Governance," in *The Oxford Handbook of Climate Change and Society* 653 (John S. Dryzek et al. eds. 2011).

26 As a reminder, modern researchers do not try to prove the veracity of a theory or statement. Instead, this book tries to show how no one has yet falsified such a theory or statement. *See* Jonathon Hill, "Comparative Law, Law Reform and Legal Theory," 9 *Ox. J. Legal Stud.* 101 (1989) (providing superlative statement of this approach).

particular international organizations like the World Bank may affect these international organizations' activities, such as lending.[27] Others look at the way that membership in certain international organizations may correlate with certain aspects or outcomes of a state's governance.[28] Many studies seek correlations between the existence of international organizations, or their underlying treaties, and the topic the treaty seeks to regulate.[29] Few, if any, studies look at the texts forming these international organizations. What principles do the framers think they are embedding in these institutions? Do different international organizations hold different values and act according to different principles?[30] A quantitative understanding of these questions could lead to rethinking the way we want international organizations law to develop and how we want the organizations to function.[31]

This book compares the values supposedly pursued by international organizations (as espoused by leading textbooks on international organizations) and quantitative textual analysis from these international organizations' constitutions. In terms of methodology, the authors have distilled the major

---

27 *See* Daniel L. Nielson & Michael J. Tierney, "Delegation to International Organizations: Agency Theory and World Bank Environmental Reform," 57 *Int'l Org.* 241 (2003); Daniel Nielson & Michael Tierney, "Principals and Interests: Common Agency and Multilateral Development Bank Lending," Working Paper, Nov. 2006.
28 *See* Axel Dreher & Stefan Voigt, "Does Membership in International Organizations Increase Governments' Credibility?: Testing the Effects of Delegating Powers," 39 *J. Comp. Econ.* 326 (2011).
29 *See* Eric Neumayer, "Do International Human Rights Treaties Improve Respect for Human Rights?" 49 *J. Conflict Prev.* 925 (2005) (providing a focus on human rights). The US specializes in researchers looking at how international organizations spread democracy, or vice versa in the case of Mansfield and Pevehouse. *See* Jon Pevehouse, "Democracy from the Outside-In? International Organizations and Democratization," 56 *Int'l Org.* 515 (2002); Edward Mansfield & Jon Pevehouse, "Democratization and International Organizations," 60 *Int'l Org.* 137 (2006).
30 The study by Anderfuhren-Biget and co-authors of the actual values employees of these organizations follow obviously seems incomplete without data about the values these international organizations' constitutions encourage them to adopt. *See* Simon Anderfuhren-Biget et al., "The Values of Staff in International Organizations," *in Routledge Handbook of International Organization* ch. 20 (Bob Reinalda ed. 2013).
31 Probably the most obvious use of such data might lie in measuring the extent to which survey respondents think various international organizations actually uphold the values and principles in their constitutions. Such data would particularly help authors like Norris, who tries to measure the extent to which various populations opine that the UN upholds various values. *See* Pippa Norris, "Confidence in the United Nations: Cosmopolitan and Nationalistic Attitudes," *in The International System, Democracy and Values* 17 (Yilmaz Esmer & Thorleif Pettersson eds. 2009).

principles from the textbooks that supposedly guide or shape international organizations. These principles include aspiration, authority, autonomy, communication, cooperation, efficiency, equality, executive staff, staff, peace, recommendation and representativeness.[32] The authors have then calculated the frequency of these principles or values from international organizations' constitutions and compared their incidence across various types of organizations. While the basic primers, and even the latest literature, make assumptions about the way these values shape international organizations, this book provides a more balanced picture on account of its entirely inductive approach. It shows which international organizations stress cooperation – surprisingly, universal, comprehensive organizations more than regional ones.[33] It also shows the increasingly important role that values, like equality, play in the conceptualization of international organizations in the new millennium.

Distilling principles from major international organizations law textbooks

Finding major principles

What values and principles guide international organizations? This quest started with six important textbooks in the field. Henry Schermers and Niels Blokker's 1,273-page *magnum opus* represents, if not the final say on the subject, certainly one of the longest.[34] Their coverage of every aspect of an international organization's operations, from voting to finance and beyond, provides a thorough overview of the field.[35] Firmly based in the international law tradition, they base their narrative on the interaction

---

32 These principles are described in more detail below.
33 "Surprisingly" because some authors claim that regional international organizations focus more on cooperation instead of other values like inclusiveness or representativeness, on account of the greater ease in negotiating cooperation among a limited number of parties. These types of questions are discussed in greater detail below.
34 *See generally* Henry G. Schermers & Niels M. Blokker, *International Institutional Law* (5th rev. ed. 2011).
35 Other, smaller treatments try to use specific international organizations as concrete examples of various ways of theorizing about the broader environment of international relations in which these organizations make a contribution. Hurd's book, probably the undergraduate version of Schermers and Blokker's treatise, similarly dedicates specific chapters to specific organizations, while also describing the realist, liberal, constructivist and even Marxist ways of rationalizing these organizations into existence. *See* Ian Hurd, *International Organizations: Politics, Law, Practice* (3d ed. 2017).

between these organizations and the evolution of international law.[36] Weighing in at a far more reasonable 388 pages, Jan Klabbers' textbook covers the essentials by discussing the cases that form many of the principles commonly accepted, as well as some of the politics locking in the way we think about international organizations law.[37] The book takes a strong tack against the functionalist approach used to analyze international organizations.[38] Probably the most functionalist of all the textbooks, Philippe Sands and Pierre Klein's reads more like a taxonomy and less like an argument for the way international organizations positively or normatively develop.[39] Providing an overview of the major organizations (centered on the UN) and a discussion by region, their book rejects much of the analogy drawing and attempts to reduce these organizations to common themes and principles.[40] Nigel White's far more structuralist textbook, at least the first portion, looks at the role and nature of these organizations in society.[41] Arguing against the positivist framework hemming in most authors, he admirably looks at realist, liberalist, functionalist, constructivist and even critical theories of these organizations.[42] Nevertheless, even in critiquing positivism as an explanation for how the world is, rather than

36 *See generally* José E. Alvarez, *International Organizations as Law-Makers* (2006).
37 *See* Jan Klabbers, *An Introduction to International Organizations Law* (3d ed. 2015).
38 Klabbers has long used and critiqued the functionalist roots of international organization theory. *See, e.g.*, Jan Klabbers, "The Emergence of Functionalism in International Institutional Law: Colonial Inspirations," 25 *Eur. J. Int'l L.* 645 (2014). Like Long and Ashworth, it is not possible to successfully argue for or against the functionalist roots of international organizations without more than cherry-picked examples from the organizations studied. *See* David Long & Lucian Ashworth, "Working for Peace: The Functional Approach, Functionalism and Beyond," *in New Perspectives on International Functionalism* 1 (Lucian Ashworth & David Long eds. 1999).
39 *See* Philippe Sands & Pierre Klein, *Bowett's Law of International Institutions* (6th ed. 2009).
40 The four institutional problems they identify for international institutions represent the exception to their refusal to force the literature into a set of common themes. These four problems relate to the law governing their activities, their legal personality, membership and finance.
41 *See generally* Nigel D. White, *The Law of International Organisations* (2d ed. 2016). White, like all the other authors reviewed in this section, fails to recognize and use the same tools to analyze international nongovernmental organizations as for their intergovernmental counterparts. The emergence of these entities necessarily points to a failure of international organizations to live up to the values their constitutions espouse. *See* Anna-Karin Lindblom, *Non-Governmental Organizations in International Law* (2005).
42 The diversity of analytic methods he uses suffers from an *embarras de richesses*. Without any empirical way to choose between these competing perspectives, there

how it should be, the author lacks a population census upon which to base his claims.[43]

Other textbook authors try to enumerate the principles and values driving international organizations' development. By tracing the way various treaties create international organizations, Chittharanjan Amerasinghe seeks to identify the legal principles driving their development.[44] For example, in his consideration of non-judicial organizations he describes their duties to consider, to cooperate, to comply and to assist as basic values underpinning their operational acts, if not their constitutive acts.[45] Similarly, each chapter attempts to derive the sources of law underpinning international organizations of various kinds.[46] Klabbers invites the reader, at the end of his opus, to rethink the law of international organizations.[47] However, without a systematic survey of these organizations, or the legal principles and values they support, at least on paper, such a reimagining seems premature. How can one reimagine the international organization landscape without an

---

is no way of determining which worldview best explains the organizations observed in the world. As Coicaud notes, such a lack of objective, quantifiable information extends far beyond the simple assessment of how well these organizations work. Such a lack colors our very understanding of these organizations and their function. *See* Jean-Marc Coicaud, "Evaluation, International Organizations, and Global Policy: An Introduction," 7 *Global Pol.* 420 (2016).

43 Indeed, as Kammerhofer notes, even a simple description of the major international organizations cannot ignore their aspirations and the normative aspects of their existence. *See* Jörg Kammerhofer, "International Legal Positivism," *in* The *Oxford Handbook of the Theory of International Law* 407 (Anne Orford & Florian Hoffmann eds. 2016).

44 *See* Amerasinghe, *supra* note 9.

45 *See id.*, ch. 6.

46 Tracing the sources of law and pinning values to each organization represent two very distinct activities. Indeed, as far back as 1995 Bennett looked for such principles, not only in intergovernmental organizations, but across the spectrum, nongovernmental, private, regional and so forth. Such a wide scope of analysis allowed for deeper thinking about the values and principles these organizations uphold and how they work together in a system (or not). *See, e.g.*, Alvin Le Roy Bennett, *International Organizations: Principles and Issues* (1995). Unfortunately, few authors since have tried to make their analyses as comprehensive.

47 Jan Klabbers, *Advanced Introduction to the Law of International Organizations* (2015) [hereinafter *Klabbers Advanced*]. Like most authors in the field, Klabbers uses historical narrative to explain whence the principles and values of various international organizations derive. Just like Bennett and Oliver, historical analysis blinkers his analysis, as the values these organizations adopt seem the inevitable consequence of history. A more dispassionate analysis, using data and quantitative indicators, could help to reduce the historical determinism that seems to color the textbooks in this field.

accurate map of these organizations' values and principles as they are at the present time?[48]

To find the values and principles targeted by each organization's constitution, the authors of this book identified six basic aspects of the international organizations which these textbooks analyzed.[49] First, the formal rules (including guidelines and laws) governing these international organizations were identified. All of the textbooks carefully referenced the laws bringing these organizations into existence, and their main elements.[50] Second, the reasoning or motivation for creating a rule, practice or organ was traced.[51] Third, with the advent of cross-border politics based on human rights considerations, any reasoning or motivation for creating rules based on these rights was identified separately.[52] Fourth, the parts of these textbooks

---

48 Emadi-Coffin takes the bold step of asking citizens to rethink their citizenship to traditional states. *See* Barbara Emadi-Coffin, *Rethinking International Organisation: Deregulation and Global Governance* (2002). Wessel, in turn, asks us to imagine world legislation. *See* Ramses A. Wessel, "Towards World Legislation? The Exercise of Public Authority by International Institutions," Paper Presented at the Conference World Legislation: Perspectives from International Law, Legal Theory and Political Philosophy, Vrije Universiteit Amsterdam, Nov. 12, 2010, *available at* www.utwente.nl/en/bms/pa/research/wessel/wesselconf6.pdf (last visited Mar. 25, 2020). If states' constitutions provide the values and principles by which state entities exercise power, then these international organizations' constitutions represent the next best thing – their overall sum as a kind of constitution for the world. However, without a census of these values (and constitutions), no one can definitively state what values and principles comprise the whole of the international organizational firmament.

49 The authors of this book charted all six elements with colored highlighters, with each element receiving its own special color.

50 As Dekker and Wessel point out, the normative basis for an organization extends far beyond these agreements – to cover a host of decisions and even non-binding rules. While not downplaying the significance of such a normative basis, this book focuses on founding constitutions in order to keep the project within reasonable bounds. For more on the way these other norms affect the values and principles guiding an international organization, *see* Ige F. Dekker & Ramses A. Wessel, "Governance by International Organizations: Rethinking the Normative Force of International Decisions," *Governance and International Legal Theory* 215 (Ige F. Dekker & Wouter G. Werner eds. 2004).

51 The authors of this book acknowledge the factors identified by authors like Barnett and Finnemore, who show how a multitude of reasons, especially unstated ones, can drive the creation of these kinds of rules. *See* Michael Barnett & Martha Finnemore, *Rules for the World: International Organizations in Global Politics* (2004). This book takes each textbook author at face value, using other textbook authors to round out the underlying reasons for many rules.

52 Concerning the drafting of these international organizations' rules, authors like Steiner and colleagues point out that, in light of modern concerns, textbook authors

describing the implementation of practices and the execution of procedures (and/or laws) – including customary/informal laws and interpretations of rules and/or practices by an internal or external judicial body – was marked.[53] Fifth, passages relating to the external and/or political influence upon decisions and actions taken by an international organization or its member states were marked. "Power, norms, preferences, and problems" represent such obvious influences.[54] The sixth and last topic marked in these textbooks related to the costs and benefits of these international organizations' activities.[55]

Within each of these elements, key words representing the major principles and values were identified and marked in the textbooks, as described below. To create the database needed to search for these terms, the major principles and values from these books were identified. From that list, the terms (and derivatives) representing those terms were identified. For example, the word "cooperation" and derivatives such as "cooperate,"

>may ascribe human rights motivations where none existed. *See* Henry J. Steiner et al., *International Human Rights in Context: Law, Politics, Morals* (2008). The authors of this book also considered that many textbook authors took uncritically stated concerns about human rights in these constitutions at face value. Indeed, Petersmann shows how the issue has gained importance only in recent years. *See* Ernst-Ulrich Petersmann, "Time for a United Nations 'Global Compact' for Integrating Human Rights into the Law of Worldwide Organizations: Lessons from European Integration," 13 *Eur. J. Int'l L.* 621 (2002).

53 What counts as implementation has bedeviled any discussion about international organizations since their inception. Do meetings count as activity? What about speeches? While the textbooks analyzed in this book seem to divide rules and activities cleanly, these activities in themselves make the rules far more often than rules make the activities. *See* Ian Johnstone, "Law-Making through the Operational Activities of International Organizations," 40 *Geo. Wash. Int'l L. Rev.* 87 (2009). Decisions and regulations about producing decisions and regulations represent a particular output of international organizations that have value, although they defy classification as either a rule or action. *See* Jochen von Bernstorff, "Procedures of Decision-Making and the Role of Law in International Organizations," *in* The *Exercise of Public Authority by International Institutions* 777 (Armin von Bogdandy et al. eds. 2010).
54 Such a succinct list conceals the power dynamics at play between developing and developed economies as well as between these groups themselves. For an overview of the issues, *see* John W. McArthur & Eric Werker, "Developing Countries and International Organizations," 11 *Rev. Int'l Org.* 155 (2016).
55 Again, the authors of this book simply code the arguments of others. Most scholars understand the problems in even identifying – much less quantifying – these costs and benefits. Indeed, commentators like Dai might argue that states join international organizations to obtain benefits (and bear costs), which cannot be estimated. *See generally* Xin-yuan Dai, *International Institutions and National Policies* (2007).

"cooperates" and so forth were searched through computer-assisted text analysis, with the frequency of these terms being noted. In order to ensure the usefulness of the term, the database of constitutions at the heart of this book was searched. This was to ensure that at least 20 percent of the constitutions – or 38 of the 191 included in the study – used the term. Naturally, concepts like sovereignty and equity underpin most of these constitutions, although not quantitatively enough to serve this book's purposes.[56] From this process, nine principles or values were gleaned from these textbooks: (1) aspiration; (2) authority; (3) communication; (4) cooperation; (5) efficiency; (6) equality; (7) peace; (8) recommendation; (9) representativeness.[57] The next subsection provides a brief explanation of all of these principles or values.

Explaining the major principles

Most international organizations' constitutions aspire to various goals. Such aspirations reflect a longer-term vision or goal that member states (and their citizens) may wish the international organization to bring about.[58] Such aspirations usually represent shared abstract concepts describing the mission of the organization; they may reflect final economic or social outcomes, such as gender equality, peace or even broader themes like enhanced

---

56 The authors of this book do not dispute the pivotal role of many values and principles not on this list – especially respect for state sovereignty, universal values held by the "community of civilized nations," and so forth. As the authors aim to quantitatively study values, the authors do not impose weights on values that they so richly deserve. This is left for future researchers. Instead, the authors prefer not to apply weights to the variables because they want the data to suggest which principles have more prominence. Moreover, they believe that imposing a given weight could be based only on current scholarly conclusions, which they argue in this book are fundamentally flawed.
57 Some databases do provide data on these international organizations. *See, e.g.*, Erik Gartzke & Christina Schneider, "Data Sets and Quantitative Research in the Study of Intergovernmental Organizations," *in The Routledge Handbook of International Organization* 41 (Bob Reinalda ed. 2013). However, none focuses on these international organizations' constitutions.
58 UN conventions and agreements often couch environmental goals and other goals in aspirational terms. For example, the Joint Convention on the Safety of Spent Fuel Management refers to radioactive waste management "now and in the future, in such a way that the needs and aspirations of the present generation are met without compromising the ability of future generations to meet their needs and aspirations (Art. 1)." Barbara Kwiatkowska et al., *International Organizations and the Law of the Sea: Documentary Yearbook* ¶ 298 (1997).

cooperation.[59] As demonstrated later in this book, peace represents a core aspiration of a substantial number of these international organizations.[60]

International organizations' constitutions provide for *de jure* autonomous authority. Most constitutions describe the authority required of an international organization in order to bring about the aspirations of its members.[61] However, *de facto* authority comes from a transfer of sovereignty, or at the bare minimum member states' consent to follow or otherwise implement these organizations' decisions.[62] While various researchers may debate whether international organizations have the necessary level of authority to achieve particular aspirations, like global environmental targets, none debates the necessity of transferring some basic amount of sovereignty in order to achieve collective goals.[63] This book does not represent the first attempt to measure such authority.[64] Regardless, measuring such authority may open up new avenues of research, like finding out if higher levels of authority actually engender more political contestation from member states and others.[65]

Promoting interstate communication, and even enhanced communication within the international organization, represents an obvious value

---

59 Some might dispute the "shared" aspect of these shared aspirations. Authors such as Anand argue that organizations like the UN do not reflect the aspirations of states such as India, which represented colonial outposts at the time of the UN's founding. *See generally* R. Anand, "The Formation of International Organizations and India: A Historical Study," 23 *Leiden J. Int'l Law* 5 (2010).

60 Many trace the rise of international organizations as a key form of interstate relations to the universal aspiration for world peace after the world wars. If the founders of the UN and the modern system of international organizations saw peace *primus inter pares* among core international values, later authors have derided the naïveté of using international bureaucracy as a vehicle for achieving world peace. For a history of these views, *see* David Mitrany, *A Working Peace System: An Argument for the Functional Development of International Organization* (1944).

61 *See* Dan Sarooshi, "Some Preliminary Remarks on the Conferral by States of Powers on International Organizations," Jean Monnet Working Paper 4/03 (2003).

62 Such authority may exhibit schizophrenic traits, as member states set agendas with sometimes incompatible aims. *See generally* Xu Yi-Chong & Patrick Weller, *The Working World of International Organizations: Authority, Capacity, Legitimacy* (2017).

63 Guzman represents one scholar who thinks states have delegated too little authority. *See* Andrew Guzman, "International Organizations and the Frankenstein Problem," 24 *Eur. J. Int'l L.* 999 (2013).

64 *See* Liesbet Hooghe et al., *Measuring International Authority: A Postfunctionalist Theory of Governance* (2017).

65 For development of this thesis, *see* Michael Zurn et al., "International Authority and its Politicization," 4 *Int'l Theory* 69 (2012).

for international organizations. Most researchers see issuing formal communications, like reports and assessments, as one of the core functions of most international organizations.[66] States could not organize international relations or the relevant structures or rules needed to carry out international relations, as well as monitoring and enforcement of those rules, without the broader communication that precludes the "random consequence of informal interaction."[67] The complexity inherent in most international organizations makes broad communication both a means and an end for most of them.[68]

All international organizations supposedly cherish cooperation. Most authors of the textbooks analyzed for this book use the EU as an example of an institution whose *raison d'être* revolves around cooperation between member states, and even with other groups like nongovernmental organizations, political parties, regions and other non-state actors. Klabbers describes the EU basically as an "intensive form of cooperation."[69] International organizations like the EU provide the fora, the bureaucratic structures and physical places where representatives of state actors may cooperate on the gambit of policies – from fishing policy to child welfare.[70] Cooperation on law enforcement represents the most obvious form of cooperation in the EU.[71] However, the creation of an entirely new supranational law, and a deep and profound law at that, developed cooperatively between the EU members represents one of the greatest modern fulfillments of the aspiration of cooperation enshrined in a constitution of this kind.[72]

---

66 All the textbooks that the authors of this book reviewed placed an emphasis on such communication. See Amerasinghe, *supra* note 9, at 59–60; White, *supra* note 19, at 97–98, 184, 192, 219, 223; Sands & Klein, *supra* note 39, at 23, 306, 320–28; Schermers & Blokker, *supra* note 5, at 881, 883, 909; Klabbers, *supra* note 37, at 111.
67 David Armstrong et al., *International Organisation in World Politics* 1 (3d ed. 2004).
68 Most commentators underestimate the complexities involved in bureaucracies dealing with other bureaucracies, as well as the value of information as a coordinating mechanism. See Jarle Trondal et al., *Unpacking International Organisations: The Dynamics of Compound Bureaucracies* (2010).
69 Klabbers, *supra* note 37, at 27.
70 See *id.*; White, *supra* note 19, at 52; Sands & Klein, *supra* note 39, at 171; Schermers & Blokker, *supra* note 5, at 1091, 1107.
71 Commentators tend to focus on law enforcement when analyzing cooperation in these kinds of treaties and texts because the texts themselves abundantly refer to "cooperation." Indeed, the spirit of many of the more modern agreements seems to stress cooperation for cooperation's own sake. See, e.g., Florian Geyer, *Security Versus Justice?: Police and Judicial Cooperation in the European Union* (2016).
72 Commentators argue that EU law represents a field in its own right. See Joanne Scott & David Trubek, "Mind the Gap: Law and New Approaches to Governance

Few international organizations could appear and continue to exist without deference to efficiency. Do international organizations use their budgets and other resources as efficiently as possible? Ancillary rules about the use of these budgets, reporting and accountability underlie this concern for efficiency.[73] The drive for international organization efficiency belies the deeper problem of monitoring or even defining effectiveness.[74] However, many accept that some international organizations operate more efficiently than others.[75] How can we measure the efficiency of international organizations if we do not even have a census of international organizations' constitutions requiring such efficiency?[76]

Like efficiency, equality represents a value to which many international organizations ascribe. Equality remains a core principle of international organizations, even if few give voting or other powers according to the one-country-one-vote principle.[77] Many international organizations, like the international financial organizations of the World Bank and International Monetary Fund (IMF), define such equality in terms of proportionate

---

in the European Union," 8 *Eur. L.J.* 1 (2002). If that is the case, then certainly the law of international organizations merits its own epistemologically separate classification.

73 The problems in even defining efficiency – much less effectiveness – in an international organization context make any assessment of such efficiency almost impossible. Few can estimate (or even know) the actual benefits and drawbacks of seemingly inefficient behavior. *See* Heidi Hardt, *Time to React: The Efficiency of International Organizations in Crisis Response* (2014).

74 More than a century after the launch of the first modern international organizations, scholars and practitioners still lack a means of defining such effectiveness (as the extent to which these organizations achieve their goals). For a recent attempt to tackle this question, *see* Vinicius Lindoso & Nina Hall, "Assessing the Effectiveness of Multilateral Organizations," Oxford University Blavatnik School of Government Working Paper BSG-WP-2016/013, Apr. 2016, *available at* www.bsg.ox.ac.uk/ (last visited Mar. 25, 2020); Jonas Tallberg et al., "The Performance of International Organizations: A Policy Output Approach," 23 *J. Eur. Pub. Pol'y* 1077 (2016).

75 *See* Tamar Gutner & Alexander Thompson, "The Politics of IO Performance: A Framework," 5 *Rev. Int'l Org.* 227 (2010).

76 The current approach consists of assuming that all international organizations strive for maximum efficiency – ignoring the politics and unseen plans of members and other stakeholders in these organizations. For an example of such a quantitative assessment, *see* Ranjit Lall, "Beyond Institutional Design: Explaining the Performance of International Organizations," 71 *Int'l Org.* 245 (2017).

77 Many trace the self-interested motives behind giving lip-service to such equality. Giving representation to small states and actors in international organizations gives them greater incentives to adopt policies they otherwise would not. *See*

contribution to the organization and proportionate representation of that state's population or economic output.[78] More nefariously, some researchers have argued that international organizations promote equality by reducing economic, social and cultural differences between states.[79] However, before one can analyze the prevalence or even desirability of propounding equality as a value of international organizations (both within and between them), it first is necessary to have sufficient data upon which to make an assessment.[80]

Many international organizations' constitutions refer to peace. However, whose peace remains unclear. The liberal peace of a plurality of states differs from the enforced peace of a hegemon, even a hegemon negotiated and controlled by its membership.[81] If peace represented an uncontested value, resistance to peace would make no sense.[82] References to peace in these

---

Kenneth Abbott & Duncan Snidal, "Why States Act through Formal International Organizations," 42 *J. Conflict Res.* 3 (1998).

[78] As such, these organizations have redefined equality, such that inequality reflects a broader proportional equality between members. Through such conversion, again, these organizations help to co-opt smaller members to adopt policies they would not otherwise adopt. *See* Stephen Zamora, "Voting in International Economic Organizations," 74 *Am. J. Int'l L.* 566 (1980).

[79] In an interesting parallel to the work of this book, Boli and Thomas use a census of nongovernmental organizations to look for similarities and differences in the way they work and their effects. *See* John Boli & George M. Thomas, "World Culture in the World Polity: A Century of International Non-Governmental Organization," 62 *Amer. Soc. Rev.* 171 (1997).

[80] Statistical analysis of voting in international organizations misses the point. If an international organization espouses equality, adopts proportionate voting and has a few states making the majority of the decisions, the question still remains as to whether the voting system itself helps the organization to achieve the values in its constitution. Without analyzing the constitutions themselves, authors like Payton see the positive results – rather than normative desired effects – of such voting. *See* Autumn Payton, "Building a Consensus (Rule) for International Organizations," Paper Prepared for the Annual Conference on The Political Economy of International Organization (2014), *available at* wp.peio.me (last visited Mar. 25, 2020). In this light, authors like Posner and Sykes completely miss the boat. *See* Eric A. Posner & Alan O. Sykes, "Voting Rules in International Organizations," 15 *Chicago J. Int'l L.* 195 (2014).

[81] The authors of this book cannot hope to review the studies of peace as a value in international organizations' constitutions in one paragraph. For a minimum conception of these differing concepts of peace, *see* Oliver P. Richmond, *Peace in International Relations* (2008).

[82] For an understanding of why many may oppose such supposed peace, *see* Roger Mac Ginty, *International Peacebuilding and Local Resistance: Hybrid Forms of Peace* (2011).

international organizations' constitutions need interpretation in context.[83] Does peace merely consist of the restraint "from the threat or use of force against the territorial integrity or political independence of any state"?[84] As few studies of any kind of international law look at quantitative aspects of referrals to peace, it is virtually impossible to know.[85]

The value of recommendation consists in an international organization's authority and legitimacy to make recommendations to member states, to other international organizations and even to itself. Any discussion about the value of such recommendations must include the role of soft law in the wider field of international organizations law.[86] Researchers and even constitution drafters themselves view the role of such recommendations as ranging from mere facilitator of formal contract between states to the contract itself.[87] Many researchers may consider such recommendations the purview of international technical standards bodies.[88] However, it is important to assess the pervasiveness of such recommendations

---

83 Underneath the contested nature of peace lies politics. At the very least, before analyzing the politics driving any conception of peace, one must understand the term in context in international organizations' constitutions. *See* Katharina Coleman, *International Organisations and Peace Enforcement: The Politics of International Legitimacy* (2007).
84 *See* UN Charter, art. 4(2).
85 For a discussion about the paucity of such analyses, *see* Ghassem Bohloulzadehl, "The Nature of Peace Agreement in International Law," 10 *J. Pol. & L.* 208 (2017). For an example of such a study, *see* Nicholas Sambanis, "Short-Term and Long-Term Effects of United Nations Peace Operations," 22 *World Bank Econ. Rev.* 9 (2008).
86 Couched in the technocratic language of technical norms and compliance, such soft law represents a core way that international organizations exercise influence. *See* Dinah Shelton, *Commitment and Compliance: The Role of Non-binding Norms in the International Legal System* (2003). As with the other principles discussed in this book, no one way serves as a guide to understanding the meaning of such recommendations in international organizations' constitutions. For several perspectives, *see* Ilhami Alkan Olsson, "Four Competing Approaches to International Soft Law," 58 *Scand. Stud. L.* 177 (2013).
87 In other words, soft law either helps hard law or serves as the law promulgated and used by international organizations. For the first approach, *see* Armin Schafer, "Resolving Deadlock: Why International Organizations Introduce Soft Law," 12 *Eur. L.J.* 194 (2006); Gregory Shaffer & Mark Pollack, "Hard vs. Soft Law: Alternatives, Complements, and Antagonists in International Governance," 94 *Minn. L. Rev.* 706 (2010). For the second viewpoint, *see* Fabián Augusto Cárdenas Castañeda, "A Call for Rethinking the Sources of International Law: Soft Law and the Other Side of the Coin," 13 *Mex. Ybk Int'l L.* 355 (2013).
88 While many scholars focus on technical standards for products and technological items, such standards also include the supposed "standards" by which governments regulate public security and financial systems. For a discussion of the wide ambit of

before it is possible to tie this principle to its supposed effects on state behavior.[89]

Representativeness is the final value distilled from the leading textbook authors' main principles for international organizations law. Perhaps few other values hold such importance for researchers and the member states of these international organizations than does representation.[90] The methods of representation in the international organization's constitution affect the organization's legitimacy, besides obviously its authority and ability to act in international relations.[91] Many states have representation in a wide range of international organizations. As such, many consider such multi-organizational representation – and the offer of such representation by these international organizations themselves – as a means of competing for power and resources.[92] If many authors have quantitatively analyzed such representation, few, if any, have analyzed the landscape of international organizations that refer to such representation in their constitutions, as this book does. With these principles in mind, the following section explains how this book defines and categorizes international organizations.

such supposedly merely technical standards, see Leonardo Borlini, "Soft Law, Soft Organizations e Regolamentazione 'Tecnica' di Problemi di Sicurezza Pubblica e Integrità Finanziaria," 27 *Rivista di Diritto Internazionale* 356 (2017).

89 Many researchers have tried to quantify and find causalities between international organizations pursuing their value of recommendation and its effects. If the assessment of UN Security Council resolutions reflects authority from the evaluative form of recommendation, the assessment of zinc deficiency represents the other extreme. See Bruno de Benoist et al., "Conclusions of the Joint WHO/UNICEF/IAEA/IZiNCG Interagency Meeting on Zinc Status Indicators," 28 *Food & Nutrition Bull.* S480 (2007); Marko Oberg, "The Legal Effects of Resolutions of the UN Security Council and General Assembly in the Jurisprudence of the ICJ," 16 *Eur. J. Int'l L.* 879 (2005).

90 Authors like Cogan stress the vital role that constitutions play in defining such representation, as well as the vital role that informal relations play in undermining these constitutions. See Jacob Katz Cogan, "Representation and Power in International Organization: The Operational Constitution and Its Critics," 103 *Am. J. Int'l L.* 209 (2009).

91 For a discussion about the role of such legitimacy, see Jonathan Symons, "The Legitimation of International Organisations: Examining the Identity of the Communities that Grant Legitimacy," 37 *Rev. Int'l Stud.* 2557 (2011). For a description of the way that representation molds the multilateralist project, see Robert Kissack, *Pursuing Effective Multilateralism: The European Union, International Organisations and the Politics of Decision Making* (2010).

92 For a brutally direct analysis, see Malte Brosig, "Overlap and Interplay Between International Organisations: Theories and Approaches," 8 *S. Af. J. Int'l Aff.* 147 (2011).

Accounting for international organizations

The who and how of international organizations

How many international organizations exist? Estimates vary from 170 to 700, depending on each author's own view of what constitutes an international organization.[93] The simplest and broadest legal definition of an international organization comes from the International Law Commission, which defines them as all intergovernmental organizations referred to in the Vienna Convention on the Law of Treaties.[94] Using this definition, the Union of International Associations lists 246 intergovernmental organizations worldwide.[95] More recent work by the International Law Commission has narrowed this definition by requiring at least a few states as members, the governance of international law and the existence of at least one organ with a will of its own.[96] Such a definition adds considerable flexibility to the membership arrangements of these entities, while at the same time limiting them to those entities with bona fide international legal personality.

Compiling the list of these organizations required time and effort, which involved first searching the official websites of these 246 entities for their constitutions and then contacting organizations by e-mail, mail and telephone to ask for their establishing agreement (treaty) as well as headquarters agreement, privileges and immunities agreements, rules of

---

93 Amerasinghe places the number somewhere between 500 and 700, while Klabbers cites estimates at around 170. See Amerasinghe, *supra* note 9, at 10 n 2; Klabbers, *supra* note 37, at 1.

94 Vienna Convention on the Law of Treaties art. 2(i), May 23, 1969, 1155 UNTS 331, 8 ILM 679.

95 *See* Union of International Associations, "Yearbook of International Organizations," *at* https://uia.org/yearbook (last visited Nov. 17, 2020).

96 Under this more comprehensive definition, an international organization "refers to an organization established by a treaty or other instrument governed by international law and possessing its own international legal personality .... International organizations may include as members, in addition to States, other entities." International Law Commission, "Report on the Work of its Fifty-Fifth session: The Responsibility of International Organisations," UN Doc. A/58/10, 2003, ¶ 53. *See also* Giorgio Gaja, "International Law Commission: First Report on the Responsibility of International Organizations of the Special Rapporteur," UN Doc. A/CN.4/532, 2003, ¶ 34 (defining international organization as "an organization which includes States among its members insofar it exercises in its own capacity certain governmental functions"); Schermers & Blokker, *supra* note 5, at 26 (defining international organizations as "forms of cooperation founded on an international agreement usually creating a new legal person having at least one organ with a will of its own, established under international law").

procedure and staff rules. Naturally, many organizations did not or could not provide these other documents, so this book has had to focus specifically on the establishing treaty, inasmuch as all of the organizations possess such a document. Collecting these required also collecting the amendments to the originals. Inactive and/or defunct international organizations were excluded, except when they had transferred their functions to a successor organization, in which case the successor organization was included. Non-English documents that arrived were read through Google Translate. After removing organizations governed by domestic law, lacking at least one organ with its own agency or lacking the ability to interact with civil society in the most basic of ways, the final number of international organizations included in this study came to 191.[97]

This book's statistical analysis of international organizations' constitutions shows which constitutions refer to which principles more frequently. Figure 1.1 shows the constitutions with the most references to each principle. For example, the Economic Community of West African States' constitution mentions authority most often as a proportion of other words in the document. The Arab League's constitution mentions autonomy more often than do others' constitutions. Some constitutions, like the UN Charter, mention both authority and peace more often than do others – with the UN Charter ranking fifth for authority and first for peace. The Arab League ranks in the top ten for autonomy and representativeness. The Intergovernmental Committee for the Coordination of Rio de la Plata Basin Countries represents one of the most important organizations in terms of citing principles in its constitution. The Committee appears in the top ten list for mentioning efficiency, staff issues, communication, joint issues (all first place), equality and representativeness (second place) and cooperation (third place). These statistics do not indicate whether these organizations actually tried to achieve or did achieve work on these principles,[98] merely that their constitutions mention these principles often.

Figure 1.1 shows the organizations whose constitutions referred most frequently, as counts of thousands rounded to the nearest 0.1 of all the words

---

97 In most of these excluded cases, governments' foreign ministries handle the organization's administrative matters on a rotating basis, like the G20. In some cases, one organization relies on another to serve as its secretariat, like the International Grains Council does for the Food Aid Committee.
98 As previously mentioned, the attempts to measure the extent to which international organizations achieve certain performance targets remain in their infancy. As this book asserts, without a map of principles, how can any researcher measure an organization's success in achieving those principles? For one such attempt at measuring international organizations' performance, see Lall, *supra* note 76, at 245.

Authority	Cooperation	Executive Staff	Peace
Economic Community of West African States (9.7k)	Indian Ocean Rim Association for Regional Cooperation (25k)	Asia Pacific Association of Agricultural Research Institutions (18k)	UN (4.5k)
International Union for Protection of New Varieties of Plants (2.9k)	South Asian Association for Regional Cooperation (20k)	International Sericultural Commission (17k)	Permanent Court of Arbitration (1.7k)
Food and Agriculture Organization (2.3k)	Gulf Cooperation Council (17k)	Islamic Educational Scientific and Cultural Organization (17k)	NATO (1.7k)
ILO (1.9k)	Comite Intergubernamental Coordinador de los Paise de la Cuenca del Plata (13k)	International Criminal Police Organization (16.5k)	Organization of the Islamic Conference (1.4k)
UN (1.8k)	Nordic Council of Ministers (12k)	International Organization for Migration (16k)	Organization of American States (1.2k)
Council of Europe (1.5k)	Economic Cooperation Organization (10k)	Association of Agricultural Research Institutions in the Near East and North Africa (15.6k)	African Union (1.1k)
International Criminal Police Organization (1.5k)	OECD (8k)	Centre for Agriculture and Biosciences International (15.3k)	Organization of Ibero-American States (1k)
International Civil Defense Organization (1.4k)	Economic Community of Central African States (7k)	International Organization of Vine and Wine (15k)	League of Arab States (1k)

Figure 1.1 Organizations with the most frequent mentions of each principle.

Authority	Cooperation	Executive Staff	Peace
International Tribunal for the Law of the Sea (1.3k)	South Centre (7k)	Asian Productivity Organization (13k)	ASEAN (0.9k)
League of Arab States (4k)	Comite Intergubernamental Coordinador de los Paise de la Cuenca del Plata (7.8k)	Comite Intergubernamental Coordinador de los Paise de la Cuenca del Plata (21k)	OECD (1.6k)
Organization of the Islamic Conference (2.4k)	Association of Caribbean States (4.2k)	Court of Justice of the Andean Community (7k)	ASEAN (1.3k)
South Asian Association for Regional Cooperation (1.8k)	Food and Agriculture Organization (3.2k)	International Commission on Civil Status (7k)	Council of Europe (1.1k)
World Bank Administrative Tribunal (1.7k)	World Customs Organization (3.2k)	African Development Bank Administrative Tribunal (6k)	Centre for Agriculture and Biosciences International (0.7k)
Organization of American States (1.4k)	European Organisation for the Safety of Air Navigation (2.8k)	World Bank Administrative Tribunal (6k)	Africa Rice Centre (0.7k)
South Centre (1.2k)	Caribbean Postal Union (2.8k)	Association of Natural Rubber Producing Countries (5k)	European Central Bank (0.7k)
International Whaling Commission (1k)	International Regional Organization for Plant and Animal Health (2.8k)	International Organization of Legal Metrology (4.5k)	Mano River Union (0.7k)

Secretariat of the Pacific Community (0.9k)	South Centre (2.7k)	Ibero-American Social Security Organization (4.3k)	UN (0.6k)
African Court of Human and People's Rights (0.9k)	International Bank for Economic Cooperation (2.7k)	Organization for Joint Armament Cooperation (4.3k)	UNIDO (0.6k)
Comite Intergubernamental Coordinador de los Paise de la Cuenca del Plata (6.5k)	Caribbean Telecommunications Union (3.4k)	Comite Intergubernamental Coordinador de los Paise de la Cuenca del Plata (4k)	International Organization of Vine and Wine (3.8k)
Islamic Educational Scientific and Cultural Organization (5.7k)	Comite Intergubernamental Coordinador de los Paise de la Cuenca del Plata (2.6k)	Inter-American Tropical Tuna Commission (3.3k)	Comite Intergubernamental Coordinador de los Paise de la Cuenca del Plata (2.6k)
ILO (5k)	Banco del Alba	Mano River Union (2.9k)	Ibero-American Social Security Organization (2.2k)
International Organization of Vine and Wine (3.8k)	International Organization of Vine and Wine (2.1k)	Benelux Econ. Union (2.8k)	Association of Natural Rubber Producing Countries (1.7k)
International Development Law Organization (2.9k)	Eurasian Economic Commission (2k)	Council of Europe (2.5k)	Asian African Legal Consultative Organization (1.7k)
International Cotton Advisory Committee (2.7k)	Nordic Council of Ministers (1.8k)	Andean Community (1.8k)	Nordic Council of Ministers (1.7k)

Figure 1.1 Continued

Authority	Cooperation	Executive Staff	Peace
Association of Agricultural Research Institutions in the Near East and North Africa (2.7k)	South Asian Association for Regional Cooperation (1.7k)	Nordic Council of Ministers (1.5k)	League of Arab States (1.5k)
African Court of Human and People's Rights (2.7k)	Indian Ocean Rim Association for Regional Cooperation (1.4k)	Gulf Cooperation Council (1.5k)	Organization of the Petroleum Exporting Countries (1.4k)
International Commission on Civil Status (2.6k)	Organization of the Islamic Conference (1.4k)	East African Community (1.4k)	Association of European Public Postal Operators (1.4k)
Support			
Advisory Centre on World Trade Organization Law (3k)	International Association of Supreme Administrative Jurisdictions (2.3k)	West African Development Bank (1.8k)	Organization of the Islamic Conference (1.4k)
Association of Postal and Telecommunications Operators of the Portuguese Speaking Countries and Territories (3k)	International Fusion Energy Organization (2.2k)	Organization of Ibero-American States (1.8k)	Islamic Educational Scientific and Cultural Organization (1.3k)
Bank for International Settlements (1.2k)			

Figure 1.1 Continued

in their constitutions, to the principles shown in the figure. For example, the Advisory Centre on World Trade Organization Law's constitution referred to support most frequently, or about 3,000 times for every 100,000 words in the constitution.

Analyzing principles by the type of international organization

Among the six textbooks analyzed for this book, authors tended to group – or stratify – international organizations in five ways. Figure 1.2 shows the ways they stratify international organizations and the statistically significantly different mentions of principles in these subgroups' constitutions. For example, universal international organizations' constitutions statistically significantly referred to executive staff more differently than did their regional counterparts. On balance, their regional counterparts referred to authority more than simple accident can explain.[99] Limited competence international organizations have – as a group and for a specific level of statistical confidence – no principles statistically significantly distinguishing this group.

Figure 1.2 shows the categorization of international organizations suggested by a review of six prominent textbooks in the field of the law of international organizations. It shows the area of such a categorization – for example, by scope, competence, financial, judicial and EU affiliation. It also shows the dichotomous breakdown within each category – for example, international organizations have either a universal or regional scope for the purposes of this book. The figure also shows the number of international organizations of each type in this book's sample – for example, the book's database has 52 constitutions of universal-scope international organizations. Later sections in this book show which values statistically significantly correlated with each category – determined by running a statistical procedure known as a Mann-Whitney U test. To take the example of international organizations' scope, the procedure estimated that the frequency of mentions of authority in regional international organizations' constitutions (per 1,000 words) exceeded the number of these mentions in universal organizations' constitutions. The test indicates that random variation would explain these differences in less than 5 percent of all the sample data like this.

---

99 Statistical procedures like the "Mann-Whitney U test" look for differences in the way these constitutions reference these principles. While this book cannot provide an entire statistics core, a "statistically significant" result indicates that a constitution's mention of principles differs by more than simple random fluctuation would account for.

Scope		Judicial	
Universal: 52 Executive staff	Regional: 139 Authority	Judicial: 14 Autonomy	Non-judicial: 177 Cooperation
Competence		**EU Affiliated**	
General: 22 Cooperation Peace Executive staff Support	Limited: 169 None	EU: 13 Aspiration Autonomy Efficiency Staff Recommendation	Non-EU: 178 Communication Executive staff Representativeness
Financial			
Financial: 43 None	Non-Financial: 148 Cooperation Peace		

Figure 1.2 Number of international organizations studied and the major values associated with those organizations.

The first grouping of international organizations consists of the scope of the international organization. Universal organizations have an open membership criterion, with the aim of having states join. Universal membership organizations strive for wide representation, as illustrated in their criteria and procedures for appointing senior officials like the secretary general and judges in tribunals from various countries,[100] although membership often falls short of being actually universal, usually due to political reasons.[101] Regional organizations have specific criteria for determining eligibility membership. These regional organizations have specialized criteria for

---

100 Such a dichotomy naturally ignores intermediary organizations like clubs and networks. Not quite universal, some organizations have a membership that does not exactly fit into geographical bounds. The authors of this book accept the limitations of such a geography-based dichotomy, and they refer readers interested in the subject to the following source: Michele U. Fratianni & John C. Pattison, "International Organisations in a World of Regional Trade Agreements: Lessons from Club Theory," 24 *World Econ.* 333 (2001). In any event, this book's operational definition of what counts as an international organization does not include clubs and networks, thus they were already ignored prior to the stratification.
101 For more information on such political matters involving UN membership, *see generally* James D. Fry & Agnes Chong, "Membership in the United Nations," *in Leading Judicial Decisions of the Law of International Organizations* 138 (Ramses A. Wessel et al. eds. 2015).

membership, based on the "common bond of policy" that the specific international organization addresses.[102]

The second grouping consists of the international organization's competence. International organizations with a general competence do not primarily focus on a specific task, policy or agenda. Such an organization – like the UN – provides services to its members in a variety of areas, from social and economic to security-related areas.[103] However, not all universal international organizations have general competencies. The Arab League and the Gulf Cooperation Council represent examples of international organizations with general competencies but focus on a regional scope. Organizations with limited competence focus on specific activities. For example, member states of the International Bureau of Weights and Measures "act together on matters related to measurement science and measurement standards."[104]

The third categorization comes from whether the international organization has financial or non-financial objectives and goals. International financial organizations – particularly universal financial organizations such as the IMF and the World Bank – may have values that differ from other organizations inasmuch as they often represent the pooling of resources rather than any attempt to manage particular transnational policies.[105] Diffuse governance – with one delegate sometimes representing many

---

102 *See* Sands & Klein, *supra* note 39, at 151. The EU shows why such regional organizations may have universal aspects to both their membership and aspirations. *See* Ramses Wessel & Steven Blockmans, *Between Autonomy and Dependence: The EU Legal Order Under the Influence of International Organisations* (2012).

103 As Grek shows, these competencies may slide over time. *See* Sotiria Grek, "International Organisations and the Shared Construction of Policy 'Problems': Problematisation and Change in Education Governance in Europe," 9 *Eur. Edu. Res. J.* 396 (2010).

104 International Bureau of Weights and Measures, "The Role and Objective of the BIPM," *at* www.bipm.org/en/about-us/role.html (last visited Mar. 25, 2020). As competences continue to evolve and shift between levels of government, the need for a census of such organizations with general versus limited competences has never been more pressing. *See* Jonathan Joseph, "Governmentality of What? Populations, States and International Organisations," 23 *Global Soc.* 413 (2009).

105 One cannot yet judge the definitive veracity of such a statement without data about these organizations' constitutions. The reaction of members' populations to the imposition of governance requirements by some of these institutions clearly showed that many expected these institutions to serve as self-help entities rather than as the imposers of particular rules. *See* Devesh Kapur & Richard Webb, "Governance-Related Conditionalities of the International Financial Institutions," G-24 Discussion Paper 6, United Nations Conference on Trade and Development, Aug. 2000, *available at* www.pdfs.semanticscholar.org (last visited Mar. 25, 2020).

member states – and very specific areas of work make this type of international organization supposedly different from non-financial organizations.[106] However, different does not always mean better, given the din of cries for reforming the major international financial organizations.[107] Never has a need for identifying the values behind these organizations' organic laws been more pressing.

The fourth categorization revolves around whether an international organization exercises judicial authority or responsibilities. Such organizations include international courts and tribunals established through a separate agreement, rather than from a resolution within a parent international organization like the UN, and not subject to national law (thus, excluding most hybrid courts).[108] Inherently, international judicial organizations differ from non-judicial ones due to their authority to rule on cases under international law – in effect contributing to international law.[109] Many of these organizations appear for specific purposes (such as to rule on war crimes) and become inactive after a period of time.[110] Understanding the values that these organizations work under would contribute towards understanding the values driving lawmaking at the international level.

The last category involves affiliation with the EU. The EU's unique bureaucratic, and more importantly supranational, nature makes organizations formed under or by EU law distinct from other international

---

106 *See* Ariel Buira, *Reforming the Governance of the IMF and the World Bank* (2006).
107 Again, the need for a catalogue of these institutions' values has never seemed more pressing. If literally hundreds of articles have appeared urging the reform of these organizations, none has had recourse to a scientific study of the values enshrined in their (and their peers') founding constitutions. *See* Ngaire Woods, "The Challenge of Good Governance for the IMF and the World Bank Themselves," 28 *World Dev.* 823 (2000).
108 If the international financial institutions have generated a large amount of negative criticism and controversy, researchers and policymakers alike have greeted international judicial institutions with more enthusiasm. *See* Armin von Bogdandy & Ingo Venzke, "Beyond Dispute: International Judicial Institutions as Lawmakers," 12 *German L.J.* 979 (2011).
109 Their part in creating – as well as working under – international law represents a key differentiator between these kinds of organizations and other specialized entities. The organic development of a broader architecture for such law represents one of the most fascinating areas of law in this area. *See* Richard Goldstone et al., *International Judicial Institutions: The Architecture of International Justice at Home and Abroad* (2015).
110 However, the number of these bodies does not remain steady by any means. *See* Cesare Romano, "The Proliferation of International Judicial Bodies: The Pieces of the Puzzle," 31 *N.Y.U. J. Int'l L. & Pol.* 709 (1999).

organizations. Most of the textbook authors acknowledge the special nature of EU supranational institutions by dedicating a special chapter to them. A vibrant sub-discipline exists for studying the mutual effects of EU law on international organizations and vice versa – making an understanding of the values in their constitutions so much the more important.[111]

Naturally, this book analyzed attributes like the size, age and location of each organization. The sections later in this chapter describe exactly how these attributes vary with the values. However, it is important to note here that all three of these variables statistically significantly vary with these international organizations' scope (universal or regional). International financial organizations and EU-affiliated organizations generally have incorporated later than non-financial organizations. Findings like these show that some international organizations' constitutions adhere more to some principles than to others. It is possible to see groupings in even these simple data, with the implication being that these patterns run far deeper.

Findings of the book

Patterns present in international organizations' constitutions are hard to spot. Figure 1.3 shows the lack of any obvious relationship in the way that international organizations' constitutions mention communication, efficiency and equality. If some constitutions referred to these principles more than others, one would expect to see some kind of relationship in these data. For example, there might be a cluster of dots representing universal organizations or a straight-line relationship showing how constitutions that mention communication more also refer to equality more often, as a percentage of all the words in that constitution.[112]

However, when using the categories discussed above, some patterns start to emerge. When the data is stratified (or separated) by organizational

---

111 Indeed, many of the authors of the textbooks analyzed in this book have studied this issue well beyond the topics discussed in their respective textbooks. *See* Jan Klabbers, "*Sui Generis?* The European Union as an International Organization," *A Companion to European Union Law and International Law* 1 (Dennis Patterson & Anna Södersten eds. 2016); Christine Kaddous, *The European Union in International Organisations and Global Governance: Recent Developments* (2015).
112 Even with the sub-discipline of the law of international organizations, some of the literature posits a relationship between culture and such law. If true, then differing cultures would show up in the scatter plot as either different groups or clumps of data or as different linear relationships in this data. None of these patterns exists in this figure. For a discussion of this literature, *see* Stephan Sberro, "Culture and International Law," 20 *Eur. J. Int'l L.* 463 (2009).

30 *The values of international organizations*

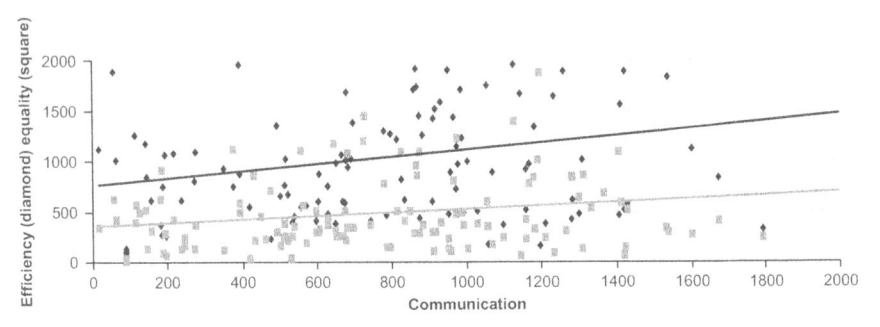

Figure 1.3 No apparent groups of constitutions mention communication and/or efficiency more than others. The figure shows the (lack of) apparent relationship between constitutions' mentions of efficiency, equality and communication. Each dot represents a different organization's constitution. We see no obvious relationships at all.

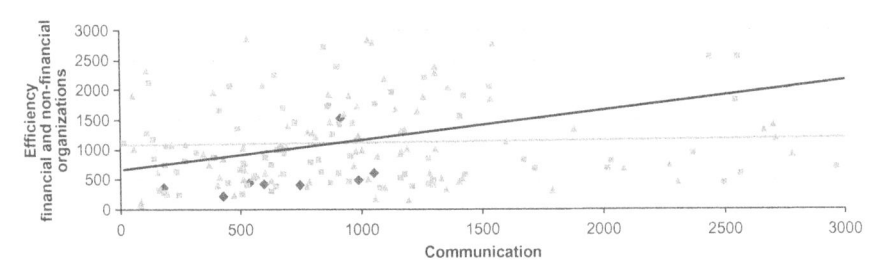

Figure 1.4 The start of principles "clustering" for different groups of organizations. The figure shows the extent of references to efficiency and communication in various international organizations' constitutions. The **diamond** refers to universal financial organizations. The **triangle** refers to universal non-financial organizations. The **square** refers to regional financial organizations. We clearly observe the start of grouping characteristics – with different lines of best fit between universal financial and regional non-financial organizations. These data also show why we need to use more complex statistical methods to find structure.

scope and whether the organization represents financial topics or not, some rudimentary patterns start to emerge.[113] Figure 1.4 shows the different ways that four subgroups of international organizations' constitutions refer to communication and efficiency. Not only does some limited clustering appear (see the larger clusters of triangles towards the origin of the graph), but one also can see different relationships between the ways that constitutions that often refer to communication also refer to efficiency, as

---

113 The authors of this book choose these two stratifying categories – namely, the scope and whether the organization possessed financial objectives – on a whim. The stratification of the data can illustrate such pattern formation.

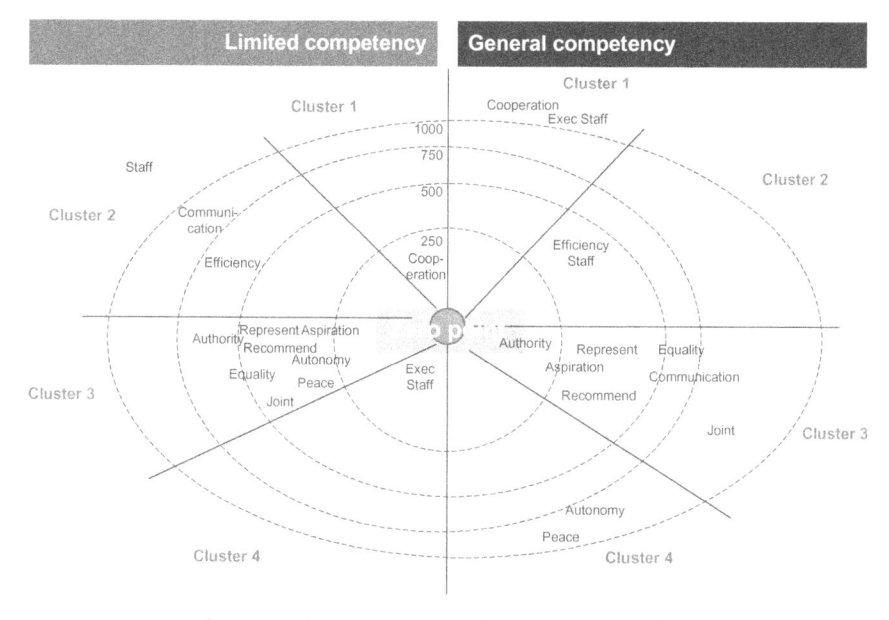

Figure 1.5 Cluster analysis shows that different organizations promulgate different principles. The figure shows the most likely clusters in the dataset, using k-clusters analysis, with the "k" being chosen to minimize variation within groups and maximize variation between groups. Both limited competence and general competence organizations have four optimal clusters. Each cluster represents groups of principles that likely characterize, or define, that cluster. For example, cooperation defines Cluster 1's character for limited competency organizations (as there is little distance or variation in its values). Staff characterizes Cluster 2 for this same organizational grouping of limited competency organizations. However, staff mentions' high distance indicates that staff principles only weakly characterize the cluster.

shown by the lines with different slopes. The research has not yet tested these patterns to see if they arise at random or represent "statistically significant" patterns, which is a phrase that the reader often will see in this book. Ige Dekker and Ramses Wessel qualitatively analyze the trend observed in this figure – that some international organizations take different decisions and act in different ways because of differences in their core principles.[114] In other words, the data and quantitative analysis support their more anecdotal observations.

With more advanced statistical procedures, clearer patterns in the data can be observed. Figure 1.5 shows the way that this book has divided

---

114 *See* Dekker & Wessel, *supra* note 50, at 215.

international organizations' constitutions – merely by looking at the variance in their citations of principles.[115] Using this method, it is possible to figure out which groups of principles belong together. Do efficiency and staff principles belong to a similar "idea," as they seem to for Cluster 2 characterizing general competence organizations in the figure? Such a technique enables an *objective* lumping together of these principles for the organizations existing in the world.

With algorithms able to detect these kinds of clusters, it is possible to imagine the ability to slice-and-dice international organizations by their principles. What happens if a clustering or grouping algorithm is asked to find the number of groupings that international organizations fall into, and what importance does each grouping give to various principles? Figure 1.6 shows the results of such an algorithm, and the next chapter provides more details about the results and methods. One might characterize a grouping (made entirely by computer algorithm) of constitutions with high mentions of staff, efficiency and communication principles as constitutions stressing efficient international organizations. If executive staff trying to make aspirations come true does not represent a "technocratic" – although not necessarily bureaucratic – organization, it is entirely unclear what does.

Of course, any purely quantitative analysis of words in a constitution will fail to understand the true developing jurisprudence of international organizations law. Throughout this book, quantitative and qualitative analysis of these constitutions is mixed to arrive at an empirically driven map of international organizations' principles that transcends the cloying generalities in the popular textbooks of our time. Figure 1.7 provides one example of such an analysis. The figure looks qualitatively at the jurisprudential traditions, theories and "structures" (for lack of a better word) using the tools of a jurist. The jurisprudence around the use of the term "authority" in many constitutions tends to incorporate the principles of communication, making recommendations and authority into "discursive modules," "semantic objects" and legal theories.[116] This book uses the tools of a jurist to find

---

115 Space limitations make it impossible to discuss cluster analysis in this book. For the uninitiated reader, they only need know that such analysis looks at the ways that principles vary together across constitutions. The clustering algorithm analyzes such variance and indicates the most likely clusters these constitutions belong to.
116 The legal tradition studying these nexuses of words that come together to make unique meaning – as well as confer unique rights and obligations – has a long tradition. Space limitations do not allow for an explanation of semiotic theory, either in its original postmodern origins or its recent quantitative rehash. For further background on these methods, *see* John Conley & William O'Barr, *Just Words: Law, Language, and Power* (2005).

Efficient organization		Dictating organization		Harmony organization		Peace-loving organization		Technocratic organization		Equal-rights organization		Dreaming organization	
Staff	0.718	Equality	0.276	Executive staff	0.361	Peace	0.418	Aspiration	0.650	Equality	0.444	Peace	0.282
Efficiency	0.645	Representation	0.187	Communication	0.308	Executive staff	0.373	Executive staff	0.324	Recommend	0.276	Recommend	0.277
Communication	0.619	Cooperation	0.180	Aspiration	0.224	Autonomy	0.339	Cooperation	0.315	Executive staff	0.185	Aspiration	0.236
Representation	0.590	Autonomy	0.177	Representation	0.124	Communication	0.252	Representation	0.158	Communication	0.169	Efficiency	0.217
Joint	0.580	Staff	0.056	Efficiency	0.090	Representation	0.199	Recommend	0.150	Peace	0.163	Staff	0.179
Equality	0.501	Joint	0.053	Staff	0.066	Efficiency	0.085	Autonomy	0.095	Representation	0.137	Communication	0.075
Cooperation	0.499	Communication	0.005	Joint	-0.058	Equality	0.077	Equality	0.065	Joint	0.026	Joint	0.072
Executive staff	0.418	Efficiency	-0.101	Authority	-0.067	Aspiration	-0.016	Joint	-0.092	Cooperation	0.026	Equality	-0.027
Aspiration	0.256	Aspiration	-0.276	Equality	-0.296	Authority	-0.031	Peace	-0.096	Authority	-0.156	Representation	-0.053
Authority	0.194	Peace	-0.277	Recommend	-0.318	Staff	-0.112	Communication	-0.175	Efficiency	-0.231	Autonomy	-0.098
Autonomy	0.122	Executive staff	-0.287	Cooperation	-0.448	Recommend	-0.279	Staff	-0.179	Staff	-0.284	Executive staff	-0.275
Peace	0.107	Authority	-0.624	Peace	-0.630	Cooperation	-0.334	Authority	-0.325	Aspiration	-0.390	Cooperation	-0.354
Recommend	0.040	Recommend	-0.665	Autonomy	0.654	Joint	-0.587	Efficiency	-0.370	Autonomy	-0.482	Authority	-0.568

Figure 1.6 The seven kinds of international organization (according to their principles). The figure shows the best number of factors able to capture the variation in mentions of the principles we analyzed in this study. Namely, seven factors maximize the percentage variation explained in our data (about 75 percent). We show the factor-loadings (or importance) of each principle in explaining each statistically independent factor.

34 *The values of international organizations*

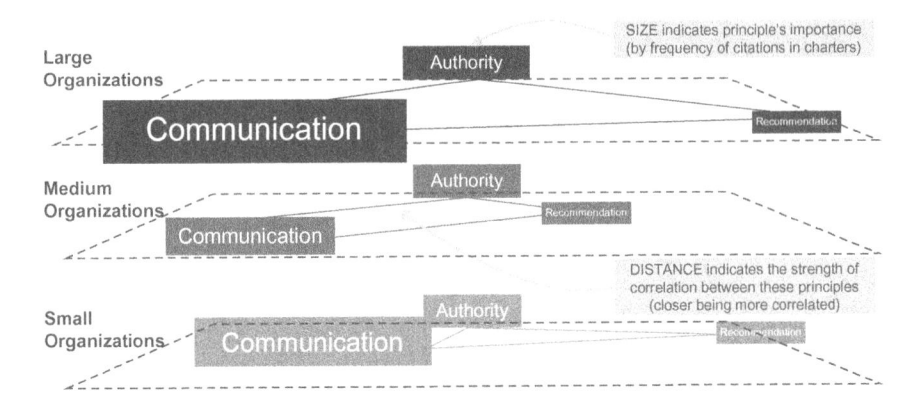

Figure 1.7 An example of different "tracks" of authority by organizational size. The figure shows the data on different levels or conceptions of each of the values shown in the figure (authority, communication and recommendation).
We show the importance of each value as the size of the value and the correlation between these values by the distance between them. We show these differences for the sizes of international organizations to illustrate our general point. Sizes ranged from small to large: Authority (303, 514, 533), Recommendation (124, 129, 152), Communication (960, 894, 1073). Corrections as distances. Small: A-to-C (0.31), A-to-R (0.01), C-to-R (-0.07), A-to-C (-0.01). Medium: A-to-R (0.26), C-to-R (-0.11). Large: A-to-C (0.10), A-to-R (0.08), C-to-R (-0.09).

these connections first. However, this book also illustrates these connections graphically, using quantitative analysis.

The quantitative analysis in Figure 1.7 shows how different groups of international organizations' constitutions seem to form patterns in the way they use words. For large international organizations, their constitutions frequently refer to communication. These references to communication coincide or correlate with references to authority and to the issuing or use of recommendations. The correlation between references to these three principles in these constitutions forms *stable and predictable* patterns. These patterns differ from those in medium-sized organizations' constitutions, which refer to communication less. However, references to such communication tend to coincide more frequently with references to recommendations. This is not just any communication. Indeed, if large organizations use authoritative communications to make recommendations, medium-sized organizations' constitutions see the issuing of recommendations as a way of developing authority. There are links between principles using quantitative methods that only deep reading of these texts can discover, after Herculean efforts. Groups, networks and tracks of references to principles in these international organizations' constitutions form their own patterns and meanings of interest to legal researchers, international civil servants and the people whom they regulate.

Principles in international organizations' constitutions clearly form their own networks of meaning. If the analysis above looks only at how words or groups of words appear together in international organizations' constitutions, network analysis shows the deep "effect" or deep correlations between these words and principles. Figure 1.8 provides an example of such a network. Such analysis shows how references to peace correlate

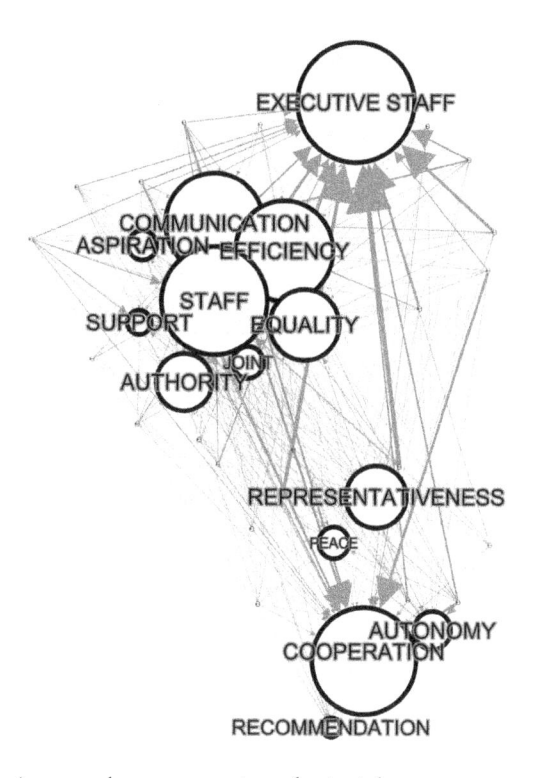

Figure 1.8 A network representation of principles across organizational constitutions. The figure shows the network relationship between principles in international organizations' constitutions. It was constructed by starting with a spreadsheet containing the frequency of mentions of each principle for each international organization. For example, the African-Asian Rural Development Organization has "links" with communication (about 376 mentions per 100,000 words), cooperation (32,000 per 100,000), efficiency (about 750 mentions per 100,000 words) and so forth. The mentions tell how important each link is or, rather, the weight of each link. The OpenOrd algorithm was used to display the network, an algorithm that shows similar principles closer together and less similar principles farther apart.

(or literally "link") to efficiency. Nevertheless, such links take into account the way that efficiency links to the principle of support, authority and all the other principles in these constitutions. Cooperation and authority may relate to each other or work together, to use non-legal language. Nevertheless, their effects on each other already include the effects of authority and other principles.

Removing links to each organization and looking at the pure links between these principles provides a much clearer picture of the way these principles relate to one other. Figure 1.9 shows the way that each principle mentioned in an international organization's constitution links to other principles in that same constitution. If a constitution mentions communication more than cooperation, the link between these principles becomes directed towards communication. Because all of these links have a direction, it is possible to trace through – mathematically if not jurisprudentially – the way that the principle of efficiency impacts on executive staff principles through their effect on cooperation, or at least through the way they mention such cooperation.[117] Mentions of representativeness in these constitutions correlate with mentions about executive staff. However, without network analysis it would be impossible to detect how these mentions of representativeness and cooperation relate to the mentions of communication, which eventually correlate with mentions of executive staff. The stress on executive staffing principles in these constitutions becomes all the clearer only with this most advanced form of mathematical analysis.

The reader should see three broad pictures emerging from this analysis. First, the mentions of particular principles within and across international organizations' constitutions form patterns that social scientists can analyze. This chapter has provided a taste of the complexity in the way that these principles group, link and otherwise work together in these constitutions. The term "cooperation" does not mean one thing to all international organizations. The way that these constitutions refer to cooperation and other principles, like efficiency and communication, depends on some unknown way that these organizations work, fit or conceptually exist together as groups or clusters. The rights, obligations, instructions, prohibitions and all the other "stuff" that law deals with conveyed by these principles depends on who uses the term, where, when and how. From this point of view, the

---

117 Remember that this book does not measure these international organizations' actual results, only words in their constitutions. Thus, it is impossible to make any statements about the way actual efficiency in these organizations affects cooperation, or vice versa. This book can only refer to the way that the more frequent mention of some of these principles in their constitutions correlates with the less frequent mention of others.

Principles 37

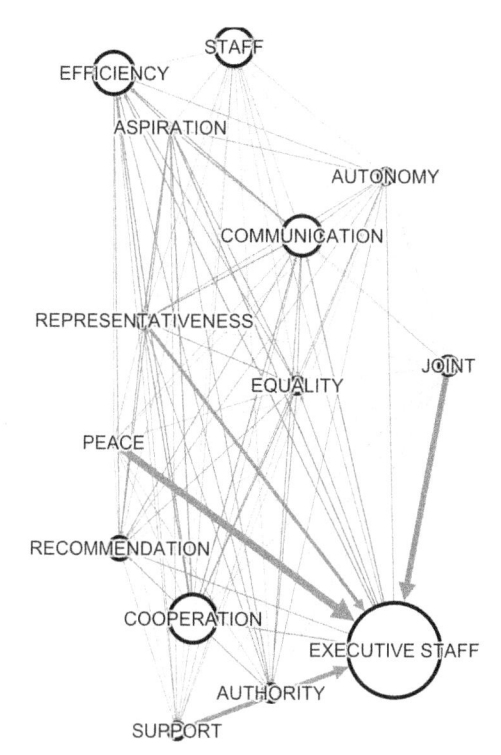

Figure 1.9 A pure representation of principles in international organizations' constitutions (obvious patterns). The figure shows the relationship between principles cited in the database of international organizations' constitutions. This figure was calculated by finding the relative frequency with which each constitution mentions each of these principles. These principles then were "linked" in each constitution, such that if a constitution mentioned cooperation and communication, these two principles are linked. The proportion of references in that constitution to communication, relative to cooperation, determines the direction and magnitude of that link. The OpenOrd algorithm was then applied to the network database, which is an algorithm that gives some distance to similar principles, yet draws in less similar values. The sizes of the links, otherwise known as "edges," in the figure show the relative extent or frequency with which these principles appear together in various constitutions.

nascent study of these principles offers much for the would-be international lawyer, jurist or political scientist to decode.

Despite all of the seemingly quantitative precision that these figures provide, jurists and social scientists of all kinds have a long way to go to make sense of these road maps. This book provides theories, suppositions and arguments about the meaning of these groupings of principles, with great effort to cite others' opinions and ideas. However, without an empirical map of these principles, no one could even try to flesh out either a common law or a treaty-based understanding of them. It is impossible to know, at this early stage, what these links and groupings mean. Nevertheless, there is one thing that is known: treating these principles like immutable, universal objects – as the authors of the popular textbooks in this field do – hurts more than helps in terms of understanding reality. With these points in mind, the following section explains why the language of international organizations' constitutions matters.

The meaning of constitutional language

Why should anyone study the number of times international organizations' constitutions mention particular principles? Critics will assert that it is more important to look at the ways that these constitutions impact on the international organizations they guide. Moreover, they will assert that this book should be more interested in the number of times these constitutions' provisions actually involve the principles of autonomy or equality, for example, rather than simply looking at the number of times the constitutions use the words "autonomy" and "equality." These critics presumably will see this book's approach as creating methodological and substantive problems. They also might point to the innovativeness and value of such research. After all, without traditions and institutions in place to uphold the rights and obligations incumbent on international organizations, words are just words.[118] This section provides explanations for and rebuttals to the more likely critiques that will arise from both academics and practitioners, starting with the methodological criticisms and proceeding to the more substantive criticisms.

Methodological criticisms

Why count words like "autonomy" when provisions that help to ensure such autonomy never mention the word? Provisions protecting international organizations from lawsuits in national courts (or even international

---

118 The use of some treaty provisions may seek to create a type of soft law, which treaty framers might have hoped would later congeal into hard law. This book does not discuss the problems involved with turning soft, unimplementable international organizations law into the implementable kind. For more on this issue, *see* Jan Klabbers, "Institutional Ambivalence by Design: Soft Organizations in International Law," 70 *Nordic J. Int'l L.* 403 (2001).

fora) may not explicitly refer to the organization's autonomy.[119] A highly participatory voting structure may not refer to authority or representativeness explicitly.[120] Some provisions referring to equality may allude to a wide range of issues – from workplace equality between genders to the equality of voting rights between types of members.[121] For example, the Statute of the International Court of Justice points out, "In the event of an equality of votes among the judges, the eldest judge shall have a casting vote."[122] Yet, such a provision deals far less with equality than with simple staff issues. Most – if not all – of these international organizations' implied powers do not appear at all in their constitutions, and so they do not appear in any count of the organization's "authority." It must not be forgotten that this book focuses on principles, not powers per se.[123]

Such a criticism puts the proverbial cart before the horse. It is important to measure laws before measuring their effects. This book represents the first comprehensive census of these constitutions and the principles contained within them. The fundamental motivation here is to move international

---

119 Simply counting the number of times a treaty refers to "autonomy" cannot compare with the in-depth treaty analysis done by some commentators, with whom this book does not compete. Instead, this book offers a complementary view of the issue by using these counts to start a broader debate on how to quantify aspects of the constitutions of international organizations.

120 Authors like Rapkin et al. argue that we have such a long way to go before understanding such representativeness in international organizations' voting arrangements that even basic empirical work will represent a solid step forward. For more on this plea (and on their plea for better conceptualization of constitutional principles), see David P. Rapkin et al., "Representation and Governance in International Organizations," 4 *Pol. & Gov.* 77 (2016).

121 Authors like Bohman might argue that these principles do not lie inertly in the words of constitutional provisions, waiting for legal scholars to discover them and their meaning. See James Bohman, "International Regimes and Democratic Governance: Political Equality and Influence in Global Institutions," 75 *Int'l Aff.* 499 (1999). Following Krook and True, this book gives greater or lesser weight to certain principles – and our understanding of the legal content of these principles may change radically over time. See Mona-Lena Krook & Jacqui True, "Rethinking the Life Cycles of International Norms: The United Nations and the Global Promotion of Gender Equality," 18 *Eur. J. Int'l Rel.* 103 (2010).

122 Statute for the International Court of Justice art. 12(4), June 26, 1945, 59 Stat. 1055, 33 UNTS 993 [hereinafter "ICJ Statute"].

123 International organizations' constitutions benefited greatly from the move away from enumerated powers in the pre-Second World War era towards implied powers in the post-war period. While debates rage about the reasons for and limits of implied powers, almost no scholarly discussion has focused on the *principles* driving that debate. For more of an explanation, see Viljam Engstrom, *Constructing the Powers of International Institutions* (2012).

organizations law from an analysis of effects to one of measurements, just as modern chemistry emerged when scientists turned away from phlogiston.[124] The modern era in chemistry appeared with Antoine-Laurent de Lavoisier when he turned away from measuring effects (like the heat from elements composed of elemental fires) towards more careful measurement, much like the jurimetricians of today are doing.[125] Modern legal scholars seek to measure the words and forms of written law, just like Lavoisier measured the properties of chemicals themselves, rather than try to measure them by the effects they cause.[126]

The main question is: how can one measure the authority of an international financial organization like the IMF or World Bank, for example? Many might claim that their authority – or at least the coercive part of it – comes from loan conditions, not provisions within a constitution. To be more precise, critics might argue that these international organizations' advice and recommendations hold sway because they can restrict funding to a needy government, not because the recipient government signed a treaty vesting authority in the Fund or Bank.[127] However, where should one look for such authority? Lending conditionalities hardly appear – if

---

124 Phlogiston theory – as popularized by Lavoisier's predecessor Georg Ernst Stahl – held that we could measure the amount of a combustible substance (called phlogiston) in any object by measuring its flammability. Pre-empirical chemistry focused on measuring the results of chemicals, such as air, earth, fire and water, rather than the chemicals themselves. Many modern legal scholars seem to view international organizations law in a similar light – as the pre-empirical. If the discipline is to progress and mature, it must start measuring laws themselves before measuring their effects. The authors of this book do not wish to weigh in on this debate, only to note that this idea has a larger following than the authors of this book. *See, e.g.,* Kylie Burns & Terry Hutchinson, "The Impact of 'Empirical Facts' on Legal Scholarship and Legal Research Training," 43 *Law Teacher* 153 (2009).
125 If authors, like Loevinger, argue that such measurements represented the start of an empirical revolution in law in the 1960s, the growth of empirical work in law mushroomed just a decade later. *See* Lee Loevinger, "Jurimetrics: The Methodology of Legal Inquiry," 28 *L. & Contemp. Prob.* 5 (1963); Lee Loevinger, "Jurimetrics: The Next Step Forward," 12 *Jurimetrics J.* 3 (1971).
126 De Mulder et al.'s title says it all. *See* Richard De Mulder et al., "Jurimetrics Please," 1 *Eur. J. L. & Tech.* 135 (2010) (showing the usefulness of measuring laws).
127 Legal scholars certainly would not agree with these critics. Following good practice in legal analysis (and pointing to the need for better thinking as well as better empirical data about these constitutions), Ciorciari finds the authority exercised in World Bank and IMF lending in their constitutions. *See* John Ciorciari, "The Lawful Scope of Human Rights Criteria in World Bank Credit Decisions: An Interpretive Analysis of the IBRD and IDA Articles of Agreement," 33 *Cornell Int'l L.J.* 331 (2000).

at all – in the articles of association of the two institutions.[128] Moreover, handbooks lack the binding authority of law. Executive directors' decrees do not form durable, binding law, just as ministerial decisions represent an unclear part of administrative law; declarations and recommendations form a soft, gray informal law.[129] The jurimetrician has no place to go to analyze black-letter law, except for the language of international organizations' constitutions.[130]

Only references to specific words represent an objective, independently verifiable start at quantitatively, empirically studying international organizations law. Therefore, this project needed an approach that all observers could agree upon and a measure that different scholars working in different legal contexts could agree upon.[131] To date, scholars have accepted only measures of the frequency and context of word use in legislation and other

---

[128] As already noted, they – like human rights obligations – appear only constructively in these constitutions – meaning only if a jurist intends to draw a link where no obvious link seems to exist. For more on the way that governments have constructively interpreted these constitutions, based on the dominant principles of the times, *see* Victorial Marmorstein, "World Bank Power to Consider Human Rights Factors in Loan Decisions," 13 *J. Int'l L. & Econ.* 113 (1979).

[129] Few jurimetricians have even tried to quantify this flocculent level of rulemaking, given the soft rights and obligations such rules create. Goldenziel's failed (though impressive) attempt to look at how human rights regulations are promulgated by international organizations illustrates the need for scholars to back up and start measuring the basics of such law. See Jill I. Goldenziel, "Regulating Human Rights: International Organizations, Flexible Standards, and International Refugee Law," 12 *Chi. J. Int'l L.* 453 (2014).

[130] Indeed, leximetricians – not to be confused with jurimetricians – would argue that quantitative measurements of laws represent a prime way for understanding social and administrative institutions. This book does not provide a background of leximetric/jurimetric thought, as the preference is to focus on this book's narrower scope. For more information on the leximetric intellectual project, *see* Zoe Adams et al., "The CBR-LRI Dataset: Methods, Properties and Potential of Leximetric Coding of Labour Laws," Working Paper 489, Centre for Business Research, University of Cambridge, *available at* https://ideas.repec.org/p/cbr/cbrwps/wp489.html (last visited Mar. 25, 2020).

[131] Authors like Barabucci and co-authors specifically argue for European initiatives aimed at making words in EU legal texts manipulable by statistical software, on the grounds that qualitative methods do not allow for cross-country comparison. See Gioele Barabucci et al., "Managing Semantics in XML Vocabularies: An Experience in the Legal and Legislative Domain," Paper Presented at the Balisage Markup Conference in Montreal, Canada, Jan. 2010, *available at* www.researchgate.net/profile/Silvio_Peroni/publication/256766569_Managing_semantics_in_XML_vocabularies_an_experience_in_the_legal_and_legislative_domain/links/02bfe50d48d3b9543d000000.pdf (last visited Mar. 25, 2020).

legal texts.[132] Such "semantic analysis" of legal texts has led to a burgeoning field of legal inquiry, quite separate from any analysis of the way laws impact on the real world.[133] This project extended this empirical process on the most solid footing available – by looking at the black-letter law contained in international organizations' constitutions.[134]

The subjectivity involved in interpreting constitutions and treaties makes such black-letter law even more useful. One potential criticism of this project could be that a purely textual analysis would completely miss concepts like the implied powers that form the basis of international organizations' authority.[135] However, even Anglo-Saxon legal scholars cannot agree on the specifics of this doctrine, with the definition and common

---

132 For an example of the initiatives aimed at making legislation and other law amenable to quantitative analysis, *see* Mariangela Biasiotti et al., "Legal Informatics and Management of Legislative Documents," Global Centre for ICT in Parliament Working Paper No. 2, Jan. 2008, *available at* pdfs.semanticscholar.org (last visited Mar. 25, 2020).

133 One obvious area – besides looking at "word networks" – consists of measures of legal complexity. For one example, *see* Bernhard Waltl & Florian Matthes, "Towards Measures of Complexity: Applying Structural and Linguistic Metrics to German Laws," Jurix: International Conference on Legal Knowledge and Information Systems in Krakow (2014), *available at* pdfs.semanticscholar.org (last visited Mar. 25, 2020).

134 Who could argue that analyses like Gruenberg's do not represent solid contributions to the literature? *See* Justin S. Gruenberg, "An Analysis of United Nations Security Council Resolutions: Are All Countries Treated Equally?," 41 *Case W. Res. J. Int'l L.* 469 (2009) (looking at the frequency of various words appearing in UN Security Council resolutions). An analysis of international organizations' constitutions would sit on more theoretical solid ground, as constitutions sit in the hard-law area of international law, while these types of resolutions might not be as hard. *See, e.g.,* Martti Koskenniemi, "The Police in the Temple: Order, Justice and the UN," 6 *Eur. J. Int'l L.* 325, 327 (1995) (asserting that the Security Council's power to force states to act a certain way does not make such actions and edicts law); Gabriël H. Oosthuizen, "Playing the Devil's Advocate: The United Nations Security Council Is Unbound by Law," 12 *Leiden J. Int'l L.* 549, 550 (1999) (highlighting how Security Council resolutions are different from law).

135 The authors of this book do not wish to go in depth into any particular theory of international organization so as not to privilege any view of such international organizations. To grossly oversimplify, the implied powers doctrine arose from the common-sense notion that states place certain obligations on international organizations to engage in, or accomplish, certain tasks. Therefore, these states must endow these organizations with "implied" powers to engage in activities further to their ends. Otherwise, why set up these organizations in the first place? For deeper background on the concept, *see* A.I.L. Campbell, "The Limits of the Powers of International Organisations," 32 *Int'l & Comp. L.Q.* 523 (1983).

understanding among jurists shifting significantly over time.[136] Legal scholars like Andrew Guzman would emphasize this project's supposed inability to measure such powers through analyzing constitutions' texts. However, this does not represent a flaw in this project's design but, rather, stems from the nebulous and almost chimerical way that drafters have written these constitutions in the first place.[137]

Consider the subjective attempt to classify a simple UN Charter provision subjectively. A simple provision from that constitution states, "Each Member shall have not more than five representatives in the General Assembly."[138] Which principle from this project's list of 13 principles distilled from the major textbooks in the area best describes the driving purpose behind such a restriction on representatives? Jurists can only classify this provision subjectively. The limit of five persons arguably might bolster the efficiency of the organization, as too many representatives can lead to inefficient meetings.[139] However, representativeness also plays a role, as such a number helps to ensure representation by internal groups, ethnicities and political constituencies.[140] Such a number might foster communication, inasmuch as each member state has enough representatives to attend meetings, as well as to communicate the member state's position in a range

---

[136] Even as early as the 1970s, scholars from around the world noted the widespread subjectivity involved in using this concept. *See* Manuel Rama-Montaldo, "International Legal Personality and Implied Powers of International Organizations," 44 *Brit. Y.B. Int'l L.* 111 (1970).

[137] Guzman specifically refers to this as the Frankenstein problem, whereby member states of the international organization accede to vague constitutions on the grounds that such ambiguity will help the member states rein in the organization at a later date. *See* Guzman, *supra* note 63, at 999.

[138] UN Charter, *supra* note 7, art. 9(2).

[139] Even this statement would draw skepticism, as there are only "best practices" and fuzzy interviews upon which to decide. For one of the only scholarly sources available that discusses such a performance question, *see* Ngaire Woods et al., "Effective Leadership in International Organizations," World Economic Forum Global Agenda Council on International Governance Systems, Ref. No. 211014, Apr. 2014, *available at* www3.weforum.org/docs/WEF_Effective_Leadership_International_Organizations_report.pdf (last visited Mar. 25, 2020).

[140] Indeed, the lack of minority representation in international organizations leads some scholars like Martinez-Diaz to conclude that such organizational designs explicitly seek to promote efficiency and autonomy at the expense of representativeness. See Leonardo Martinez-Diaz, "Boards of Directors in International Organizations: A Framework for Understanding the Dilemmas of Institutional Design," 4 *Rev. Int'l Orgs* 383 (2009). Until more data like the data at the heart of this book becomes available, scholars cannot test the veracity of such claims.

of committees and to the public in general.[141] Giving all members the same number of representatives also might help to promote the member states' autonomy, as they do not need to share representatives as do the smaller economies within World Bank and IMF executive board meetings.[142] Any subjective interpretation of constitution provisions – even done by the best legal minds of our times – must involve assumptions about member states' interests, motivations and goals, not only at the time of signature but also in the present.[143] Indeed, this project eschews such a subjective approach in favor of the only aspect of such law that all seem to be able to agree on – the words actually agreed to by all of the parties, as contained in the constitution itself.[144]

Other critics of semantic analysis of these constitutions also might point to cases where such analysis picks up too many different types and

---

141 Authors like McArthur and Werker represent the perfect potential "consumers" of research like the research provided in this book, inasmuch as they ask scholars to quantify four dimensions of international organizations' communication as they seek to explain these organizations' engagement with their policy environments. See McArthur & Werker, *supra* note 54, at 155. These dimensions include power, norms, preferences and problems, although such a quantification seems difficult to imagine without preliminary attempts like the one provided in this book. See *id.*

142 Such sharing of board representatives has been a controversial practice since its start. For more on the perceived slights to a state's autonomy from having such "voice-sharing" structures in international organizations like the World Bank and the IMF, see Jakob Vestergaard, "Voice Reform in the World Bank," Danish Institute of International Studies Working Paper 2011/1 (2011).

143 Even by the early 1960s, academics realized the difficulty of interpreting constitutional provisions. Hexner's detailed study showed that even the same international organizations cannot interpret their own constitutional provisions. See Ervin P. Hexner, "Interpretation by Public International Organizations of their Basic Instruments," 53 *Am. J. Int'l L.* 341 (1959). Without guidance and without even internal agreement on the principles motivating certain provisions, external assessors and experts have little chance of compiling a database that can help to understand the underlying principles driving international organizations' constitutions.

144 Leaving aside inferences about the deep underpinning principles guiding constitutional provisions, even technocratic interpretation of these words can run afoul of differences in the way analysts think about international legal jurisprudence. For example, states and jurists interpret a basic constitutional concept – like "threat to the peace" – "in conformity [with the jurists' own understanding of the] rules of the Vienna Convention on the Law of Treaties of 1969 and in accordance with the principles and purposes of the United Nations Charter." See Mónica Lourdes de la Serna Galván, "The Security Council's Interpretation of UN Charter Article 39 (Threat To The Peace): Is the Security Council a Legislator for the Entire International Community?" 11 *Mex. Y.B. Int'l L.* 147 (2011). Such subjectivity makes any objective, replicable analysis of such a threat impossible.

interpretations of the same principle. For example, as a later chapter explains in greater detail, international organizations' constitutions refer to equality in voting rights between members, equality of genders during recruitment and even procedures to follow in case of "equality of votes" – namely, a tied vote.[145] The quantitative analysis at the heart of this book distinguishes between different meanings of such equality only to the extent that such analysis finds *patterns* of similar usage. As the previous section explained, this book has found some similarities in these constitutions' structures and language, with equality being used in similar contexts and places within the text, for example. This book shows how having a map of provisions using these words allows for deeper *qualitative* analysis, as reflected in Chapters 3 to 5. Any preliminary map of these constitutions – and the way they use words – can form the basis for further analysis where these constitutions do not explicitly refer to certain principles.[146]

This book intentionally is limited to illustrating diversity in the law of international organizations' constitutions. Critics might prefer it to study the *actions* of international organizations themselves in order to understand such law. For example, they might prefer that it analyze the autonomy of international organizations by measuring whether international organizations – like the European Organization for Nuclear Research (CERN) – accept gifts and bequests.[147] While CERN's constitution explicitly mentions such gifts, others – like that of the World Intellectual Property Organization (WIPO) – do not define the matter so clearly.[148] Nevertheless, both receive private sector funding.[149] So many problems immediately

---

145 See "ICJ Statute," *supra* note 122, art. 12(4) ("In the event of an equality of votes among the judges, the eldest judge shall have a casting vote").

146 Shaffer and Ginsburg, in their literature review of empirical approaches to law, presumably would classify this book as the vital first step in categorization that allows for further work looking for causality and real-world impacts. *See* Gregory Shaffer & Tom Ginsburg, "The Empirical Turn in International Legal Scholarship," 106 *Am. J. Int'l L.* 1 (2012).

147 For a press account of the policy, *see* Elizabeth Gibney, "Charity Begins at CERN," *Nature*, July 15, 2014," available at www.nature.com/news/charity-begins-at-cern-1.15558 (last visited Mar. 25, 2020).

148 The WIPO Convention allows for funding by member states, referred to as Unions due to inheriting the language of an 1883 Paris Convention for the Protection of Industrial Property. *See* Convention Establishing the World Intellectual Property Organization art. 11, July 14, 1967, 21 U.S.T. 1749, 828 UNTS 3. Nothing in the constitution forbids member states from using private funds as part or all of their contributions.

149 Only recently has the WIPO started regulating such funding, at a level that any jurist might consider hard law, in its Financial Regulations. *See* WIPO, *Proposed*

emerge if one tries to compare specific legal provisions across international organizations. Is it possible to compare provisions in the constitutions of international financial organizations with provisions in the constitutions of other types of international organizations? Do these organizations' practices – unremarked on in their constitutions – actually constitute part of their law?[150] Comparing the practices of international organizations tells us nothing about their laws.[151]

Substantive criticisms: putting word counting into perspective

The biggest critique of this book likely will be that it neglects to explain how international organizations' constitutions impact on the international organizations' structure, strategy and activity. To be clear, the authors of this book have only delayed analysis of this aspect of international organizations law to a later time. Understanding the value of this book requires a deeper look into the way this research into international organizations law likely will evolve over time. Figure 1.10 shows the way that this research fits into the larger research program of trying to trace international organizations law to all aspects of the organizations that exist around us. Critics will ask for a relationship between one specific aspect of international organizations law (as contained in their constitutions) and environmental policy, the legal responsibility for harms to specific groups of persons or effects on the

---

Amendments to WIPO's Financial Regulations and Rules (FRR), Program and Budget Committee Twenty-Sixth Session Geneva, July 10–14, 2017, *available at* www.wipo.int/edocs/mdocs/govbody/en/wo_pbc_26/wo_pbc_26_ref_frr.pdf (last visited Mar. 25, 2020).

150 Conservative jurists consider these practices as basically agency problems, whereas the international organization engages in actions unknown to their principals, the member states. Liberal jurists might consider these practices as soft law, having little applicability to other organizations. For a description of the autonomy that each organization exercises in creating its own law, *see* Erin R. Graham, "International Organizations as Collective Agents: Fragmentation and the Limits of Principal Control at the World Health Organization," 20 *Eur. J. Int'l Rel.* 366 (2013).

151 As Wood notes, scholars do not agree on whether the building blocks of customary international law – namely, generating state practice and evidencing *opinio juris* – apply to the law of international organizations. *See* Michael Wood, "The International Tribunal for the Law of the Sea and General International Law," 22 *Int'l J. Marine & Coastal L.* 351 (2007). Unlike states, international organizations' practice may not represent custom (as the practice of member states, rather than their agents, often forms the basis of such law). As the concluding chapter of this book discusses, international courts and tribunals have exercised considerable reluctance in giving opinions (which jurists might mistake as law) about international organizations' practices.

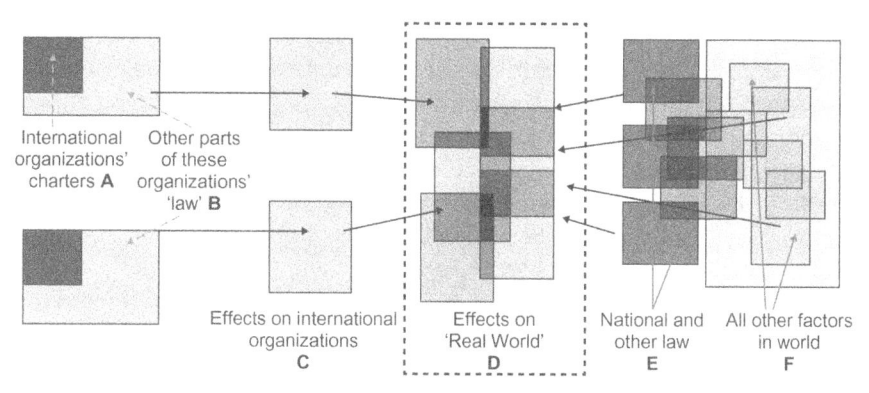

Figure 1.10 A diagrammatic illustration of why we measure words in international organizations' constitutions. The figure shows why we measure the frequency of words appearing in international organizations' constitutions, rather than something else. We can all agree that the ideal research design consists of mapping constitution law (marked A) to real-world outcomes (marked D). Yet, we can measure these effects only by international organizations' actions (marked C) – effects which depend also on other international law and decisions (marked B). These real-world effects, though, also depend on national and other law (marked E) and a wide range of other factors – D, E or F right now. We propose to start by providing a first measure of A – letting other scholars fill out this schema, just as the first empiricists of the twentieth century did for the physical sciences.

"real world." Such research requires well-defined and accurately measured independent variables that reflect some aspect of international organizations' constitutions, which is labelled "A" in the figure.[152] So far, researchers have not even managed to do this, which is a prerequisite to finding a relationship.

Understanding the way that international organizations' constitutions affect other parts of an organization's internal law (or law developed across these organizations) must represent the next stage of such research. How can a social scientist trace through the effect of international organizations law on the real world without understanding this wider constellation of

---

152 An independent variable represents a known factor, and researchers look for a relationship between an independent variable and a dependent variable (or the variable that the researcher attempts to explain). Thinking about laws as independent or dependent variables may offend some classically trained jurists, who might see the law as the result of legal reasoning as well as political debate between judges and parliamentarians. For an example of such analysis, *see* Adam S. Chilton & Eric A. Posner, "Treaties and Human Rights: The Role of Long-Term Trends," 81 *L. & Contemp. Prob.* 1 (2008).

internal regulation, which is labelled "B" in the figure? For better or for worse, this book's measure represents the first census of these constitutional principles. Jurists and social scientists may now revise this project's dataset, taking subjective aspects of these principles into account.[153]

Clearly, even tracing through the effects of international organizations' constitutions on organizational characteristics and functions represents a leap too far for this book. The part of the figure labelled "C" represents the extent to which international organizations consult with civil society, organize conferences, fight for human rights or any of the millions of things that international organizations are and do. This project simply cannot engage in such an analysis here because of the interactions, confounding effects and otherwise obscuring factors involved in parts of the figure labelled "E" and "F."[154] To take a simple example, modeling the effects of international organizations law on peace would require controlling for states' level of economic development, shared histories and cultures, military spending and a wide range of factors.[155] Without an MECE (mutually exclusive, collectively exhaustive) measure of our independent variable – namely, aspects of international organizations law – none of this subsequent work can reliably take place.[156]

Using this project's data, this book can only characterize such a constitution-based international organizations law, without making causal statements. If the book were to advance a hypothesis beyond the four corners of the constitutions included in the dataset, such as whether the

---

153 The authors of this book do not ascribe unrealistic importance to seminal databases in the field. Two influential datasets have led to over 30,000 citations in the field of comparative corporate law. See Rafael La Porta et al., "Investor Protection and Corporate Valuation," 57 *J. Fin.* 1147 (2002); Rafael La Porta et al., "Law and Finance," 106 *J. Pol. Econ.* 1113 (1998).

154 In other words, it is not possible to simply tie the existence or type of constitutional provisions to specific organizational attributes, like having a constitutional requirement for gender diversity and the proportion of women working in an international organization. Other, outside (or "confounding") variables would affect this relationship.

155 Without controlling for these confounding variables, statistical results would show wrong results for the "pure" effects of international organizations law, something that this book does not even attempt. For one obvious example, see William J. Dixon, "Democracy and the Management of International Conflict," 37 *J. Conflict Res.* 42 (1993).

156 Such MECE models refer to frameworks where it is possible to identify factors uniquely (not as fuzzy combinations of factors), and factors influencing the dependent variables are not omitted. This book's dataset represents a first step towards collecting such a MECE set of statistics that international law scholars can use for decades to come.

importance of executive staff correlates with these organizations' budgets, it might have a section that plots the number of times that constitutions refer to executive staff and organizational budgets. However, without a common measure of the importance of executive staff, others cannot check this work. Others cannot assess the reliability (or variance) of this book's estimates or check to see how statistically controlling for staffing levels affects the relationships discovered. Without objective, independently variable information, it is impossible to falsify this book's hypotheses and others' hypotheses, and the debates would continue in endless circles.[157] Therefore, the dataset at the heart of this book represents the first – and hitherto only – step towards falsifying statements and hypotheses in the field of international organizations law.

Critics might also ask why this book does not provide a complete lexicon or compilation of the statistics generated for this book for every organizational type, region and so forth. After all, if the aim is to survey the principles in every international organization's constitution, should not this book provide all of these relationships in something like an atlas? The authors posit that the largest value of this book would not come from simply describing these international organizations' constitutions in an atlas. Instead, the overarching goal consists of *disproving* the existence of a common, unitary law of international organizations. As a result, this book shows such differences repeatedly, throughout (especially in Chapter 3), in various cluster analyses and network analyses. All of the data exists online, making the physical printing of constitutions' values by region unnecessary, for example. Any researcher interested in comparing the way that constitution principles from international organizations based in Europe differ from those based in North America needs only to search the database for these two criteria. This project could split, divide and group the data in so many different ways – by region, by type of organization and so forth – that providing a complete printed list of these summary statistics would be too distracting and tedious for the average reader.

Does looking at constitutions of international organizations, especially historical constitutions, ignore the changing nature of such a law of international organizations? One criticism will be that analyzing constitutions like the 1945 UN Charter – or even the older International Telecommunication Union's (ITU) 1865 charter – tells us little about

---

[157] Thomas Kuhn said that "normal science" even in law progresses not from proving a hypothesis correct, as such proof will be epistemologically impossible. Instead, it is possible only to fail to reject (or falsify) the finding. Falsifiability represents *the* way empirical, modern science advances. *See* Brian Leiter, "The Demarcation Problem in Jurisprudence: A New Case for Skepticism," 31 *Oxford J. Leg. Stud.* 663 (2011).

developments in international organizations law since the formation of these organizations. Admittedly, legal principles do change over time.[158] Nevertheless, comparing these older constitutions with newer ones – like the World Trade Organization's (WTO) 1995 constitution – reveals some interesting trends. For example, comparing the number of times the International Telecommunication Union's constitution and that of the WTO refer to cooperation tells us something interesting about the principles that were on the drafters' minds. This project does not compare these constitutions with their historic versions that would show changes in the way that these constitutions mention aspirations, authority and other principles, as the project already is considerably complex. The hope is that other researchers will engage in such longitudinal studies, once they have been convinced of the merits of this book's quantification scheme.

Rethinking these organizations as lawmakers

Many authors have written about international organizations' potential role as lawmakers. Chief among them stands José Alvarez's *International Organizations as Law-makers*.[159] As it is one of the most comprehensive reviews of international organizations' constitutions to date, critics presumably will expect a review comparison of this book with that book. In general, Alvarez' fine work reflects the qualitative analysis that this book seeks to further extend. While he analyzes international organizations' constitutions from the perspective of a jurist, he lacks the quantitative data needed to discover deep similarities and differences between and across these constitutions.

As if to highlight the problems with subjective analysis that this book bemoans, Alvarez's Chapter 2 immediately illustrates the problems of interpreting charter law.[160] The Vienna Convention on the Law of Treaties provides little guidance behind *jus cogens*, which Alvarez himself notes.

---

158 Numerous other academics write about such change and development. This book would not contribute much by repeating their work. For a description of this work, *see* Jost Delbrück, "Prospects for a 'World (Internal) Law'?: Legal Development in a Changing International System," 9 *J. Glob. Leg. Stud.* 401 (2002); David Held, "The Changing Structure of International Law: Sovereignty Transformed?," *in The Global Transformations Reader: An Introduction to the Globalization Debate* 161 (David Held & Anthony McGrew eds. 2003).
159 *See generally* Alvarez, *supra* note 36.
160 *See id.*, ch. 2 (calling this "institutional practice," which boils down to commonly accepted activities of international organizations). As Blokker and Wessel note, though, existing activities and traditions provide poor foundations for understanding the normative underpinnings and principles *behind* these practices. *See* Niels M.

Like most commentators in this area, he asserts that the interpretation of constitutional provisions of international organizations emerges by consensus and negotiation, a process poorly suited for legal scholars, who rely on evidence and often personal, deeply held notions of morality, jurisprudential order and meaning.[161] Implied powers and intent (other subsections of his work) fall completely outside the ambit of empirical law, as both rely on unobserved (and usually unobservable) information. However, if one accepts as true Alvarez' writings and the work of the thousands of other scholars writing in this tradition, then this project's aim to understand international organizations' constitutions represents a core piece of international law scholarship, as these establishing agreements serve as genuine constitutions for these entities and the areas of social and political activity they regulate.[162]

Alvarez' roughly fifteen-page "survey" of constitutional provisions represents the same kind of selective analysis that makes this book's analysis necessary. His survey of constitutions' provisions focuses on the areas of organizational activity that provisions regulate, and it completely ignores the deeper principles guiding these provisions. Some examples of these kinds of activity include these organizations' memberships, structure and staffing, as well as issues like funding. Alvarez chooses five issues to look at in more depth – the membership body's power over the organization's finances, the organization's legal personality, the basis in treaty law for the organization's powers, the limits on its powers and the definition of internal versus external rulemaking authority. However, without an objective measure of these provisions, Alvarez' analysis must rest on abstract reasoning. Naturally, he cannot apply such reasoning to 191 international organizations. He cannot describe – except with case studies – how powers over internal rulemaking can extend to external regulation, or even tell how

---

Blokker & Ramses A. Wessel, "Editorial: Updating International Organizations," 2 *Int'l Org. L. Rev.* 1 (2005).

161 One way of avoiding such subjectivity may consist in finding one person who everyone can agree will resolve such differences in subjective, individual interpretation. However, even an attempt to find such a final authority or expert to give authoritative judgments and interpretations of international laws runs into difficulties. For more on this problem, *see* Katharina Berner, "Authentic Interpretation in Public International Law," 76 *Heidelberg J. Int'l L.* 845 (2016).

162 Alvarez specifically dedicates the final part of the chapter to dealing with this topic. This book takes no view on this topic, other than to provide data for individuals seeking to write about the topic. For more on previous work quantifying constitutional texts, *see* Anne Meuwese & Mila Versteeg, "Quantitative Methods for Comparative Constitutional Law?," *in Practice and Theory in Comparative Law* 230 (Maurice Adams & Jacco Bomhoff eds. 2012).

many international organizations face this problem. Like all other studies of international organizations law before this one, his twenty-plus-page treatment of the subject provides no data and thus no specific comparisons and contrasts between different international organizations. The only conclusion he can reach at the end of his Chapter 3 highlights the political processes used in agreeing on the treaties, regulations and other legal instruments commonly associated with international law.[163] Unfortunately, noting the political nature of international organizations law brings us no closer to understanding these organizations quantitatively, something Alvarez does not even wish to do.

The rest of Alvarez' book deals with the way that international organizations' formation and activity impacts on international law. The UN Security Council and other UN bodies may adopt resolutions or declarations, negotiate treaties and otherwise engage in these types of rulemaking processes.[164] However, Alvarez does not address the source of their authority (in these organizations' own constitutions) to make these rules. His book discusses only ten international organizations, a far-from-comprehensive sample. The other five chapters (Chapters 5–9) describe the ways that these international organizations make laws by serving as fora for the conclusion of treaties, as well as the sites for dispute resolution.[165] None of these international organizations' constitutions provides specific rules about how they engage in such lawmaking. Thus, even ostensibly comprehensive books like Alvarez' almost completely ignore more than 90 percent of international organizations' constitutions, which severely limits the types of conclusions that can be made.

To be clear, this book does not try to give a complete, comprehensive picture of international organizations. Instead, the only goal consists in falsifying the notion of a single, unitary law of international organizations – nothing more and nothing less. Thus, the book does not need to show what these constitutions mean for the evolution of international organizations law. Moreover, the book does not need to demonstrate any links between particular aspects of these international organizations' constitutions and the structure (or conduct) of these organizations. It does not prove (or disprove)

---

163 *See* Alvarez, *supra* note 36, at 146–84.
164 Alvarez provides specific case studies looking at the International Civil Aviation Organization, International Labour Organization, International Atomic Energy Agency, Food and Agriculture Organization, the WTO and the IMF, among others.
165 Enough exciting research has come out looking at textual similarities in international courts' and tribunals' decisions, which authors like Alvarez could usefully summarize. For one example, *see* Nikolaos Aletras et al., "Predicting Judicial Decisions of the European Court of Human Rights: A Natural Language Processing Perspective," 2 *Peer J. Comp. Sci.* 93 (2016).

that these constitutions take any epistemological view of international jurisprudence. It does not try to convince the reader of any theories about the incorporation and evolution of constitutional principles. Rather, the dataset provides the first step on a long road towards fully understanding international organizations law. If anything, the book hopefully triggers much of the useful work to follow.

Lessons learned from this book

Despite the limitations of this book, it nevertheless contributes much to the field of international organizations law. In particular, the dataset falsifies, beyond any doubt, the existence of a single, generalizable international organizations law.[166] The book shows that circuits, networks, clusters or "tracks" of principles exist across international organizations' constitutions. Regardless of whether one agrees or disagrees with this book's aims and methods, one cannot deny the validity of these observations.

This book also provides the first estimates for social science entities that will require much refinement in the future. Figure 1.11 puts the book into perspective by describing the social sciences approach to jurists who are unaccustomed to the research methods adopted here. Social scientists start out by assuming the existence of some ontological fact, like the authority given by (or contained in) an international organization's constitution.[167] Greek letters are used in the figure to signify the ontological true value or principle that is being measured, as shown on the left-most side. It is possible to think of a principle such as authority or cooperation inherent in the constitution as some quantity (illustrated by the boxes). Any proxy or epistemological measurement of such a principle, which is shown as "mentioned authority" and "mentioned cooperation," will contain part of that true value that this book seeks to measure. Part of the measure will not contain the information that the book seeks to measure, which is labelled as "mistaken authority" and "mistaken cooperation." The Greek letters with the hat over them (by convention) represent this book's measurement – the values that this project actually reports. These parameters – or variables that take on specific values depending on the

---

166 A later chapter reviews the work of some of the prominent scholars in the field of international organizations law looking for such a single, unifying law.
167 The authors of this book accept the problems of assuming that such authority or communication or any other principle "exists" ontologically, waiting for us to measure it. Such authority, equality and so forth represent social constructs. *See generally* Julia Black, "Constructing and Contesting Legitimacy and Accountability in Polycentric Regulatory Regimes," 2 *Reg. & Gov.* 137 (2008).

54   *The values of international organizations*

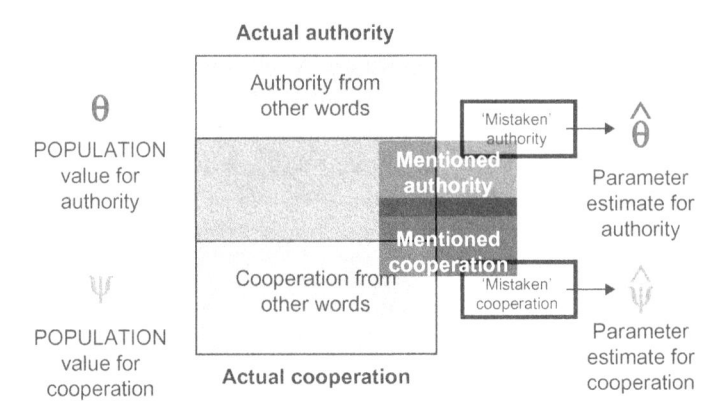

Figure 1.11 What do our measurements actually mean? Social scientists think about estimation somewhat differently than lawyers do. For social scientists, some statistics can represent some attribute of authority, cooperation and other principles. Counting words in constitutions represents one way of estimating that value (which is ontologically true, even if we cannot measure it accurately). These word-mentions will cover only a fraction of the true population/concept we look to measure (as shown by the overlap). Some of these mentions will not accurately measure the underlying concept (which we label as "mistaken" estimates). Altogether, we obtain "estimates" (shown typically by the hat above the parameter). Social scientists accept that these estimates may exhibit bias and imprecision. We accept that future scientists must improve parameter definition and measurement – rather than throwing out the project because we cannot understand the issue using lawerly tools of analysis and deduction.

constitution being measured – contain reliable information about the underlying concept and some noise. When taken together, these parameters describe the network that the next chapter illustrates.

Therefore, future researchers will need to extend this research in three ways. First, they will need to improve the definition of the underlying concept or principle that this book measures. The book purposely has not tried to define authority, cooperation or the other principles being analyzed, as such a definition would add the authors' own subjective biases to the analysis. Future scholars – who hardly can deny the existence of underlying principles in these constitutions – can debate the meaning and content of these principles for years to come.[168] Second, they will need to

---

[168] It is unknown if scholars and treaty makers can ever arrive at such definitions. For one skeptic's analysis, *see* Kyon-Gun Koh, "Reservations to Multilateral Treaties: How International Legal Doctrine Reflects World Vision," 23 *Harv. Int'l. L.J.* 71 (1983).

go through each type of provision in these constitutions (as most of them use very similar language and structures) and decide on which principles these provisions uphold. They also may amend this book's measurement scale, removing provisions that mention a principle but do not refer to the actual substantive principle as these future experts might define it.[169] Third, they may design questionnaires and other measures to "triangulate" the real measure of authority, communication and other principles in a constitution.[170] Significant econometric skill and attention needs to go into the design of surveys and other methods of measuring constitutional principles.[171]

By providing an objective dataset for the discipline, this book opens the study of international organizations to the thousands of algorithms, characterizations and modeling models available to social science researchers. Figure 1.12 provides one example of such an algorithm, which measures the diversity of principles appearing in these constitutions. Such diversity measures the extent to which a wide number of principles appear frequently in each international organization's constitution. From that it is possible to see that the Asia Pacific Association of Agricultural Research Institutions' constitution refers to more principles, in copious amounts, than does the Asian Development Bank's constitution. Moreover, it is possible to quantify exactly the extra diversity of that constitution's principles and look for other factors that correlate with that diversity. Perhaps more effective

---

169 Other advances in jurimetrics show the promise of the method proposed in this book. Thanks to early quantification work in environmental treaties, it is known how to design treaties to better bring about particular health and environmental outcomes worldwide. For a discussion, *see* Steven J. Hoffman & John-Arne Røttingen, "Assessing the Expected Impact of Global Health Treaties: Evidence from 90 Quantitative Evaluations," 105 *Am. J. Pub. Health* 26 (2014).

170 The development of the International Volunteer Impacts Survey represents just one example of an effort to measure and validate principles like "open-mindedness, international understanding … civic activism, community engagement, media attentiveness, and financial contributions," with measurement of such nebulous topics requiring a period of analysis and negotiation. See Benjamin Lough et al., "Measuring Volunteer Outcomes: Development of the International Volunteer Impacts Survey," Center for Social Development Working Paper No. 09–31 (2009), *available at* https://openscholarship.wustl.edu (last visited Mar. 25, 2020).

171 Even simple studies like Hoole's analysis of senior executive appointments at UN-related organizations requires significant attention to defining terms, obtaining objective data and tying that data to motives and intentions. *See* Francis W. Hoole, "The Appointment of Executive Heads in UN Treaty-Based Organizations," 30 *Int'l Org.* 91 (1976). Imagine the added complexity involved in trying to gauge the underlying principles guiding those appointments.

56 *The values of international organizations*

Shannon Diversity Index (H)

Organization	
Association of Natural Rubber Producing Countries	
Association of European Public Postal Operators	
Association of Caribbean States	
Association of Agricultural Research Institutions in the Near East and North Africa	
Association of African Central Banks	
Asian-Pacific Postal Union	
Asian Productivity Organization	
Asian Development Bank	
Asia Pacific Association of Agricultural Research Institutions	
African Rice Centre	
African Civil Aviation Commission	
Afro-Asian Rural Development Organization	

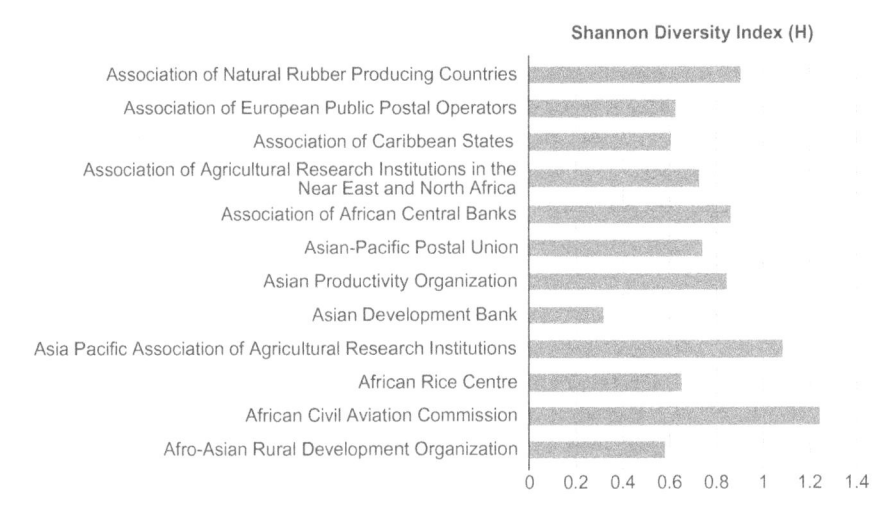

0   0.2   0.4   0.6   0.8   1   1.2   1.4

Figure 1.12 The great diversity of principles mentioned among the international organizations' constitutions. This was calculated using the ecological Shannon Diversity Index (H) approach, as the principal terms identified in this study within the constitutional documents are analogous to species in a given community/ecosystem. This demonstrates one of the many ways that social-scientific statistical approaches can supplement legal analysis through their discovery of patterns and uniqueness among the texts.

international organizations have more diverse constitutions. Perhaps they employ a more diverse workforce. With these data, it will be possible to test a wide range of hypotheses.[172]

The authors of this book naturally accept peers' criticism, especially from international law scholars who see little value in econometric and quantitative methods as applied to law. Obviously, no statistical analysis of international organizations' provisions can (yet) provide the depth of insight that classical methods of treaty analysis provide.[173] Quantitative analysis does not replace traditional analysis; it merely supplements it. Traditional

---

172 Indeed, many important studies, only marginally related to our topic, heavily rely on datasets like that of this book. For one example, *see* Emilie M. Hafner-Burton & Alexander H. Montgomery, "Power Positions: International Organizations, Social Networks, and Conflict," 50 *J. Conf. Res.* 3 (2006).
173 Critical analyses also will play an important role, which statistical analysis can never provide. For one example of such an in-depth critique, *see* Tetsuo Sato, *Evolving Constitutions of the International Organizations: A Critical Analysis of the Interpretative Framework of the Constituent Instruments of International Organizations* (1996).

international law scholars have little to fear from this book's approach to counting up the number of times international organizations' constitutions refer to specific words. Nevertheless, such counts may inspire a new generation of insights, which traditional analysis can help to clarify.[174]

The road ahead

With a census of the principles contained in international organizations' constitutions, this book maps some of the broader understandings around these principles of the law of international organizations. The major textbooks on the law of international organizations have hitherto glossed over issues like cooperation, equality and representativeness, assuming that all international organizations must hold these values similarly. However, as demonstrated in the previous sections of this chapter, different international organizations' constitutions have fundamentally different aspirations and ideas about cooperation. For example, there are different conceptions of equality, defined and actualized by the design of international organizations in different areas. At last, with the help of legal researchers, universal understandings of these values could be found.

This chapter has shown how the principles often discussed by the leading commentators in the field of international organizations law are embodied in international organizations' constitutions in ways far more complex, and interesting, than might be first assumed. The chapter has reviewed the proof for the clustering, linking and grouping of principles – and international organizations' constitutions referring to these principles – that are discussed in depth throughout the book. It has provided simple illustrations showing how the simultaneous mention of cooperation, equality and representativeness in one group of international organizations' constitutions could have a different meaning – and, more importantly, legal interpretation – than in another group of constitutions. The principles found in *all* international organizations may coincide in seven different pragmatic groupings of these institutions (as shown in Figure 1.6). However, as shown in Figure 1.5, four groupings of these principles may best exemplify the way universal international organizations' constitutions specifically refer to these principles. It is

---

[174] Multiple branches of law have benefited from the insights that quantitative analysis can bring from the 1950s onward. Work on the genealogy of legal traditions represents one area where quantitative methods allowed for widespread acceptance of theories predicated on different traditions or families of law, like common law, civil law and Germanic law. *See* Daniel N. Rockmore et al., "The Cultural Evolution of National Constitutions," 69 *J. Assoc. Info. Sci. & Tech.* 483 (2017).

important to note that this is only the beginning of understanding why these groupings emerge and what they mean.

Finding network relationships between these principles shows the complexity behind any jurisprudential attempts to define, operationalize or, especially, generalize these principles. As Figure 1.7 showed, there is a clustering of three groups of principles when looking at the links between these principles and the international organizations' constitutions in which they appear. However, when all the links between these principles are traced through, all references end up back at executive staffing principles. All principles seem to support the way executive staff work in these international organizations. If true, such a finding has obvious repercussions for how to think about international organizations' legitimacy and authority.[175] Concrete data gives us the means of fixing the basis of international organizations law in legal and general principles – for better or for worse.

The rest of the book provides the details behind any principles-based jurisprudential theory of international organizations law. Chapter 2 illustrates the extent to which various international organizations' constitutions refer to a range of principles identified in the literature. It describes the universe of these constitutions quantitatively, and it provides a first analysis of groupings of these principles. It shows how some constitutions refer to different principles more than others. It also shows how these groupings were found, as well as which organizations and principles belong to these groups. The chapter also shows the network linkages between these principles, as constitutions refer to some principles more than others. If mentions of executive staff appear dominant in traditional quantitative analysis, these mentions become all the more important in the network analysis provided. Indeed, no analysis of international organizations law can omit the principles driving executive staff, and remain relevant.

Chapters 3, 4 and 5 illustrate these quantitative links using the standard tools of legal analysis. Chapter 3 shows how references to other principles shade any legal or practical definition of authority in these international organizations. For example, the African Export Import Bank's constitution describes how the Bank's autonomy from its member states helps ensure its staff's authority. The constitutions of the Caribbean Development Bank, the

---

175 To speculate, by way of example, if the principles in these constitutions all relate to executive staff, then such staff obviously form the basis and extent of these organizations' authority. Senior staff – rather than existing philosophical personhood or existential qualities of these organizations in themselves – provide legitimacy, social contract and right-to-rule of these ill-defined international entities. While obviously silly in the light of 100 years of theorizing, the empirics could tell a different on-the-ground story.

European Bank for Reconstruction and Development and the Eastern and Southern African Trade and Development Bank also show how some constitutions use recommendations to appoint staff, while in other cases staff make recommendations to member states. Depending on the international organization, the principle of making recommendations serves different ends. In some cases, autonomy helps to provide the authority to make these recommendations. In cases like the UN, the recommendations themselves carry authority, and the authority vested in the UN gives authority to these recommendations. However, the *law* (and particularly the subsidiary and regulatory law) behind these nuanced concepts of these legal principles remains almost completely undefined.

With a detailed analysis of the mysterious workings of authority out of the way, Chapter 4 concentrates on substantive principles. The statistical analysis discussed previously identified these principles as the main drivers of international organizations law, in contrast to procedural principles. Chapter 4 shows, using the same kind of analysis as in the previous chapter, how equality, peace, representativeness and autonomy mean something together and separately, depending on the constitutions being discussed. Unequal relations between states can never form the basis of peace between states, as the UN Charter and other constitutions attest. State sovereignty may represent the ultimate type of autonomy, but representation in an international organization may actually *bolster* both the autonomy of the state and the international organization concerned. Such apparent contradictions bedevil all aspects of constitutional interpretation. Valuing these principles and knowing their value in promoting a principle like peace requires a holistic understanding of these constitutions in context.

Valuing international organizations' constitutions starts by understanding the principles driving these organizations. Only with a map of these principles in hand can we hope to build the foundations of a durable law of international organizations, if one is to be created in the future.

2

The empirics of international organizational principles

Introduction

What do the numbers describing each international organization's constitution tell us about these organizations' principles? The Caribbean Telecommunication Union's constitution may mention equality more than any other constitution, literally twice as often as the Indian Ocean Rim Association's and the Organisation for Islamic Cooperation's. How do these numbers compare with those of their peers? Do the high-frequency mentions of efficiency in the constitutions of the Association of Caribbean States or the Caribbean Postal Union mean that Caribbean-based international organizations place more emphasis on the core legal principles discussed in this book? Only hard numbers can answer questions like these.

This chapter illustrates the patterns in which international organizations' constitutions refer to the major principles in international organizations law. Indeed, it is beyond a reasonable doubt that international organizations' constitutions form regular patterns in the ways they refer to these principles, patterns that were unidentifiable before now.[1] This chapter starts by showing how different types of international organizations stress different principles in a way that mere accident cannot explain.[2] Universal organizations' constitutions differ from those of their regional peers by

---

1 This reference to a qualitative criminal test has been made to start leading the reader towards thinking statistically. In a courtroom, beyond a reasonable doubt may represent the idea of certainty. In a statistical setting, a finding of 99 percent statistical significance represents something as close to "beyond a reasonable doubt" as one will obtain in the social sciences.
2 If universal organizations referenced aspirational principles the same as regional organizations by accident (in other words, randomly), one would expect to see UN specialized organizations stressing aspiration as a core principle more often than regional cooperative organizations, like the Arab League. Therefore, it is

referencing authority, equality, executive staff and staff differently. General competence organizations reference autonomy, cooperation, equality, executive staff and other principles differently than their partners with limited competences, and so forth. These international organizations' constitutions also stress different principles, according to the size of their constitutional documents, their employment, age and location.

Other parts of this chapter contain most of the statistically causal evidence for the chapter's claims. The second section shows how the mention of some principles seems to statistically significantly correlate with others. The most basic grouping algorithms indicate a split between substantive and procedural principles. Executive staff – and staff principles in general – seem to correlate with almost everything, which hardly is surprising for documents whose purpose is to explain the governance and management of international organizations by human beings. Nevertheless, different groups of international organizations clearly prioritize different principles. One analysis shows how it is possible to split – using objective, statistical analysis – universal organizations into four subgroups. Another section breaks up all international organizations into seven groups and labels these machine-made groups as efficient international organizations, aspiring ones, dreaming ones and so forth. However, such clustering cannot look at the way principles "pass through" to other principles – namely, how constitutions that mention authority also mention cooperation as an oft-cited principle in executive staff management.

Such networks of principles clearly show how it is important to interpret networks of principles in the same way as interpreting networks of organizations, referring to particular constitutional principles. To illustrate this point, this chapter shows three groups of clusters of principles usually appearing together – cooperation and autonomy (with a bit of recommendation added in), representativeness and peace, and everything else as a third group. Nevertheless, in line with the finding that the constitutions of different groups of international organizations rely on different groups of principles, this chapter shows how these networks vary. They vary over time for the same organizations. Moreover, they vary across types of organizations. As the last figure in the chapter shows (see Figure 2.21), all roads lead back to executive staff. Ultimately, all constitutional principles relate to executive staff, which can be seen as an obvious conclusion, once one stops to think about it.

> possible to compare the average frequency with which each type of organization refers to aspirations and test to see if randomness explains such differences in these averages. This book uses a range of statistical procedures to test exactly that proposition.

62   *The values of international organizations*

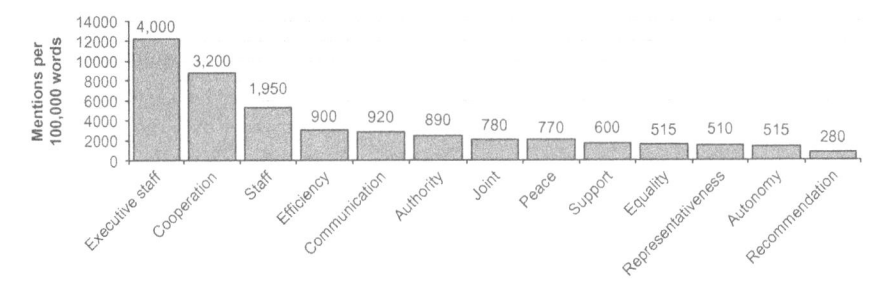

Figure 2.1 Discussions about staffing and cooperation dominate the internal organization structure. The figure shows the range of mentions of each of the principles shown. The bars show the range within which 95 percent of the values fall. Thus the top of the bar shows the range of 95 percent of all mentions for each value (calculated by adding twice each principle's standard deviation to the mean value of mentions for each principle). The bottom of each bar shows the smallest value among the constitutions we analyzed. The values above each bar show the average number of mentions.

Understanding international organizational principles statistically

Correlation between principles

International organizations' constitutions clearly reference some principles more than others.[3] Figure 2.1 shows the range of mentions of each of the principles focused on in this book. For example, all international organizations' constitutions referred to cooperation, at most 10,000 times per 100,000 words. Nevertheless, most constitutions refer to most principles fewer than 3,000 times per 100,000 words. If the mere frequency of mentions reflects, in any way, the importance these constitutions ascribe to these principles, then cooperation and efficiency far outweigh representativeness and autonomy as cherished principles. With an average frequency of about 4,000 times and 3,200 times per 100,000 words, respectively, executive issues and cooperation far outweigh references to all other principles combined.

What about the way international organizations' constitutions refer to these principles together, as in groups? Figure 2.2 shows roughly the

---

3 In other words, some constitutions may reference a principle like cooperation more than any other constitutions do. However, across the universe of all constitutions, they may on average reference a principle like attention to executive staff more than any other principle.

Variable														

Correlations (NEW values. sta)
Marked correlations are significant at p <.05000
N = 190 (Casewise deletion of missing data)

	Means	Std. Dev.	Aspiration	Authority	Autonomy	Communication	Cooperation	Efficiency	Equality	Executive Staff	Staff	Joint	Peace	Recommendation	Representation
Aspiration	204.3	368.47	1.00	0.04	-0.03	0.10	0.06	0.10	0.02	**0.19**	0.14	0.08	-0.04	0.05	0.11
Authority	465	817.74	0.04	1.00	-0.01	0.07	0.05	0.16	-0.01	0.10	0.09	0.08	0.10	0.14	0.01
Autonomy	258.3	455.07	-0.03	-0.01	1.00	-0.06	0.26	0.06	0.08	-0.08	0.08	-0.05	0.28	-0.02	0.04
Communication	989	920.13	0.10	0.07	-0.06	1.00	0.09	0.55	0.25	0.03	0.35	0.25	0.03	-0.09	0.28
Cooperation	2303.2	3155.64	0.06	0.05	0.26	0.09	1.00	0.11	0.34	0.25	0.25	0.47	0.05	0.09	0.18
Efficiency	1091.8	917.99	0.10	0.16	0.26	0.55	0.11	1.00	0.21	x	0.47	0.27	0.04	0.02	0.24
Equality	463.7	515.48	0.02	-0.01	0.08	0.25	0.34	0.21	1.00	0.06	0.21	0.18	0.16	-0.01	0.26
Executive Staff	4210	4014.09	**0.19**	0.10	-0.08	0.35	0.09	0.19	0.21	1.00	0.16	0.03	-0.03	0.04	0.26
Staff	1303.5	1934.85	0.14	0.09	0.08	0.25	0.25	0.47	0.21	**0.16**	1.00	0.38	-0.01	-0.01	0.33
Joint	237.6	578.08	0.08	0.08	-0.05	0.37	0.27	0.27	0.18	0.03	0.38	1.00	-0.01	0.08	0.22
Peace	121.5	431.66	-0.04	0.10	0.28	0.03	0.05	0.04	0.16	-0.03	0.38	-0.01	1.00	0.20	0.02
Recommendation	138.3	243.57	0.05	0.14	-0.02	-0.09	0.09	0.02	-0.01	0.04	-0.01	0.08	0.20	1.00	-0.07
Representation	366.8	492.83	0.11	0.01	0.04	0.28	0.18	0.24	0.26	0.26	0.33	0.22	0.02	-0.07	1.00

Figure 2.2 Correlations between values show that the principles of staff communication and efficiency dominate the international system. This figure shows the extent of Pearson correlations in the number of mentions of each principle. These statistics were calculated by first finding the frequency of mentions of each principle, as previously explained. All of these frequencies were then correlated over all the constitutions analyzed. The numbers in bold type correlate at a statistically significant level of 95 percent. In other words, the chances of these numbers appearing different than zero, when in fact they are zero, are less than 5 percent.

same information as in the previous figure – namely, the average extent to which constitutions refer to various principles and the variability in those references. The figure also foreshadows the later analysis in this chapter of such correlations, by showing the way these principles appear together in constitutions. The scale used in the figures ranges between –1 and 1, where 1 represents always appearing together, –1 represents never appearing together and 0 means no pattern exists in the way these mentions appear in international organizations' constitutions. A value of 0.26 for autonomy and cooperation indicates that references to these two principles in international organizations' constitutions occur more frequently than simply at random.

What are these values? Figure 2.3 foreshadows some of these more important values. As the figure shows, staffing principles correlate with nine out of the thirteen principles analyzed – aspiration, communication, cooperation, efficiency, equality, executive staff joint activities, representativeness and staff. The highest correlations occur with efficiency and the principle of engaging in joint activities, which are correlations that this book does not interpret, given the complexity of the jurisprudence behind these values.[4] However, it is possible to clearly see that staff principles hold a special place among the constellation of connected principles. It also is possible to observe that some principles always appear with others, like representativeness, efficiency and equality. Future scholarship in the field of international organizations law will be well served by understanding what these groups of principles are, why they appear together, and how they function.

Figure 2.3 shows the number of other principles with which each principle statistically significantly correlates. For example, the principle of representation statistically significantly correlates with seven other principles – communication, cooperation, efficiency, equality, executive staff, staff and joint activities. This is calculated by simply counting the number of other principles with which each principle in Figure 2.2 statistically significantly correlates.

Before dividing these international organizations' constitutions into groups, it is possible to observe a few patterns. First, and perhaps most importantly, constitutional principles do not appear to "crowd out" other principles. A basic assumption underpinning the international system is that, "with the exception of the United Nations ... most of the organizations should have mandates that are limited to specific and defined sets

---

4 Later chapters illustrate some of this complexity, which shows how groups of principles take on completely different meanings, depending on the context.

Principle	No.	Principle	No.	Principle	No.
Staff	8	Cooperation	5	Aspiration	2
Representation	7	Communication	6	Autonomy	2
Efficiency	7	Joint	6	Peace	2
Equality	7	Exec. Staff	5	Authority	1
Recommendation	1				

Figure 2.3 Which principles correlate with the most other principles? (max = 13).

of problems."[5] If a negative correlation were observed in these data, one would expect to see constitutions that mention one value (autonomy, for example) would mention another value (like peace) *less*. Therefore, such a negative correlation would strongly suggest some kind of international "division of labor" between international organizations, or at least some substitutability or replaceability of principles with others. However, such principle substitutability in these data has not been observed. To be clear, such a lack of any "division of labor," or at least a division of principles among international organizations, does not mean that certain groups of international organizations' constitutions do not favor certain principles.

Several examples from the correlation analysis portray such a grouping. Constitutions that frequently mention "efficient staff communication" (representing a convergence of correlations between efficiency, staff-related issues and communication) hold among the highest correlations among these principles. As shown in later chapters, these principles come together differently, depending on the international organization involved. "Staff representation" – again a hypothetical construct made up to represent the correlation between staff-related issues and representation – represents another pair of highly correlated principles. These two observations lead to a hypothesis: groups of principles work together to form some kind of semantic (if not legal) concept above and beyond the meaning of these principles individually.

These deeper patterns in the data can be observed by marking up Figure 2.2 to some degree. Figure 2.4 shows how to think about the way that groups of principles correlate with each other in these international organizations' constitutions. This illustrates the way that cooperation might correlate with communication. Figure 2.2 shows no statistically significant correlation in the relationship between these principles. However, when the correlation is "trace through," as shown in Figure 2.4, a slight (though extant)

---

5 Daniel D. Bradlow & Claudio Grossman, "Limited Mandates and Intertwined Problems: A New Challenge for the World Bank and the IMF," 17 *Human Rights Q.* 411 (1995).

Value	Means	Std. dev.	Aspiration	Authority	Autonomy	Communication	Cooperation	Efficiency	Equality	Exec. staff	Staff	Joint	Peace	Recommendation	Representation
Cooperation	2303.2	3155.64	0.06	0.05	0.26	0.09	1	0.11	0.16	0.09	0.25	0.37	0.05	0.09	0.18
Efficiency	1091.8	917.99	0.1	0.16	0.08	0.35	0.11	1	1	0.19	0.47	0.27	0.04	0.02	0.24
Equality	463.7	515.48	0.02	-0.01	0.08	0.23	0.24	0.21	1	0.06	0.21	0.18	0.16	-0.01	0.26
Exec. staff	4210	4014.09	0.19	0.1	-0.08	0.33	0.09	0.19	0.36	1	0.16	-0.03	-0.03	0.04	0.26
Staff	1303.5	1934.85	0.14	0.09	0.08	0.35	0.25	0.47	0.21	0.16	1	0.38	-0.01	-0.01	0.33
Joint	237.6	578.08	0.08	0.08	0.08	0.25	0.37	0.27	0.18	-0.03	0.38	1	-0.01	0.08	0.22
Peace	121.5	431.66	-0.04	0.1	-0.02	0.04	0.05	0.02	0.16	-0.01	-0.01	-0.01	1	0.2	0.02
Recommendation	138.3	243.57	0.05	0.04	-0.02	0.09	0.09	0.02	0.01	0.04	-0.01	0.08	0.2	1	-0.07
Representation	366.8	492.83	0.11	0.04	0.04	0.28	0.18	0.24	0.26	0.26	0.33	0.22	0.02	-0.07	1

Figure 2.4 The "transivity" in these correlations means we can find long-linked clusters of principles living together in groups of constitutions. The figure shows the same correlation matrix we presented in Figure 2.3. We have drawn arrows from particular correlations to others to show how to think about the group or clustering of principles which we will present at some length later in this chapter. In this case, we see that cooperation correlates with communication (perhaps more communication leads to greater cooperation or vice versa). Through this cluster we see that cooperation has a correlation coefficient of 0.26 with autonomy; autonomy has a correlation coefficient of 0.16 with equality; and so on through the linkages until arriving at representation's 0.28 correlation coefficient with communication.

relationship can be seen. Common sense might suggest an obvious relationship between cooperation and communication. Indeed, how is it possible to cooperate without communicating? Nevertheless, when deducing deep-seated legal principles and doctrines in these constitutions, common sense simply will not do. Instead, careful legal analysis of these texts is needed in order to find a relationship that transcends mere correlation.

Perhaps it is difficult to clearly see these correlations and groupings when looking at all international organizations' constitutions together. What happens if one looks for correlations and differences between *subgroups* of these international organizations? That is the topic of the following subsection.

Organizational groupings leaning towards certain principles

How does grouping these international organizations help to understand the differences in the way these groups' international organizations refer to certain principles? Figure 2.5 shows several ways of grouping international organizations, like whether they have universal or regional approaches, general or limited competence and so forth.[6] The percentages in the figure show the probability that constitutional mentions of each principle do not vary by group. For example, a 4 percent probability exists that general competence international organizations refer to autonomy just as much as limited competence organizations. International judicial organizations mention cooperation to the same extent as non-judicial organizations with only a 1.3 percent probability. References to statistically significant differences involve these kinds of findings.[7]

The figure shows two-tailed, independent samples Mann Whitney U test p-values for universal versus regional scope international organizations. Such a test tells us whether these two types of international organizations' constitutions have a statistically significantly different extent of reporting topics such as authority and autonomy. Most researchers set 5 percent as the statistically significant level of difference between these scores.

---

6 As the previous chapter explained, most legal researchers group international organizations according to their own subjective (although usually rationally based) categories. The analysis here thus explores whether their groupings tell us anything about differences in the way the constitutions refer to legal principles and values.
7 Most social scientists accept a 5 percent probability as the limit for deciding on the statistical significance of a result. Such a 5 percent means that the test in this chapter will wrongly indicate that two groups' constitutions (like EU versus non-EU) mention a particular principle (like equality) differently, when in fact no real statistically significant difference exists.

Principle	Universal/ regional Probability of same	General/ limited competence Probability of same	Financial/ non-financial	Judicial/ non-judicial	EU/ non-EU
Aspiration	60.5%	7%	94.5%	95.6%	1%*
Authority	0.00%*	20%	31.9%	55.9%	25.4%
Autonomy	6.9%	4%*	13.2%	1.1%*	0.6%*
Communication	42.4%	59%	12.9%	81.1%	0.6%*
Cooperation	47.8%	0.00%*	0.2%*	1.3%*	15.4%
Efficiency	7.8%	4%	84.3%	57.5%	0.1%*
Equality	1.2%*	1.2%*	10.1%	93.1%	52.8%
Executive Staff	0.1%*	2%*	6.3%	6.1%	1.5%*
Staff	1.1%*	12%	34.4%	34.3%	0.4%*
Peace	20%	0.00%*	0.9%*	5.7%	94.9%
Recommendation	49%	0.1%*	56.5%	45.6%	1.4%*
Representativeness	9.1%	0.1%*	71.2%	56.2%	3.4%*

Figure 2.5 Difference in mentions of each legal principle between types of international organization. Cells with asterisks are statistically significant.

Note: * This has not been adjusted for repeated statistical tests (false discovery).

Therefore, if a difference has less than 5 percent probability of appearing due to random fluctuation, there is a statistical reason to think that universal and regional constitutions mention a particular topic more or less. This table shows "asymptotic" p-values, which shows such significance *as if* there were a large sample size.

A first, though wrong, glance at these correlations shows several patterns already.[8] These differences in the way international organizations refer to principles seem to impact on EU versus non-EU international organizations more frequently than other types of organizations. Mentions of aspirations, autonomy, communication, efficiency, executive staff and ("normal") staff – six of the thirteen principles analyzed in this book – appear to statistically significantly differ between EU and non-EU entities. Differences in the extent to which various international organizations refer to cooperation appear to dominate the groupings of these organizations, with only universal organizations failing to show some statistically significant

---

8 As described later in this book, these simple correlations do not take into account the *systemic* nature of these correlations. In other words, international organizations' constitutions may frequently mention cooperation and making recommendations together because of frequent mentions of the organization's authority. Social scientists refer to these simple, two-variable correlations as partial correlation.

Empirics 69

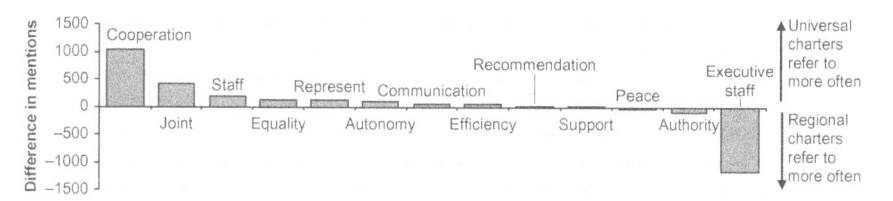

Figure 2.6 Regional organizations tend to mention almost all principles more frequently than do their universalist peers. The figure shows the difference between the number of times universalist organizations mention each of the principles shown and the number of times regional organizations' constitutions refer to them. For example, universal organizations' constitutions refer to cooperation about 1,000 times per 100,000 words – more often than do regional organizations' constitutions.

difference from regional organizations in mentions of such cooperation. Mentions about executive staff do not appear to differ much between financial and non-financial, or judicial and non-judicial, organizations. As the book shows throughout, however, executive staff principles play a vital role in the network of legal principles contained in the constitutions of these international organizations.

Differences exist in the ways that universal and regional international organizations illustrate the nature of such statistically significant differences, particularly for jurists unschooled in the ways of statistically significant relationships. Figure 2.6 shows the differences in the ways that universal and regional organizations refer to the legal principles in this book. Differences in the ways that these constitutions mention cooperation and executive staff represent the largest differences in the dataset. While differences in universal international organizations' mentions of executive staff statistically significantly differ from those of their regional peers, mentions of cooperation do not. As Figure 2.1 shows, the variation in mentions of cooperation fluctuates wildly, with the most cooperation-centric constitutions mentioning the principle almost 12,000 times per 100,000 words.[9] Variations in the ways that constitutions refer to these principles have far more predictive power than simply comparing differences in the ways these constitutions refer to principles.

---

9 As a reminder, cooperation (the second bar from the left in Figure 2.1) has a mean value of 4,000. This book later shows that there is a 3,150-word standard deviation of these mentions of cooperation, far higher than aspiration's 368 or peace's 431. Such standard deviation mentions the variability of data, with higher values meaning more variable data.

70   *The values of international organizations*

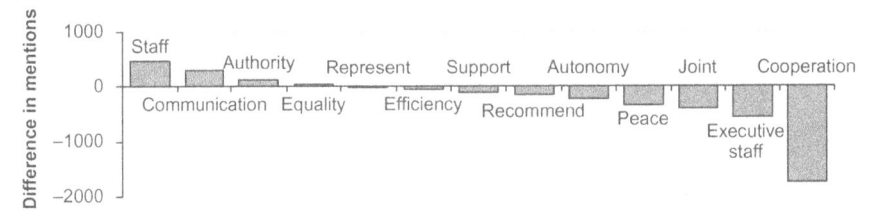

[Bar chart showing Difference in mentions ranging from -2000 to 1000, with bars for: Staff, Communication, Authority, Equality, Represent, Efficiency, Support, Recommend, Autonomy, Peace, Joint, Cooperation, Executive staff]

Figure 2.7 Limited competence organizations refer to most principles more often than do their general competence organizations. The figure shows the number of times (per 100,000 words) that general competence organizations' constitutions refer to the principles shown in the figure more than limited competence organizations' constitutions do. For example, general competence organizations' constitutions referred to staff principles 470 times more frequently (on average) than do those of limited competence organizations. The large number of negative-valued bars shows that most principles are referred to more often by limited competence organizations.

The way international organizations' constitutions mention cooperation also can teach us other things about interpreting these data. Continuing with the example in Figure 2.7, there appears to be a large difference in the way limited competence organizations refer to cooperation, compared with general competence ones. Differences in the ways these constitutions refer to representativeness and equality hardly even appear in the figure. However, statistically significant differences exist in the way limited competence and general competence international organizations refer to these principles *because of the way the data vary across constitutions*.

Another graphical method can illustrate the importance of such variance. As previously stated, variance matters more than averages or levels for statistically understanding international organizations' constitutional principles. Figure 2.8 illustrates such variance in the ways that groups of international organizations' constitutions refer to the principles that this book analyzes. Principles mentioned more often in international organizations' constitutions undoubtedly vary much more than less-mentioned principles, as illustrated by the larger bands or bars around the dots towards the top of each graph in the figure. However, for EU versus non-EU organizations and judicial versus non-judicial organizations, there is a high variance in principles that are less referenced. Without the aid of a statistical test and its numerous assumptions, there would appear to be far fewer statistically significant differences across groups.[10] Even this simple illustration shows

---

10 The statistics in Figure 2.2 come from a Mann-Whitney U test. In contrast, these graphs simply show the ranges within which 95 percent of constitutions mentioning the principles shown in the figure fall.

Empirics 71

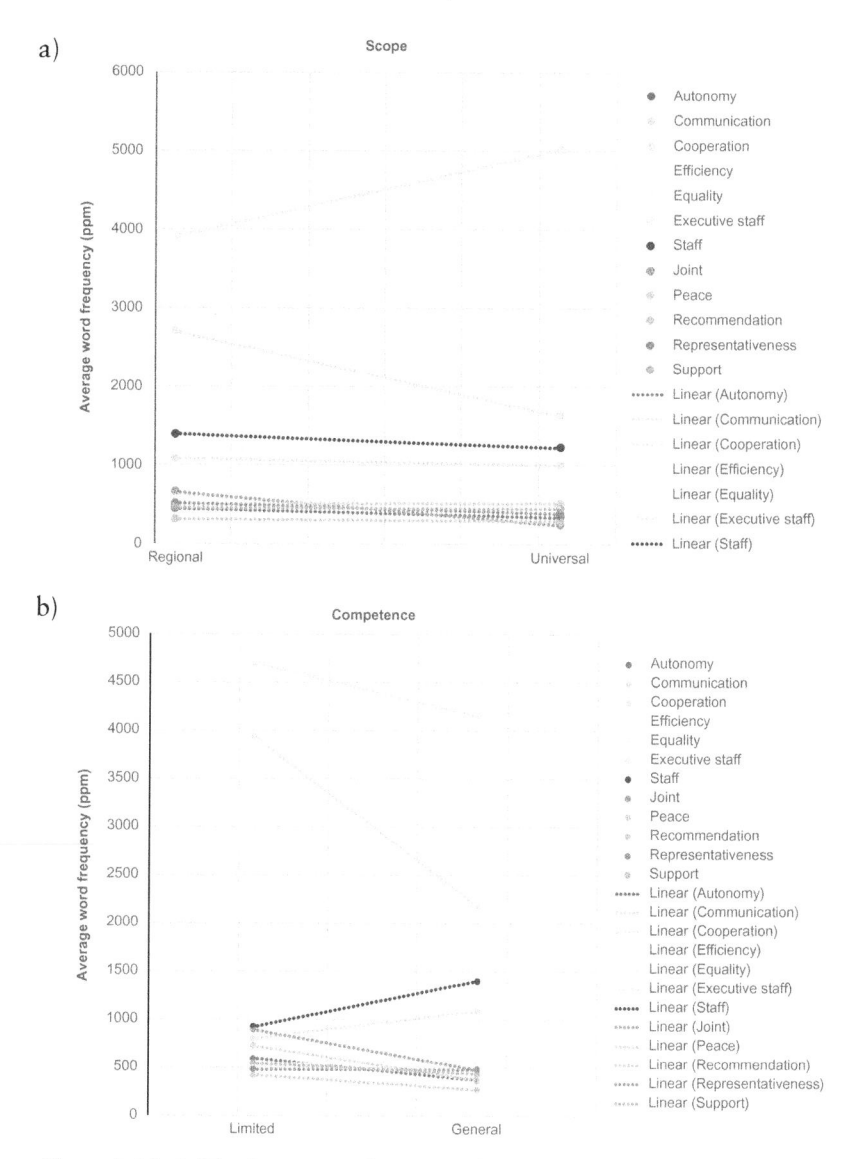

a)
[Chart: Scope — Average word frequency (ppm) vs Regional/Universal, showing series: Autonomy, Communication, Cooperation, Efficiency, Equality, Executive staff, Staff, Joint, Peace, Recommendation, Representativeness, Support, with linear trend lines]

b)
[Chart: Competence — Average word frequency (ppm) vs Limited/General, showing series: Autonomy, Communication, Cooperation, Efficiency, Equality, Executive staff, Staff, Joint, Peace, Recommendation, Representativeness, Support, with linear trend lines]

Figure 2.8A–E The frequency of citation of most principles does not differ across types of organizations. The figure shows the difference between the average frequencies with which international organizations' constitutions refer to each principle, as separated by type of organization. The lines around each average show where 95 percent of constitutions' values lie. If these lines overlap across types (for example, if the 95 percent interval of aspiration for EU organizations overlaps with the same frequency as non-EU organizations), then it is possible to claim a statistically significant difference in such citations. The y-axes refer to the frequency of mentions (per 10,000).

The values of international organizations

c)

Financial

- Autonomy
- Communication
- Cooperation
- Efficiency
- Equality
- Executive staff
- Staff
- Joint
- Peace
- Recommendation
- Representativeness
- Support
- Linear (Autonomy)
- Linear (Communication)
- Linear (Cooperation)
- Linear (Efficiency)
- Linear (Equality)
- Linear (Executive staff)
- Linear (Staff)
- Linear (Joint)

Average word frequency (ppm) — Financial, Non-Financial

d)

Judicial

- Autonomy
- Communication
- Cooperation
- Efficiency
- Equality
- Executive staff
- Staff
- Joint
- Peace
- Recommendation
- Representativeness
- Support
- Linear (Autonomy)
- Linear (Communication)
- Linear (Cooperation)
- Linear (Efficiency)
- Linear (Equality)
- Linear (Executive staff)
- Linear (Staff)
- Linear (Joint)
- Linear (Peace)
- Linear (Recommendation)
- Linear (Representativeness)
- Linear (Support)

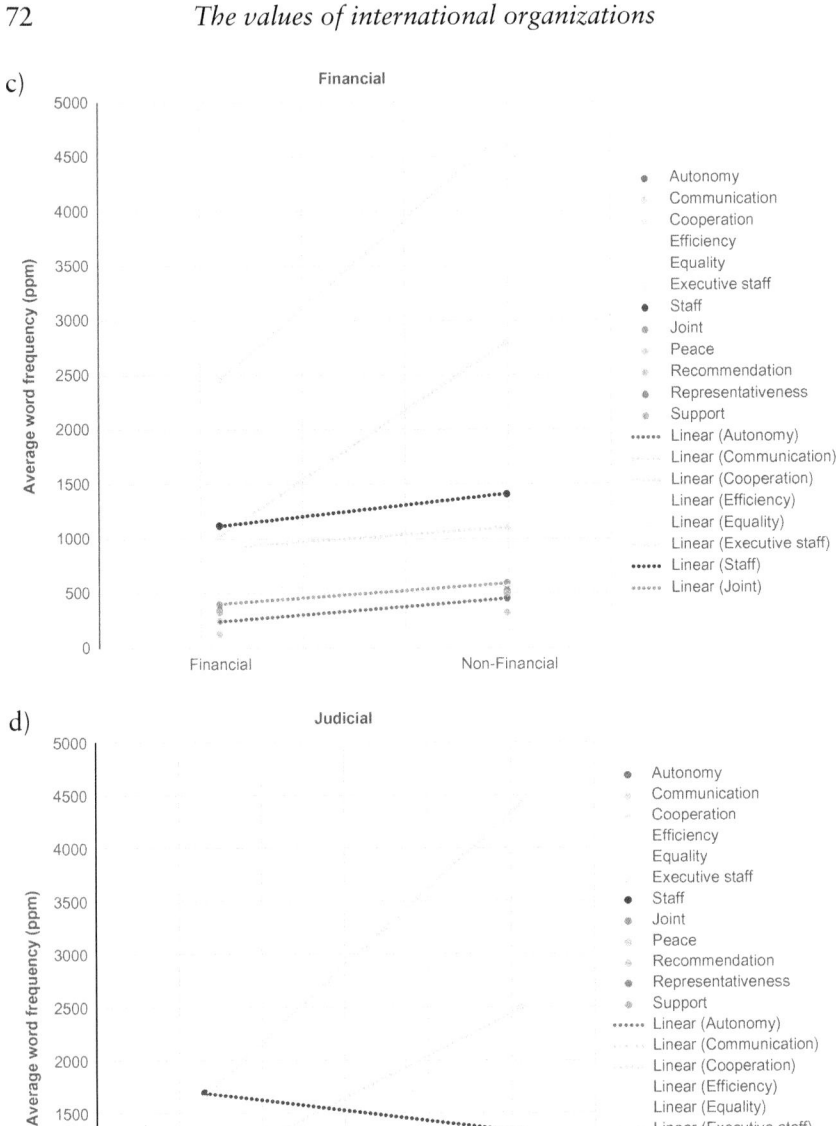

Average word frequency (ppm) — Judicial, Non-judicial

Figure 2.8A–E Continued

Empirics 73

e)

EU affiliation

[Chart showing average word frequency (ppm) vs EU affiliation (Yes/No), y-axis 0 to 5000, with legend listing: Autonomy, Communication, Cooperation, Efficiency, Equality, Executive staff, Staff, Joint, Peace, Recommendation, Representativeness, Support, and Linear trend lines for each.]

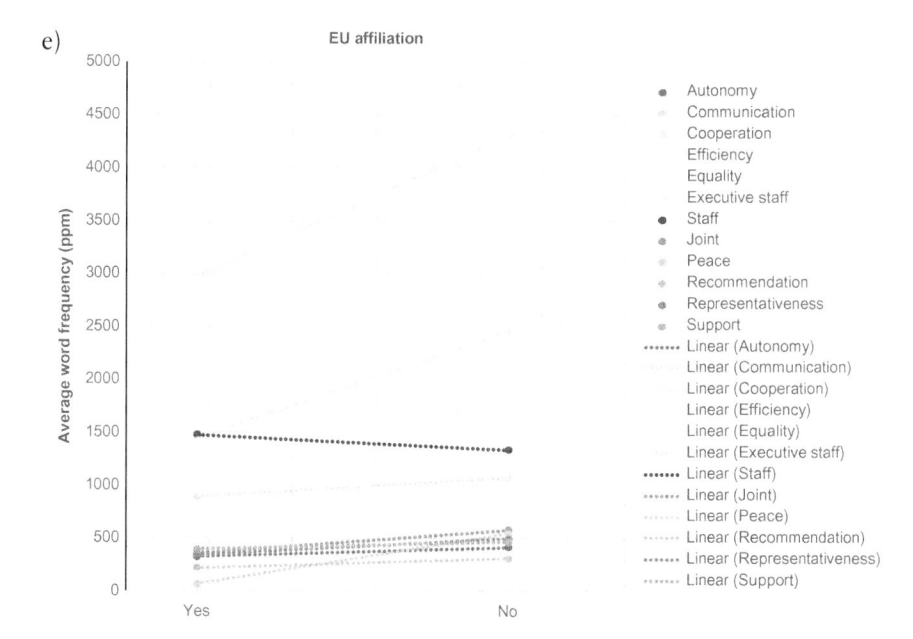

Figure 2.8A–E Continued

the importance of using a range of tools, tests and plots, rather than relying on one simple method in order to tell the story of international organizations' values.

Understanding the practicalities of variance

What these differences mean practically (or legally) differs from what they mean statistically. International organizations that are universal in scope have constitutions that mention authority and equality statistically significantly more often than do those of regional international organizations. As Chapter 3 describes, researchers such as White argue that such authority stems from the need to demonstrate the unequivocal ability to make rules that directly bind member states, as well as the need to possess the authority to enforce their own decisions.[11] However, how does equality enter into

---

11 *See* White, *supra* Chapter 1, note 19, at 60. Other scholars have attempted to quantitatively assess such authority in international organizations. *See, e.g.*, Liesbet Hooghe & Gary Marks, "The Authority of International Organizations: The Effects of Scope and Scale," UNC Chapel Hill Working Paper, 2013, *available at* www.unc.edu (last visited Mar. 25, 2020).

the picture? Moreover, how do mentions of authority and equality differ for universal organizations, as opposed to regional organizations?

A comparison between the ways that the WTO and the Arab Bank for Economic Development in Africa refer to authority illustrates these differences. In particular, both constitutions may similarly refer to authority frequently. However, such mentions refer to completely different legal ideas, rights and even principles. The WTO's constitution gives its "Ministerial Conference ... the authority to take decisions on all matters under any of the Multilateral Trade Agreements."[12] Therefore, the WTO's authority lies in its Ministerial Conference, and so it implicitly lies in the authority of its member states.[13] In contrast, the main source of the authority of the Arab Bank for Economic Development in Africa stems from the rather flimsy definition of the "international status of staff members."[14] The relevant provision from the Bank's constitution requires such staff members to "refrain from any act that is contrary to the international character of their jobs or to their independence."[15] Therefore, such staff members' authority derives from their "international character" rather than necessarily from any derived authority their member states grant to these individuals.[16] Both of these international organizations' constitutions vest individuals working in them with authority. However, the fountainhead of such authority – and thus the nature of such authority – lies in completely different legal conceptions of authority.

What about the principle of equality, which general competence international organizations' constitutions hold in high regard, or at least refer to often? Figure 2.8 shows that both universal scope and general competence international organizations statistically significantly refer to equality more frequently than do their regional scope and limited competence

---

12 Marrakesh Agreement Establishing the World Trade Organization art. IV, Apr. 15, 1994, 1867 U.N.T.S. 15 [hereinafter "WTO Agreement"].
13 The constitution does not mention where such authority comes from. As this book describes, most researchers have thus deduced that such authority stems from the authority granted to their member state governments.
14 Agreement Establishing the Arab Bank for Economic Development in Africa, July 2009, *available at* www.badea.org (last visited Mar. 25, 2020).
15 *Id.*, art. 30.
16 The provision falls a long way away from those giving the Bank the same authority as, say, the UN or World Bank, with their internationally and diplomatically protected civil servants. Such differences in authority may stem from these organizations' limited accountability to larger populations, as authors like Wouters and co-authors suggest. *See* Jan Wouters et al., "Managerial Accountability: What Impact on International Organisations' Autonomy?," *Leuven Ctr. for Glob. Gov. Stud.* 43 (2010), *available at* https://ghum.kuleuven.be (last visited Mar. 25, 2020).

counterparts. Nevertheless, as described later in this book, many of these international organizations call for some form of "limited" equality.[17] For example, organizations like the IMF treat member states' votes equally in the Orwellian *Animal Farm* sense – with richer and larger members' votes being more equal than others.[18] If detractors point to the role of power in explaining such differences, more neutral observers point to the increased legitimacy that such "unequally equal" governance gives the international organizations.[19] Nevertheless, the fact remains that such a system represents a far cry from the idea of "pure" equality as one state one vote, as often caricatured in the UN Charter.

General competence international organizations also differ from their limited competence peers by their focus on peace. However, as described in Chapter 4, if many of these organizations seek peace, as opposed to war, others have a different view of such peace. Many organizations, even general competence ones, focus on the peacekeeping that comes from the pledge to enforce collective security.[20] Collective security represents some-

---

17 The literature seems to have hit a dead end in talking about equality between international organizations shortly after Briggs' rumination about power differences between member states as an inherent barrier to the international equality so desperately sought by the UN Charter's founders. However, the frequent mention of this principle by international organizations law textbook authors still gives hope to a next generation of researchers pursuing this thread of research. For that seminal and last-of-its-kind article, *see* Herbert Briggs, "Power Politics and International Organization," 39 *Am. J. Int'l L.* 664 (1945). For original arguments around equality between international organizations, *see* Hans Kelsen, "The Principle of Sovereign Equality of States as a Basis for International Organization," 53 *Yale L.J.* 207 (1944).
18 Authors have ignored the issue of equality between international organizations, focusing on social equality between peoples (and particularly gender equality). While important, such a diversion has moved attention from equality between peoples to equality within peoples – something known since the early 1990s. *See* Sandra Whitworth, *Feminism and International Relations: Towards a Political Economy of Gender in Interstate and Non-Governmental Institutions* (1994).
19 Many do not even see a dichotomy between the two values. Providing perhaps one of the strongest arguments for this book, d'Aspremont and De Brabandere argue that the legitimacy of an international organization's exercise of authority comes from the legitimacy of its origins. *See* Jean d'Aspremont & Eric De Brabandere, "The Complementary Faces of Legitimacy In International Law: The Legitimacy of Origin and the Legitimacy of Exercise," 34 *Fordham Int'l L.J.* 190 (2011). How surprising it is that so few researchers have systematically or quantitatively studied the values and principles of these constitutions.
20 Many have commented on the "false promise" of international values that seek to maintain peace by promising war. *See* John Mearsheimer, "The False Promise of International Institutions," 19 *Int'l Sec.* 5 (1995). Pacts of collective security differ

thing far different than peace, as such security emerges from arms and, ultimately, armed conflict.[21] Simply counting the number of times a constitution refers to peace may miss the completely opposite meaning, in the war-mongering bend of national security and collective security.[22] Indeed, if international organizations truly seek peace, why do not more take the form of international organizations that are limited to particular types of peacekeeping and mutual aid in defense?[23]

To understand *practically* (as opposed to statistically) why states do not use limited competence organizations more to maintain the peace, it is important to look at the ways these international organizations view cooperation, through the lens of their founding constitutions.[24] If Klabbers views most, if not all, international organizations as "vehicles for interstate

  from pacts promising peace – a fact neither lost on the authors of the textbooks that were analyzed to generate this book nor the discipline in general.
21 Most researchers do not state the matter as bluntly. Koskenniemi hides behind this ugly reality by referring to abstract generalities, in that *de maximis non curat praetor*: "Today, most lawyers have accepted that if law has a role to play in matters of security, it is as a handmaid to state power and interest, a facilitator for politics to take its natural course … ." Martti Koskenniemi, "The Place of Law in Collective Security," 17 *Mich. J. Int'l Law* 455, 488 (1996). *See also* Martti Koskenniemi, *The Politics of International Law* ch. 3 (2011). War, though, is what most researchers call politics by a different name.
22 This book refers to the axiomatic, direct, relationship between security and preparedness for war, and not to more diffuse theories about the way collective security agreements and the concept of "national security" help to encourage the weaponization of states and the use of such arrangements to exploit other states. For these arguments and evidence, *see* Mark Duffield, *Development, Security and Unending War: Governing the World of Peoples* (2007).
23 If the North Atlantic Treaty Organization clearly represents an organization dedicated to peace, the UN does less so. However, from this data, "general purpose" organizations' constitutions seem far more focused on peace. This might be because international humanitarian law spans such a large range of issues – from the protection of non-combatants to promoting material and emotional relief – that only large, general purpose organizations can deal with the multifaceted issues involved in promoting peace. The debate continues. *See* Tristan Ferraro, "International Humanitarian Law's Applicability to International Organisations Involved in Peace Operations," *in Proceedings of the Bruges Colloquium* 42 (College of Europe ed. 2012).
24 Interestingly, peace results as the by-product of member states using international organizations completely removed from having peace as a goal or principle. *See* Sara Mitchell, "Cooperation in World Politics: The Constraining and Constitutive Effects of International Organizations," Paper Presented at the Conference Intergovernmental Organizations in Action, Mar. 26–27, 2006, *available at* ir.uiowa.edu (last visited Mar. 25, 2020).

cooperation," then we must ask what kind of cooperation that entails.[25] As Chapter 4 notes, many international organizations define such cooperation within the more narrowly defined mandate to share information, scientific knowledge and technical know-how.[26] Authors at the OECD say it best when they note that international organization activity most actively focuses on the "exchange of information and experience, data collection, research and policy analysis, discussion of good regulatory practices, development of rules, standards and guidance, negotiation of international agreements, enforcement activities including imposition of sanctions, dispute settlement and crisis management."[27] Clearly, trading arms and promises to attack an enemy with nuclear weapons fall outside such a remit for general competence organizations. The combination of multiple principles may lead to a different practical or legal understanding of any particular principle. In this case, *peace* plus *cooperation* can, in practice, equal *war*.

Other examples show how the confluence of principles in international organizations' constitutions can represent something different from the independent pursuit of ideals like representation and aspirations, which are principles analyzed in this book. The statistical analysis concludes that general competence international organizations value representativeness (or simply representation) more than their limited competence cousins do. As Chapter 4 shows, such representativeness may be purely aspirational, as international organizations' founders seek representativeness in support of the broader values of inclusion and participation that such representation brings.[28] However, as the analysis above indicates, the shared mention of these two principles in many constitutions shows how these international organizations' framers saw these principles as complements, and not just as representativeness being subservient to the broader aspiration of increasing

---

25 *See* Klabbers, *supra* Chapter 1, note 37, at 27.
26 Besides sharing ideas and knowledge (and even trust), stable cooperation comes about from managing shared resources such as lakes. For a review, *see* Maurice Schiff & L. Alan Winters, "Regional Cooperation, and the Role of International Organizations and Regional Integration," World Bank Policy Research Working Paper 2872, July 2002, *available at* http://documents.worldbank.org/ (last visited Mar. 25, 2020).
27 Celine Kauffmann, "International Regulatory Co-operation: The Role of International Organisations in Fostering Better Rules of Globalisation," OECD, 2016, at 15, *available at* www.oecd.org (last visited Mar. 25, 2020).
28 Such representativeness might also emerge from politics. Understandings of even such a seemingly neutral value may change over time as politics evolve. *See* Marieke Louis & Coline Ruwet, "Representativeness from Within: A Comparison between the ILO and the ISO," 14 *Globalizations* 535 (2017).

participation in international organizations.[29] It is possible to dig into the treaty debates to find out why these framers envisioned such complementarities, or at least that they did not merely put these words together at random. However, few legal theories can explain the inclusion of principles like representation, aspiration and efficiency in the same constitution.

International financial organizations and, to a lesser extent, their judicially focused siblings espouse none of the values that this book looks at more than their generalist peers do. Figure 2.8 shows that generalist organizations mention values that relate to their executive staff and to cooperation far more than financial *and* judicial organizations. These mentions of executive staffing issues may not statistically significantly differ between these types of organizations. However, the differences shown in the figures clearly bear more research, particularly in the case of international judicial organizations with a sample size of only fourteen organizations. As Chapter 4 describes, such executive staff and cooperation seek to promote the autonomy, impartiality and independence of courts and tribunals, which are core features and, indeed, the *sine qua non* of any judicial body.[30] If the European Court of Human Rights' constitution considers such autonomy as "self-legitimizing," then the International Criminal Court's (ICC) constitution views the notion of credibility being linked to judicial autonomy.[31]

---

29 The authors of this book try not to discuss pair-wise comparisons of these values until the individual chapters of the book. However, no discussion of representation in any organizational setting may occur without a consideration of the practicalities of running meetings. To illustrate the problems, imagine if parliaments had direct representation in international organizations. Such a thought experiment most vividly illustrates the pros and cons of expanding representation through participation. *See* Jofre Rocabert et al., "The Rise of International Parliamentary Institutions? Conceptualization and First Empirical Illustrations," Presentation at the European Consortium for Political Research Joint Sessions in Salamanca, Apr. 10–15, 2014, *available at* www.polsoz.fu-berlin.de/ (last visited Mar. 25, 2020).

30 A lawyerly reading of international judicial organizations' constitutions easily reveals the goals of such executive staff and cooperation, and ultimately the role of autonomy in these organizations' work. However, few studies have tried to study these principles empirically. To the extent that such studies attempt to quantify the importance of such principles, fewer still look to these organizations' constitutions to provide the guiding principles driving these organizations. For a discussion of such measurement, and the lack of links to any evaluation taking the original organizations' constitutions into account, *see* Michael Bauer & Jorn Ege, "Bureaucratic Autonomy of International Organizations' Secretariats," 23 *J. Eur. Pub. Pol'y* 1019 (2016).

31 Autonomy does not lie outside the realm of politics or institutional change. Indeed, many scholars mix up autonomy and independence, often arguing that neither can

The EU provides a unique example, in its own right, of a supranational international organization set up supposedly reflecting most of the values enshrined in the international organizations' literature.[32] However, the data tells a different story. Other international organizations' constitutions refer to the values of aspiration, autonomy, communication, executive staff, recommendation and representativeness more frequently than do the EU organizations' constitutions analyzed. Instead, the EU organizations' constitutions refer to the values most associated with the Union – namely, efficiency and staff.[33] International organizations like the EU may demand efficiency, as the husbanding and proper management of financial resources is given to the organization.[34] Procedures dealing with member states failing to pay dues (where applicable), regulations requiring audits and, particularly, communications allowing citizens and other third parties to oversee EU spending all represent key parts of the rules aiming at such efficiency, as embodied in these treaties.[35] A sample size of only thirteen organizations

> exist for an international judicial body. For a review of some of the issues, *see* Erik Voeten, "International Judicial Independence," *in Interdisciplinary Perspectives on International Law and International Relations: The State of the Art* 421 (Jeffrey L. Dunoff and Mark A. Pollack eds. 2013).
>
> 32 Most see the EU at the vanguard of developing international law and certainly as a role model for multilateral organizations. See Petersmann, *supra* Chapter 1, note 52, at 621. For probably the best overview of the legal issues involved with the EU (as an international organization) dealing with others, *see The European Union and International Organizations* (Knud Erik Jørgensen ed. 2009).
>
> 33 Legitimacy and, especially, efficiency represented the two values Nedergaard stressed most in 2006 for the EU. For all of Kochenov and Amtenbrink's discussion of the way the EU has most impacted on other international organizations, the discussions in their book always turn back towards efficiency. *See* Peter Nedergaard, *European Union Administration: Legitimacy and Efficiency* (2006); Dimitry Kochenov & Fabian Amtenbrink, *The European Union's Shaping of the International Legal Order* (2013).
>
> 34 The ordinary EU citizen may not associate the Union with efficiency, but efficiency always has remained a key and guiding principle for the Union's institutions. For a recent statement of this long-cherished principle, *see* European Commission, "College Sets Out Options for an Efficient EU and its Future Budget," *Weekly Meeting Comm.*, Feb. 14, 2018, *available at* https://ec.europa.eu/commission/news/college-sets-out-options-efficient-eu-and-its-future-budget-2018-feb-14_en (last visited Mar. 25, 2020).
>
> 35 The flood of research into the EU's efficiency – and EU leaders' acceptance of the importance of efficiency as a principle – illustrates the centrality of the principle. For recent examples of scholarly analysis of the ways the Union policy can support this Treaty principle, *see* Gian Luigi Tosato, "How to Pursue a More Efficient and Legitimate European Economic Governance," Institute for International Affairs Working Paper 16/03 (2016), *available at* www.iai.it/sites/default/files/iaiwp1603.

may severely limit the applicability of any conclusions in this book about EU-related international law. Nevertheless, the data shows that EU-related organizations' constitutions do not militate for many more principles than do those of non-EU organizations.

Emergence of principles from organizations' characteristics

Even the most hardened legal scholar must at least test the dictum from international organizational theory – that structure follows strategy.[36] Do the structures of international organizations change or adapt in pursuit of the principles and values their organizing treaties contain? International organizations' creators design international organizations differently. Some are bigger or smaller, newer or older, geographically focused or global in span. What do an organization's size, age and location say about the principles the international organization espouses? Are there relationships that shed light on the ways we think of the evolution of the law of international organizations?

Even the most rudimentary analysis shows some patterns in the ways different types of international organizations' constitutions refer to principles. Figure 2.9 shows the results of a statistical analysis known as the Kruskal–Wallis test for group means.[37] The test looks at the extent to which the mention of various principles statistically significantly differs between

<blockquote>
pdf (last visited Mar. 25, 2020). <i>See also</i> David Garcia & Paolo Vacca, "Improving the Efficiency, Democracy and Legitimacy of the EU Institutions within the Current Treaties: Possibilities and Limits," Union of European Federalists Policy Brief, Feb. 2016, <i>available at</i> www.federalists.eu/fileadmin/files_uef/POLICY/Policy_Briefs/2016/Policy_Brief_Improving_efficiency_democracy_and_legitimacy_of_the_EU_institutions_within_the_current_Treaties_20_proposals.pdf (last visited Mar. 25, 2020).

36 If few organizational theorists and social scientists have grappled with the factors driving the organizational design and change of international organizations, legal scholars have completely ignored the issue. Laws may dictate the UN's structure, for example. However, what legal values encouraged the framers to choose one design over that of another? Hopefully, the data associated with this book will inspire more scholarship in this area. For probably one of the most comprehensive overviews in this area (although not from a legal perspective), <i>see</i> Daniel Wehrenfennig & Christopher Balding, <i>Theorizing International Organizations: An Organizational Theory of International Institutions</i> (2011).

37 The Kruskal–Wallis test uses the ranking in each organization's constitution of references to each of the principles shown. Using ranks (namely, which organization ranks first in mentioning authority, which ranks second, third and so forth) helps to overcome the problems of using word counts. In other words, these word counts do not follow a normal distribution when plotting the number of organizations' constitutions mentioning each principle. Statistical analysts must use special tests – like
</blockquote>

Empirics 81

Principle	Size of international organization	Year of international organization	Region/location of international organization
Aspiration	0.074	9.379*	8.554
Authority	10.221*	4.737	12.862*
Autonomy	0.713	11.170*	15.523*
Communication	3.333	3.653	10.920
Cooperation	0.128	3.345	1.278
Efficiency	0.546	3.835	9.926
Equality	0.507	10.870*	4.059
Executive staff	16.386*	1.239	7.111
Staff	4.265	0.888	10.938*
Peace	5.502*	11.991*	5.085
Recommendation	2.073	1.336	11.634*
Representativeness	4.059	8.857*	7.002

Figure 2.9 Difference in mentions of each legal principle between characteristics of international organizations. Asterisked numbers are statistically significant at the 95 percent level.

small, medium or large numbers of members in these organizations.[38] The higher the number in the figure, the larger the statistically significant differences between subgroups like size, year of incorporation or region in which the organization operates. For example, the score of 10.22 indicates much larger differences between the average number of times different sizes of organizations refer to authority in their constitutions. A score of 3.33 for differences in the mentions of communications in these organizations' constitutions remains too small to indicate a 95 percent likelihood (or larger) of statistically significant differences in the amount of times small international organizations' constitutions refer to communication, when compared with medium-sized or larger organizations' constitutions.

This figure shows two-tailed, independent samples Chi-squared values for Kruskal-Wallis tests of similarity between the various levels of the variables shown. Values with asterisks show statistically significantly different values of the principle described for the varying levels of the column variable. For example, the statistically significant value for the number of

the Kruskal–Wallis rank test – for data like this that does not follow well-known statistical distributions. Such a "non-parametric test," as statisticians call it, helps to compare two or more independent samples, without worrying too much about differences in sample sizes.
38 The figures describe in more detail the categories of each variable analyzed as well as the statistical procedures used.

aspirational mentions in international organizations' constitutions by age means that constitutions for organizations incorporated before the 1900s had statistically significantly more mentions of aspirational values than constitutions from organizations incorporated later. Asterisked values mean that one would expect such a significant value only 5 percent of the time if these differences came about only by random luck. These tests of significance were not adjusted for repeated statistical tests (false discovery). Fifty-two international organizations are small in size, 47 are medium in size and 90 are large. Six international organizations were established before 1900, 20 were established between 1900 and 1945, 148 between 1946 and 1999, and 15 from 2000 onward.

It is possible to better understand such differences by taking a closer look at the numbers of principles cited in the constitutions of international organizations located in different areas of the world. Figure 2.10 shows the range in the number of times that constitutions from various geographical areas mention each of the principles studied in this book. The figure shows how organizations in all regions refer to executive staffing more often than other principles, as shown by the gray line that sits above all of the other lines. However, significant differences between regions exist when looking

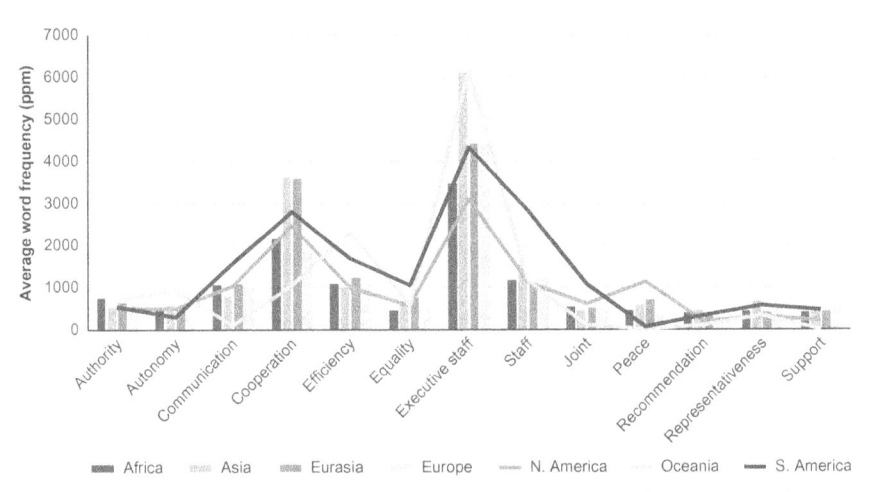

Figure 2.10 Difference in mentions of each legal principle for location of the international organization. This figure shows the 95 percent confidence interval in the number of times organizations from each region refer to each of the principles shown in the figure. For example, Asian-based organizations refer to cooperation roughly between 2,000 and 5,000 times per 100,000 words in their organizational constitutions. In contrast, European organizations refer to such cooperation only between 1,500 and 2,500 times for every 100,000 words.

at the range in the frequency of mentioning a particular principle in one area, which does not overlap with the range in the frequency that constitutions in another part of the world mention the same value. Looking closely, one might see that Asian and Eurasian international organizations focus on equality far more than do the international organizations located outside these areas. Asian international organizations focus on the practical need for cooperation in the functioning and authority of the executive staff and staff. If any region's international organizations militated for peace, somewhat ironically, North American international organizations' constitutions most frequently mentioned such peace. Also somewhat surprisingly, African international organizations that sit in the region with some of the worst conflicts in the post-war period do not have such frequency. Naturally, given the large number of Western, as opposed to non-Western, international organizations, such a picture does not do justice to either these non-Western international organizations or the increasingly important place that these non-Western organizations occupy in the constellation of global international organizations.[39]

Correlation analysis might unearth relationships that were undetectable by comparing groups of international organizations. Figure 2.11 shows the results of such correlation analysis, which looks at the extent to which mentions of each principle in international organizations' constitutions correlate with the number of words in the constitution, the age of the international organization and the number of member states belonging to the organization.

Larger constitutions, or, rather, constitutions with more words, have fewer mentions of equality, communication, staff and executive staff. Older organizations tend to mention peace and autonomy less often, statistically significantly speaking. International organizations with more member states tend to mention joint activities and authority less frequently in their constitutions. The other principles analyzed in this book did not correlate with any of these characteristics. At first glance, this data suggests that organizational characteristics influence the principles enshrined in these international organizations' constitutions, or vice versa.[40]

---

39 This book's database analyzes 191 organizations' constitutions, with only about 60 coming from outside of North America and Europe. The database's focus on Western international organizations reflects broader discourses on such organizations. *See* Madeleine Herren, "Towards a Global History of International Organization," in *Networking the International System: Global Histories of International Organizations* 1 (Madeleine Herren ed. 2014).

40 The "vice versa" here refers to the adage that correlation does not tell us anything about causality. In other words, simple correlation cannot indicate whether these

Principle	Words	Age	Members	Principle	Words	Age	Members
Significant variables				Insignificant factors			
Equality	−0.16*	−0.05	−0.08	Aspiration	−0.01	−0.03	−0.01
Communication	−0.19*	−0.01	−0.03	Cooperation	−0.12	−0.08	−0.14
Executive staff	−0.19*	−0.01	0.13	Efficiency	−0.14	−0.07	−0.01
Staff	−0.16*	−0.07	−0.08	Recommendation	−0.08	−0.05	−0.04
Representation	−0.15*	−0.06	−0.01	Words	1.00	0.01	0.13
Peace	−0.05	−0.22*	0.11	Age	0.01	1.00	−0.04
Autonomy	−0.08	−0.19*	−0.03	Members	0.13	−0.04	1.00
Joint	−0.06	0.01	−0.16*				
Authority	−0.06	−0.02	0.16*				

Figure 2.11 No theory can explain why organizations' size, age and membership would influence constitutional principles.

However, such simple analysis ignores a number of problems, as explained below.

Figure 2.11 shows the Pearson correlation coefficient for the number of times international organizations' constitutions mention the principles shown in the rows and the variables shown in the columns. For example, a statistically significant correlation coefficient describes the relationship between the number of times all international organizations' constitutions mention equality and the number of words in these constitutions. Such a relationship means that longer constitutions mention equality statistically significantly less often than do shorter constitutions.

Any analysis of the relationship between international organizations, their constitutions and their characteristics needs to consider the ways that constitution drafters insert principles as a systemic whole. Constitution drafters do not insert principles into constitutions without thinking about all of the principles they want to insert into the document.[41] Any correlation looking

---

organizations' framers set up certain types of organizations (like large versus small ones) in order to live up to certain principles. Correlation also cannot corroborate the converse relationship – namely, whether certain principles *follow* from these framers' design of these institutions. This book does not attempt to establish such causality.

41 Much legal research has described the motivations, mental models and legal theories driving the drafters of international organizations' constitutions, like the UN Charter. For a fascinating discussion of the way the UN Charter's framers considered principles as a holistic system, see Bardo Fassbender, "The United Nations Charter as Constitution of the International Community," 36 *Colum. J. Transnat'l L.* 529 (1998).

at constitutional references to representativeness and the organization's age must consider, at the same time, the extent to which these framers refer to authority, peace and other principles.[42] Therefore, simple correlation fails to explore the links between principles.

Searching for meaning in structures and networks of principles

Accounting for structures in principles through clustering

How do groups of principles correlate with each other in international organizations' constitutions? Finding groups of these principles comprises one important way of knowing which principles tend to appear together in organizations' constitutions. Figure 2.12 shows the results of a popular statistical technique known as joining tree analysis. In such an analysis, an algorithm looks for the extent to which principles tend to appear together in constitutions.[43] Just by eyeballing the distance (or the extent to which principles appear together), it is possible to see two main groups of principles, which are labeled here as inspirational and practical.[44] Readers may debate the interpretation of the distances shown in the figure. Nevertheless, no one can debate a fundamental truth: some groups of principles appear together

---

42 Authors like Kratochwil and Ruggie might refer to this collection of principles driving an international organization – and thus the policy environment the organization seeks to influence – as an "international regime." If international organizations drive such regimes, and constitutional principles drive such organizations, by transitivity, such principles must drive the broader legal regime governing international law and the law of international organizations. *See* Friedrich Kratochwil & John Ruggie, "International Organization: A State of the Art on an Art of the State," 40 *Int'l Org.* 753 (1986).

43 The algorithm looks for the words appearing the most frequently together. It proceeds to find the next principle appearing with this combination of two words. Such a statistical approach adds new principles to the "tree," according to the extent to which other principles appear with the groups the algorithm has previously identified. As such, principles "join" the tree based on the extent to which they appear in these constitutions. The less often new principles correlate with groups already identified, the "farther" away they appear on the tree.

44 This statistical approach can identify statistical patterns, but it cannot interpret the groups it finds. This book offers a plausible interpretation (or categorization) for these groups. The exact division between these two lists of principles does not matter for this book's discussion. The book merely wants to show that mentions of some principles appear more closely with others, and that differences in the extent that constitutions mention these principles provide a useful way of thinking about these divisions.

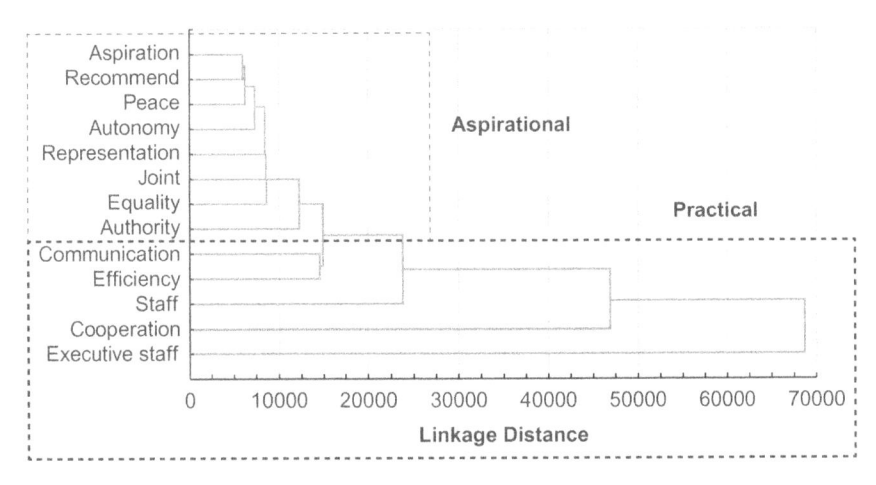

Figure 2.12 Joining tree by values. The figure shows the linkage distances in a standard Euclidian joining trees analysis. We do not discuss how to interpret the distances on the x-axis or the method, as we use this graph mostly for illustrative purposes. We show that some values (like peace and autonomy) have citations across chapters *statistically* more in common with each other than with cooperation. We divide aspirational and practical values by eye-balling the other values (rather than using a dividing or other algorithm).

more often in international organizations' constitutions. Understanding such patterns represents a new and exciting area of study for legal researchers working on international organizations law.

How else could one interpret these two major groupings of international organizations' constitutions? Knowing the members of each group would facilitate such an interpretation.[45] For example, if it were known which constitutions mentioned more aspirational principles and which referenced practical principles, then interpreting these groups would be possible. Figure 2.13 shows the results of a statistical method known as cluster analysis. Similar to the joining trees approach, the algorithm looks at which

---

45 Researchers from all walks of the social sciences have searched for an objective method for grouping international organizations since at least the early 2000s. Barnett and Finnemore – political and social scientists – used their intuition and common sense to arrive at such a grouping. *See* Michael Barnett & Martha Finnemore, *Rules for the World: International Organizations in Global Politics* (2004). Such common sense has guided legal researchers like the ones this book reviewed for at least as long.

Members of cluster 1	Dis.	Members of cluster 2	Dis.
International Tropical Timber Organization	245	Latin American Fisheries Development Organization	621
International Coffee Organization	299	Desert Locust Control Organization for East Africa	633
Caribbean. Meteorological Organization	311	Parliamentary Union of the OIC Member States	773
Advisory Centre on World Trade Organization Law	323	Pan African Postal Union	798
Latin American Energy Organization	334	International Civil Defense Organization	819
European Organisation for Astronomical Research in the Southern Hemisphere	340	International Sugar Organization	831
Northwest Atlantic Fisheries Organization	367	World Intellectual Property Organization	841
IMF	377	UNESCO	913
International Olive Oil Council	381	Southeast Asian Ministers of Education Organization	924
Latin American Centre for Physics	396	Commonwealth Secretariat	931
Central American Court of Justice	399	World Meteorological Organization	968
International Organization of Space Communications	400	Caribbean Postal Union	972

Figure 2.13 Top dozen members of each cluster of organizations.

principles appear more often together in international organizations' constitutions. The procedure builds two groups, which are as different from each other as possible. These two groups ostensibly seem similar. Both groups consist of very specific, practical organizations that focus on tropical timber and coffee (for the first group) and fish as well as locusts (for the second group), for example. Nevertheless, the underlying principles in their constitutions could not be more different.

The figure shows the members of each cluster, which were found by looking for the closest membership in terms of principles in their constitutions and the frequency of references of those principles. Such cluster analysis further showed that two clusters represented the best amount for the dataset, as the number that minimized differences from what was expected in the extent to which various constitutions mentioned principles.

Such simple analysis leads to a conclusion that flies in the face of twenty years of practice – namely, it is not possible to group international organizations by what they purportedly do or should do. Conventional thinking about classifying international organizations traditionally has identified them as legal, political, by type of impact and in contrast with transnational organizations.[46] Klabbers' own attempt at categorizing them – a project that he admits remains highly subjective – ranges from trying to classify organizations created between states, created on the basis of a treaty, as possessing an organ with a distinct will, by function, by membership, as political versus technical and so forth.[47] The categorization conundrum has let researchers like Ian Hurd avoid categories altogether – leaving him to conveniently present large international organizations as unique entities in themselves.[48] Nevertheless, grouping international organizations by the similarities in their constitutional principles clearly provides a practicable and useful way of grouping these organizations.

The use of statistics and subjective interpretation by legal researchers shows that no one answer exists to the question of how many groupings of international organizations exist. Figure 2.14 shows the results of another (different) grouping method called factor analysis. Such factor analysis presumes that associations between principles help to detect underlying "factors" that explain the data. For example, mentions of staff and efficiency in international organizations' constitutions associate with the factor related to organizations labeled as efficient international organizations. The factors stressed by international organizations' constitutions that are labeled as peace-loving (unsurprisingly) are peace and related principles.[49]

Based on the profiles of principles shown by groups of constitutions, this book identifies seven groups of international organizations. Efficient organizations place an emphasis on staffing and efficiency. For authors like Gayl Ness and Steven Brechin, efficiency represents one of the few

---

46 *See, e.g.*, Union of International Associations, Types of International Organizations, *at* https://uia.org/archive/types-organization/cc (last visited Mar. 25, 2020).
47 *See* Klabbers, *supra* Chapter 1, note 37, chs. 1–2.
48 *See* Hurd, *supra* Chapter 1, note 35.
49 Scholarly support has grown since the year 2000 for categorizing international organizations according to the principles they espouse. For a discussion of the UN as a "peace-loving" entity, and other international organizations' own characterizations of their principles by the community of researchers at large, *see* Michael N. Barnett, "The New United Nations Politics of Peace: From Juridical Sovereignty to Empirical Sovereignty," 1 *Global Gov.* 79 (1995).

Empirics 89

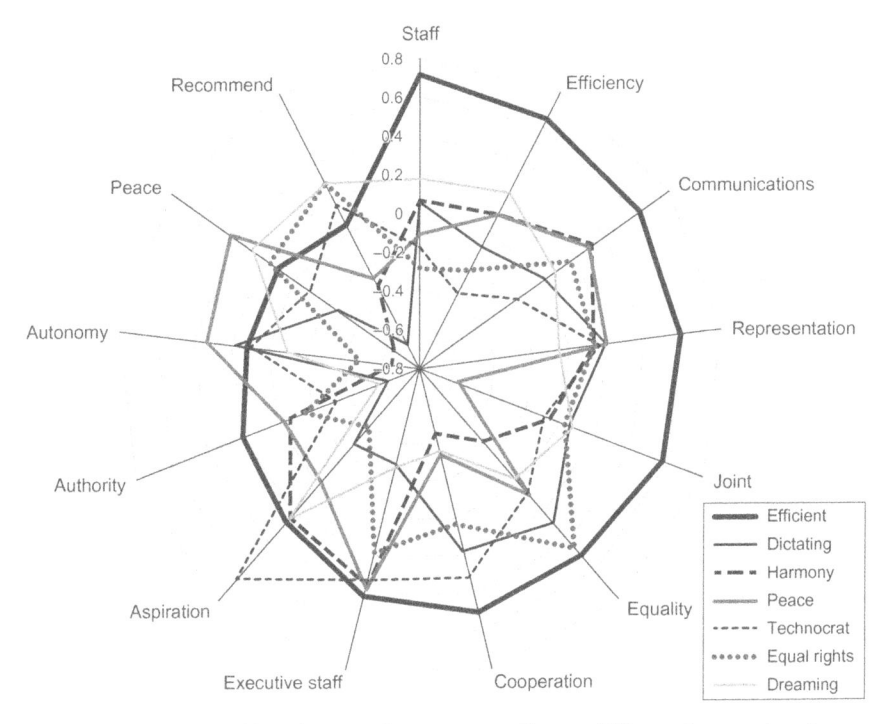

Figure 2.14 Profiles of principles corresponding to different international organization types. This figure shows the factor weightings (or extent of the importance) of each principle for each factor identified in this book's analysis. In particular, there are seven factors as represented by the different lines. Each factor (or line) weighs the importance of a different combination of principles. The interpretation of these factors is described later in the book.

principles that all international organizations – as organizations in the sociological meaning of the term – have in common.[50] Dictating organizations place a large emphasis on making recommendations, authority and staff.[51] Authors like Beth Simmons and Lisa Martin might see these international organizations as the influencers, setting the standards

---

50 *See* Gayl Ness & Steven Brechin, "Bridging the Gap: International Organizations as Organizations," 42 *Int'l Org.* 245 (1998).
51 Such factor analysis places principles on an axis with two extremes. Extreme negative weights for principles in each factor represent the factor just as much as large positive values. The authors of this book chose to define the factor by the large negative weights attached to principles associated with that factor just as much as the positive values. Naturally, interpreting a collection of weights attached to a factor remains a highly subjective exercise.

for international regimes driving international organizations' activities.[52] Harmony organizations – or organizations striving for harmony, or at least consensus among members – represent communicating organizations with aspirations towards the representation of interests in the body equally, if not fairly.[53] Authors like Barbara Koremenos, Charles Lipson and Duncan Snidal, in stark contrast with most of the profession, place such harmonious cooperation at the heart of international organizational design.[54] In the empiricist's tradition, they compile a database to show how international organizations strive to cooperate as their *primus inter pares* goal.

The other factors identified by this book's analysis suggest other groupings or categories of international organizations. Technocratic organizations, as a category, reflect the widely argued premise that some international organizations focus on a specific goal, like controlling locusts or helping to manage tropical timber worldwide. Authors like Ernst Haas would argue that such an attempt to group international organizations by their function or activity represents a useful, if flawed, functional conception of the system of international organizations.[55] Equal-rights organizations have equality and making recommendations as core constitutional principles. As Robert Dahl might argue, such organizations do not seek equality or rights for themselves but, rather, for certain classes of beneficiaries.[56] Finally, dreaming organizations place aspirations and recommendations at the core of their constitutional principles. Authors like Akira Iriye have argued for international organizations' role in promoting – usually globalist-oriented and led – progress.[57] Aspiring international organizations, aspiring founders

---

52 *See* Beth Simmons & Lisa Martin, "International Organizations and Institutions," *in Handbook of International Relations* 192 (Walter Carlsnaes et al. eds. 2002).
53 Put less prosaically, the factor weighting communication, aspiration and representation – particularly among its senior staff – represents these organizations.
54 *See* Barbara Koremenos et al., "The Rational Design of International Institutions," 55 *Int'l Org.* 761 (2001).
55 *See* Ernst Haas, *Beyond the Nation-State: Functionalism and International Organization* (1964).
56 Dahl conflates equality with democracy and participation, in effect arguing that international organizations cannot attain democracy, and thus merit-based equality between individuals and entities enfranchised in such a democracy of international organizations. For all the problems with Dahl's analysis, his critique of participation in international organizations leading to more equality between the individuals and groups served by the organization remains as valid today as in the past. *See* Robert A. Dahl, "Can International Organizations Be Democratic? A Skeptic's View," *in Democracy's Edges* 19 (Ian Shapiro et al. eds. 1999).
57 In Iriye's telling, aspirational international organizations (and international organizations with progressive aspirations) have led the way towards the development

and members of these organizations create a place in the firmament of international organizations unique to their calling.

While grouping principles and thus organizations in this way has its benefits, such groupings ignore the dynamic, shifting and group-specific nature of the way principles appear together in international organizations' constitutions. Authors like Hans Kelsen would decry any attempt to sift through customs and treaty law in an attempt to create a set of single values and principles.[58] International organizations' constitutions for the most part represent treaties that underpin existing international law. Nevertheless, the values and principles they contain branch out, forming new meanings and containing meanings unique to subsets of international organizations, which change over time.[59] Fortunately, advances in statistical methods, particularly relating to semantic networks, can capture some of the complexity hitherto impossible to analyze without generalizing.[60]

Accounting for the way principles depend on principles through networks

Rather than grouping legal principles, jurimetricians can identify network relationships in the way constitutions refer to these principles.[61] For such an analysis, the relationship between any pair of constitutions or principles

---

of a global community. Such a community has enfranchised business and civil society to bring about revolutionary changes in the way global governance operates. Behind such a change lie the aspirations of these international organizations and their founders. See Akira Iriye, *Global Community: The Role of International Organizations in the Making of the Contemporary World* (2002).

58 Kelsen would refer to such an attempt as monism. *See generally* Hans Kelsen, *Principles of International Law* (1952).

59 Both Kelsen and Malanczuk would argue for such a pluralism of values and principles. Indeed, Malanczuk pays tribute to such complexity by refusing to generalize about types of international law influenced by international organizations. Instead, he takes each organization as it is, and analyzes its contribution to international law as it is. *See* Peter Malanczuk, *Akehurst's Modern Introduction to International Law* (7th rev. ed. 1997).

60 Indeed, researchers had wished to do the kind of analysis contained in this book for decades. For analyses of how much more one could understand by conducting network analysis of international organizations law and texts, *see* Anthony Judge, "International Organization Networks: A Complementary Perspective," *in International Organizations: A Conceptual Approach* 381 (Paul Taylor & A.J.R. Groom eds. 1977). *See also* David C. Ellis, "Theorizing International Organizations: The Organizational Turn in International Organization Theory," 1 *J. Int'l Org. Stud.* 11 (2010).

61 Despite many successful analyses of international organizations, and particularly their membership, network analysis remains a highly underused tool in the field of

holds less interest than in the long-distance linkages between them – "through" other principles. Figure 1.8 illustrates the idea with a network analysis of the international organizations' constitutions from this book's database. As shown, many constitutions link cooperation, autonomy and recommendation together in the same document. Authority, aspiration, communication and the other principles sit almost on top of each other in the graph, which suggests that these principles frequently appear together. Peace and representativeness seem the odd-man-out principles, linking to both major groupings of other principles. Such patterns suggest a completely different way to group principles. Such a network approach shows the ways that principles associate with others – not in the same document – but in other constitutions that contain at least one of the same principles.

How are we to understand this "long-linking" nature of principles in international organizations' constitutions? Consider the extent to which the Advisory Centre on WTO Law refers to autonomy roughly 242 times for every 10,000 words in its constitution and to communication roughly 726 times for every 10,000 words. The African Civil Aviation Commission's constitution, in contrast, does not refer to autonomy at all. However, the African Civil Aviation Commission's constitution does refer to communication – roughly 430 times for every 10,000 words. Both constitutions share references to communication. By extension, the African Civil Aviation Commission's constitution then links with a constitution mentioning autonomy "through" its similarity with the Advisory Centre on WTO Law's mentions of communication in its constitution. Some constitutions share similarities with other constitutions, which may mention particular principles more or less often. The African Civil Aviation Commission's constitution does not mention autonomy. However, it shares commonalities with the Advisory Centre on WTO Law's constitution, which does.

Such an approach allows quantification of how international organizations' constitutions "link" to particular principles, not by mentioning them but by sharing similarities with constitutions that do mention these principles. Mathematics can help to quantify the extent to which international organizations' constitutions share commonalities with other constitutions that share commonalities with other constitutions that refer to certain principles. Figure 2.15 demonstrates the method, which illustrates how jurimetricians calculate the eigencentrality of a principle in these constitutions. The eigencentrality of a constitutional principle measures the importance of the principle, in light of the importance of the other principles associated with it in other international organizations' constitutions. As shown in the figure,

international organizations. For one such interesting study, *see* Hafner-Burton & Montgomery, *supra* Chapter 1, note 172, at 3.

Organization name	Authority	Autonomy	Communication	Cooperation	Efficiency	Equality
Afro-Asian Rural Development Organization [2007 + 2012 declarations]			376.435	3199.699	752.870	1129.305
Advisory Centre on WTO Law		242.248	726.744	1453.488	1453.488	1211.420
African Civil Aviation Commission			420.942	1939.237	861.883	861.883
African Court of Human and People's Rights (establishing protocol + charter)		900.437	2701.312	1157.705	1414.973	1414.973
African and Malagasy Council for High Education	433.651	433.651	1300.954	3035.559	433.651	
African Development Bank	266.720	133.360	666.800	533.440	600.120	266.720
African Development Bank and Administrative Tribunal	416.320	416.320	416.320	832.639	1665.279	
African Export Import Bank	384.333	489.151	628.909	314.454	489.151	419.273
African Intellectual Property Organization	414.614	207.307	956.800	382.720	896.014	111.627
African Regional Intellectual Property Organization			1310.616	1638.270	2293.578	

Figure 2.15 Understanding long-linked "eigencentralities" in international organizations' constitution principles. The figure shows the 'links through links' of the Africa Rice Center's constitution mentions of authority with the African Regional Intellectual Property Organization and the African Telecommunications Union. The Rice Center constitution shares similarities with the African Development Bank Administrative Tribunal's (ADBAT) constitution mentions of communication and thus its mentions of efficiency (tracing the red arrows and boxes in the figure). The Rice Center's constitution also shares similarities with the Arab Bank of Economic Development in Africa's (ABEDA) constitution's extent of referring to communication. The ADBAT's constitution refers to communication much less than the ABEDA's – making the weight of the Tribunal's constitution mentions of efficiency less important than the Arab Bank's. Eigencentralities "trace through" all of these associations – in effect looking at the weight of the African Telecommunication Union's constitution references to communication and so forth.

Organization name	Authority	Autonomy	Communication	Cooperation	Efficiency	Equality
Africa Rice Center	388.878		1166.634	1361.073	972.195	777.756
African Telecommunications Union	188.430		1601.658	2449.595	1130.582	282.646
African Union		712.589	475.059	1662.708	232.530	712.589
Agency for the Prohibition of Nuclear Weapons in Latin America	170.213	510.638	1191.489	851.064	1021.277	1021.277
Andean Community [Andean Subregional Integration Agreement]	72.653	145.307	1307.759	2688.172	1017.146	145.307
Arab Bank for Economic Development in Africa	568.909	568.909	1280.046	568.992	426.682	853.364
Asia Pacific Association of Agricultural Research Institution			978.953	1468.429	978.953	489.476

Figure 2.15 Continued

Empirics 95

the Africa Rice Center constitution's mentions of authority "link" more strongly to efficiency through the path of association drawn out by the gray path because of the high frequency of communication in the Arab Bank for Economic Development in Africa's constitution. Both constitutions share relatively frequent mentions of communication. However, tracing through the weight of these links, as shown by the frequency of mentions of each principle in these international organizations' constitutions, allows for a calculation of the relative association of authority to efficiency in the Africa Rice Center's constitution by tracing through its similarities with communications – and thus efficiency – in other, similar constitutions. The eigencentrality algorithm traces through all these similarities, for all principles in all international organizations, to find the relative importance of each principle *in the overall constellation of principles for all international organizations.*

Four groupings of principles emerge when considering the transitivity of principles across international organizations' constitutions. Figure 2.16 shows the eigencentralities of the book's database of constitutional principles. Cooperation and executive staff principles lie at the center of such a network of principles, with both principles scoring eigencentralities of unity. Communication and efficiency appear transitively quite frequently with mentions of executive staff. Equality appears relatively frequently with

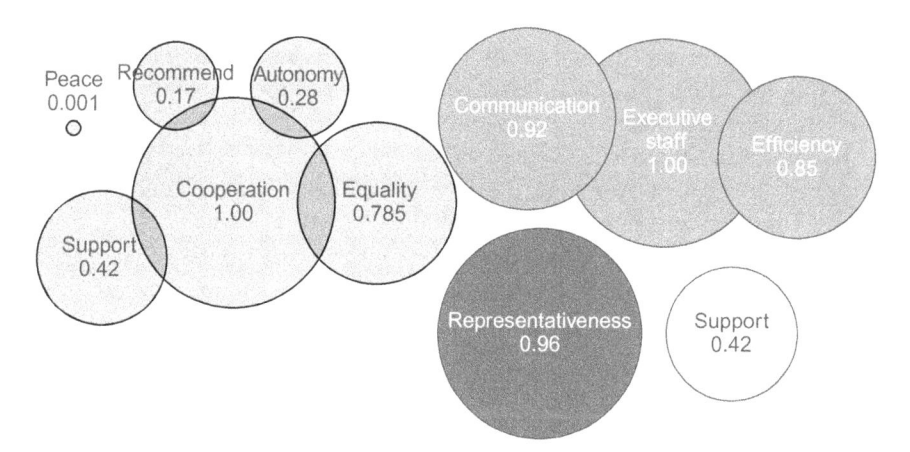

Figure 2.16 Mapping the long-linkedness of constitution principles. The figure shows the four groups of principles identified by network analysis of the principles contained in international organizations' constitutions. We applied the OpenOrd algorithm to the network constitutions' principles weighted by each principle's citations per 10,000 words. We found the four main modules in the network and the eigencentrality of each principle. We rescaled these eigencentralities between 0 and 1. The bubble graph shows the value of each centrality in the whole network.

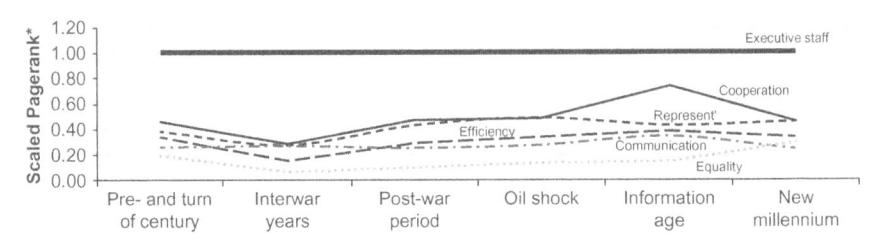

Figure 2.17 Principles change in importance depending on the time period. The figure shows the extent to which each principle gained or lost importance in the "network" of principles formed by principles contained in international organizations' constitutions for the time periods shown. We calculated these values by finding the Pagerank value for each principle in each time period's data. We then rescaled these Pagerank values between 0 and 1. Executive staff represents the group of principles they most closely belong to. We report on these modularity changes in a separate figure.

cooperation in these constitutions, after tracing through all the ways that these two principles share commonalities across all constitutions. While peace seems to connect with almost no other principles, eigencentrality analysis shows that the principle associates with the group associated with cooperation. The principles of representativeness and support appear as important principles, yet they do not often transitively associate with these other principles in the book's database. Such analysis provides another way to group organizations, or at least the principles in their constitutions, by their importance in the overall "network" of principles.

How does the importance of these principles in international organizations' constitutions change over time? As international organizations incorporate later in time, the content of their constitutions changes. Principles in these constitutions associate with different principles (or to a greater or lesser extent) in similar constitutions. Figure 2.17 shows the statistic similar to eigencentrality, which shows the extent to which certain principles transitively associate more or less with other principles. For all international organizations created during the interwar years, the centrality of principles like cooperation, representativeness, efficiency and communication falls, in some cases quite significantly. From 1940 onward, these principles' centrality in the overall "fabric" of principles in international organizations' constitutions expanded. The principle of cooperation declined in importance as a principle associated frequently with other principles. Efficiency rose, indicating a more technocratic bent to international organization design and motivation.[62]

---

[62] Helfer's historical analysis of the ILO illustrates just how much the Organization reflects these trends at the micro-level. See Laurence Helfer, "Understanding Change

Empirics

These changes can be illustrated by showing the network of international organizations' constitutional principles changing over time. Figures 2.18A–F show the network of values in six time periods. In the nineteenth century and up to the First World War, like in all time periods, mentions of executive staff remain central to these international organizations' constitutions, not only individually but across all constitutions. Representativeness and cooperation represent important principles in opposition to efficiency and communication. No principle appears dominant in this projection.[63] In the interwar years, international organizations' constitutions give greater weight to communication and authority, as a collective of all constitutions.[64] The interwar years also saw the rising importance of principles, such as equality and the other principles, more closely allied with executive staff principles and rules.

Constitutions drafted in the post-war years exhibited tremendous similarity in their principles and the extent to which they associated with others between and across international organizations' constitutions. The thick arrows shown in the figure signify the importance of specific principles to specific international organizations. The extent that non-overlapping sets of international organizations' constitutions mention certain principles more frequently supports the oft-cited notion that some international organizations support particular principles and values more than others. The patchiness of links between principles across constitutions in the oil shock years shows that, even if such a division of principles by particular organizations existed, such associations of particular organizations with particular principles proved short lived. Nevertheless, the conclusion remains: certain time periods coincide with the rising importance of certain sets or networks of principles in these international organizations' constitutions.

International organizations' constitutional principles have evolved significantly since the 1980s. Figures 2.18A–F continue to show the links between these principles. In the last two decades of the twentieth century a

---

in International Organizations: Globalization and Innovation in the ILO," 59 *Vanderbilt L. Rev.* 649 (2006). The ILO underwent changes reflecting changes in broader principles and values occurring across the international organizational landscape. *See id*.

63 This figure uses the OpenOrd graphing method. Such an approach gives distance to very similar principles, but draws in principles a bit less similar. As such, it becomes possible to observe groupings more clearly, without dominant principles all lumping together.

64 Since network analysis like this looks at the weight of principles across all constitutions, the graph shows the way principles are associated as a group across all constitutions. Naturally, patterns applicable to the system as a whole might appear much less prominently in individual constitutions.

98 *The values of international organizations*

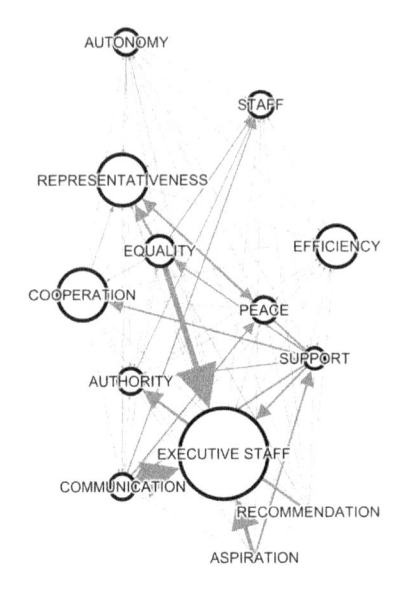

Figure 2.18A Principles coming into their own over the past 100 years: turn of the century (pre-1900 to 1917). Representativeness and cooperation represent important principles in opposition to efficiency and communication.

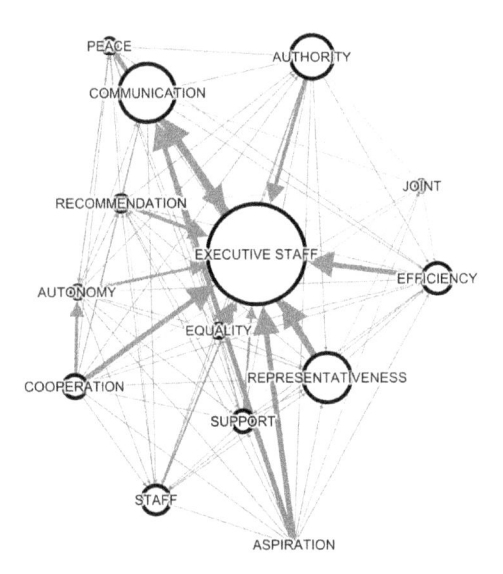

Figure 2.18B Principles coming into their own over the past 100 years: interwar years (1918 to 1945). Communication and authority rise in importance when linked to principles such as equality and the other principles more closely allied with executive staff.

Empirics 99

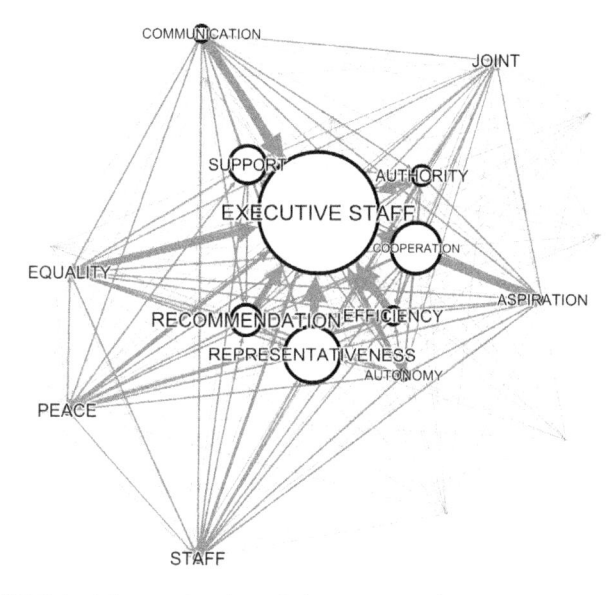

Figure 2.18C Principles coming into their own over the past 100 years: post-war years (1946 to 1972). Principles become closely aligned after the Second World War, with "division of labour" the most visible across organizations, as represented by the thick arrows to particular principles.

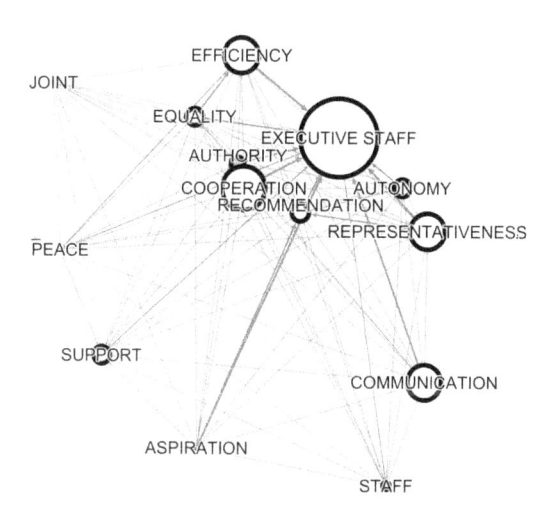

Figure 2.18D Principles coming into their own over the past 100 years: oil shock years (1973 to 1980). Principles do not align as simply as before. Greater emphasis appears in relation to representativeness, and authority, cooperation and other principles serve as a better counter-balance against constitutions focused on executive staff.

100   *The values of international organizations*

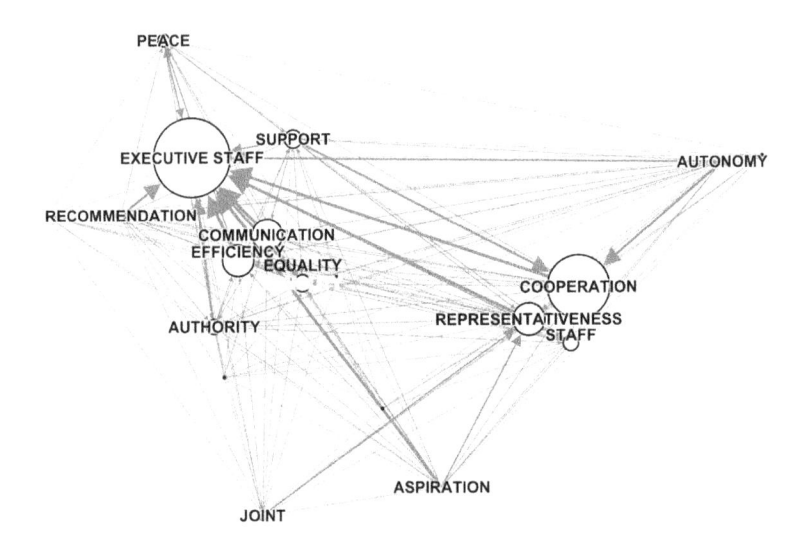

Figure 2.18E Principles coming into their own over the past 100 years: information age (1980 to 1999). A clear separation of constitutions by interest in staffing versus cooperation and representativeness is apparent. Never has a dichotomy in values been so apparent.

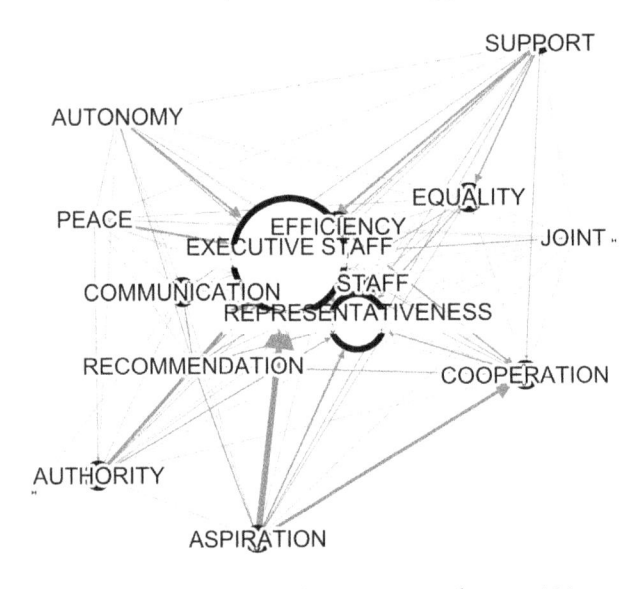

Figure 2.18F Principles coming into their own over the past 100 years: the new millennium (2000 to 2020). The post-2000 era sees constitutions focused on efficiency and communication, with each value having almost its own power base among different organizations, as represented by large nodes diametrically opposed to other values.

clear division of associations appears in constitutions, between interest in staffing, cooperation and representativeness. Such a division might have led to the widely held attempt to generally classify organizations as technocratic versus aspirational. Such an attempt by the authors of international organizations law textbooks has confused a pattern exhibited in the latter part of the twentieth century with a general pattern for all international organizations. Such a division in mentions of principles by international organizations' constitutions morphed into a division between a set of constitutions focused on efficiency and others on communication.

Figures 2.18A–F illustrate network analysis of the book's dataset for the time periods shown. The graphs were made by using the OpenOrd algorithm on a dataset measuring the frequency with which international organizations' constitutions refer to each of the principles shown in the figures.

Looking at these networks of constitutional principles in certain types of international organizations illustrates the futility of trying to generalize classifications and theories about international organizations. Figures 2.19A–B show the same kind of network analysis of principles in international organizations' constitutions, albeit dividing organizations by their jurisdiction. Universal international organizations' constitutions focus heavily on executive staff issues, with all other principles playing minor roles in supporting this value. In regional organizations' constitutions, in contrast, cooperation, efficiency and representativeness play much larger roles for different groups of regional organizations. Any analysis of international organizations' principles must consider these differences in organizational types and characteristics, which defy the generalities of academic analysis to date.

Removing international organizations from the analysis and focusing exclusively on principles provides the clearest picture of these principles yet. Figure 2.20 shows this picture, which was constructed by associating principles from each constitution with other principles.[65] Using only principles in the analysis makes it possible to see that all principles seem to "support" executive staff, in that mentions of such staff far outstrip

---

65 The previous network analyses showed the links formed by the name of the organization and the principle involved. For example, one binary pair might consist of the Advisory Centre on WTO Law paired with autonomy (with a link weight of 242, corresponding to the number of mentions per 10,000 words). The next pair appearing in the dataset would consist of Advisory Centre on WTO Law and communication, with a link weight of 726. In contrast, this dataset consists of autonomy and communication (with a link weight of 3, meaning autonomy appears in the Advisory Centre's constitution three times more often). The pair autonomy and cooperation would appear as the next datum, with a link weight of 6.

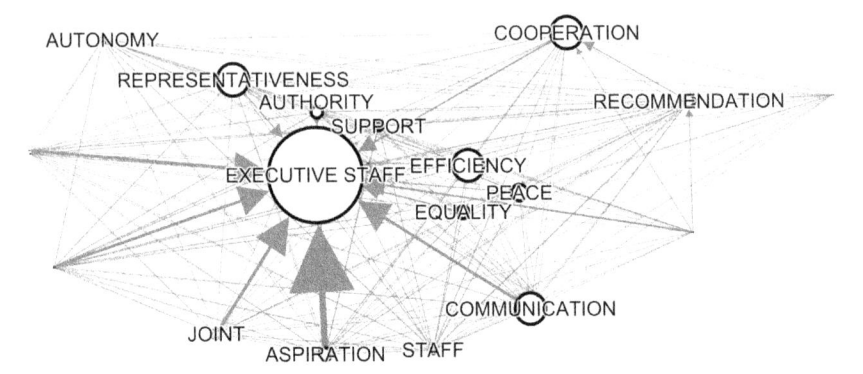

Figure 2.19A Different kinds of international organizations clearly have different constitutions that prioritize and "link" different principles: universal international organizations. These organizations' constitutions focus far more heavily on executive staff and give far less prominence to other values. Authority tends to support such staff, whereas communication clearly refers to something outside of staff issues. Autonomy and recommendations appear literally sidelined.

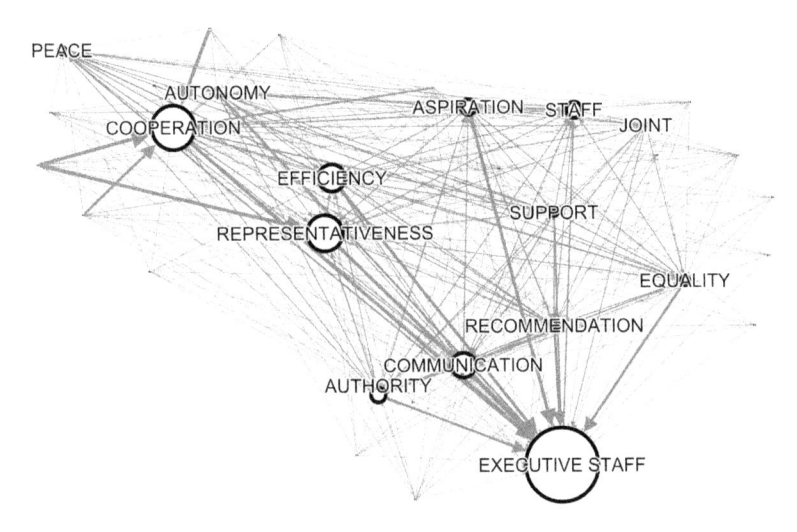

Figure 2.19B Different kinds of international organizations clearly have different constitutions that prioritize and "link" different principles: regional international organizations. These organizations' principles show marked distinction between those focusing on executive staff issues (and the ways that recommendations, authority and equality support such staff) as well as cooperation and autonomy, which literally are at the other end of the figure. Efficiency and representativeness represent their own principles, neither of which is often connected with either "camp" of values.

Empirics 103

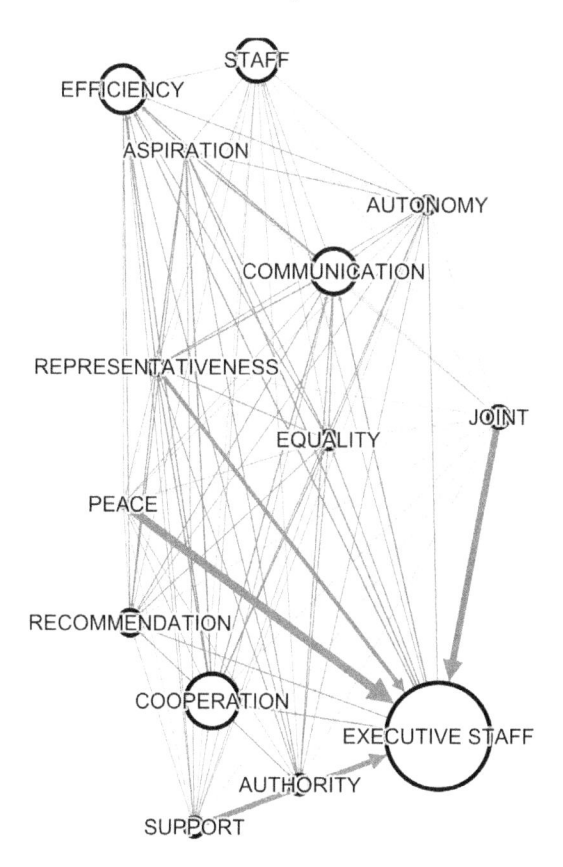

Figure 2.20 All principles lead back to international organizations' executive staff. The figure shows the linkages between principles in international organizations' constitutions from the book's database. This data was constructed by creating a list of all the principles appearing in the same constitution as all other principles. For each set of associations (authority/autonomy, authority/representativeness and so forth), the analysis involved dividing the number of mentions of the first principle by the number of mentions of the second principle. In this way, a constitution mentioning support twice as often as cooperation would have a support/cooperation link weight of 2. All possible bilateral pairings of principles in each constitution – 17,580 pairs – were used.

other principles. Principles like cooperation, autonomy and authority directly link to such staff. Other principles like efficiency link to other principles like staff, which then link to executive staff. Analyzing principles in this way shows how references "flow" to executive staffing. Cooperation appears to represent a linch-pin in the network, with many principles linking to cooperation before such mentions of cooperation link to executive staff. This book does not show similar graphs for subsets of organizations or specific time periods, so as not to lose the general lesson from this graph – particular principles play significant, and quantifiable, key and supporting roles in organizational constitutions, with executive staffing principles serving as the "end" or key principle in the network of principles.

Conclusion

Quantitative analysis of principles in international organizations' constitutions provides some insights into the ways that different organizations promote cooperation, their own authority, autonomy and so forth. Every textbook on international organizations law includes a general section trying to classify, group and otherwise organize international organizations by function or values. The analysis of this book demonstrates the futility of making such generalizations without hard data. This chapter has shown how certain principles like staffing issues, cooperation, efficiency and representation correlate with each other within constitutions. It has also shown how, because of such close correlations, it is impossible to simply compare these principles pair-wise, or two by two. Instead, it was necessary to look at groups and networks of principles to understand the entire "system" of principles driving international organizations.

The chapter has shown that each grouping, classification or type of international organization has its own groups of principles driving their own meanings and purposes. The analysis started by grouping principles into aspirational and practical valued principles, with such groupings being determined exclusively by objective algorithms. The analysis showed how other, more detailed groupings could be found. Using more sensitive grouping methods yielded seven types of categories of international organizations, judging by the principles that appear together in their constitutions. Network methods allowed the analysis to "trace through" the way that principles correlate indirectly with each other. These methods show that these principles appear together in different ways for different types of organizations and in different time periods. Cooperation, efficiency and representativeness feature much more prominently in regional international organizations' constitutions than in those of universal ones. If these constitutions referred to principles relatively equally in the organizational environment after the Second World War, constitutions divided into those stressing efficiency and technical issues (for one set of organizations' constitutions) and those stressing aspirational and political cooperation (for another set of organizations' constitutions). The prominence of these principles changes over time, and it does depend on how others' constitutions refer to these principles.

Most importantly, this chapter's analysis identified the core role played by executive staffing principles in these organizations. It showed that all principles seem to lead to executive staff, which means that groups of principles always support staffing issues. The result of the analysis, having shown us where to look and the important networks of principles in these constitutions, is that jurists can start to apply their tools to understand what these associations mean for international organizations law.

3

Patterns of authority in international organizations' constitutions

Introduction

Statistics can take us only so far. Inspired by statistical analysis, this chapter illustrates how the associations, groups and networks from the data translate into international organizations law.[1] Such law consists of principles that, combined together, result in particular rights, obligations and the jurisprudence of international organizations law.[2] Authority, one of the international system's cornerstone principles, appears frequently with other principles as well as representing a statistically important principle in its own right.

Much of the authority vested in international organizations derives from agreements and events determined outside of the founding constitution, but what about the authority derived from their founding constitutions?[3] Such authority may come from subsequent treaties and agreements clarifying, expanding or restricting the international organization's authority to decide and act on certain issues.[4] Many have tried to measure the way such author-

---

1 *See also* James D. Fry, *Termination of Secretaries General* (forthcoming 2022) (providing similar illustrations). Other researchers are hereby invited to use this book's dataset at www.law.hku.hk/academic_staff/dr-james-d-fry to generate their own illustrations and to try to falsify the findings contained in this book.
2 *See* Chester Brown, "The Cross-Fertilization of Principles Relating to Procedure and Remedies in the Jurisprudence of International Court and Tribunals," 30 *Loy. L.A. Int'l & Comp. L. Rev.* 219 (2008).
3 For some researchers, such authority results even from the unforeseen and accidental result of interstate rivalries, where states vest authority (but often not) to achieve cooperative outcomes not available to these states working individually. Following the tradition of this book, Hooghe and Marks at least use a dataset to test assertions about the authority of international organizations. *See* Hooghe & Marks, *supra* Chapter 2, note 11.
4 Authors like Röben describe the ebbs and flows of such authority in the area of cross-border law enforcement, while authors like Ecker-Ehrhardt describe the never-ending

ity in international organizations changes over time.[5] However, few have tried to survey such authority, let alone provide a practical, legal analysis of the way that mentions of authority in these international organizations' constitutions relate to other principles mentioned in the same constitution, as this chapter provides.

To be more precise, this chapter provides a more rounded picture of the way international organizations refer to authority in their founding constitutions. Such a picture should shed light on how the drafters of these international organizations' constitutions envisioned the vesting and exercise of authority by and in these organizations, if at all.[6] The patterns found through this book's analysis consist of a complex mesh of legal values and subsidiary principles, as well as relationships between them.[7] Member states may vest one international organization with wide-reaching authority, competencies for communicating with other bodies and making recommendations implicitly backed up by the use of force from one or more member states, like the UN. Other constitutions may grant organizations, like the WTO, little actual authority. There, member states take virtually all the decisions in meetings and leave the organization devoid of much technocratic authority to communicate and make recommendations. However, these polar opposites do not represent the only options. All kinds of sinewy jurisprudential "links" may allow some organizations to make high-impact recommendations affecting the development of international law, without

---

politics driving such change. *See* Volker Röben, "The Enforcement Authority of International Institutions," 9 *Germ. L. Rev.* 1965 (2008); Matthias Ecker-Ehrhardt, "Why Parties Politicise International Institutions: on Globalisation Backlash and Authority Contestation," 21 *Rev. Int'l Pol. Econ.* 1275 (2014).

5 We cannot hope to provide a complete overview of the attempts to qualify the authority of international organizations. Authors like Hooghe and Marks (already referred to above) have made large strides in providing such data. Their upcoming opus will probably provide enough background to satisfy most readers' curiosity about – and for – such measurements. *See* Hooghe et al., *supra* Chapter 1, note 64. For their data, *see* Gary Marks, "International Authority," *at* http://garymarks.web.unc.edu/data/international-authority/ (last visited Mar. 25, 2020).

6 The qualifier "if at all" is added, as forty-seven of the treaties analyzed have no significant explicit mention of authority. The lack of explicit mention of such authority has perplexed academics for decades. For a discussion, *see* Randall W. Stone, "Informal Governance in International Organizations," 8 *Rev. Int'l Org.* 121 (2013).

7 This book does not critique or describe the conflicts in these values. As mentioned in the introductory chapter, this book aims to provide a census of values, leaving further work and critique to peers. For the critical reader interested in some of the clashes and overlaps in these values, *see* Michael N. Barnett & Martha Finnemore, "The Politics, Power, and Pathologies of International Organizations," 53 *Int'l Org.* 699 (1999).

actually vesting much authority in the organization itself.[8] All the variation in the way framers put together these values and principles into international organizations' constitutions makes for a rich and variegated frame of jurisprudence guiding our international organizations.

The first section of this chapter reviews the thinking about authority in these constitutions and confronts that thinking with the quantitative data on the constitutions that this book has analyzed. Despite the popularity of general theories of authority, actual constitutions refer to authority in very different ways.[9] Even when the text of one constitution mimics another, the "interaction" of these mentions with other legal principles – like communication and recommendation – makes generalization impossible.[10] Instead, the idea of an ecosystem seems apt, or a wide array of circuits that connect all different kinds of authority, authority to communicate and authority to make recommendations. Some of these connections may even give rise to *jus gentium* or *jus cogens*, which arguably form the backbone of jurisprudence about international organizations.[11]

The second section of this chapter provides in-depth analysis of the ways that international organizations' constitutions refer to authority. At one end

---

8 Many researchers, even non-postmodern researchers, might take umbrage at this book's attempt to even find these principles. These researchers might argue that the book looks for constitutional (or constitution-like) principles in agreements never meant to face the same kind of interpretation as constitutions. For one statement of this position, *see* Aoife O'Donoghue, "International Constitutionalism and the State," 11 *Int'l J. Const. L.* 1021 (2013).

9 Other authors have had similar findings. Bezuijen conducts one of the most extensive surveys of authority in international organizations, finding a similar tapestry of variation. However, she treats organizations as a sociologist rather than a lawyer – looking for apparent similarities and differences by types of organization instead of looking at the deeper legal principles defining difference and structure. *See* Jeanine Bezuijen, "Governance Above the State: Explaining Variation in International Authority," Ph.D. Thesis at Vrije Universiteit Amsterdam (2015), *available at* https://research.vu.nl/ws/portalfiles/portal/42152383 (last visited Mar. 25, 2020).

10 Many of these attempts at generalizing the value of authority in international organizations come from the lack of any alternative theory or framework that might allow for heterogeneous, multiple views of such authority, with the EU experience providing one of the only case studies providing for such variegation. *See* Armin von Bogdandy, "General Principles of International Public Authority: Sketching a Research Field," 9 *Germ. L.J.* 1909 (2008).

11 As a reminder to readers outside of this field, much of international organizations law comes from widely recognized rules that no one has necessarily defined in treaties. The ability of international organizations to contract represents an obvious example. *See* Kristina Daugirdas, "How and Why International Law Binds International Organizations," 57 *Harv. Int' L.J.* 325 (2016).

of the spectrum, some constitutions make sure that international organizations remain devoid of the authority to act as separate actors in international relations. Constitutions that almost encourage semi-independent authority, to the extent allowed in a principal–agent approach to law, occupy the other end of the spectrum. In many cases, authority remains tightly governed, from member states and principals to organizations as their agents. In other cases, constitutions themselves provide for narrow gaps in such a pass-through of authority.[12] In all cases, some vestige of authority might stay with the international organization in order for it to participate in the firmament of international organizations.[13]

The third section of this chapter explores the ways that authority allows for some international organizations' autonomy. Gaps in the delegation of authority clearly allow for limited organizational autonomy. Part of that autonomy comes from unique jurisprudential concepts only available in international law, like the existence of international legal personality for international organizations, which helps to guarantee the autonomy of officials working in international organizations. The recognition of external authorities, besides states, also cements the acceptance in international law of agents who may act like, if not are, principals.

The fourth section treats international organizations' authority to communicate to authorities in states as well as within and between their own bureaucratic structures. For many international organizations, the right and ability to communicate helps to constitute membership in the international organization. Other international organizations' *raison d'être* consists of issuing recommendations, and some issue recommendations as part of their internal governance and management. Various stakeholders, usually in the board of member state representatives and in senior management, have their say over appointments, particularly those of senior staff.

The fifth section deals with international organizations' authority to issue recommendations. Some recommendations come to form part of the soft

---

12 Such a finding confirms others' qualitative analysis. At the risk of gross oversimplification, Sarooshi divides such a pass-through into three levels, basically full, medium and little, if any. See Dan Sarooshi, *International Organizations and their Exercise of Sovereign Powers* (2007).

13 The non-lawyerly way of seeing authority as a quantity that states retain or may pass through to international organizations helps us to understand such variation, even if researchers might object to treating authority like a measurable and divisible attribute. However, as the OECD notes, international organizations could not set up the extensive network of cross-organizational *regulatory* cooperation without retaining some authority, even devolved or delegated. See OECD, "International Regulatory Co-Operation: The Role of International Organizations," *GOV/RPC(2016)5/REV1* (2016), *available at* www.oecd.org (last visited Mar. 25, 2020).

law underpinning international law. Other recommendations represent the way that international organizations, or stakeholders in them, share authority. The most obvious examples include the UN General Assembly recommendations or the UN Economic and Social Council's recommendations to the World Health Organization (WHO) and other specialized bodies. Some recommendations focus on internal operations and staffing as a way of getting an international organization to do something, like make loans or harmonize railway standards.

The final section concludes by reviewing findings about the multitrack values and principles enshrined in words like authority, autonomy, communication and recommendation. Valuing international organizations' constitutions consists partly of calculating and deducing how values govern the legal instruments governing their inception. Values like authority represent something different for almost every organization's design. Only by understanding how these values work empirically is it possible to understand how international organizations law works.

How constitutions refer to authority

The textbook approach to authority

How to define international organizations' authority? While not providing an exact definition, White describes six ingredients for an international organization to exercise authority.[14] First, the international organization's decisions must bind member governments.[15] Second, organizations taking such decisions need not require unanimous participation by all member states, even if some do not agree to the decision.[16] Third,

---

14 *See* White, *supra* Chapter 1, note 19, at 60.
15 White should have qualified the statement with the qualification that such law should bind them "as much as possible." The fount of such a binding – the Vienna Convention on the Law of Treaties – that governs such rule-following has no real enforcement mechanism, besides states' acting in good faith and voluntary arbitration. In the case of the Vienna Convention on the Law of Treaties between States and International Organizations or between International Organizations, not enough states have ratified this almost carbon copy of the Vienna Convention on the Law of Treaties in order to bring that convention into force. *Compare* Vienna Convention on the Law of Treaties, May 23, 1969, 1155 U.N.T.S. 331, 8 I.L.M. 679, with Vienna Convention on the Law of Treaties between States and International Organizations or Between International Organizations art. 66, Mar. 21, 1986, UN Doc. A/CONF.129/15, *at* https://treaties.un.org (last visited Mar. 25, 2020).
16 For example, such a situation may arise when a constitution allows decisions taken by majority (or super-majority) rule. As alluded to in this chapter, such voting has

these organizations' rules should directly bind citizens of participating member states.[17] Fourth, organizations must have the power to enforce their decisions. Fifth, organizations should have some degree of financial autonomy.[18] Sixth, the organization's constitution and other rules should not allow for unilateral withdrawal from the organization. Such authority obviously requires the consent of member states' "sovereign will."[19] As such, if a constitution mentions any or all of these points, the constitution defines – at least "mentions" for the purposes of this book's textual analysis – authority.[20]

The UN Charter represents an example of a treaty mentioning authority, for the purposes of this book. Roughly speaking, the UN Charter compels members of its General Assembly to comply with decisions of the

---

implications for the way international organizations may "game" votes in order to assure outcomes different from the principals' own preferences. *See* Göran Ahrne et al., "The Paradox of Organizing States: A Meta-Organization Perspective on International Organizations," 7 *J. Int'l Org. Stud.* 5 (2016).

17 Ingredients three and four come from the Vienna Convention, making White's yardstick for judging whether an international organization exercises authority tautological. For the power to bind and enforce decision on their own citizens, *see* Vienna Convention on the Law of Treaties, art. 29 (for White's third ingredient) and art. 27 (for his fourth ingredient).

18 Many studies subsequent to White's six-part test for international organizations' exercise of authority show the foresight he exercised in including the requirement for financial autonomy. Ege and Bauer, as well as Bryant, provide evidence showing that lack of financial autonomy undermines an international organization's authority. *See* Jörn Ege & Michael W. Bauer, "How Financial Resources Affect the Autonomy of International Public Administrations," 8 *Glob. Pol'y* 75 (2017); Katherine Bryant, "Agency and Autonomy in International Organizations: Political Control and the Effectiveness of Multilateral Aid," Paper Presented at the 8th Annual Conference on the Political Economy of International Organization, Sept. 30, 2015, available at http://wp.peio.me/wp-content/uploads/PEIO9/102_80_1443656227537_KatherineBryant30092015.pdf (last visited Mar. 25, 2020).

19 *See* White, *supra* Chapter 1, note 19, at 129 ("Consent is an expression of sovereign will.").

20 This book takes a principal–agent view of the way authority "flows" between organizations. At first glance, such a view seems to conflict with the primacy of *jus cogens* (that traditional practices in international law vest international organizations with authority far more than contractual transfers of such authority). Indeed, the Vienna Convention on the Law of Treaties clearly gives primacy to *jus cogens* over any treaty provisions created, either in the Vienna Convention on the Law of Treaties or in other treaties governed by this Convention. For the supremacy of *jus cogens* as investing authorities with authority, see Vienna Convention on the Law of Treaties, arts. 53 & 64.

organization, and specifically the Security Council.[21] Member states' agreement to comply clearly accounts for the bulk of the UN's authority.[22] The Charter envisions enforcement though potential sanctions, both internal and external.[23] While the UN's deliberations and legislative capacities (such that they are) may exclude many nations, charter protections do allow these potentially excluded members to participate in deliberations, if not through actual voting.[24] White does not mention limits to such authority in his ingredients, and any constitution defining limits to the use of such authority must obviously create such authority, as a constitution.[25] The UN Charter builds in protections against the use of such authority by Security Council

---

21 While article 25 provides the clearest language, derogations to the article have piled up over the years. This book does not cover post-Charter rulemaking in any detail, as it focuses on constitutions themselves. Article 25 specifically mandates that "[m]embers of the United Nations agree to accept and carry out the decisions of the Security Council in accordance with the present Charter." UN Charter, *supra* Chapter 1, note 7, art. 25; *id.*, ch. VII (for details on the types of decisions the Security Council may call upon general members to follow). For the legal case for and against *de jure* and *de facto* UN authority under Chapter VII, and subsequent lawmaking with regard to the International Court of Justice, *see* David Schweigman, *The Authority of the Security Council Under Chapter VII of the UN Charter: Legal Limits and the Role of the International Court of Justice* (2001).

22 *See* White, *supra* Chapter 1, note 19, at 193 ("A Council resolution adopted under Article 41 is binding by virtue of Article 25 of the UN Charter, but the actual implementations and therefore effectiveness of the action will ultimately depend upon States themselves implementing measures within their own legal order and enforcing them against their own citizens and companies.").

23 Internal sanctions may include sanctions that affect the member state's (or states') position in the body by removing voting privileges or funding support or by other members refusing to cooperate and vote with the member state involved. As authors like Franck show, external sanctions represent a large and specialized area of the subject, lying outside the remit of this book. *See* Thomas M. Franck, "The 'Powers of Appreciation': Who Is the Ultimate Guardian of UN Legality?," 86 *Am. J. Int'l L* 519 (1992).

24 White constructs such a theory of the legislative effect of UN decision by "the combination of Article 25, which provides for binding effect of Security Council (SC) decisions, and Article 103 is the basis for the SC's *supra*national competence." White, *supra* Chapter 1, note 19, at 186. Authors like Talmon clearly agree, seeing UN Security Council resolutions and other decisions as the outlines of international legislation. *See* Stefan Talmon, "The Security Council as World Legislature," 99 *Am. J. Int'l L* 175 (2005).

25 For example, how can a constitution define limits on authority that does not exist? How can any other previous document create such authority if, by definition, the organization's own constitution defines these limits?

members against other members.[26] Why propose such protections if the original document did not define authority in the first place?[27]

Behind the authority – or lack thereof – of international organizations lies their power to make recommendations.[28] Members ultimately must implement these recommendations, in one way or another.[29] As discussed later in this chapter, the UN Charter frames the decision-making powers of the Security Council as issuing recommendations to the General Assembly.[30] Roughly translating the spirit of the 1969 Vienna Convention on Law of Treaties, as authority comes from traditional practice (first) and mutual consent (second), recommendations represent soft law obligations

---

26 In particular, articles 25 and 31 of the UN Charter provide the UN authority over member states, some of whom may object to its decisions. Article 31 states, "Any Member of the United Nations which is not a member of the Security Council may participate, without vote, in the discussion of any question brought before the Security Council whenever the latter considers that the interests of that Member are specially affected." UN Charter, *supra* Chapter 1, note 7, art. 31. Under Article 25, "Members of the United Nations agree to accept and carry out the decisions of the Security Council in accordance with the present Charter." UN Charter, *supra* Chapter 1, note 7, art. 25. A jurist may use these two articles in combination to argue that the UN Charter must grant authority to the UN as the organization promulgates decisions, which some members may disagree with.

27 Admittedly the Security Council has more voting powers than the General Assembly. However, such differences do not negate the overall conclusion – that the UN members grant decision-making powers, and thus *authority*, to the international organization as a separate entity. This book does not consider all the ways that structure and politics impose informal limits on authority that are not codified in organizations' constitutions. For a discussion of these limitations on international organizations' authority, *see* Scott Cooper et al., "Yielding Sovereignty to International Institutions: Bringing System Structure Back In," 10 *Int'l Stud. Rev.* 501 (2008).

28 Researchers still cannot reconcile the recommendations, and "soft law" admonitions of states making recommendations through international organizations, with the unenforceable and often abstract "law" of treaties and international agreements. This chapter assumes that recommendations impose contractually made, mutually agreed obligations (sometimes problematically on third-party states), without the force of custom or expectations of enforcement present with treaties and other "harder" law. For a defense of this position, *see* Andrew T. Guzman & Timothy Meyer, "International Soft Law," 2 *J. Legal Analysis* 171 (2010).

29 However, recent research sees soft law supporting the wider system of treaty law, rather than just as cheap talk or wishful thinking. Such support, then, makes for systemic enforcement, rather than enforcement by powerful nation-states, and gives even weaker member states broader authority to make recommendations. For a case study and analysis, *see* Mary E. Footer, "The (Re)Turn to 'Soft Law' in Reconciling the Antinomies in WTO Law," 11 *Melb. J. Int'l Law* 241 (2010).

30 This book does not want to complicate the analysis by discussing the tension between the organization's authority and respect for members' sovereignty.

for member states, who should consider their implementation with the same good faith as other law.[31] Naturally, most international organizations have the internal authority to recommend staff appointments and operational decisions in their own bureaucracies. However, beyond this trivial case of authority, recommendations seem like a main way that international organizations exercise authority.[32]

Nevertheless, not all international organizations exercise their authority by issuing recommendations. Universal financial organizations, such as the IMF, WTO and the International Bank for Reconstruction and Development (or World Bank), do not issue recommendations that bind member states.[33] Instead, given the widespread impact of their activities on member states' economic, political and social institutions, member states themselves particularly monitor these organizations' adherence to their own internal rules.[34] Thus, any constructionist reading of international organizations' authority must view an organization's ability to make recommendations as part and parcel with its authority. In other words, constitutions mentioning authority also should mention the power to make recommendations, particularly among universal organizations.

Communication represents another way that international organizations can both gain and use authority. International organizations like the United Nations Educational, Scientific and Cultural Organization (UNESCO) exist to communicate, with members communicating priorities

31 See Amerasinghe, *supra* Chapter 1, note 9, at 181.
32 See Jochen Abr. Frowein, "The Internal and External Effects of Resolutions by International Organizations," 49 J. For. Pub. L. & Int'l L. 778 (1989).
33 Amerasinghe, in particular, highlights the limits to these organizations' authority, as institutions like the World Bank Group, which "could not issue binding rules to govern the conduct of member states in any field." Amerasinghe, *supra* Chapter 1, note 9, at 188. Decades of research from authors like Nielson and Tierney has shown how member states have worked around the controls incorporated into these organizations' constitutions, giving them the authority to bind member states' environmental and other policies. See Nielson & Tierney, *supra* Chapter 1, note 27, at 241.
34 While Schermers and Blokker describe these organizations' "most explicitly" following their own rules, and particularly those rules governing elections to their boards of directors and/or governors, Woods and Narlikar represent one example of a litany of voices showing how these organizations adopt decisions that deeply change member states. Schermers & Blokker, *supra* Chapter 1, note 5, at 234; Ngaire Woods & Amrita Narlikar, "Governance and the Limits of Accountability: The WTO, the IMF, and the World Bank," 53 *Int'l Soc. Sci. J.* 170 (2001). How could so many researchers document the wide-reaching authority of these institutions if such authority did not actually exist?

to the organization and the organization communicating priorities out.[35] Communication between member states, between their agents (like international organizations) and among these agents underpins the cooperation, the functions attributed to them, the political mandate to arbitrate competing interests and even defines their membership.[36] However, for all the theorizing about international organizations, their legal basis for communicating, the authority for such communication and the very existence of the international organization form as a "technology" of reducing information costs remains sorely neglected.[37]

Statistical links of authority, communication and recommendations

How frequently do international organizations' constitutions refer explicitly to authority? Naturally, simply counting words does not tell the whole story.[38] Nevertheless, any empirical analysis of the concepts underlying international organizations' constitutions must start with measurement. Figure 3.1 shows the number of international organizations' constitutions

---

35 For a fascinating study of such communications' richness, *see* Hassan Nafaa, "The Study of Relationships Between the International Organizations and the Member States: A System Approach," 7 *Int'l Interactions* 337 (2008).

36 Klabbers says as much, yet fails to see his own insight. In his textbook's rudimentary overview of classifying international organizations and explaining why they cooperate, he makes resort to all kinds of realist, constructivist and other theory. *See* Jan Klabbers, *An Introduction to International Institutional Law* 21–31 (2d ed. 2009). However, at the heart of every item he mentions stands the need to communicate, the content of that communication and the medium *as* the message. This chapter explains what this means, using these organizations' own laws.

37 Social scientists seem to have quarantined the study of information, communication and international organizations in the realm of international regimes. For more on these regimes, *see* Robert O. Keohane, "The Demand for International Regimes," 36 *Int'l Org.* 325 (1982). These regimes, existing to minimize information and transactions costs, also exist to provide a battleground for discourses of power that serve the interests of stakeholders in these international organizations. All the textbook authors analyzed for this book failed to engage with communication at any level.

38 Modern jurimetrics and legal researchers increasingly forget that words work together to create meaning in legal texts. Similar words can represent completely different ideas in agreements with different structures. While the authors of this book do not wish to exaggerate the importance of the frequency of citing words, many studies show insights from the exercise when analyzed judiciously (no pun intended). See Todd Allee & Manfred Elsig, "Are the Contents of International Treaties Copied-and-Pasted? Evidence from Preferential Trade Agreements," World Trade Institute Working Paper 8, Aug. 2016, *available at* https://boris.unibe.ch (last visited Mar. 25, 2020); Mark S. Manger & Clint Peinhardt, "Learning and the Precision of International Investment Agreements," 43 *Int'l Interactions* 920 (2017).

116 The values of international organizations

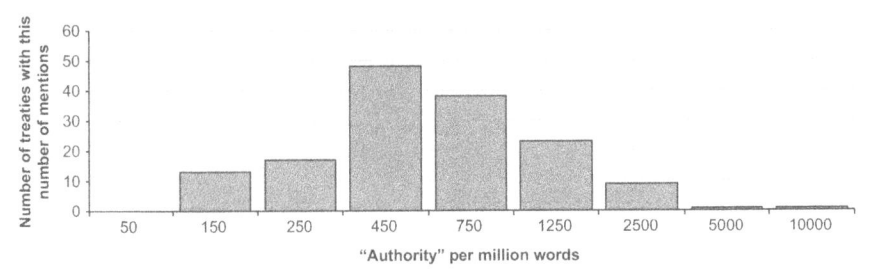

Figure 3.1 Most international organizations' founding constitutions refer to authority about 550 times per million words. The figure shows the number of times per million words that international organizations' founding constitutions mention the word "authority". We compiled these figures by looking at all the international treaties matching criteria we outlined earlier – namely, at least two states as members, the governance of international law and the existence of at least one organ with a will of its own. We calculated the number of mentions of authority divided by the total number of words in the treaty and multiplied that ratio by one million in order to get a figure with a workable number of significant digits.

corresponding to various amounts of references to the word "authority." The average constitution has 550 references to authority per million words, with roughly ninety constitutions having between 450 and 750 mentions of authority per million words.[39] The Inter-Parliamentary Union and the East African Development Bank have less than 90 mentions per 10,000 words. However, one constitution has almost 1,000 mentions per million words – the Economic Community of West African States.

How do mentions of authority stack up to other values mentioned in international organizations' constitutions? Figure 3.2A shows the extent to which these international organizational constitutions refer to authority, rather than other values. The source and uses of authority remain a middling value for international organizations' constitutions. This analysis shows the log values of these mentions, as the mentions of executive staff far exceed those of other values. Figure 3.2B shows the range of these mentions across constitutions. Each line shows the values of 95 percent of the constitutions' mentions for a particular value. The axis for Figure 3.2B also shows the actual number of mentions, rather than the log number of mentions. Despite serious differences in these averages, an actual statistically

---

39 As described previously, this chapter uses one million words as the comparison in order to cite figures easy to read. No treaty has one million words. However, the reader might struggle with an actual incidence of authority for the African and Malagasy Council for High Education of 0.0004337.

Patterns of authority 117

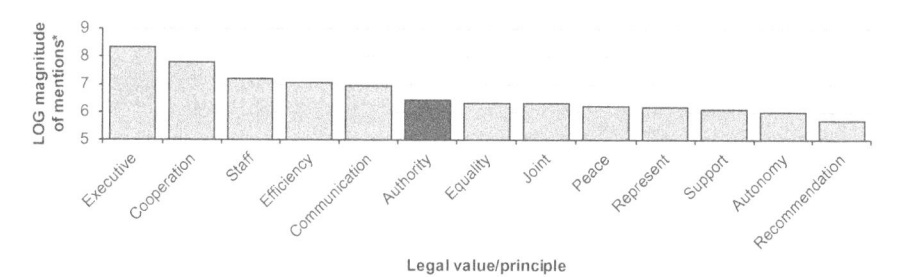

Figure 3.2A Authority a middle value among international organizations' constitutions. The figure shows the log value of ratio of the number of times international organizations' founding constitutions mentioned the values shown in the graph divided by the total number of words in their respective treaties, multiplied by one million. As we showed the range of mentions before (see Figure 2.1), we do not give 95 percent confidence intervals here.

significant difference probably does not exist, allowing for random chance.[40]

What effect does the type of organization have on mentioning authority? Figure 3.3A seems to show that these differences in citations by international organization type do not matter, whether large or small organization, new or old, financial or EU-affiliated. These constitutions refer to authority at about the same rate: 750 mentions for every million words. The large amount of overlap in the spread of these mentions shows high variation, and thus a low likelihood that the average mention of authority actually differs much across types of international organizations.[41] Nevertheless, first glances can deceive. Figure 3.2B shows the results of more advanced techniques used to test differences between these types of international organizations. To be sure, most of these differences result from random chance. However, the difference between the frequency of references to authority in the constitutions of universal organizations and those of

---

40 Figure 3.2B shows that the standard deviations around these values extend far out. As such, it is impossible to statistically significantly differentiate the number of mentions in these values. A procedure called a Friedman ANOVA (a procedure looking at differences in the averages of pooled variables like ours) does not show actually likely differences in these values. In other words, despite all the apparent variation, the differences in these overall averages come from random fluctuations. However, when this data is divided by group, there are actually statistically significant differences.
41 These bands show the number of mentions of authority for 95 percent of the constitutions in a particular class. For example, 95 percent of millennial international organizations (started in 2000 or later) mention authority in their constitutions anywhere between not at all (0) and 1,000 times per million words.

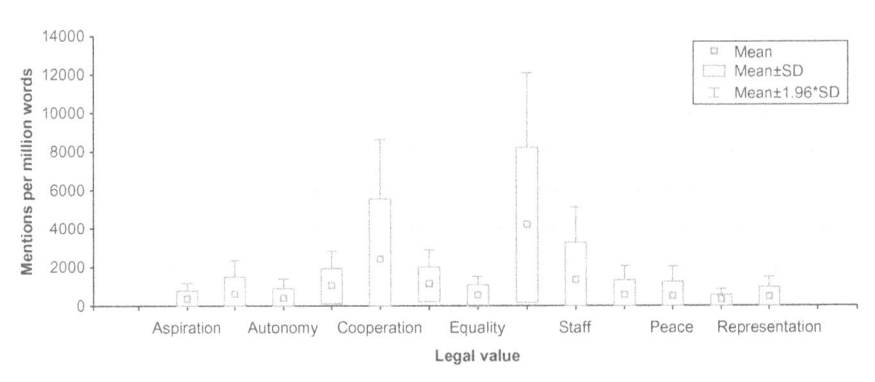

Figure 3.2B Statistical analysis of values

regional organizations does not arise due to random chance.[42] Matching the discussion in the literature, universal organizations have greater frequency rates of authority than do regional organizations. However, general versus limited competence international organizations do not.[43]

However, authority does coincide with some values more than others. Figure 3.4 shows the correlation between authority and the other values this book studied. At first glance, high frequencies of mentioning authority correlate heavily with high incidences of mentioning efficiency, recommendation and executive staff. However, as the previous chapter showed, the systemic links between these values make recommendation, communication and the organization's autonomy linked concerns, despite having low bilateral scores.[44] Efficiency seems the only organizational value that statistically significantly correlates with authority.

Constitutions and authority

The references of most international organizations' constitutions to authority follow a rather standard formula. One hardly can peruse the constitutions of entities like the Islamic Development Bank's Articles of Agreement and

---

42 All of them have at least 99 percent certainty.
43 Such a finding varies with authors like Lenz and co-authors, who find significant differences in what they call task-specific versus general international organizations. *See* Tobias Lenz et al., "Patterns of International Organization: Task Specific vs. General Purpose," RSCAS 2014/128, 2014, *available at* https://papers.ssrn.com/sol3/papers.cfm?abstract_id=2554275 (last visited Mar. 25, 2020). As non-lawyers, they simply leave differences in values completely unaddressed.
44 This analysis shows how values cluster (to use the proper statistical word) together. Please refer to Chapter 2 for more details.

Patterns of authority

[bar chart showing mentions of authority by type of international organization, with categories including Interwar, Millennial, Prehistoric, Interwar, Post-war pre-OPEC, Post-war OPEC, Post-war post-OPEC, Africa, Europe, N. America, S. America, Eurasia, Oceania, Asia, Medium, Large, Small, Regional, Universal, Limited, General, Financial, Non-financial]

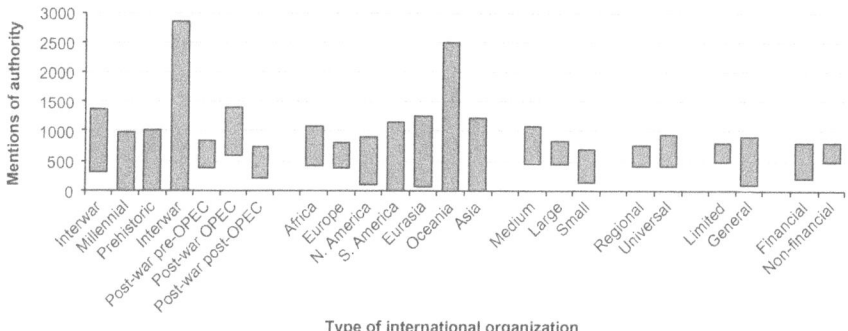

Type of international organization

Figure 3.3A Authority as a middle value among international organizations' constitutions. The table displays log ratios of the values, which is the number of times international organizations' constitutions mentioned the values divided by the total number of words in their respective treaties, multiplied by 1,000,000. As Figure 2.1 shows the range of mentions, we do not give 95 percent confidence intervals here.

Type of international organization	Probability same	International organization's characteristics	Distance*
Universal/regional	0.00%*	Size	10.221*
General/limited competence	20%	Year of incorporation	4.737
Financial/non-financial	31.9%	Region/location	12.862*
Judicial/non-judicial	55.9%		
EU/non-EU	25.4%		

Figure 3.3B Difference in mentions of authority by various kinds of international organizations. Cells with asterisks statistically significant. The left-hand side of the figure shows the probability that the average number of mentions of authority between types of international organizations actually does not differ between these types. For example, if we believe the results of these Mann-Whitney tests, there is a 0 percent probability that universal international organizations' higher number of mentions of authority (compared to regional international organizations' constitutions) results from pure chance. By convention, a probability of less than 5 percent indicates statistically significant differences between the groups. The right-hand side of the figure shows the extent of these differences, with asterisks indicating the two groupings (by size and location) where these international organizations' constitutions statistically significantly differ from each other.

120   *The values of international organizations*

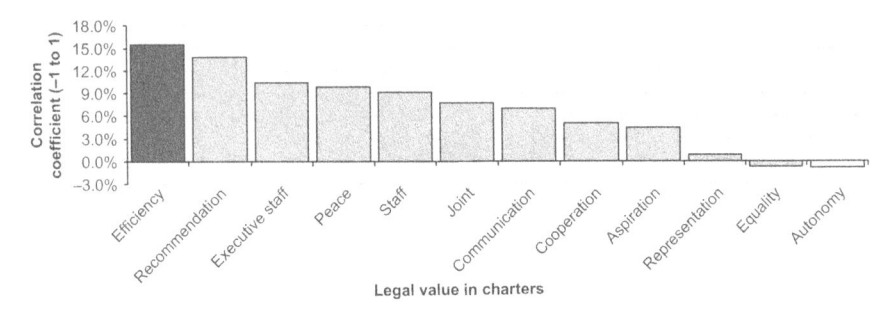

Figure 3.4 Mention of authority most closely correlates with efficiency and recommendation. The figure shows the correlation between coefficients between the number of mentions of authority in international organizations' constitutions and the values shown. Only efficiency statistically differs from zero – though we report all the correlation coefficients. We obtain these figures by calculating Pearson correlation coefficients between authority and each value bilaterally. We do not (here) remove the effects of semi and partial correlation (removing the "second order" effects of the way other values may influence the values shown here).

the New Development Bank's constitution without noting striking similarities in words, provision order and values. The formulaic approach to constitution drafting dealing with authority usually consists of four parts:

1. an early provision in the treaty refers to the organization's governing group or body, describing the delegation of their authority to executive staff;
2. articles concerning operation and management define executives' and general staffs' scope of authority;
3. many articles in these constitutions mention authority and recommendation, often when describing appointment procedures and a chain of command;
4. many provisions refer to communication and authority when describing (a) channels of communication; (b) privilege for communication; and (c) constitutional amendments.

At first glance, many constitutions almost seem like copies of each other. For example, the IMF's Articles grant privilege for communications, noting that "the official communications of the Fund shall be accorded by members the same treatment as the official communications of other members."[45] The African Export Import Bank's privilege for communications grants

---

45 *See* Articles of Agreement of the International Monetary Fund art. IX, sec. 7, Dec. 27, 1945, 160 Stat. 1401, *as amended* April 1, 1978, 29 U.S.T. 2203, 2 UNTS 39 [hereinafter "IMF Agreement"].

Name	Authority	Communication	Recommendation	Autonomy
International Development Association	Art VI, sec. 2 (BoG) Art. VI, sec. 5, (Ops and Man)	Sec 10	Art. V, Sec. 1(d).	Art. VI, sec. 5
International Finance Corporation	Art. 2(c) Sec. 5(b)	**	**	**
IMF	Art. XII, sec. 2 and sec. 4	Art. XII (8).	**	Sec. 4(c)
WTO	Art. IV Art. VI	**	Art. IX*** Art. XIII***	Art. VI

Figure 3.5 Legal provisions governing principles in universal and regional financial international organizations. Asterisked cells not applicable.

that "official communications of the Bank shall be accorded by each Participating State the same treatment and preferential rates that it accords to the official communications of international organizations."[46] Little differences can mean a great deal. For example, why does the African Export Import Bank's constitution accord communications the preferential treatment "of international organizations" whereas the IMF accords them the same treatment as "other members"? Do these differences reflect deep-seated views about the nature of authority and privilege, as the Fund does not accept that international organizations possess their own inherent rights and privileges, whereas the African Export Import Bank does? Do such distinctions exist only in the minds of academic jurists?

The similarity of international organizations' constitutions makes cataloging these values and references to them possible. Figure 3.5 shows the provisions from universal international financial organizations' constitutions where references to authority, communication, recommendation and autonomy occur. The differences in wording are analyzed later in this chapter. In some cases, these constitutions do not substantially refer to these principles, reflecting modification of the template, if such a template actually exists.

---

46 Agreement for the Establishment of the African Export-Import Bank, art. IX, May 8, 1993, *available at* https://afreximbank.com/wp-content/uploads/2014/12/Bank-Agreement-December-2012-English.pdf (last visited Mar. 25, 2020) [hereinafter "AEIB Agreement"].

122 *The values of international organizations*

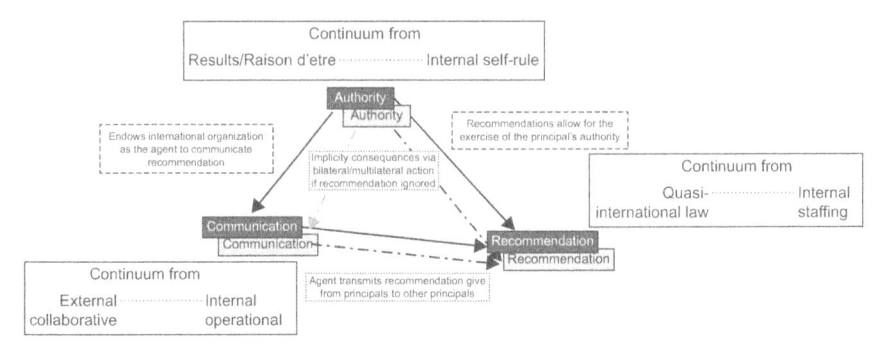

Figure 3.6 The nexus of authority, communication and recommendation in international organizations law. The figure shows the different levels or conceptions of each of the values shown in the figure (authority, communication and recommendation). While there are links between these values in international organizations' constitutions, they may exist at many levels. For example, organizations with wide-ranging authorities to act semi-independently may have very limited powers of communication.

As the next sections show, when taken together, authority, communication and recommendation form a relationship that differs between organizations. Figure 3.6 provides a diagrammatic representation of the relationships described below. In some international organizations, a more outward-focused authority endows international organizations with the ability to make recommendations that bind (in a limited sense) member states. In others, such authority covers only their ability to communicate with their own staff and, in limited cases, operational communications when making loans or doing what the organization should do. No relationship necessarily exists between international organizations' constitutions that stress authority and their authority to communicate or make recommendations. Figure 1.7 illustrates this model using actual data from this book's dataset. In short, large international organizations' constitutions refer to authority more often than do small organizations' constitutions. However, for smaller organizations' fewer mentions of authority and communication, they refer to both principles more often in the same constitution than large organizations' constitutions do. In theory, and in practice, many combinations exist between these variables.

The next section treats each of these values separately. That section shows how authority may differ, from outward-focused, results-oriented authority to a very limited authority over self-rule. Some international organizations use communication to promote collaboration across member states. Others use communication to promote collaboration internally. Recommendations range from quasi or soft international law (having the implicit backing of force of a member state) to recommendations only about staffing. Organizations with outward authority may not have the authority to issue "powerful" recommendations. However, these combinations disprove the generalizations made by most researchers of international organizations law.

Authority, from controlling member states to quasi-independence

The extent to which member states in an international organization vest authority (if at all) differs from organization to organization. This section explores these differences, between retaining authority, vesting wide latitudes of authority and what these decisions reveal about the ways these constitutions' framers view such authority.

One end of the spectrum: member states retaining authority

The WTO represents an international organization whose very limited authority consists mostly of facilitating dialogue among its member states.[47] Such authority comes from the organization's member states, negotiating in the organization's managing council, and the international organization itself has little if any of that authority. The WTO's Ministerial Conference "shall have the authority to take decisions on all matters under any of the Multilateral Trade Agreements."[48] Legal researchers have argued that subsequent agreements under the WTO have greatly expanded the WTO's authority.[49] However, to sum up the philosophy of the WTO's governance (albeit grossly taking the provision out of context), its Director-General and staff of the Secretariat are required not to "seek or accept instructions from any government or any other authority external to the WTO."[50]

---

47 The WTO results from a long history of trade agreements aiming at reducing tariff and non-tariff barriers to trade. For readers interested in the workings and law of the organization, Dillon still provides a concise, if dated, overview. See Thomas J. Dillon Jr., "The World Trade Organization: A New Legal Order for World Trade?," 16 *Mich. J. Int'l L.* 349 (1995).
48 *See* "WTO Agreement," *supra* Chapter 2, note 12, art. IV § 1.
49 Many researchers particularly point to the supposed latitude of the WTO's appellate body and its other decision-making rules. However, besides being adopted after the Marrakesh Agreement (defining the inception of the Organization), many argue that the Organization houses and provides services only for member-state adjudicators and other officials and specialists who take these decisions. For a discussion on this subsequent law, and the arguments for and against, *see* David Palmetear & Petros Mavroidis, "The WTO Legal System: Sources of Law," 92 *Am. J. Int'l L.* 398 (1998).
50 "WTO Agreement," *supra* Chapter 2, note 12, art. IV § 4.

The Ministerial Conference may accept recommendations from particular councils overseeing the functioning of a particular agreement.[51] Member states settle grievances between themselves by making recommendations in Council or Conference, rather than by leaving such recommendation powers up to the organization itself.[52] The WTO and the law governing the investiture and use of its authority is far more complex than is the case with an organization like the Intergovernmental Organisation for International Carriage by Rail.[53] However, the WTO has little authority to engage in action, make recommendations or even communicate without member states' approval.[54]

The International Labour Organization's (ILO) constitution similarly keeps authority with member states, and its structure leaves little doubt as to whether any authority actually "transfers" to the organization.[55] The ILO's Convention requires that "each of the Members undertakes that it will … bring the Convention before the authority or authorities within

---

51 This is a paraphrasing, with the original reading, the "Ministerial Conference and the General Council … shall exercise their authority on the basis of a recommendation by the Council overseeing the functioning of that Agreement." *Id.*, art. IX. While not exactly a recommendation as this chapter envisions it, the Agreement gives the Director General the authority to recommend a budget to the Council of member states. *See Id.*, art. VII.
52 *See id.*, art. XIII § 4 ("The Ministerial Conference may review the operation of this Article [on the non-application of multilateral trade agreements between particular members and] in particular cases at the request of any Member and make appropriate recommendations."). Such authority thus clearly stays with member states themselves, rather than passing to the organization.
53 Another organization with a long and fascinating history, the Intergovernmental Organization's 1893 predecessor organization – the Central Office for International Carriage by Rail – centralized authority for negotiating rail standards with its General Assembly. Although the Organization's subordinate bodies provide useful input like a committee of experts, authority still remains with member states. *See* Convention Concerning International Carriage by Rail, May 9, 1980, 1397 UNTS 2, amended by Protocol of 3 June 1999.
54 The Appellate Body shows how member states that design an international organization to have very limited authority can subsequently revise its rules to extend such authority. Indeed, future empirical work following this book's model may wish to incorporate these changes over time into any count of the number of times that international organizations' laws mention authority. For the evolution of this authority in the WTO, *see* Gregory Shaffer et al., "The Extensive (But Fragile) Authority of the WTO Appellate Body," 79 *L & Contemp. Prob.* 237 (2016). For a fascinating case study and analysis of such authority, *see* Julia-Ya Qin, "Judicial Authority in WTO Law: A Commentary on the Appellate Body's Decision in China-Rare Earths," 13 *Chin. J. Int'l L.* 639 (2014).
55 The short answer is no.

whose competence the matter lies, for the enactment of legislation or other action."[56] As each member has no authority, either to direct the ILO or its own state's government, the Convention requires only that the member report to the ILO Director-General "the position of its law and practice in regard to the matters dealt with in the Convention, showing the extent to which effect has been given, or is proposed to be given, to any of the provisions of the Convention by legislation, administrative action, collective agreement or otherwise and stating the difficulties which prevent or delay the ratification of such Convention."[57] The large differences between member states' legislation and the conventions and recommendations the ILO promulgates show just how little authority the ILO ultimately possesses.[58]

Member states in a number of other international organizations also clearly wanted, through the design of their constitutions, to keep international organizations on a short leash. The International Union for Protection of New Varieties of Plants clearly vests authority in member states, and not in the Union. The Union's Convention requires that members "maintain an authority entrusted with the task of granting breeders' rights or entrust the said task to an authority maintained by another Contracting Party."[59] Indeed, the Convention formally defines "authority" in the definitions section of the text as "any Contracting Part[ies]."[60] The Convention makes no assumptions about authority, instead requiring that "*it shall be understood* that ... each State or intergovernmental organization must be in a position, under its laws, to give effect to the provisions of this Convention."[61] Member states define authority and give it effect in this Convention.[62] The Asian Infrastructure Investment Bank's authority

56 Constitution of the International Labour Organization art. 19(5)(b), Oct. 9, 1946, 62 Stat. 3485, 15 UNTS 35 [hereinafter "ILO Constitution"].
57 *Id.*, art. 19(5)(e).
58 For example, Weissbrodt and Mason describe the very large differences between the US's labor code and the provisions in ILO conventions and recommendations; more similarity between these rules would exist if the ILO possessed more authority. *See* David Weissbrodt & Matthew Mason, "Compliance of the United States with International Labor Law," 98 *Minn. L. Rev.* 1842 (2014).
59 *See* Convention of the International Union for Protection of New Varieties of Plants, art. 30.1(ii), Dec. 2, 1961, *available at* www.upov.int/ (last visited Mar. 25, 2020).
60 *Id.*, art. 30(1).
61 *Id.*, art 30(2) (emphasis added).
62 In the case of the International Union, as well as the European Chemicals Union, such a lack of authority does not necessarily imply a lack of effectiveness or usefulness. As Dijkstra notes, states may benefit even from weak secretariats. *See* Hylke Dijkstra, "Collusion in International Organizations: How States Benefit from the Authority of Secretariats," 23 *Glob. Gov.* 601 (2017).

stretches only so far as its own organizational structure and development, with the Bank's constitution vesting authority in the Board of Governors and allowing for delegation to the Board of Directors.[63] The Benelux Court of Justice's authority, similarly, allows the Court's Committee of Ministers to discipline Registrar staff as necessary, who fall under the Registrar's direct line of command and only indirectly under the Court's.[64]

Some constitutions grant the limited use of authority, only to keep authority in the organization's decision-making body. For example, the Eastern and Southern African Trade and Development Bank's constitution makes a special point to note that, even though the Board of Governors may delegate authority to the Board of Directors, these Governors "retain full power to exercise authority over any matter delegated to the Board of Directors" and other bodies.[65] The Inter-American Development Bank similarly keeps member states in the driver's seat, giving them the ability to overturn decisions made by the organization's agents, in that "the Board of Governors shall retain full power to exercise authority over any matter delegated to the Board of Executive Directors."[66] In the case of the regional international organization CERN, "the Council ... delegate[s] to the Directors-General, either separately or jointly, authority to act on behalf of the Organization in other matters."[67] However, such delegation occurs only with the approbation of "two-thirds majority of all the

---

63 In particular, Article 23(3) gives the Board of Governors full power to exercise authority over any matter delegated to the Board of Directors under para. 23(2), which describes the Bank's governance structure and delegation of authority. Article 26 describes such delegated powers in directing the Bank's general operations, work given by the Board of Governors, establishing internal policies and ultimately delegating authority to the Bank's president. *See* Articles of Agreement of the Asian Infrastructure Investment Bank, June 29, 2015, *available at* www.aiib.org (last visited Mar. 25, 2020) [hereinafter "AIIB Agreement"].

64 The Court handles judicial matters between the three Benelux states Belgium, Netherlands and Luxembourg. *See generally* Treaty on the Establishment and Status of a Benelux Court of Justice, Mar. 31, 1965 [hereinafter "Benelux Court of Justice Treaty"]. The Court exercises disciplinary competence, except when these staff belong to the Secretariat-General. *See id.*, art. 3(a)(6)–(7).

65 The Board of Governors represents the decision-making body and the Board of Directors represents the executive body. *See* Charter of the Eastern and Southern African Trade and Development Bank art. 26(4), July 12, 1985 [hereinafter "ESATDB Charter"].

66 Agreement Establishing the Inter-American Development Bank art. VIII.2(c), Feb. 9, 1996 [hereinafter "IADB Agreement"] (providing the Board of Governors as the head governing body).

67 Convention for the Establishment of a European Organization for Nuclear Research art. VI, July 1, 1953, 200 UNTS 150 [hereinafter "CERN Convention"].

Member States."[68] Such a rule clearly demonstrates a hesitance to delegate authority.[69]

Pass-through authority in international organizations

The UN Charter best illustrates the pass through of authority in international organizations' constitutions. The UN Charter clearly refers to the delegation of authority from the General Assembly to the Economic and Social Council.[70] For their part, the ICC's Articles show how authority may pass or transfer from one organization to another, defining both the extent of the Court's authority to self-regulate and substantive authority to regulate on behalf of (and in the interests of) its member states.[71] In both the Registrar's and Prosecutor's offices, the Articles give relative authority to self-govern. The Registrar's authority passes simply from the Court's President to the Registrar.[72] The Registrar runs the office under such authority. Regarding the Office of the Prosecutor, the Articles allow the Prosecutor to "have full authority over the management and administration

---

68 *Id.*
69 To belabor the point, these initial provisions outlining member states' initial views on authority have changed over time for a wide range of organizations. Indeed, Heldt and Schmidtke measure the change of their "empowerment" over time, which increases as the number of issue areas member states delegate to them increases, as they provide more financial resources and as they hire more staff. *See* Eugénia Heldt & Henning Schmidtke, "Measuring the Empowerment of International Organizations: The Evolution of Financial and Staff Capabilities," 8 *Glob. Pol.* 51 (2017).
70 *See* UN Charter, *supra* Chapter 1, note 7, art. 60 ("Responsibility for the discharge of the functions of the Organization ... shall be vested in the General Assembly and, under the authority of the General Assembly, in the Economic and Social Council."). This is to say nothing about the pass-through authority that often can be seen in practice. *See, e.g.*, James D. Fry, "Early Security Council Efforts at Nuclear Non-Proliferation Law and Policy: Cooperation Forgotten," 21 *Transnat'l L. & Contemp. Probs.* 337, 345–46 (2012) (discussing how the very first resolution of the UN General Assembly created the Atomic Energy Commission, which was made up of the Security Council's membership plus Canada and had the Security Council as the main authority over that entity). The study of such pass-through authority outside of the context of organizations' founding treaties is reserved for future research.
71 Such substantive authority specifically refers to the conditions under which the Court may use its authority. These Articles cover both the Court and specific institutions attached to the Court, such as the Court's Registrar and Prosecutor.
72 The Articles stipulate that "the Registrar shall exercise his or her functions under the authority of the President of the Court." The Registrar represents the principal administrative officer of the Court. *See* Rome Statute of the International Criminal Court art. 43(2), July 17, 1998, 2187 UNTS 90 [hereinafter "Rome Statute"].

of the Office, including the staff, facilities and other resources thereof," presumably derived from the authority from the Court itself.[73] Regarding the actions of the Prosecutor, "pending a ruling by the Pre-Trial Chamber, or at any time when the Prosecutor has deferred an investigation under this article, the Prosecutor may, on an exceptional basis, seek authority from the Pre-Trial Chamber to pursue necessary investigative steps for the purpose of preserving evidence."[74] The provisional authority to pursue an investigation emanating from the Court includes cases where defendants may have tampered with evidence, where it is necessary to finish taking evidence when a defendant challenges the Court's jurisdiction, and where it is necessary to prevent flight of suspects for whom the prosecutor already has sought a warrant for arrest.[75] Despite extensive criticism of the Court's over-reaching authority, these represent the main provisions describing the way the Court uses such authority, at least directly using the word "authority."[76] Such arrangements resemble the ILO's vesting of authority to a Commission of Inquiry as well as its Governing Body.[77]

Regional organizations like the EU have similar transfers of authority in place. The Treaty on the Functioning of the European Union particularly shows how authority moves in international organizations, bifurcating and even giving the institution certain independent authority. The Treaty "provides for the conclusion of agreements between the community and one or more states *or international organizations*" such that "the Council ... shall *authorize* the Commission to open the necessary negotiations."[78] The Commission conducts the negotiations, clearly as authorized by the Council.[79] However, the authority given to member states to interact with

---

73 Authority comes from member states to the Court and onward to the Prosecutor, or directly from member states to both the Court and Prosecutor simultaneously. *See id.*, art. 42(2). Similarly, the same provision makes it unclear whether Deputy Prosecutors "shall be entitled to carry out any of the acts required of the Prosecutor" directly from the Statute, or from the authority derived from the Prosecutor. *Id.* The wording of the Articles suggests the former interpretation.
74 *Id.*, art. 18(6).
75 *See id.*, art. 19(8)(a)–(c).
76 To repeat a leitmotif of this chapter, values endowed by subsequent treaties may alter the way initial constitutions envision the application of principles like authority. Casey's case against the ICC in particular shows how treaties can result in authority that even state governments may not (or should not) endow. *See* Lee A. Casey, "The Case Against the International Criminal Court," 25 *Fordham Int'l L.J.* 840 (2001).
77 *See* "ILO Constitution," *supra* this chapter, note 56, arts. 24, 26.
78 Consolidated Version of the Treaty on the Functioning of the European Union art. 228(l), 2012 O.J. C 326/162 [hereinafter "Treaty on the Functioning of the EU"] (emphasis added).
79 *See id.*, arts. III-139, 302, 309(2), 311 (for the authority of the Council).

third-party states hints at the *independent* authority of the EU.[80] Authority clearly vests in the EU and devolves to subordinate bodies in a far more extreme way than the UN's or the ICC's authority ever could.[81]

However, in most cases the delegation of authority represents the prosaic shift of operational authority to senior management. Similar to the African Export Import Bank, the Bank of Central African States' constitution grants relatively narrow authority to its governing body, the Monetary Policy Committee and its governor.[82] CERN's constitution refers to operational authority to manage the organization's finances. CERN's constitution provides up front in the description of the CERN directors-general that for "each Laboratory a Director-General ... shall be the chief executive officer of the Organization and its legal representative."[83] The European Chemicals Agency may "rely on the competent authorities of Member States," and "[i]n carrying out an evaluation of a substance, the competent authorities may appoint another body to act on their behalf."[84] While having authority over the evaluation of these chemicals, the Agency does not have *exclusive* authority.[85] Clearly, some international organizations, especially the EU as

---

80 *See id.*, arts. 73(a)–(h), 100(c), 109(c), 126, 127.
81 The power to devolve authority relies on the explicit vesting of such authority in the Union from member states in the first place, as required in the Treaty on the Functioning of the European Union. However, even if rules governing the (re)delegation of authority are devolved back to the states or Union-wide subordinate bodies, such a discussion would well exceed any chapter-sized treatment that can be written in this book. For more on the complexities of such authority, *see* Renaud Dehousse, "Delegation of Powers in the European Union: The Need for a Multi-Principals Model," 31 *W. Euro. Pol.* 789 (2008); Sami Andoura & Peter Timmerman, "Governance of the EU: The Reform Debate on European Agencies Reignited," European Policy Institutes Network Working Paper 19, Oct. 2008, *available at* www.files.ethz.ch/isn/92938/WP%20019.pdf (last visited Mar. 25, 2020).
82 *See* Treaty Establishing the Economic and Monetary Community of Central Africa art. 47, June 25, 2008 [hereinafter "BEAC Treaty"]. As with other international organizations, other provisions describe the delegation of such authority to its Board of Directors (executive staff) and the Governor of the Bank.
83 "CERN Convention," *supra* this chapter, note 67, art. VI.
84 "Concerning the Registration, Evaluation, Authorisation and Restriction of Chemicals (REACH)," Reg (EC). No. 1907/2006, Dec. 18, 2006, art. 45, *available at* osha.europa.eu (last visited Mar. 25, 2020) [hereinafter "European Chemicals Agency Regulation"].
85 Unlike with international organizations, EU bodies have a well-worn tradition of establishing shared versus unique competencies. Maybe universal international organizations could learn something from the efficient way the EU treats the separation of competences and thus the allocation of authority. For more on this point, *see* Marta Simoncini, "Paradigms for EU Law and the Limits of Delegation: The Case of EU Agencies," 9 *Persp. Federalism* 47 (2017).

a regional international organization, regularly assign authority with such delegation, devolution and transfer in mind.

The different ways and voting rules that international organizations use to vest and use authority show the complex ways that such authority passes through to these international organizations. If the UN uses a headcount rule for voting, ignoring the dynamics of the ways the Security Council and General Assembly interact, while the IMF and World Bank use contributions to determine voting weights, then such differences in power clearly signal differences in the extent to which member states vest authority in these institutions.[86] The Russia-based International Investment Bank illustrates the issues involved. The Bank's member states vest authority in the Bank Council as the "highest authority of the Bank responsible for the general management of its activities."[87] However, unlike other institutions, this international financial organization draws authority from member states in headcount, rather than proportionately to economic or other power, as "each member irrespective of the amount of its quota in the authorized capital has one vote in the Council of the Bank."[88] Why would an economic organization use a voting model that is at odds with the way all other international banks vote? What do these differences tell us about differences in the extent and distribution of authority *from* member states, if anything?[89]

The other end of the spectrum: highly devolved authority

Several international organizations' design explicitly gives them authority. Indeed, the word is included in the organization's name, such as the International Seabed Authority. The Authority's authority comes from its

---

86 Hooghe and co-authors bump upon this problem when quantifying authority pooling versus delegating in international organizations. We merely signal the issue here, rather than trying to find a theory or model explaining how voting might affect/distort the allocation of authority to international organizations (assuming that authority can be "allocated"). See Hooghe et al., *supra* Chapter 1, note 64.

87 Agreement on the Establishment of the International Investment Bank art. 19(1), July 10, 1970 [hereinafter "IIB Agreement"].

88 *Id.*

89 By selecting a different model for exercising member states' authority in Council meetings, the Bank's constitution clearly shows different preferences for passing through authority – from member states to Bank policy and thus from Bank policy to executives' action. Stone provides a fascinating account of such pass through, showing how even member states' informal authority pass through to and through the international organizations. *See* Stone, *supra* this chapter, note 6, at 121.

"international legal personality and such legal capacity as may be necessary for the exercise of its functions and the fulfillment of its purposes."[90] Strictly enumerated powers and objectives endow the Authority with the authority of its member states.[91] The Convention also enumerates authority in the specific conditions of prospecting, exploring and exploiting the sea.[92] Concrete limitations define the limits of the Authority's authority.[93] However, the Authority may borrow funds, which represents an innovation, certainly among non-financial international organizations.[94] The Authority also may encourage cooperation with other international organizations.[95] The Authority of the Common Market also represents a similar case, which is the body established under a treaty establishing a preferential trade area in Eastern and Southern Africa.[96]

Several examples show the extent to which international organizations' constitutions may vest authority in these entities. The IMF's constitution gives the Fund special authority to distribute special drawing rights to members.[97] At its most extreme, the European Bank for Reconstruction and Development's constitution gives its Board of Directors the pre-existing authority to suspend or adjust any member's access to resources "in cases where a member might be implementing policies which are inconsistent with Article 1 of this Agreement, or in exceptional circumstances."[98] These examples clearly show how some international organizations' constitutions envision the greater exercise of authority by these institutions.

The ICC's Articles also define times when the Court exercises rather wide latitude in the use of its authority. The Court's Articles specifically give the Court's Pre-Trial Chamber the authority to authorize, or, rather,

90 United Nations Convention on the Law of the Sea art. 176, Dec. 10, 1982, 1833 UNTS 397 [hereinafter "UNCLOS"].
91 *See id.*, art. 274.
92 *See id.*, annex III art 17.
93 *See id.*, art. 189 ("The Authority's jurisdiction with regard to [its] decisions.").
94 *See id.*, art. 174 (as with corporations, member states extend authority to the Authority to borrow funds, but do not take upon themselves the obligation to repay them).
95 *See id.*, pt. XIV § 2 & art. 273.
96 *See* Treaty Establishing the Authority of the Preferential Trade Area for Eastern and Southern African States art. 7, Dec. 21, 1981 (article setting up the Authority of the Common Market). The Treaty also sets up the Eastern and Southern African Trade and Development Bank, which is described later in this chapter.
97 *See* "IMF Agreement," *supra* this chapter, note 45, art. XV. The Articles place restrictions on the allocation of these rights in Article XVIII (as per point a) of Art. XV, § 1, while a separate Schedule M dictates the allocation of these rights. *See id.*
98 Agreement Establishing the European Bank for Reconstruction and Development, art. 8(3), May 29, 1990, 29 I.L.M. 1083 [hereinafter "EBRD Agreement"].

delegate authority, to the Prosecutor to take specific investigative steps in a territory of a State Party when no authority exists in the state to answer a request for judicial cooperation.[99] Law enforcement bodies in a custodial state may release a suspect on bail so long as that custodial state has an authority capable of exercising such authority.[100] The Articles give the Court the authority to request evidence.[101] As such, the Court has no authority from the member state that is unable to give such authority, lacking such authority over their territory. The Court has the authority to request cooperation without orders from member states, which is a type of autonomous authority, yet it does not necessarily have discretion to decide on the channel of such communication.[102] The offer of immunity from prosecution to witnesses, and to experts from arrest, represents perhaps the strongest form of independent authority.[103] These narrow margins of authority hardly seem like the basis for exercising the kind of oppression many detractors of the Court argue against.[104]

The principle of unity-of-authority

Whether the organization avails itself of a little or a large measure of authority from its member states, international organizations law clearly

---

99 *See id.*, art. 57.2(d). As such, the Pre-Trial Chamber possesses authority that remains unexercised until or unless the superseding authority, in the member state, either does not or cannot vest such authority directly.
100 A five-part test qualifies such authority in whether the person arrested matches the person sought by the Court, whether the arrest followed the proper process, whether the arrest procedure respected the arrestee's rights, whether the arrestee has the right to apply for bail (interim release) and whether the competent authority can ensure the eventual arrestee's surrender to the Court. *See id.*, art. 59(1).
101 *See id.*, art. 69.3(3) ("All evidence that [the Court] considers necessary for the determination of the truth.").
102 *See id.*, art. 87.1(a) (the channel of communication "shall be transmitted through the diplomatic channel or any other appropriate channel as may be designated by each State Party upon ratification, acceptance, approval or accession," and so the articles "lock in" this channel of communication).
103 *See id.*, art. 93(2) (such an offer provides that these persons "will not be prosecuted, detained or subjected to any restriction of personal freedom by the Court in respect of any act or omission that preceded the departure of that person from the requested State").
104 Indeed, authors like Caserta and Cebulak note that international courts like the ICC have avoided public backlashes because of their narrow range of authority. *See* Salvatore Caserta & Pola Cebulak, "The Limits of International Adjudication: Authority and Resistance of Regional Economic Courts in Times of Crisis," 14 *Int'l J. L. in Context* 275 (2018).

accepts the principle of unity-of-authority.[105] Most international organizations' constitutions establish clear unity of authority – from member states to the international organization's staff.[106] For example, the International Development Association's Articles of Agreement create an authority placed in the Board of Governors and delegated to the Executive Directors, who use such authority, except to modify the structure of decision making in the Association.[107] The agents of those executive directors – the president, officers and staff – "owe their duty entirely to the Association and to no other authority."[108] The widespread nature of these provisions suggest a broader principle of unity-of-authority, such that international organizations owe their authority and thus their activity to one fount or source of such authority, as embodied in one discrete constitution. Like the International Development Association, the International Finance Corporation's Articles of Agreement vest authority in a Board of Governors, who may delegate it

105 The principle of unity-of-command comes from the writings after the Second World War of organizational theorist Henri Fayol. *See generally* Henri Fayol, *General and Industrial Management* (1949). While widely accepted in large organizations, the customary nature of international organizations law does not need the same transfer of authority from principal to agent as required in a strict contract-centered view of organizational relations. However, the principal still permeates international organization design. The International Law Commission even has conducted an assessment of the extent to which clear lines of authority (and thus reporting and responsibility) exist in and among international organizations. See International Law Commission, "Responsibility of International Organizations: Comments and Observations Received from International Organizations," Doc. A/CN.4/545, June 25, 2004.

106 Economists and organizational theorists like Epstein and O'Halloran have extended this idea, elaborating complex models of the way and interests of delegating authority. *See* David Epstein & Sharyn O'Halloran, "Sovereignty and Delegation in International Organizations," 71 *L & Contemp. Prob. Winter* 77 (2008); Nielson & Tierney, *supra* Chapter 1, note 27, 241; Andrew T. Guzman & Jennifer Landsidle, "The Myth of International Delegation," 96 *Cal. L. Rev.* 1693 (2008). The authors of this book accept Nielson and Tierney's as well as Guzman and Landsidle's criticism of principal–agent theory as a way of viewing international organization law. However, the texts undeniably show at least an influence of such contractualism in the minds of these international organizations' constitutional drafters.

107 In particular, such an authority prohibits the executive directors from admitting new members, authorizing additional subscriptions, suspending members, interpreting and deciding appeals for interpretations of the Agreement, cooperating with other international organizations and dissolving the Association. See International Development Association Articles of Agreement, art. VI, § 2(c)(i)–(vii), Sept. 24, 1960.

108 *Id.*, art. VI, § 5(c). Later sections in this chapter talk about this duty, usually concomitantly acquired with the "international character" of their duties.

to a Board of Directors, with the exception of the same kinds of restrictions imposed on the International Development Association.[109] Similarly, such a unity-of-authority principle compels the president, officers and staff to "owe their duty entirely to the Corporation and to no other authority ... [and] refrain from all attempts to influence any of them in the discharge of their duties."[110] Clearly, both the Association and the Corporation in these two examples have an authority that can be delegated and to which executive officials hold a duty.[111]

In the case of the Southern African Development Community, a Summit of Heads of State or Government of all Member States make the Community's policies and decisions.[112] While these heads of state or government adopt legal instruments developed under the Community's auspices, they may delegate their authority to their own ministers who make up the Community's Council.[113] These ministers recommend the appointment of an executive secretary and deputy executive secretaries to the Council.[114] As such, the authority of the Council simply consists of the delegated authorities present in the member states, assuming that the head of government similarly delegates authority to ministers.[115] Similarly, the Council

---

109 *See* Articles of Agreement of the International Finance Corporation, art. IV, § 2(c), May 25, 1955, T.I.A.S. No. 3620 [hereinafter "IFC Agreement"]. For example, besides restrictions on determining or affecting membership, directors may not affect the organization's capitalization through raising capital, distributing dividends and so forth. *See id.* The similarity of these provisions likely comes from their combined membership in the World Bank Group.

110 *See id.*, art. VI, § 5(c).

111 Researchers question the nature of this duty, as fiduciary duties (and international civil servants' fidelity) cannot attach to an entity whose legitimacy and even legal personality come from traditional *jus cogens* norms. *See* Donald Feaver, "Fiduciary Principles and International Organizations," *in Fiduciary Duty and the Atmospheric Trust* 165, 177–81 (Charles Sampford et al. eds. 2011).

112 *See* The Consolidated Text of the Treaty of the Southern African Development Community art. 10, Aug. 17, 1992, *available at* www.sadc.int (last visited Mar. 25, 2020) [hereinafter "SADC Treaty"].

113 *See id.*

114 *See id.*

115 Such a view of authority in government has its detractors. Government authority, like parliamentary authority in a parliamentary system, may come from the elected government *as a whole*, and not from delegated powers of the prime minister or head of government. To the extent that a constitution or other organic law gives competencies to ministers, one may not see these competencies as derived or delegated as assumed in the Southern African Development Community model (if the intentions of the Southern African Development Community's framers have been understood correctly). The authors of this book were unable to find the

uses its authority to recommend amendments and the adoption of treaties in its protocols, circularly implying that the Summit cannot consider these protocols unless their delegated agents in the Council recommend them for consideration.[116] Such circularity naturally poses problems for any doctrine or principle trying to show the "delegatability" of authority, as how can a Summit delegate authority to a Council, but lack the subsequent power to consider protocols, except on the recommendation of the Council?[117]

However, most international organizations uncontroversially vest the authority to appoint and delegate authority to staff. In the Caribbean Development Bank Agreement, a Board of Governors delegates authority to its Board of Directors.[118] The European Bank for Reconstruction and Development's constitution provides for unity-of-authority:

> [U]nder the direction of the Board of Executive Directors and the President of the Bank, the Executive Vice President shall exercise such authority and perform such functions in the administration of the Bank as may be determined by the Board of Executive Directors. In the absence or incapacity of the President of the Bank, the Executive Vice President shall exercise the authority and perform the functions of the President.[119]

Any non-staff members appointed by CERN's Council still work under the director-general's authority, despite not being appointed by that director-general.[120] Indeed, no one can work in an international organization unattached to the ultimate authority of member states.[121]

    deliberations of the drafting committee setting up article 10, and so anything further would be speculation on their views of authority.

116 *See id.*, art. 22(2) ("Each Protocol shall be approved by the Summit on the recommendation of the Council.").

117 As shown throughout the chapter, the Southern African Development Community does not represent the only international organization designed with such issues. However, the question remains whether this represents an exception to a coherent principle of the unity-of-authority, or if it is just one of many constitutions treating authority incoherently, thereby vitiating the idea of a generalizing unity-of-authority principle.

118 *See* Agreement Establishing the Caribbean Development Bank, art. 27(3), Oct. 18, 1969 [hereinafter "CDB Agreement"].

119 *See* "EBRD Agreement," *supra* this chapter, note 98, art. VIII § 5(b).

120 *See id.*, art. VI(3).

121 Lake describes every combination and variation in such authority, rightly noting that states exercise authority over the international organization, even though they do not exercise authority over each other, suggesting that international organizations represent very different things than other legal persons/fictions. *See* David A. Lake, "Authority, Coercion and Power in International Relations," in *Back to Basics: State Power in a Contemporary World* 55 (Martha Finnemore & Judith Goldstein eds. 2013).

Autonomy through authority

If authority only delegated to international organizations from member states, they would have little scope for true autonomy. Such authority would define the terms of their autonomy, making true autonomy impossible.[122] Nevertheless, international organizations' constitutions contain references to their autonomy, and such autonomy is observed in the real world. What do their constitutions tell us about the way their framers thought about autonomy? Do regular mentions of autonomy reveal underlying principles or shared ideas about the way authority vests and *jus gentium* or *jus cogens* interact to provide for such autonomy?[123]

The authority for self-governance as a principle

All international organizations have some level of authority to govern themselves, in the way they execute tasks, to structure their bureaucracy and so forth. For example, the founding articles for the African Export Import Bank describe in unusual detail the extent to which the Bank's executives exercise a degree of autonomy from member states. The Articles specifically give the Bank "in the territories of African countries[,] branch offices which shall exercise such functions and *operational authority* as shall be determined from time to time by the Board of Directors."[124] The Bank's autonomy, effectuated via transfer of authority from the Board of Directors to an Executive Committee, allows for the Bank's executive staff "including in particular[,] commitment authority in respect of financing, guarantee and investment proposals".[125] The Board of Directors retains authority over

---

122 Even if the organization managed to engage in hidden action or played members off against each other, the organization must still act within the confines of its authority institutions and structures – something social scientists of all kinds accept as structuralism. For a fuller statement on this point, *see* Mark Pollack, "Principal–Agent Analysis and International Delegation: Red Herrings, Theoretical Clarifications and Empirical Disputes," Bruges Political Research Papers No. 2, Feb. 2007, *available at* http://aei.pitt.edu/7344/ (last visited Mar. 25, 2020).

123 While one might view a continuum between norms of *jus cogens* on the one hand and principal–agent theory on the other, a wide range of views about such autonomy exist. *See generally* Jean d'Aspremont "The Multifaceted Concept of the Autonomy of International Organizations and International Legal Discourse," *in International Organizations and the Idea of Autonomy* 63 (Richard Collins & Nigel D. White eds. 2011).

124 "AEIB Agreement," *supra* this chapter, note 46, art. 4(2) (punctuation added to improve clarity).

125 *Id.*, art. 24(1) (punctuation added to aid readability). These Articles delegate author-

broader issues related to share capital, internal governance and relations with domestic and national authorities.[126]

In many cases, such authority derives from powers granted to make recommendations and communicate about issues affecting the organization. Continuing with the African Export Import Bank, appointments to key positions proceed from recommendations by senior staff.[127] In the case of the Arab Bank for Economic Development in Africa, recommendations come from the Board to management, rather than the other way around, with management's narrow margin to ignore such recommendations defining its margin of autonomy.[128] The Asian Infrastructure Investment Bank's Agreement mentions such recommendations only in the appointing of a Vice President "by the Board of Directors on the recommendation of the President," defining a narrow margin for exercising even possible autonomy by simply ignoring the recommendation.[129] Narrow rules governing communication, like those defining the Southern African Development Community's Secretariat's margin for autonomy, focus on facilitating communication between member states, to ensure that all member states are aware of the new regulations, recommended policies and projects.[130]

Presumptions about an international organization's autonomy sneak into even the most unlikely places. Provisions related to income from gifts

---

ity to a President and an Executive Secretary who reviews and countersigns (with the company seal) the President's decisions. Article 25(4) gives the President the delegated authority from the Board of Directors "in respect of financing, guarantee and investment proposals up to such amounts as the Board of Directors shall determine from time to time." *Id.*, art. 25(4). Article 27 gives the Executive Secretary the authority to affix the company seal. *See id.*, art. 27.

126 *See id.*, art. 14 (for rules of transfer of shares) and art. 21(8) (for the composition of the Board of Directors). Much more like a private sector bank, Article 21(8)(i) restricts any director's capacity to serve as a director, recognizing "any regulatory authority to which he may be subject." *Id.*, art. 21(8)(i).
127 *See id.* The Board of Directors receives recommendations for the alteration of capital (art. 8(1)), appointment and removal of the President (art. 17), vice-president as recommended by the president (art. 25(1)) and senior executives (art. 22(viii)). This does not include provision, but it instead just aims to give the reader a sense of all the supposed recommendations.
128 The Board of Directors' ability to make recommendations about the way management handles special funds, their power, along with the Director General's recommendation, to recommend deputy directors general, and the Board of Governors' authority to recommend the use of profits to increase bank reserves, shareholders' equity or other uses. *See* Agreement Establishing the Arab Bank for Economic Development in Africa, arts. 13(iii), 28, 36, Feb. 18, 1974 [hereinafter "BADEA Agreement"].
129 *See* "AIIB Agreement," *supra* this chapter, note 63, art. 30.
130 *See* "SADC Treaty," *supra* this chapter, note 112, art. 14.

and bequests perhaps best bolster CERN's autonomy and thus its autonomous authority. Only "to the extent of the authority delegated to him ... and subject to any directions given by the Council, a Director-General may accept gifts and legacies to the Organization provided that such gifts or legacies are not subject to any conditions inconsistent with the purposes of the Organization."[131] Such a provision helps to break the financial grip of member states on CERN, which offers the organization at least a possibility of funding activities to which member states may not contribute.[132] As explained below, nothing affects such autonomy as much as the ad hoc international tradition affording protections to organizations with an international character.

The principle of international character and autonomy

Most international organizations' constitutions refer to principle of international character, which guarantees their limited autonomy.[133] Such a principle, usually defined as the Arab Bank for Economic Development in Africa Articles do, guarantees autonomy by requiring that staff "owe their duty entirely to the Bank and to no other authority."[134] The Caribbean Development Bank's constitution similarly refers to its "international character" and similarly requires that executives and staff "owe their duty entirely to the Bank and to no other authority."[135] If duty, as a categorical imperative, defines such a duty of fidelity, then most constitutions like

---

131 *Id.*, art. VII (Financial Contributions).
132 This chapter does not discuss regulations or experiences outside of these constitutions. Nevertheless, some authors like Abbott and Snidal have argued that such funding may help to promote member states' interests. *See* Abbott & Snidal, *supra* Chapter 1, note 77, at 3. *See* also White, *supra* Chapter 1, note 19, at 151–56. If true, such a finding would invalidate at least one of White's "ingredients" regarding the authority of an international organization.
133 This phrase comes from Article 100 of the UN Charter, almost verbatim in every instance of the constitutions analyzed in this book. To date, neither the UN Charter nor subsequent theorizing by bodies attached to the UN has clarified the source of such a duty to respect this international character and provide a working definition of such an international status, except by means of diplomatic rows caused by espionage committed by diplomatic officials attached to the UN. *See* United Nations, "International Character of Secretariat," 13 *Dig. Int'l L.* 858 (1968). As Schwebel describes in detail, such a principle extends into the murky depths of *jus cogens* norms established before and during the days of the League of Nations. *See* Stephen Schwebel, "The International Character of the Secretariat of the United Nations," 30 *Brit. Y.B. Int'l L.* 71 (1953).
134 "BADEA Agreement," *supra* this chapter, note 128, art. 30.
135 "CDB Agreement," *supra* this chapter, note 118, art. 35(3).

the Arab Bank for Economic Development in Africa's invoke the "international character of their jobs" and a natural "independence" inherent in the organization by virtue of possessing such an international status.[136] The European Bank for Reconstruction and Development's constitution, for its part, refers to an "international character of this duty" to the Bank and to no other authority.[137] Similarly, the Asian Infrastructure Investment Bank refers to an "international character" as the guarantor of the Bank's staff and management's duty to the institution, rather than to particular member states.[138] Such an international character for the Caribbean Development Bank, again by way of definition, includes the duty of undivided fidelity and duty to resist attempts to undermine such fidelity.[139] The Charter similarly imposes on the Bank's staff a "duty to respect" the international character and the "obligation to refrain" from outside influences. Such a duty *defines* autonomous authority.[140]

---

136 *Id.* ("They shall refrain from any act that is contrary to the international character of their jobs or to their independence."). However, as the Bank does not belong to the UN system, one must question whether the tradition developed from the UN Charter applies to non-UN entities. The treaty founders tend to think so.
137 *See* "EBRD Agreement," *supra* this chapter, note 98, art. 32. After long negotiations between government officials about the form and characteristics of such a Bank, most participating members agreed that traditional international law, along with its standard immunities and duties of loyalty, should with an institution with member states apply to even "commercial" entities like banks "with an international character." For the history of this, *see* John Linarelli, "The European Bank for Reconstruction and Development: Legal and Policy Issues," 18 B.C. *Int'l & Comp. L. Rev.* 361 (1995).
138 *See* "AIIB Agreement," *supra* this chapter, note 63, art. 31. Such a distinction allows for active shareholder oversight of basically a government institution. For more on the reconciling of UN notions of such an international character with more inclusive non-government elements of governance, *see* Whitney Debevoise, "International Financial Institution Governance: The Role of Shareholders," *AIIB Y.B. Int'l L* 29 (2018).
139 "CDB Agreement," *supra* this chapter, note 118, art. 35(3) ("The President, officers and staff of the Bank, in the discharge of their offices, owe their duty entirely to the Bank and to no other authority. Each member of the Bank shall respect the international character of this duty and shall refrain from all attempts to influence any of them in the discharge of their duties.").
140 Often international organizations need to resort to the court of international public opinion to secure their claim as an international organization with an autonomous international character. The Inter-Parliamentary Union's experience, and its use of law professors to bolster its claim, represents an interesting example. *See* Ian Brownlie & Guy S. Goodwin-Gill, Joint Opinion Prepared on the Instruction of Mr. Anders B. Johnsson Secretary General Inter-Parliamentary Union, May 31, 1999, *available at* www.ipu.org (last visited Mar. 25, 2020).

While not exactly a conventional international organization per se, the International Fusion Energy Organization's (ITER) Agreement similarly notes that "the responsibilities of the Director-General and the Staff in respect of the ITER Organization shall be exclusively international in character."[141] Such a phrasing is noteworthy because it qualifies the international character of the organization's authority – and thus autonomy – to cases "in respect of the ITER Organization" and qualifies the exclusive nature of such an international character. While the first part of the phrase opens the door to potentially non-international activities by International Fusion Energy Organization officials, the second part notes that, if done for the Organization, the work is deemed *in its entirety* international. The International Fusion Energy Organization's constitution puts all the elements analyzed in this section together, besides "in respect to" and "exclusively," by requiring staff not to "seek or receive" instructions from governments or external authorities, and includes the admonition not to try to influence these staff.[142]

Several constitutions provide three qualifications to the jurisprudence on these organizations' international character. First, similar to the Islamic Development Bank, the Inter-American Development Bank's constitution explicitly accepts the existence of and need to contain political activity.[143] Such an admonition attempts to draw a clear divide between politics at the Board level and execution at the administrative and executive levels. Such an unusual worry about such political activity further cements jurisprudence about the division of politics and execution.[144] Second, such an international character derives from the intangible and tautological position as international officials with an international character of responsibilities.

---

141 Agreement on the Establishment of the ITER International Fusion Energy Organization for the Joint Implementation of the ITER Project art. 7(6), Nov. 21, 2006. The Organization shows haziness with the line between international organization and private cross-border organization. While it is a self-declared private sector "project," its articles use much the same language as other international organizations' constitutional language.

142 *Id.*

143 The Islamic Development Bank specifically includes the "prohibition of political activity." Articles of Agreement for the Islamic Development Bank, art. 37, Oct. 1975.

144 As with most concepts addressed here, these treaties nowhere define such political activity. To make matters worse, no legal scholar has ever dared to acknowledge or write about such political activity. Writing laws containing such politics represents the next, great project in international organization law. *See generally* Matthew Parish, "An Essay on the Accountability of International Organizations," 7 *Int'l Org. L. Rev.* 277 (2010).

For example, the ILO Charter refers to a "position as international officials," and the "international character of responsibilities," by insisting that staff "refrain from any action which *might reflect* on their position as international officials responsible only to the Organization."[145] Such a qualification makes sense when considering the importance of *perceived* autonomy. International officials have responsibilities possessing an international character. Taking action that might put that in jeopardy hurts not just the organization but the entire tradition of applying this principle in international organizations.[146] Third, the official, being fallible, can try to achieve such a position only by "undertaking to respect" the character of his or her work, or similar phrasing. In a subsequent point, the Charter seeks to bolster such an international character by requiring that "[e]ach Member of the Organization *undertakes to respect* the exclusively international character of the responsibilities of the Director ... ."[147] The ILO formulation represents one of the few constitutions explicitly recognizing that such respect demands loyalty, which does not come about automatically.[148]

The recognition that influence occurs both ways still remains absent from the international constitutions. If most constitutions admonish international officials against member states' or others' influence, the WTO treaty admonishes *member states* themselves not to "seek to influence them in the discharge of their duties."[149] Such a formulation represents a novelty because such phrasing recognizes the two-way process by which such influence might occur. However, such an approach also opens a Pandora's box, as such influence may come from other organizations through policy work as well as informal meetings.[150]

---

145 "ILO Constitution," *supra* this chapter, note 56, art. 20(1)(4) (emphasis added).
146 Constructivist scholarship of international organizations has seen such a premise as self-evident for decades. Nevertheless, perceptions make the *jus cogens* norms of our times, and shifting perceptions may put certain rights and privileges of international organizations, like the immunities and duties to resist outside influence, at risk. See Bryan Schwartz & Elliot Leven, "International Organizations: What Makes Them Work?," 30 *Can. Y.B. Int'l L.* 165 (1992).
147 "ILO Constitution," *supra* this chapter, note 56, art. 20(2)(5) (emphasis added).
148 Again, as with most of the finer points of international organization law, few scholars have grappled with the obligations that civil servants acquire by virtue of their international status and character.
149 "WTO Agreement," *supra* Chapter 2, note 12, art. VI § 4.
150 In particular, to what extent does politics legitimately contribute to customary international law, or does it represent a corruption of such law? For a fascinating consideration of the former position, *see* Ramses A. Wessel & Steven Blockmans, "The Legal Status and Influence of Decisions of International Organizations and other Bodies in the European Union," *in The European Union's External Action in Times of Crisis* ch. 7 (Piet Eeckhout & Manuel Lopez-Escudero eds. 2016).

The CERN constitution provides a unique case study of a regional organization having resort to the same principles underlying international organization jurisprudence by resorting to the same "*exclusively* international character" of staff when deciding on their status.[151] However, the Agreement may not simply conjure such an international character but, rather, relies on the fact that "each Member State shall request the international character of the responsibilities of the Directors-General and the staff, and not seek to influence them in the discharge of their duties."[152] Again, the CERN constitution stipulates that "in the discharge of their duties they [Directors-General and staff] shall not seek or receive instructions from any government or from any authority external to the Organization."[153] However, such a formula seems to divide the fount or source of authority. On the one hand, the member states grant authority to the director-general and his or her staff. On the other hand, their exercise of authority and the consequent autonomy hail from their international character.

While most constitutions refer to such an international character, neither the constitutions themselves nor researchers have attempted to define the nature and origin of such a special status, at least not in the same way that they have theorized their international legal personality.[154] Indeed, international NGOs similarly perform activities of "international character."[155] However, perhaps reflecting the politics of governments refusing to give up authority to organizations not directly under their control, the status of these international NGOs still remains unsettled after almost 100 years.[156] Legal researchers will need to flesh out a theory of such a status and the underpinnings for such a status in the principal-agency theory relationship between international organizations and their member states. Why does the work of the World Bank's officials have an "international character," while the work of the World Bank member organization the International Finance Corporation compels the president, officers, and staff to "owe

---

151 "CERN Convention," *supra* this chapter, note 67, art. VI(4).
152 *Id.*
153 *Id.*
154 *See* James D. Fry, "Rights, Functions, and International Legal Personality of International Organizations," 36 *B.U. Int'l L.J.* 221 (2018).
155 As early as 1983, authors like Merle had noted such an international nature and inquired as to what makes international organizations with governments, rather than non-government members, derive such an international nature. *See* Marcel Merle, "International Non-Governmental Organizations and their Legal Status," 1 *International Associations Statutes Series* appendix 3.5 (1988).
156 *See generally* Rephael Harel Ben-Ari, *The Legal Status of International Non-Governmental Organizations: Analysis of Past and Present Initiatives (1912–2012)* (2013).

their duty entirely to the Corporation and to no other authority ... [and] refrain from all attempts to influence any of them in the discharge of their duties"?[157] Only further empirical work will figure this out.

The recognition of external authority

Provisions in international organizations' constitutions dealing with arbitration provide a fascinating glimpse at the assumed foundations of international organizations' authority. If international organizations derived their authority only from the member states and possessed no true authority of their own, then they would not be competent to arbitrate in cases where international organizations dissolve or in other matters.[158] For example, the Asian Infrastructure Investment Bank's Articles allow for an external authority to participate in the arbitration of disputes when the Bank winds up or when a claimant or respondent member state has already terminated its membership. Such an external authority shall be submitted to "unless the parties otherwise agree, by the President of the International Court of Justice or such other authority as may have been prescribed by regulations adopted by the Board of Governors."[159] The Articles do not require the International Court of Justice (ICJ) or its President in particular to serve as arbitrator, or even for this arbitrator to serve alone.[160] Nevertheless, the underlying assumption that authority vests in another institution when the authority of the organization itself ends represents a peculiarity of the Asian Infrastructure Investment Bank's constitution,

---

157 "IFC Agreement," *supra* this chapter, note 109, § 5(c).
158 A complex tissue of law governs this area. These organizations' international legal personality may be enough to make them competent to serve in international arbitrations and other adjudications. However, the intent of personality clearly lies in establishing responsibility. No serious scholar would argue for personality to make international organizations sovereign. Nevertheless, accepting these organizations' binding decisions in international adjudications is tantamount of accepting their limited authority in international affairs. See James E. Hickey, Jr., "The Source of International Legal Personality in the 21st Century," 2 *Hofstra L. & Pol'y* 1 (1997).
159 "AIIB Agreement," *supra* this chapter, note 63, art. 55.
160 The language "unless the parties otherwise agree" and "or such other authority as may have been prescribed by regulations adopted by the Board of Governors" clearly suggests to parties to try other options. Moreover, the article envisions that such an arbitrator serves on a board of three persons (the others being chosen by the Bank and the respondent/claimant, respectively). If the parties chose their arbitrators "rationally," the one chosen by the President of the ICJ would represent the most independent among the three.

which represents one of the newer international organizations in this book's database.[161]

Other constitutions combine the possible use of an ICJ-appointed arbitrator with other kinds. The (Brazil, Russia, India, China and South Africa) New Development Bank does not require the third arbitrator to come from another institutional organization, such as the ICJ, but merely "an authority as may be approved by the Board of Governors."[162] Such ambiguity gives any "authority" eligibility to serve as arbitrator, without clarifying whether international organizations represent "authorities" in their own right. The Caribbean Development Bank's constitution mixes up this formula, allowing each party to appoint an arbitrator and then having the two arbitrators appoint their own chairperson.[163] Only if the parties fail to appoint arbitrators in time, or they fail to find a chairperson in time, does the organization "request the President of the International Court of Justice, or such other authority as may have been prescribed by regulations adopted by the Board of Governors, to appoint an arbitrator."[164] As such, authority never leaves the Board while it is still relying on outside authorities.

Communication as law, membership or operational act?

Communication between international organizations and their members serves many purposes. This section takes an expansive look at the ways that international organizations' constitutions refer to communication. The standard view of such communication focuses on the everyday transmission of speech, transactions and other operational "speech" needed to run an international organization. However, deconstructing the use of the word in context often reveals a structural context or a constructed meaning that means far more.[165]

---

161 The Asian Infrastructure Investment Bank, the New Development Bank, and the European Bank for Reconstruction and Development all refer to the President of the ICJ. For the European Bank for Reconstruction and Development Agreement's mention of the authority of the ICJ President to arbitrate, see "EBRD Agreement," *supra* this chapter, note 98, art. 58.
162 See "Agreement on the New Development Bank," art. 46, July 15, 2014.
163 "CDB Agreement," *supra* this chapter, note 118, art. 60.
164 *Id.*
165 Even non-constructivist authors from the 1970s see communication as the way an organization includes or excludes agents (or authorities, in the language of many of these constitutions) in decisions. Therefore, the medium, or form of organization, often dictates the message. *See* Robert O. Keohane & Joseph S. Nye, Jr.,

Communication roles as membership

Many international organizations' constitutions use "communication" to refer to the right or way of communicating with member states. For example, the Asian Infrastructure Investment Bank's constitution basically refers to member states as a channel of communication, representing "an appropriate official entity with which the Bank may communicate in connection with any matter arising under [the] Agreement."[166] The "authority" serves as contact point, and "communication" for facilitating the Bank's operation. Such a view does not contradict very much the intuitive sense of communication, as authors like David Epstein and Sharyn O'Halloran argue:

> The more countries that belong to [international organizations, IOs], the more benefits accrue to all members. In this sense, IOs display increasing returns to scale, similar to many social or Internet-based resources.[167]

The European Bank for Reconstruction and Development's constitution requires that "each member shall designate an official entity for purposes of communication with the Bank on matters connected with this Agreement."[168] The "channel of communication," as the constitution refers to them, determines in practice membership in the international organization.

Communication literally represents the method by which international organizations designate the authority of the member state. Consider the International Finance Corporation's Agreement and its provision establishing a channel of communication:

> Each member shall designate an appropriate authority with which the Association may communicate in connection with any matter arising under this Agreement. In the absence of any different designation, the channel of communication designated for the Bank shall be the channel for the Association.[169]

"Transgovernmental Relations and International Organizations," 27 *World Pol.* 39 (1974).
166 "AIIB Agreement," *supra* this chapter, note 63, art. 33.
167 Epstein & O'Halloran, *supra* this chapter, note 106, at 78.
168 "EBRD Agreement," *supra* this chapter, note 98, art. XIV § 3 (Channel of Communication).
169 "IFC Agreement," *supra* this chapter, note 109, art. IV § 10. The other mentions of communication as paired with authority occur in Article X (Interpretation and Arbitration), Article VIII § 7 (privilege for communication), and Article IX (Amendments). *Id.*

Unlike in the case of the European Bank for Reconstruction and Development case, the International Finance Corporation's Agreement states that the member designates – in actual fact nominates, identifies and places – authority in and with the Corporation, with the drafters deliberately using of the word "authority." The "channel of communication" for the Bank naturally serves as the same one for the Association, as the authority and the members are the same.

Interestingly, the Arab Bank for Economic Development in Africa's constitution represents one of the rare attempts to outline the authority for making such communication. Statements must be "made by a designated appropriate official authority in connection with any matter arising under [the] Agreement."[170] These Articles do not take for granted the authority's capacity or authority to represent the member, as "any statements made by such authority to the Bank shall be deemed to have been made by the member concerned."[171] The authority to communicate clearly represents an under-researched value in international organizations law.

Rather than providing details about who may communicate, as in the Arab Bank for Economic Development in Africa's case, some international organizations' constitutions detail the path of such communication, especially when revising the constitution itself. For example, the European Bank for Reconstruction and Development's constitution requires:

> [A]ny proposal to amend this Agreement, whether emanating from a member or the Board of Executive Directors, shall be communicated to the Chairman of the Board of Governors, who shall bring the proposal before the Board of Governors. When an amendment has been adopted, the Bank shall so certify in an official communication addressed to all members. Amendments shall enter into force for all members three months after the date of the official communication unless the Board of Governors shall specify a different period.[172]

The right to exercise *authority to communicate* represents a different right than the simple right to communicate. The IMF's Articles allow the Fund to "*at all times* have the right to communicate its views informally to any member on any matter arising under this Agreement."[173] Such a right comes closest to the similar right of natural persons to exercise their authority in society.[174] Instead, more like in the ILO's case, communications represent

---

170 Such a phrasing rewords the original in the Agreement. *See id.* at art. 50.
171 *Id.*
172 *See* "EBRD Agreement," *supra* this chapter, note 98, art. XII, amendment (c).
173 "IMF Agreement," *supra* this chapter, note 45, art. XII (8) (emphasis added).
174 Many have hotly disputed this right. *See, e.g.*, Howard C. Anawalt, "The Right to Communicate," 13 *Denv. J. Int'l L. & Pol'y* 219 (1984). It appears to have fallen out of fashion in academic circles.

Patterns of authority 147

"relations with governments" as representatives of government departments or "such other qualified official."[175] A channel of communication represents membership in the organization and the exercise of the member state's authority. To what extent the kind of "right to communicate its views informally" represents the exercise of the Fund's authority remains an open question.

Privilege for communication and intrinsic authority

What does the privilege accorded to communications tell us about these constitutions' implicit assumptions about authority? The Asian Infrastructure Investment Bank's constitution, in contrast, simply requires member states to give communications "the same treatment that it accords to the official communications of any other member."[176] The European Bank for Reconstruction and Development's constitution provides similar treatment, in that "the official communications of the Bank shall be accorded by each member the same treatment that it accords to the official communications of other members."[177] The Caribbean Development Bank only asks for "most favored status," compared with members' communications with each other.[178] Such an approach basically gets around the question of international organizations' authority by not making resort to the tenuous authority of international organizations, which may or may not actually exist.

Other constitutions do recognize international organizations' customary privilege to receive information. The African Export Import Bank's constitution requires that each of the Bank's members should provide "the same treatment and preferential rates that it accords to the official communications of international organizations."[179] Such a provision obviously recognizes the privileges accorded with international organizations and recognizes them as preferential, although they do not define whether they are preferential in relation to other member states' communications or simply with non-diplomatic communications.[180] The Eastern and Southern African Trade and Development Bank Charter takes both routes, requiring

---

175 "ILO Constitution," *supra* this chapter, note 56, art. 11.
176 "AIIB Agreement," *supra* this chapter, note 63, art. 49.
177 "EBRD Agreement," *supra* this chapter, note 98, art. XI § 7.
178 *See* "CDB Agreement," *supra* this chapter, note 118, art. 53 ("Official communications of the Bank shall be accorded by each member treatment not less favourable than that it accords to the official communications of any other member.").
179 "AEIB Agreement," *supra* this chapter, note 46, art. XI.
180 Shortly after the IMF's version of this provision came into effect, the Fund had already sought to rely on such preferential treatment in seeking discounts from

communication accorded "by each Member State the same treatment that it accords to the official communications of other Member States *or* international organizations including diplomatic missions."[181]

These calls to give international organizations preferential terms for communication may tell us nothing about their authority. The Caribbean Development Bank's constitution, as with the Eastern and Southern African Trade and Development Bank's constitution, mixes these values. Nevertheless, such a constitution does not refer to authorities, but to communications of and by an "official entity."[182] Naturally, mentions of communications to an authority obviously represent the authority – as a governmental institution – named to correspond with the organization. However, it still is impossible to say for sure what authority (in the normative sense) lies behind constitution writers' conception of an authority (in a positive sense).

Communicating operational information and staff changes

More prosaically, most communication refers to transmitting changes to these constitutions, recommendations and other legal instruments. Adopting the standard language for communication, the ILO Charter requires that any "convention will be communicated to all Members for ratification."[183] The Asian Infrastructure Investment Bank's Articles address communication in the way members may amend the Articles, adding rules for the handling of such communication by transmission from a member of the Board of Directors to the Chairman of the Board of Governors and then back to all members, if and when amended.[184]

A wide range of treaty provisions describe operational communications. The European Chemicals Agency, in the context of communicating exemptions from the general obligation to register for product- and process-orientated research and development, (besides obviously communicating with the producer of the chemicals) "shall also communicate this information to the competent authority of the Member State(s) concerned."[185] The

---

U.S. cable companies. *See* Ervin Hexner, "Interpretation by Public International Organizations of Their Basic Instruments," 53 *Am. J. Int'l* L. 341, 361 (1959).

181 "ESATDB Charter," *supra* this chapter, note 65, art. 43 (emphasis added).
182 "CDB Agreement," *supra* this chapter, note 118, art. 37.
183 "ILO Constitution," *supra* this chapter, note 56, art. 19 (5)(a) (provided as "Obligations of Members in respect of Conventions").
184 *See* "AIIB Agreement," *supra* this chapter, note 63, art. 53(3).
185 "European Chemicals Agency Regulation," *supra* this chapter, note 84, arts. 9(3), 22(1) (for general registration), 59(6) (for communicating evaluations).

Agency's constitution also deals with communication with the public.[186] For example, "[C]ommunication of technical advice to support risk management [of hazardous materials] should be encouraged in the supply chain, where appropriate."[187] Such communication should "include describing, documenting and notifying in an appropriate and transparent fashion the risks stemming from the production, use and disposal of each substance."[188] Nevertheless, the European Chemicals Agency's constitution refers to communication far more than do most international organizations' constitutions.

Many international organizations have at least passing references to such operational communication, no matter the nature of the organization. Communication between the UN Economic and Social Council and these other agencies consists of transmitting recommendations, obtaining reports on steps taken to implement these recommendations and its own views of these steps taken.[189] The provisions of the ICC's constitution relating to communication deal with such communication between the accused and the Court during the trial and afterwards.[190] For the Benelux Court of Justice, authorities must communicate the exercise of that authority in enforcements or refusals to enforce other judgments.[191] The African Export Import Bank's articles clearly refer to the more everyday meaning as operational communication, including operational decisions undertaken by directors.[192] These constitutions possibly single out these types of communication as relevant to the exercise of authority, rather than just to describe ways the organization should talk.[193]

---

186 *See id.*, arts. 20, 22, 36 (emphatically stating the necessity of the constant communication between registrants, manufacturers, importers, distributors, downstream users and the Agency concerning the information on the safety and care of the chemical substances marketed, transferred and used).
187 *Id.*, art. 69(17).
188 *Id.*, art. 69(25).
189 *See* UN Charter, *supra* Chapter 1, note 7, art. 64. The UN Economic and Social Council can communicate its views to the agency concerned or to the General Assembly, presumably with a copy of the original report they are responding to.
190 *See* "Rome Statute," *supra* this chapter, note 72, art. 63(2) (for communication during the trial), 106 (for communication after the trial).
191 *See* "Benelux Court of Justice Treaty," *supra* this chapter, note 64, art. 11(5)(a).
192 Article 23 illustrates the intent behind such communication, whereby board-level directors may adopt resolutions "by correspondence, by any means of communication in the form of one or more documents signed or approved in writing" in the same way as *in camera*. *See* "AEIB Agreement," *supra* this chapter, note 46, arts. 23, 34.
193 Such a statement begs the question whether communication represents the exercise of authority, and does the exercise of authority require communication.

However, in a wide variety of cases, communication refers to what amount to staff appointments. The Asian Infrastructure Investment Bank's constitution, like several other constitutions, requires its president to recommend a vice-president.[194] The Caribbean Development Bank's constitution stipulates that the Board of Directors appoints a vice-president on the recommendation of the president.[195] The Bank of Central African States' constitution also mentions recommendations, like many others, in the context of staff appointments.[196] Perhaps the most important staff appointment in the international organization system, the UN Secretary General's appointment relies on "recommendation of the Security Council."[197] These communications represent the exercise of authority, albeit to what extent remains to be theorized.[198]

Recommendations: substantive and banal

Recommendations as the basis for international lawmaking

One view of international organizations posits that they represent legal technologies for making recommendations.[199] The UN Charter further describes how its Economic and Social Council *may* use such authority to "make recommendations with respect to any such matters to the General

---

Alternatively, does the exercise of authority *define* such communication? For more on the issues involved, *see* Tony Prosser, "Constitutions as Communication," 15 *Int'l J. Const. L.* 1039 (2017).

194 *See* "AIIB Agreement," *supra* this chapter, note 63, art. 30. In other cases, the president recommends the appointment of a vice-president. In order to keep the text lean, the authors of this book do not catalogue the treaties that take one approach or the other.
195 *See* "CDB Agreement," *supra* this chapter, note 118, art. 34(1).
196 See "BEAC Treaty," *supra* this chapter, note 82, arts. 30, 63, 65, 66, 71.
197 UN Charter, *supra* Chapter 1, note 7, art. 97.
198 Researchers have started to consider these issues in the context of national constitutions, although in an international law context it remains far more problematic. *See* Corey Rayburn Young, "Constitutional Communication," 96 *B.U. L. Rev.* 303 (2016).
199 The extent to which making recommendations serves as a responsibility of international organizations remains an open question. Such a responsibility would rely on international law's treatment of the potential harm (or gain) to the third parties receiving these recommendations, something that neither the Vienna Convention on the Law Treaties nor customary international law directly tackle. *See* Ki-Gab Park & Kyong-Wha Chung, "Responsibility of International Organizations," 2 *Kor. U. L. Rev.* 1 (2007).

Assembly, to the Members of the United Nations, and to the specialized agencies concerned" and "recommendations for the purpose of promoting respect for, and observance of, human rights and fundamental freedoms for all."[200] Such delegated authority also allows the Economic and Social Council to specially "make recommendations" to UN specialized agencies, the General Assembly and to UN member states.[201]

Do recommendations form a basis for international law? The Arab Bank for Economic Development in Africa's preamble cites decisions taken at the VIth Arab Summit in 1973 and recommendations made by the Economic Council at its session in December 1973 as the basis for the Bank's articles.[202] In contrast, the Eastern and Southern African Trade and Development Bank's constitution claims authority from a treaty – the Treaty of the Authority of the Preferential Trade Area for Eastern and Southern African States.[203] Both organizations seem to work just fine. Moreover, the ILO Charter treats recommendations like law, or at least conventions like recommendations.[204] The ILO Charter requires members to bring ILO recommendations in front of their competent authorities, just as they must for amendments to the ILO Charter or any other "hard" ILO law.

Other provisions show how the "authority to recommend" represents perhaps the highest authority to make law in the system of international organizations. The UN Charter requires: "Each Member of the United Nations undertakes to comply with the decision of the International Court of Justice in any case to which it is a party."[205] Nevertheless, failure to comply does not invoke punishment from the UN, the Security Council or member states with expansive military powers directly. Instead, the Charter grants that "the other party may have recourse to the Security Council, which may, if it deems necessary, make recommendations or decide upon measures to be taken to give effect to the judgment."[206] As such, enforcement depends on Security Council members' recommendations and decisions. Little is known about the way international organizations obtain such an authority to recommend, what powers such

---

200 UN Charter, *supra* Chapter 1, note 7, art. 62(1)–(2).
201 The same provision allows the UN Economic and Social Council "co-ordinate the activities of the specialized agencies through consultation with [them]." *Id.*, art. 63(2).
202 *See* "BADEA Agreement," *supra* this chapter, note 128, preamb.
203 *See* "ESATDB Charter," *supra* this chapter, note 65, preamb.
204 *See* "ILO Constitution," *supra* this chapter, note 56, 20(1)(6).
205 UN Charter, *supra* Chapter 1, note 7, art. 94(1).
206 *Id.*, art 94(2).

recommendations involve and how international organizations may delegate such authority.[207]

Recommendations as mechanism for exercising shared authority

Several international organizations' design shows the intermingled relationship between authority and making recommendations. While the UN General Assembly takes the decision on states applying for UN membership, the General Assembly does so only "upon the recommendation of the Security Council."[208] For non-members of the UN seeking to join the ICJ, the General Assembly has the authority to set down conditions and rules for such membership, again upon the recommendation of the Security Council.[209] In the European context, the Treaty on the Functioning of the European Union "provides for the conclusion of agreements between the community and one or more states *or international organizations*" such that "the Commission shall make *recommendations* to the Council, which shall *authorize* the Commission to open the necessary negotiations."[210] Such an authority-to-recommend represents an important aspect of authority in these examples.

The authority-to-recommend helps to provide for co-management of international organizations in other ways. The ICJ's constitution grants, in cases where a member does not obey an ICJ ruling, that "the other party may have recourse to the Security Council, which may, if it deems necessary, make recommendations or decide upon measures to be taken to give effect to the judgment."[211] As such, enforcement depends on Security Council members' recommendations and decisions. Recommendations regarding the coordination between "custodial states" and the ICC include the Pre-Trial Chamber making recommendations about granting bail (or interim release) to a custodial state's competent authority, as well as

---

207 In practice, the answer to these questions depends on power. However, moving away from might-is-right will rely on international legal scholars coming up with more normative jurisprudence. For the way a lack of such legal foundations makes power an all-important concept in international organizations' recommendations, see Adrien Schifano, "Distribution of Power within International Organizations," 14 *Int'l Org. L. Rev.* 346 (2017).
208 UN Charter, *supra* Chapter 1, note 7, art. 4(2). For more information on the ICJ advisory opinions that emphasize the importance of Security Council recommendations with membership, see Fry & Chong, *supra* Chapter 1, note 101, at 138.
209 UN Charter, *supra* Chapter 1, note 7, art. 93(2).
210 "Treaty on the Functioning of the EU," *supra* this chapter, note 78, art. 228(l) (emphasis added).
211 UN Charter, *supra* Chapter 1, note 7, art 94(2).

Patterns of authority 153

recommendations on ensuring that the suspect does not flee before the Court renders its decision.[212] CERN's Council keeps a tight rein on even its operational authority, reserving the right to authorize the appointment and dismissal of all staff (even clerical staff) assisting the director-general with the recommendation of the director-general.[213] The International Finance Corporation, instead of giving recommendations, *receives* recommendations, specifically recommendations from a "competent committee" on financing.[214] Therefore, such authority-to-recommend comprises an important element of consensual management in potentially politically divisive organizations.[215]

Operational and staff "recommendations"

While high-profile recommendations from the UN General Assembly hoard the news, most recommendations referred to in international organizations' constitutions relate to workaday operational and staff decisions. The only time mentions of making any recommendation occur in the Caribbean Development Bank's constitution relates to times where the President recommends, or refuses to recommend, a loan or guarantee to the Board of Directors.[216] The European Bank for Reconstruction and Development's President recommends particular investments to the Bank's Board.[217] The Eastern and Southern African Trade and Development Bank's constitution asks the Board of Directors to make recommendations about operational decisions to the Bank's Board of Governors.[218] The Russia-based

---

212 *See* "Rome Statute," *supra* this chapter, note 72, art. 59(5).
213 "CERN Convention," *supra* this chapter, note 67, arts. VI(2)–(3).
214 "IFC Agreement," *supra* this chapter, note 109, art. V § 1(d).
215 Such a functionalist view belies the politics involved and might give more weight to these recommendations than they merit, as many decision bodies take the kinds of recommendations cited here uncritically. However, the design undoubtedly reflects a pre-existing worldview in the minds of these constitutions' drafters. For more on the functionalist value of even seemingly small decisions taken by international organizations, *see* Lisa L. Martin & Beth A. Simmons, "International Organizations and Institutions," *in Handbook of International Relations* 192 (Walter Carlsnaes et al. eds. 2002).
216 *See* "CDB Agreement," *supra* this chapter, note 118, art. 15(c).
217 *See* "EBRD Agreement," *supra* this chapter, note 98, ch. III, art. 13(vi).
218 Such recommendations from the Board of Directors to the Board of Governors include asking to call shares in (as per art. 7(4)), recommending reinvestment or paying dividends from net income (as per art. 22(1)), dismissing the president (art. 30(4)) and distributing net assets to members (art. 41(1)). Such recommendations from the President to the Board of Directors come from extending credit or investment (as under art. 16(j)). *See* "ESATDB Charter," *supra* this chapter, note 65.

International Investment Bank's Council "passes recommendations on [the] increase in the authorized capital of the Bank [and] amendments of the Statutes of the Bank."[219] In contrast, recommendations *to* the Bank Council consist of "recommendations regarding increase in the authorized capital of the Bank, [and] recommendations on amendments of the Bank's Statutes."[220] These constitutions provide the authority to recommend, not the authority to order or require, which suggests something consensual about the nature of authority in these international financial organizations.[221]

Sometimes the power to recommend does not come explicitly as a recommendation. For example, CERN's director-general serves as agent representing the interests of the member-state principals when making recommendations to the Finance Committee. In regard to financial administration, "[the director-general] act[s] in accordance with the provisions of the Financial Protocol annexed to this Convention."[222] While the financial protocol gives CERN's Finance Committee the authority to effect "transfers within the budget," "the exact form of the estimates shall be determined by the Finance Committee on the advice of the Directors-General."[223] Such "advice" clearly represents a recommendation in this case.

The international courts pose no exception to this general observation. For example, the ICC's judges "elect the Registrar by an absolute majority by secret ballot, taking into account any *recommendation* by the Assembly of States Parties."[224] A super-majority of judges can *recommend* to state parties the dismissal of another judge, and the prosecutor can *recommend* to them the dismissal of a deputy prosecutor.[225] The Pre-Trial Chamber may *recommend* to investigators procedures to follow and *recommend*

---

219 "IIB Agreement," *supra* this chapter, note 87, art. 20(i). Article 29 repeats the power of the Council to recommend changes to the Agreement. See *id.*, art. 29.
220 *Id.*, art. 20(i)(2).
221 Where some see consensual governance, others see politics. If recommendations provide for shared oversight over international financial organizations, why did so many succumb to regulatory capture if not for politics? See Andrew Baker, "Restraining Regulatory Capture? Anglo-America, Crisis Politics and Trajectories of Change in Global Financial Governance," 86 *Int'l Aff.* 647 (2010).
222 "CERN Convention," *supra* this chapter, note 67, art VI(1)(1).
223 See "CERN Convention," Finance Protocol, *supra* this chapter, note 67, art. 1(3).
224 "Rome Statute," *supra* this chapter, note 72, art. 43(4) (emphasis added). They similarly elect "in the same manner" a Deputy Registrar "upon the recommendation of the Registrar." *Id.* The text does not shed light on the apparent contradiction of electing these officials by a secret ballot while taking the recommendations of the Assembly of State Parties into account.
225 See *id.*, art. 46(2)(a).

judges from the pre-trial or trial divisions to make *recommendations* aimed at preserving evidence and questioning suspects during investigations.[226] State parties may consider and adopt *recommendations* of the Court's Preparatory Commission.[227] Finally, the Assembly of States Parties may make *recommendations* on settling a dispute between two or more state parties concerning the Court's judicial functions.[228]

However, most of these recommendations, like many communications reviewed in an earlier section, relate to executive appointments. The UN Secretary General's appointment relies on "recommendation of the Security Council."[229] The European Bank for Reconstruction and Development's President uses the "full power to exercise authority over any matter delegated or assigned to the Board of Directors" to recommend vice-presidents to the Board of Executive Directors.[230] The Inter-American Development Bank's constitution gives its president similar powers using similar wording.[231]

Conclusion

What do international organizations' constitutions tell us about the jurisprudence of authority in these constitutions? Member states vest authority in international organizations, and their constitutions reflect such investiture. Nevertheless, the extent to which international organizations act as agents, or exercise agency of their own, depends. The IMF has a law that may implicitly accept a proto-authority emerging in the international organization itself. Such implicit recognition of external authority in international organizations themselves allows these international organizations to contract with others and even accept judgments from them. However, in most, the wording around the organization's authority remains strict and circumspect. These organizations clearly do only what their member states tell them.

---

226 *See id.*, art. 56(2).
227 *See id.*, art. 112(2).
228 *See id.*, art. 119(2).
229 UN Charter, *supra* Chapter 1, note 7, art. 97.
230 *See* "EBRD Agreement," *supra* this chapter, note 98, art. 24(3) (for the authority) and art. 31 (for the power of recommending vice-presidents).
231 "IADB Agreement," *supra* this chapter, note 66, art. VIII § 5(b). A further provision provides, "In addition to the Vice President referred to in Article IV, Section 8(b), the Board of Executive Directors may, on recommendation of the President of the Bank, appoint other Vice Presidents who shall exercise such authority and perform such functions as the Board of Executive Directors may determine." *Id.*, art. VIII § 5(c).

156 *The values of international organizations*

The research reflected in this chapter shows an emerging, spontaneous order among international organizations' constitutions. The similarity between these constitutions clearly shows general understandings about phrases like having an "international character" or hiring staff "on the recommendation of" a senior official. These phrases impart real rights and obligations, clearly forming part of the firmament of international law. However, other similarities represent common principles or doctrines. The authority-to-recommend, the principle of unity-of-authority and others represent common drafting templates that appear across international organizations' constitutions, with only minor variations. This book's statistical census of these constitutions uncovered commonalities that qualitative experts have hitherto overlooked. Regardless of the type of international organization, its age, location and so forth, these constants suggest a "common law" of international organizations, which the authors of popular textbooks on international organizations law have overlooked.

Nevertheless, the statistical analysis also identified differences between texts in the links between authority, communication and recommendation, which this chapter has explored in depth in the analysis of the texts. To explain these different links between international organizations' constitutions, this book has described the values embedded in international organizations' constitutions and the tracks or circuits between them. Some international organizations' constitutions give these organizations wide-reaching authority to intervene in their member states, but little authority to communicate or make the kinds of recommendations that become part of international law. Some constitutions give these organizations authority over only their own staff and organization, but the authority to encourage the kinds of communication between members that change the international political economy. All kinds of combinations exist, and they defy researchers' attempts to classify or generalize them.

A number of tacit principles and ideas emerge from a close reading of international organizations' constitutions, which the textbook authors have failed to pick up on. Authority does not represent a value in itself but, rather, *combines* with other values analyzed in this book. There are authority-to-communicate, semi-autonomous authority and authority-to-recommend, and undoubtedly others would have been found if the statistics pointed in that direction. Such authority passes through (giving credence to principal–agent theorists' idea of unity-of-authority). However, customary law gives certain authority to international organizations and the autonomy to use it. In particular, the principle of an international character gives autonomy that member states have not strictly defined *ex ante*, or before signing the constitution. The implicit recognition of external authority, particularly in arbitration clauses, illustrates the impact of such a customary acceptance of autonomous authority.

The way that authority interacts with communication and recommendations in these constitutions points to tacit principles that the famous international organization law textbook authors have failed to dissect. Communication helps to make international law and cements the basis for membership in international organizations, as well as helps an international organization to undertake its operations and appoint senior staff. Constitutional provisions granting privilege for communications might show how authority-to-communicate comes from customary law, rather than authority delegated from member states. International organizations' constitutions accept that recommendations clearly form some, even "soft," basis for international law, even if many researchers do not accept this. Nevertheless, making recommendations also serves as a way to share authority in international organizations. The person or organization making the recommendation has a voice in policy and the operational aspects of the organization's work, but not total veto control.

The next chapter provides a similar, although less detailed, look at other principles highlighted in Chapter 2, focusing on the aspirational principles identified by statistical group analysis described in Chapter 2. In particular, the next chapter shows the limits of the analysis provided in Chapter 2, inasmuch as it exposes the many principles that Chapter 2 failed to unearth. It also shows how different conceptions of equality can appear in international organizations' constitutions. To take one example, one international organization may strive for equality between individuals, leading to equal representation in the organization that is required to engender peace worldwide. Jay-Z's complaints about the lack of African American individuals on the arbitrator roster of the American Arbitration Association come to mind.[232] However, other international organizations' constitutions may view such equality from the standpoint of equality between organizations or member states, which helps to guarantee their autonomy and representation in international affairs, thereby promoting peace. The complex conceptions of these principles and the ways that constitutions apply them illustrate some of the reasons for the complex networks and groups analyzed in Chapter 2.

---

232 See Lauren Berg, "Jay-Z Slams Arbitration Group's Lack of Diversity in IP Row," *Law* 360, Nov. 28, 2018.

4

The jurisprudence of organizations' aspirational values

Introduction

To what principles do different international organizations aspire? Do some values "hang together," such as the desire to promote peace with the desire to ensure state sovereignty? This chapter takes a deep look at the law around each principle analyzed in this book. Most international organizations' constitutions expound a nexus of values at first glance. Often strung along, international organizations claim to promote prosperity, peace, human rights, gender equality and just about every other "good" mentionable. However, peel back the claims, and it is possible to see that these constitutions adhere to different accents, different understandings and different "tracks" or groupings of values, which have been described in Chapter 2 and elsewhere in this book. A thin gray line separates values and principles, with values representing instrumental goals or conditions, while principles seem to represent final end states or purposes of the organization. Without striving to attain the principle (and almost always a track of principles) involved, the organization loses its *raison d'être*.

This chapter describes the different views that international organizations have of the aspirational principles already analyzed statistically. The first section describes the nexus of values most international organizations' constitutions purport to uphold. It argues against the "kitchen sink" method of endowing organizations with principles, usually located in a list at the constitution's beginning. This section also describes the many principles that were not analyzed in Chapter 2, since the popular international organizations law textbooks did not identify them often enough. Progress, harmony, humanity and, particularly, human rights represent some of these principles.

The other sections of this chapter analyze specific aspirational principles. The second section looks at how constitutions treat equality. Some constitutions stress equality between persons, while others stress equality between states. The section shows examples of the ways that principles work together in constitutions, with some constitutions advocating equality as a means towards more effective representation. Others constitutions stress equality as the path to other aspirations, such as progress, peace and human rights. The chapter's third section shows how peace serves as a final goal for some organizations, and as a necessary condition for others. Peace comes through justice for some, and peace represents a state of justice for others. Constitutions focusing on freedom see peace as the means to achieving such freedom, while it is vice versa for other constitutions. The same is true for the principle of security. The fourth section looks at representation and autonomy, and it shows how representation serves as means of inclusion in policy and decisions for some and as a means of ensuring participation in policy execution for others. Representation also may help to ensure justice or equality. If autonomy works in the service of efficiency or effectiveness for judicial bodies, some organizations see *restrictions* on autonomy as the means of achieving independence. However, the source of such autonomy remains contentious, with some seeing the member states as the seat of authority, and others seeing the organization itself as the seat of authority.

Determining which principles an international organization represents

One cannot divide international organizations into groups depending on their principles.[1] For example, the UN does not simply advocate peace, whereas the African Intellectual Property Organization simply strives towards efficiency. Most international organizations' constitutions contain groups of principles, and the values supporting them. As this book describes, different "tracks" or patterns of principles emerge across various types of international organizations' constitutions. Nevertheless, many constitutions contain principles completely undiscussed by the leading researchers in this area. This chapter illustrates the "nexus of principles" that most constitutions contain. In particular, it describes how some principles represent

---

1 Many have wrongly tried to convert the analogy of a "division of labor" across international organizations into a hard and fast way of dividing organizations – namely, by the main principles guiding their creation and conduct. International organizations may focus on different issues for obvious reasons at a practical level – the North Atlantic Treaty Organization for security, the WHO on health issues, Food and Agriculture Organization on food security and so forth. However, neither this book nor any other literature has noted any reliable relationship between organization principles and the type or purpose of the organization. For a more concrete discussion, *see* Georgios Kostakos, "Division of Labor Among International Organizations: The Bosnian Experience," 5 *Global Gov.* 461 (1998).

intermediary or instrumental values, and how some principles represent standards hitherto almost completely unconceptualized, especially principles relating to human rights.

The "nexus of principles" problem

Most international organizations' constitutions do not simply focus on one principle but, rather, on a nexus of principles. For example, the Gulf Cooperation Council's objectives lie "in pursuit of the goal of strengthening cooperation and reinforcement of the links between them; Having the conviction that coordination, cooperation, and integration between them serve the sublime objectives of the Arab Nation."[2] Such cooperation, though, "endeavour[s] to complement efforts already begun in all essential areas that concern their peoples and realize their hopes for a better future on the path to unity of their States."[3] These two simple lines raise a host of jurisprudential questions. Which principles take precedence – cooperation or the sublime objectives of the Arab Nation?[4] Does coordination, cooperation or integration – which are three different ways of working together – take precedence? Does unity between states, rather than cooperation between them, represent the ultimate goal?[5] If so, can unity have a legal or moral purpose, like it might in a contract or authorization for a public sector body?[6]

What happens if an international organization's constitution lists several seemingly competing principles and values? The constitution of the

---

2 Charter of the Gulf Cooperation Council preamb., May 25, 1981, *available at* www.files.ethz.ch/isn/125347/1426_GCC.pdf (last visited Mar. 25, 2020) [hereinafter "GCC Charter"].

3 *Id. See also* Rouhollah Ramazani, *The Gulf Cooperation Council: Record and Analysis* (1988).

4 From a literal reading of the text, the latter (the sublime objectives) clearly take precedence, given that cooperation "serves" such objectives.

5 Taking unity at face value requires filling the particularly difficult circle of self-determination with the square peg of aspirational unity. For more on this practically, *see* Farah Dakhlallah, "The League of Arab States and Regional Security: Towards an Arab Security Community?," 39 *Brit. J. Middle Eastern Stud.* 393 (2012); Dimitrios Molos, "Turning Self-Determination on Its Head," 4 *Phil. & Pub. Iss.* 75 (2014).

6 Commentators like Dupuy have noted that interest in cooperation as a value has waxed and waned over time. See Pierre-Marie Dupuy, "International Law: Torn Between Coexistence, Cooperation and Globalization," *Eur. J. Int'l L.* 278 (1998). Others like Delbrück have wondered whether cooperation even represents a value, given its internationally uncritical acceptance (in public at least). *See* Jost Delbrück, "The International Obligation to Cooperate – An Empty Shell or a Hard Law Principle of International Law?," In *Coexistence, Cooperation and Solidarity in International Law* 3 (Holger P. Hestermeyer ed. 2011).

Parliamentary Union of the Organisation for Islamic Cooperation includes the values of "humanism of the Islamic civilization" as a form of equality (art. 1.1), "consultation (Shoora) in all OIC Member States" (art. 1.2), "cooperation and coordination among parliaments" (art. 1.3), dialogue among parliaments" seeking to engage in joint activities (art. 1.4) and seeking representation by resisting "attempts to impose cultural, political and economic domination" (art. 1.4) and "peace, based on justice" (art. 1.6).[7] All of these represent principles analyzed earlier in this book. Clearly, organizations can aspire to multiple values and adopt rules for the practical implementation of programs seeking to bring these values into existence.[8]

Other constitutions provide a range of principles, some of which might be shoehorned into the broader principles focused on in Chapter 2. The African Telecommunications Union espouses values and principles like "universal service and access, in addition to, full inter-country connectivity, in the most effective manner."[9] One might argue that such a value seeks to promote equality and efficiency without stretching credulity too much. However, the constitution does not specifically reference equality. In the case of the Andean Community, the Community is "based on the principles of equality, justice, peace, solidarity, and democracy."[10] How to choose among these principles, in a list without verbs or words of comparison? How to deal with justice, solidarity and democracy, which are three principles that likely promote community rather than represent the end state of community?

Many international organizations' constitutions contain principles, or sets of values. Statistical analysis and legal analysis work together when trying to sort organizations' principles when these organizations *explicitly* (not tacitly) promulgate groups of equally weighted principles. This book focuses mainly on finding such groups. Nevertheless, the jurist identifies driving principles in two other ways: (1) finding major principles by precedent, and (2) identifying values outside of the authoritative list of

---

7 *See* Statute of the Parliamentary Union of the OIC Member States preamb., June 17, 1999 June 1999, at www.puic.org (last visited Mar. 25, 2020).

8 *See id.* ("reiterating the respect for the objectives and principles provided for in the Charter of the Organization of the Islamic Conference" also includes "the sovereignty and territorial integrity of States and peaceful settlement of disputes"). Sovereignty represents another value left off the list compiled from the leading textbook authors.

9 African Telecommunications Union Constitution and Convention art. 2.2, Dec. 7, 1999, *available at* http://atu-uat.org (last visited Mar. 25, 2020) [hereinafter "ATU Constitution"].

10 Codification of the Andean Subregional Integration Agreement (Cartagena Agreement), May 26, 1969, preamb. ¶ 5, *available at* www.sice.oas.org (last visited Mar. 25, 2020) [hereinafter "Cartegena Agreement"].

principles. This chapter focuses on those other ways of identifying these driving principles.

Finding values by precedent

Finding driving principles by precedent involves analyzing a constitution's words to ascertain the major principle or values targeted by the international organization's constitution. The constitution of the Agency for the Prohibition of Nuclear Weapons in Latin America and the Caribbean – namely, in the Treaty of Tlatelolco – gives several competing values to navigate.[11] Specifically, the Treaty notes that Latin America:

(a) faithful to its tradition of universality,
(b) must not only endeavour to banish from its homelands the scourge of a nuclear war,
(c) but must also strive to promote the well-being and advancement of its peoples,
(d) at the same time co-operating in the fulfillment of the ideals of mankind,
  (i) that is to say, in the consolidation of a permanent peace based on equal rights, economic fairness and social justice for all,
  (ii) in accordance with the principles and purposes set forth in the Charter of the United Nations and in the Charter of the Organization of American States.[12]

The terms in (a) clearly represent a condition or representation. Line (b) describes peace as a goal. However, line (c) gives well-being and advancement the same stress by using the clause "must also." Line d(i) defines the third goal, defining the fulfilment of mankind's ideals as peace. This type of peace requires and relies on equality, which is another value in this book's authoritative list of values. Line (d) repeats and clarifies line (b). Line d(ii)'s conditions such as peace and the advancement of principles are found in two other treaties. These treaties also contain principles that might or might not extend the number of principles beyond the two immediately identified in the Agency's preamble in the quote above. To be clear, none of these has to do directly with nuclear disarmament, which is the primary scope of the Agency for Prohibition of Nuclear Weapons in Latin America and the Caribbean.

---

11 Treaty for the Prohibition of Nuclear Weapons in Latin America and the Caribbean (Treaty of Tlatelolco), Feb. 14, 1967, *available at* www.opanal.org (last visited Mar. 25, 2020). The quote divides up the original text for ease in explaining each section of the article.
12 *Id.*, preamb. ¶ 18 (adding division to the original in order to make it easier to analyze this provision).

Many organizations reference the UN Charter's values, which adds further complexity. The Organisation for Islamic Cooperation, another institution from before the oil shocks of the 1970s, affirms "global peace, security and harmony."[13] The Organisation for Islamic Cooperation does this through its "commitment to the principles of the UN Charter."[14] The South Asian Association for Regional Cooperation, a decidedly post-oil-shock institution, affirms that "desirous of promoting peace, stability, amity and progress in the region through strict adherence to the principles of the *United Nations Charter* and *non-alignment*, particularly respect for the principles of sovereign equality, territorial integrity, national independence, non-use of force and non-interference in the internal affairs of other States and peaceful settlement of all disputes."[15] Any jurisprudential analysis of these constitutions would need to decide how much weight to give the terms "implied" in these constitutions.

Other examples show the judgment required to place some principles above others. The Andean Community's Cartagena Agreement is "based on the principles of equality, justice, peace, solidarity, and democracy," albeit "to promote the balanced and harmonious development of the Member Countries under equitable conditions."[16] The agreement does not prioritize among these values in the service of an agreement ultimately targeting economic and social development. Nevertheless, clearly equality and its related principles serve "to promote" development, thus serving more as a condition or value than as a driving principle for the organization.

The African Court of Human and People's Rights constitution requires that "all peoples shall have the right to national and international peace and security."[17] The Court's Protocol also "recognizes that freedom, equality, justice, peace and dignity are essential objectives for the achievement of the legitimate aspirations of the African peoples."[18] The Protocol goes on to define these aspirations as "to coordinate and intensify their cooperation and efforts to achieve a better life for the peoples of Africa and to

---

13 Charter of the Organisation of Islamic Cooperation art. 1(6), Mar. 14, 2008, *available at* www.oic-oci.org (last visited Mar. 25, 2020) [hereinafter "OIC Charter"].
14 *Id.*, art. 1(7).
15 Charter of the South Asian Association for Regional Cooperation art. 1, Dec. 8, 1985, *available at* http://saarc-sec.org (last visited Mar. 25, 2020) (emphasis in original) [hereinafter "SAARC Charter"].
16 "Cartagena Agreement," *supra* this chapter, note 10, preamb. & art. 1.
17 African (Banjul) Charter on Human and People's Rights art. 23.1, June 27, 1981, *available at* www.achpr.org (last visited Mar. 25, 2020).
18 Protocol to the African Charter on Human and Peoples' Rights on the Establishment of the African Court on Human and Peoples' Rights preamb., June 10, 1998, available at www.achpr.org (last visited Mar. 25, 2020) [hereinafter "ACHPR Protocol"].

promote international cooperation [with] particular attention to the right to development."[19] Happy lives, economic thriving, comfortable living and prosperity, then, seem to represent the final principles driving a *judicial* body. A simple analysis of values would place such an organization among the economic organizations before a judicial one.

In many cases, including those already seen, some combinations of values and principles include principles or goals not on the authoritative list of principles identified by the legal researchers reviewed earlier in this book. For example, the Southern African Development Community and its member states are expected to adopt the following principles when acting:

(a) sovereign equality of all Member States;
(b) solidarity, peace and security;
(c) human rights, democracy and the rule of law;
(d) equity, balance and mutual benefit; and
(e) peaceful settlement of disputes.[20]

Equality and peace represent values from the authoritative list. Many constitutions refer to human rights, democracy and the rule of law as principles, or more often conditional values to attain to. However, what about "balance and mutual benefit," as indicated in the Southern African Development Community's constitution? What about solidarity? If it is possible to treat solidarity as a type of equality, then balance and mutual benefit represent values far harder to define, much less to quantify and count in a study such as the one provided by this book.

Principles not on the authoritative list

Analysis by precedent sometimes can lead to principles not on the authoritative list. The African Court of Human and People's Rights' Protocol starts by "considering that the Charter of the Organization of African Unity recognizes that freedom, equality, justice, peace and dignity are essential objectives for the achievement of the *legitimate aspirations* of the African peoples."[21] In other words, legitimate aspirations serve as the goal, and principles represent the instrument to achieve that goal. However, legitimate aspirations, like the pursuit of happiness or self-actualization,

---

19 Id.
20 "SADC Treaty", *supra* Chapter 3, note 112, art. 4, Nov. 21, 2014.
21 See "ACHPR Protocol," *supra* this chapter, note 18, preamb. (emphasis added). While dignity does not represent a principle that this book focuses on, the UN Charter also includes the principle in its list. For more on that principle and whether dignity should rank among other principles like peace and autonomy, *see* Oscar Schachter, "Human Dignity as a Normative Concept," 77 Am. J. Int'l Law 848 (1983).

Jurisprudence of aspirational values

represent principles almost completely unstudied in international law.[22] Even the attempt to claim a set of African or universal "legitimate aspirations" would run into theoretical and practical opposition.[23]

Progress represents another aspirational principle included in many constitutions. The Gulf Cooperation Council's constitution directly identifies progress as an objective "to stimulate scientific and technological progress in the fields of industry, mining, agriculture, water and animal resources; to establish scientific research; to establish joint ventures and encourage cooperation by the private sector for the good of their peoples."[24] Even the UN Charter requires the UN to promote "higher standards of living, full employment, and conditions of economic and social progress and development."[25] Depending on one's definition of progress, the UN Charter continues to espouse progress as "solutions of international economic, social, health, and related problems."[26] The EU's constitution cites its intention to uphold five main clusters of values "to continue along the path of civilization, progress and prosperity, [work] for the good of all its inhabitants, including the weakest and most deprived, to remain a continent open to culture, learning and social progress, to deepen the democratic and transparent nature of its public life, and to strive for peace, justice and solidarity throughout the world."[27] Arguably, all these values strive towards progress.

---

22 While self-determination has a long legal tradition, the aspirations akin to Maslow's self-actualization have received almost no attention in any kind of law, international or domestic. For an exception, *see* Melissa Hung, "Obstacles to Self-Actualization in Chinese Legal Practice," 48 *Santa Clara L. Rev.* 213 (2008).
23 Joshua Kobbah, "African Values and the Human Rights Debate: An African Perspective," 9 *Hum. Rts. Q.* 309 (1987).
24 "GCC Charter," *supra* this chapter, note 2, art. 4(4).
25 UN Charter, *supra* Chapter 1, note 7, art. 55(a).
26 *Id.*, art. 55(b). Legal researchers have completely ignored progress as a principle in international law and in these organizations' constitutions. Extremely limited studies of progress as a constitutional or international normative principle treat such progress as an indicator to achieve, akin to efficiency or effectiveness. *See, e.g.*, David H. Lempert, "A Dependency in Development Indicator for NGOs and International Organizations," 9 *Glob. Jur.* 1 (2009).
27 Treaty of Lisbon Amending the Treaty on European Union and the Treaty Establishing the European Community preamb., Dec. 13, 2007, 2007/C 306/01 [hereinafter "Treaty of Lisbon"]. These principles represent ideas so controversial and political that reaching even a political agreement beyond policies supporting them (much less a legal understanding of the rights and obligations inherent in advancing progress) remains elusive. For a broader discussion of the legal problems involved in operationalizing the EU constitutional principles, *see* John-Erik Fossum & Agustin Menendez, "Still Adrift in the Rubicon? The Constitutional Treaty Assessed," *in The European Constitution: The Rubicon Crossed?* 97 (Erik-Oddvar Eriksen et al. eds. 2005).

Other organizations' constitutions have their way of expressing progress. The International Development Association's and the UN Industrial Development Organization's (UNIDO) constitutions' preambles specifically refer to aspirations noted in the UN Charter preamble, which seek "to establish conditions under which justice and respect for ... international law can be maintained, and to promote social progress and better standards of life."[28] Adding to the UN's conception of progress, the International Development Association constitution seeks cooperation for "constructive economic purposes, healthy development of the world economy and balanced growth of international trade [to] foster international relationships conducive to the maintenance of peace and world prosperity."[29] Such a view, then, sees peace and prosperity as joint goals or values to attain.

The value, and possibly principle, of progress often appears in constitutions as something only tangentially related to such progress. For example, UNIDO's constitution describes such progress in detail as the "implementation of dynamic social and economic changes and the encouragement of necessary structural changes in the development of the world economy."[30] On the face of the text, change represents the value sought in the constitution. However, even a moment's reflection suggests that a constitution must seek change for some other reason than for itself.[31] In contrast, the Commonwealth Secretariat seeks to "contribute to the enrichment of life for all," a worthy goal if one could define "enrichment" and its substantive difference from progress.[32] As for the African Telecommunications Union,

28 UN Charter, *supra* Chapter 1, note 7, preamb.
29 IDA Articles of Agreement preamb., Jan. 26, 1960, *available at* http://siteresources.worldbank.org (last visited Mar. 25, 2020).
30 The constitution unsurprisingly sees industrialization as the means to such progress, noting that "industrialization is a dynamic instrument of growth essential to rapid economic and social development, in particular of developing countries, to the improvement of the living standards and the quality of life." Constitution of the United Nations Industrial Development Organization preamb., Apr. 8, 1979, *available at* www.unido.org (last visited Mar. 25, 2020) [hereinafter "UNIDO Constitution"].
31 For authors like Schwabach and Cockfield, change brings about the need to codify the customs that form the basis of international law. However, their discussion clearly points to progress, rather than simply change, as the reason for codifying international law and creating international institutions. *See* Aaron Schwabach & Arthur Cockfield, "The Role of International Law and Institutions," *in UNESCO Encyclopedia of Life Support Systems* (2016), *available at* www.colss.net (last visited Mar. 25, 2020).
32 *See* Agreed Memorandum on the Commonwealth Secretariat preamb., June 11, 1965, *available at* 4 I.L.M. 1108 (1965) [hereinafter "Commonwealth Secretariat Memorandum"].

Jurisprudence of aspirational values 167

two of the Union's objectives aim at developing an African Information Society and rural telecommunications development, which in effect value progress.[33] Does the value "to promote and encourage the exchange of information, expertise and technology relating to info-communications for the benefit of all Member States and Associate Members" truly aim at progress?[34] What about the separate values of technical advancement, development or growth?

Questions like these illustrate the problems of including values like progress in any list of the legal principles underpinning international organizations' constitutions. While many international organizations' constitutions discuss technical and technological progress, few national constitutions embrace this value.[35] Moreover, many critiques hold the view that organizing international programs aimed at scientific pursuits and goals leads to any kind of progress.[36] Worse yet, the desire to promote progress may, in itself, represent a "shared narrative" serving to create an international order, in the same way that nations used technology policy to forge nation-states.[37] Rather than serving to promote actual progress, such provisions in international organizations' constitutions may implicitly help to create communities within and between states that use the political discourse of progress as a way to unify voters and group interests.[38] Therefore, progress represents one of the vital values in these constitutions that legal researchers

---

33 "ATU Constitution," *supra* this chapter, note 9, art. 3(c)–(d) ("To promote programmes for the development of the African Information Society" and "To prepare special programmes for Africa's Least Developed Countries (LDC's) and rural telecommunications development").
34 *Id.*, art. 3(k).
35 China represents one exception. The Chinese constitution's face-on commitment to such progress has had significant effects on the way copyright law, among other areas of law, has evolved. For more on the values addressed in these constitutions, *see* Otto Spijkers, *The United Nations, the Evolution of Global Values and International Law* (2011).
36 *See* Ernst Haas et al., *Scientists and World Order: The Uses of Technical Knowledge in International Organizations* (1977) (providing illustrations of these criticisms).
37 A detailed analysis of this position would take this book's discussion well past any reasonable length. Suffice it to say that technology policy has served political purposes to help unify particular interests in supporting the government. *See* Martti Koskenniemi, "The Fate of Public International Law: Between Technique and Politics," 70 *Modern L. Rev.* 1 (2007).
38 Such talk may seem far better suited to a sociology book rather a legal one. However, such thinking has started to permeate legal scholarship in recent years. *See, e.g.*, Tilmann Altwicker & Oliver Diggelmann, "How is Progress Constructed in International Legal Scholarship?," 25 *Eur. J. Int'l L.* 425 (2014); Olena Sihvo, "Global Constitutionalism and the Idea of Progress," 2018 *Helsinki L. Rev.* 10 (2018).

will have great difficulty defining and using in their analysis, for years to come.

The World Tourism Organization's constitution illustrates the difficulty of simply matching legal principles to an international organization's constitution. The Organization's constitution focuses on "the promotion and development of tourism *with a view to* contributing to economic development, international understanding, peace, prosperity, and universal respect for, and observance of, human rights and fundamental freedoms for all."[39] Therefore, promoting tourism serves only a litany of goals. Only peace matches the list of principles from Chapter 2. International understanding, prosperity and respect for human rights and fundamental freedoms do not match this list. Nevertheless, given the Organization's specific focus on tourism, one wonders to what extent such general constitutional principles should apply to an organization focused on a narrow sector or interest.

Can the principles and values in an international organization focused on a particular sector, industry or group of people actually represent deeper legal principles accepted by the international community of legal researchers?[40] Sectoral international organizations like the African Telecommunications Union or the International Organization of Vine and Wine may adopt principles like equality and authority, even though they are specifically focused on an industry. For example, the International Organization of Vine and Wine's constitution seeks "to inform its members of measures whereby the concerns of producers, consumers and other players in the vine and wine products sector may be taken into consideration."[41] The Organization also strives to "improve the conditions for producing and marketing vine and wine products, and to help ensure that the interests of consumers are taken into account."[42] Such organizations and their unabashedly sectoral interests create both exceptions to the universal principles analyzed in Chapter 2 and a new way of thinking about these principles in a limited context.[43]

---

39 Statute of the World Tourism Organization art. 3(1), Sept. 27, 1970, *available at* www.unwto.org (last visited Mar. 25, 2020) (emphasis added) [hereinafter "UNWTO Statute"].
40 The impartial nature of these organizations and the universality of the principles underpinning their constitutions represent a core assumption and value for international legal researchers. Only recently have researchers like Durkee started to question the wisdom of this approach. *See* Melissa Durkee, "Industry Lobbying and 'Interest Blind' Access Norms at International Organizations," 111 *Am. J. Int'l L.* 119 (2017).
41 Agreement Establishing the International Organisation of Vine and Wine art. 2(1)(a), Apr. 3, 2001, *available at* www.oiv.int (last visited Mar. 25, 2020).
42 *Id.*, art. 2(1)(c).
43 Franck calls the codification of the customary relations between states in sectoral areas like these pedigrees. Since states accept these pedigrees as legitimate, legal

Other sectoral organizations' constitutions illustrate the difficulties in thinking about constitutional principles as universal principles. The African Telecommunications Union's "financing and funding of telecommunications development" necessarily implies, at least in the short run, choices over funding hospitals or education.[44] The same is true for the objective "to promote the establishment of info-communications industries."[45] Even if the African Telecommunications Union seeks "to promote human resources development in the field of info-communications," one might obviously ask about the alternative uses of such resources.[46] As for the Parliamentary Union of the Organisation for Islamic Cooperation, the value of "providing a framework for comprehensive and fruitful cooperation and coordination among parliaments of OIC members in international fora and organizations" means coordinating before negotiating in other places like the UN.[47] Such an objective clearly reflects sectoral-level intent to achieve better bargaining power, which is a way of getting support in other international organizations.[48]

Such sectoralism applies just as much to regional institutions as topic-based ones. For example, even though the Organization of Central American States' presidents take decisions "with regard to democracy,

---

researchers – by implication – should accept the principles in their constitutions as specific principles, rather than as deviations or distorts of universal principles. *See* Thomas M. Franck, "Legitimacy in the International System," 82 *Am. J. Int'l L.* 705 (1988).

44 Authors like Gilligan might object, noting that the gains from increased cooperation more than outweigh the harms from diverting resources from other uses. *See* "ATU Constitution," *supra* this chapter, note 9, art. 3(b). *See also* Michael Gilligan, "Is There a Broader-Deeper Trade-off in International Multilateral Agreements?" 58 *Int'l Org.* 459 (2004).

45 "ATU Constitution," *supra* this chapter, note 9, art. 3(f).

46 *Id.*, art. 3(e). Bradford might see such organizations as the way of driving change and the development of all international organizations and their constitutional principles. *See* Anu Bradford, "How International Institutions Evolve," 15 *Chic. J. Int'l L.* 47 (2014).

47 Charter of the Islamic Conference art. 1(3), Mar. 4, 1972, *available at* https://treaties.un.org (last visited Mar. 25, 2020).

48 For most social scientists like Schneider, such attempts to increase a state's or industry's bargaining power in multilateral organizations represent a rational and even positive development. *See* Christina J. Schneider, "Weak States and Institutionalized Bargaining Power in International Organizations," 55 *Int'l Stud. Q.* 331 (2011). However, from a legal perspective, authors like Benvenisti and Downs ask what beneficial, universal legal principle could possibly encourage creating factions among member states in a game designed to increase a member's influence in international organizations' decisions. *See* Eyal Benvenisti & George Downs, "The Empire's New Clothes: Political Economy and the Fragmentation of International Law," 60 *Stan. L. Rev.* 595 (2008).

development, freedom, peace and security," the Organization's Protocol makes clear that they "shall be seized of *regional* questions."[49] While all the sub-points in articles 3 and 4 focus on regional issues of that organization's constitution, several points particularly stress the Organization's exclusively regional nature. In particular, the Central American Integration System has as values "to reaffirm and consolidate Central America's self-determination in terms of its external relations" in line with "Central American identity as an active manifestation of regional interests" and "Central American solidarity as an expression of its profound independence, origins and common destiny."[50] Researchers still cannot decide what such solidarity means for the creation of legal principles governing a single international law, a single law of international organizations, or many.[51]

Sectoral principles obviously conflict with the universalist nature of international organizations law. Most academics and even international organizations accept that, while universalism may represent the ideal, regionalism and sectoralism represent a pragmatic approach towards achieving such universalism.[52] Limited resources and differences in "preferences" (values, philosophies and worldviews) necessarily militate for a regional or sectoral approach to the international law of international organizations, and thus the principles underlining such a law.[53] International principles must, by definition, aspire to universality, lest international organizations turn into the simple agglomeration of national constitutions.[54] Nevertheless, nothing requires them to aspire to more than customary understandings between states and international actors.[55]

49 Tegucigalpa Protocol to the Charter of the Organization of Central American States art. 15, Dec. 13, 1991, *available at* www.sica.int (last visited Mar. 25, 2020).
50 *Id.*, arts. 3(g), 4(c)–(d).
51 For authors like Weiss, the creation of one single international law (or law of international organizations) would run contrary to custom and to the entire international law project itself. *See* Edith Brown Weiss, "The Rise or the Fall of International Law," 69 *Fordham L. Rev.* 345 (2001).
52 For two incarnations of this argument, *see* Christoph Schreuer, "Regionalism v. Universalism," 6 *Eur. J. Int'l L.* 477 (1995); James D. Fry, "Pluralism, Religion, and the Moral Fairness of International Law," 3 *Oxford J. L & Rel.* 393 (2014).
53 Since international law in any particular situation can trace the customs and practices of groups of states interacting with each other, even "universal" law must remain regional in that such law applies to different groups of states for differing sets of topics and issues. *See* Jonathan I. Charney, "Universal International Law," 87 *Am. J. Int'l L.* 529 (1993).
54 *See* Ignacio de la Rasilla del Moral, "The Unsolved Riddle of International Constitutionalism," 12 *Int'l Comm. L. Rev.* 81 (2010).
55 *See* Jed Odermatt, "The Development of Customary International Law by International Organizations," 66 *Int'l & Comp. L.Q.* 491 (2017).

Human rights as the summum bonum *of the international order*

Most international organizations' constitutions place human rights among their core principles, either explicitly or implicitly by acknowledging the UN Charter.[56] The UN Charter, for its part, affirms a commitment to "universal respect for, and observance of, human rights and fundamental freedoms for all."[57] Other international organizations' constitutions often use a similar phrasing. For example, UNESCO's constitution aims "to contribute to peace and security ... in order to further universal respect for ... human rights and fundamental freedoms."[58] For the African-Asian Rural Development Organization, such equality also consists of "women's full enjoyment of all human rights and fundamental freedoms."[59] The Inter-Parliamentary Union's constitution specifically accords the 130-year-old organization with the explicit mandate to "contribute to the defence and promotion of human rights."[60] Such constitutions represent possibly the most important attempt by the framers of international law to change the customs and *moeurs* that usually define, rather than being defined by, such law.[61]

Even regional and sectoral international organizations profess a focus on human rights. The EU constitution states the case succinctly in that

---

56 Many attribute the widespread reference to the UN Charter's principles in other international organizations' constitutions as the same kind of authorization that national legislation receives in references to a national constitution. For an analysis of such a metaphor to domestic lawmaking, *see* Fassbender, *supra* Chapter 2, note 41, at 529.

57 The Charter includes protection for gender equality in its preamble and in Article 55(c). For more on the lawmaking around the Charter's affirmation of human rights, *see* Louis B. Sohn, "The Human Rights Law of the Charter," 12 *Tex. Int'l L.J.* 129 (1977).

58 UNESCO Constitution art. 1, Nov. 16, 1945, *available at* http://portal.unesco.org (last visited Mar. 25, 2020) [hereinafter "UNESCO Constitution"].

59 African-Asian Rural Development Organization Declaration preamb., Mar. 6, 2012, *available at* http://aardo.org (last visited Mar. 25, 2020) [hereinafter "AARDO Declaration"].

60 *See id.*, art. 1.2(a)–(d). A subsequent point affirms that the Union "shares the objectives of the United Nations, supports its efforts and works in close cooperation with it." *Id.*, art. 1.3.

61 As Chapter 5 discusses in more detail, customs and *jus cogens* in a way define international law, including the law binding international organizations' formation and conduct. However, a number of researchers have argued that human rights represents the one area where treaties have tried to actively change – rather than simply codify – existing practice. For one such analysis, *see* Ryan Goodman & Derek Jinks, "How to Influence States: Socialization and International Human Rights Law," 54 *Duke L.J.* 621 (2005).

"the Union is founded on the values of respect for ... human rights, including the rights of persons belonging to minorities."[62] The World Tourism Organization's constitution focuses on "universal respect for, and observance of human rights and fundamental freedoms for all."[63] The Southern African Development Community's constitution lists human rights among its eleven principles and values.[64] The European Court of Human Rights upholds human rights and freedoms as "the foundation of justice and peace in the world."[65] Even the World Bank and IMF have their own human rights obligations.[66] Therefore, no matter the type of organization, the respect for human rights seems a constant principle in the constitution.[67]

The promotion of human rights seems to hold a special place among international organizations' principles.[68] For some authors, human rights have taken center stage due to *jus gentium* or *jus cogens* of states and international organizations assigning these rights such a primordial role in international law.[69] For others, human rights represent the ultimate

---

62 See "Treaty of the Functioning of the EU," *supra* Chapter 3, note 78, art. 1(a). As the Treaty of Lisbon further notes, "The Union recognises the rights, freedoms and principles set out in the Charter of Fundamental Rights of the European Union of 7 December 2000 ... which shall have the same legal value as the Treaties." *Id.*, art. 6(1). Like the UN, the EU backed up its constitutional affirmation of human rights with significant lawmaking. See Sionaidh Douglas-Scott, "The European Union and Human Rights after the Treaty of Lisbon," 11 *Human Rights L. Review* 645 (2011).
63 "UNWTO Statute," *supra* this chapter, note 40, art. 3(1).
64 See "SADC Treaty," *supra* Chapter 3, note 112, art. 4(c).
65 European Convention on Human Rights preamb. ¶ 5, Nov. 4, 1950, 213 UNTS 221 [hereinafter "ECHR"].
66 See generally Sigrun Skogly, *Human Rights Obligations of the World Bank and the IMF* (2012).
67 The widespread nature of these provisions may suggest they represent what Hafner-Burton and Tsutsui call "empty promises." Emilie M. Hafner-Burton & Kiyoteru Tsutsui, "Human Rights in a Globalizing World: The Paradox of Empty Promises," 110 *Am. J. Socio.* 1373 (2005). Such language represents "window dressing" or language that constitutions should have in order to promote their legitimacy, but do not represent actual obligations to the organization. *Id.*
68 Researchers have a penchant for getting lost in taxonomies and ratings of principles underpinning these kinds of constitutions. This book argues for human rights as a *summum bonum*, not based solely on the analysis of the international organizations' constitutions, but from others in combination with the frequent mention of these rights in these constitutions. For a more detailed discussion of rights in the "hierarchy of principles," see Bogdandy, *supra* Chapter 3, note 10, at 727.
69 In other words, human rights sit at an apex of principles guiding the work and objectives of international organizations because we have deemed them to, rather than from any inherent primacy based on philosophical first principles. See Daugirdas, *supra* Chapter 3, note 11, at 325.

"collective good," which only international organizations can help to provide across borders.[70] For authors like Eyal Benvenisti and Alon Harel, if "the overriding power of constitutional law stems from its promise to individuals of being the masters of their destiny," and the "overriding power of international law is based on the importance of the state's publicly recognized duty to protect individual rights," then *by implication* international organizations must have the primary duty to uphold human rights.[71]

Why is it difficult to treat human rights like equality, autonomy or the other values cited in Chapter 2? First, the universal acceptance of such a principle makes comparison between organizations difficult. If every organization pays homage to human rights, then how is it possible to look for significant differences in principles between organizations?[72] Second, as a core principle in domestic – rather than international, universal – law, such a principle seems better placed in a study of domestic law.[73] Third, the term "human rights" evokes something controversial and even indefinable in international law. Some researchers think human rights consist of principles defined in custom, ignoring the millions of differing customs adopted by groupings of individuals worldwide.[74] The UN's *de facto* power to define human rights raises serious concerns about the politicization and true

---

70 *See* Olivier De Schutter, "Human Rights and the Rise of International Organizations: The Logic of Sliding Scales in the Law of International Responsibility," *in Accountability for Human Rights Violations by International Organizations* 55 (Jan Wouters & Eva Brems eds. 2011).
71 *See* Eyal Benvenisti & Alon Harel, "Embracing the Tension between National and International Human Rights Law: The Case for Discordant Parity," 15 *Int'l J. of Constit. L.* 36 (2017).
72 See Hafner-Burton & Tsutsui, *supra* this chapter, note 67, at 1373 (providing an analysis of such references as empty promises). Some authors have tried to create hierarchies among the principles contained usually in human rights law. For another example of this misguided approach, *see* Theodor Meron, "On a Hierarchy of International Human Rights," 80 *Am. J. Int'l Law* 1 (1986).
73 Naturally, such a position has its proponents and opponents. Neuman offers a balanced view of the import of human rights conventions' provisions into domestic constitutions through ratification, though without dissonance with local municipal jurisprudential traditions. *See* Gerald Neuman, "Human Rights and Constitutional Rights: Harmony and Dissonance," 55 *Stan. L. Rev.* 1863 (2003). Just like some authors view such provisions as window dressing at the international law level, others see them as constitutional window dressing. *See* Linda Camp Keith, "Constitutional Provisions for Individual Human Rights (1977–1996): Are They More than Mere 'Window Dressing?'," 55 *Pol. Res. Q.* 111 (2002).
74 For a headlong dive into such spurious reasoning, *see* Theodor Meron, *Human Rights and Humanitarian Norms as Customary Law* (1989).

existential, ontological existence of such terms.[75] Concerns like these likely explain why human rights principles do not appear on most researchers' lists of principles underpinning international organizations' constitutions.

Equality as an illustration of principles versus values

Equality in perspective

Many, if not most, international organizations' constitutions contain some mention of the principle of equality. From Africa alone, constitutions from a wide range of types of international organizations such as the Advisory Centre on WTO Law, the African Intellectual Property Organization, the Africa Rice Center, the African Civil Aviation Commission, the African Telecommunications Union, the African Development Bank and the African Export Import Bank mention equality. Truly global organizations include organizations as diverse as the International Bureau of Weights and Measures, the Intergovernmental Organisation for International Carriage by Rail, the International Finance Corporation, the International Fund for Agricultural Development and the IMF, representing just some examples of organizations whose constitutions mention equality. However, each organization's constitution imbues a different meaning to equality. Some value equality between persons, others between groups (like groups differing in gender) and nations, and most of these constitutions place equality in the context of other principles.

The principle of equality rarely, if ever, appears alone as a mover of international organizations law. In the Association of Caribbean States' constitution equality, and specifically equality of opportunity, joins a set of instrumental values such as "democracy, rule of law, respect for the sovereignty, territorial integrity of states and the right to self-determination of peoples," as well as "respect for human rights."[76] From its place in this list, the constitution's drafters probably intended such equality of opportunity to represent an instrumental, rather than final, value. In contrast, the

---

75 *See* Philip Alston, "Conjuring Up New Human Rights: A Proposal for Quality Control," 78 *Am. J. Int'l L.* 607 (1984).
76 Convention Establishing the Association of Caribbean States preamb., July 24, 1994, *available at* www.acs-aec.org (last visited Mar. 25, 2020) [hereinafter "ACS Convention"]. The Caribbean's unique history makes equality particularly important as a driver of international organization design and behavior. For the motivations and ways these organizations tackle the multiple conceptions of equality and the way such equality supports other principles, *see* Bob Reinalda, *Routledge History of International Organizations: From 1815 to the Present Day* (2009).

Jurisprudence of aspirational values 175

drafters of the Organisation for Islamic Cooperation's constitution probably intended equality as a final principle, although one among many.[77] The Commonwealth Secretariat's Declaration stresses equal rights rather than opportunities and the right to freely participate in political institutions.[78] As such, the term "equality" can mean many things to many organizations.[79]

Many authors of textbooks on international organizations law acknowledge the importance of equality as a value in international organizations' constitutions.[80] However, what a jurist means by "equality" can differ significantly, depending on whether the constitution refers to equality among the organization's member states' citizens (and the persons whom the organization ostensibly serves), equality within the organization, equality in staff hiring or equality in voting powers.[81] Looking specifically at the EU, authors like Trevor Hartley describe in detail the principle of equality as exhibited in the EU as equality of Commission bodies, between states

---

77 Of course, even a close reading of the constitution makes discerning the drafter's intention difficult. Nevertheless, in this case, the drafters defined the equality as one of "the lofty Islamic values of peace, compassion, tolerance, equality, justice and human dignity." "OIC Charter," *supra* this chapter, note 13, preamb.

78 "Commonwealth Secretariat Memorandum," *supra* this chapter, note 32, preamb. (specifically noting that the signatories "are committed to the principles of human dignity and equality"). For the Commonwealth, members can find such equality in individual liberty and agency: "We believe in the liberty of the individual, in equal rights for all citizens regardless of race, colour, creed or political belief, and in their inalienable right to participate by means of free and democratic political processes in framing the society in which they live. We therefore strive to promote in each of our countries those representative institutions and guarantees for personal freedom under the law that are our common heritage." *Id.*

79 This book ignores the issue of equality as a means towards democracy, and so it also ignores legal researchers who argue for equality as a means towards the democratic governance of international organizations. Such a topic would require a whole book on its own. For more on this thorny topic, *see* Bohman, *supra* Chapter 1, note 3, at 499.

80 For example, Amerasinghe addresses the principle of equality in his more general discussion of conflict between general principles of (international organizational) law and written regulations. See Amerasinghe, *supra* Chapter 1, note 9, at 295. In his example, the principle of equality has taken precedence over written rules, thus confirming the importance of principles we analyze as a more reliable basis for international organization rulemaking than simple codification. *See id.*

81 For example, Klabbers refers almost exclusively to equality between member states and refers to cases dealing with such equality. See Klabbers, *supra* Chapter 3, note 36, at 211. Klabbers specifically argues that "the UN is based on the sovereign equality of its members" although "[o]n the other hand, in real life states are of course unequal" and "[t]o insist on their equality is to neglect politics, and neglecting politics is usually something that one does only at one's peril." *Id.*

and between individuals before the law.[82] Why do organizations "need to make sure that different regions are adequately represented" within their staff, as Klabbers asserts?[83] For most of the authors reviewed in this book, the answer to questions like these comes from their understanding of equality. In this case, Klabbers argues for having such representation as a way to bolster an organization's legitimacy.[84] If international organizations exist in service to their members, then clearly equality in a context like this stems from aspirations for representativeness and efficiency. As such, the context and relationship between principles "constructs" their juridical meaning.[85]

Equality in rights, opportunity and gender between persons as condition or goal?

The UN Charter's phrasing sets the scene for any legal analysis of equality between persons. Accordingly, the organization requires "universal respect for, and observance of, human rights and fundamental freedoms for all without distinction as to race, sex, language, or religion."[86] In this phrasing, equality then consists of any policy, action or attribution – for all, without distinction – and in promotion of racial, gender, linguistic and religious equality. Therefore, the UN Charter requires the organization to work "based on respect for the principle of equal rights and self-determination of peoples."[87] However, the European Investment Bank sees equality "in all its activities, the Union shall observe the principle of the equality of its citizens, who shall receive equal attention from its institutions, bodies, offices and agencies."[88] Do the "equal rights ... of peoples" represent a condition in support of other principles, like fundamental freedoms? Alternatively, do they represent a value in themselves? For some academics, the point is moot. For some, treaties constrain expectations and serve as

---

82 *See* Trevor Hartley, *European Union Law in a Global Context: Text, Cases and Materials* 9, 25, 274 (2004).
83 *See* Klabbers, *supra* Chapter 3, note 36, at 78.
84 *See id.*
85 While most scholarship on arguments or interpretative "construction" focuses on contracts, the principles behind international organizations, as contracts, clearly shows how principles – like progress – obtain their legal meaning in international judicial fora, civil service adjudication and other areas of international organizations law. *See* Altwicker & Diggelmann, *supra* this chapter, note 38, at 425.
86 The Charter includes protection for gender equality in its preamble and in Article 55(c).
87 UN Charter, *supra* Chapter 1, note 7, art. 55.
88 Statute of the European Investment Bank art. 9, July 1, 2013, *available at* www.eib.org (last visited Mar. 25, 2020).

large, incarnate declarations of their member states' intent.[89] Arguing about their role in naming and shaming or otherwise monitoring or enforcing these rights misses the point.[90] Perhaps principles like equality, too broadly defined, hardly represent effective principles at all.[91]

Acknowledging the definitional and practical problems inherent in simply upholding the broad principle of "equality," the constitutions of organizations like the Association of Caribbean States and the International Civil Aviation Organisation aspire toward the *equality of opportunity*.[92] In the Association of Caribbean States' case, the "equality of opportunity" focuses on the goal of "strengthening the friendly relations among the peoples of the Caribbean," itself a goal reflecting equality.[93] As for the International Civil Aviation Organisation, such equality of opportunity deals with service provision, in that "international air transport services may be established on the basis of equality of opportunity and operated soundly and economically."[94] The ILO

---

89 For Simmons, treaties creating international organizations provide "screens" by which a sovereign entity declares its intentions. *See* Beth Simmons, *Mobilizing for Human Rights: International Law in Domestic Politics* (2009). Completely ignoring politics or stratagem involved in international diplomacy, Simmons sees the constitutions as a reflection of member states' credible commitment to the principles contained in such constitutions. *Id.*

90 For traditional legal researchers, organizations endowed with rights, obligations and competencies should (at least try to) enforce them. Authors like Hafner-Burton would thus strongly disagree with the "organization as intent" approach that Simmons takes up. *See* Emilie Hafner-Burton, "Sticks and Stones: Naming and Shaming the Human Rights Enforcement Problem," 62 *Int'l Org.* 689 (2008).

91 At the domestic constitutional level, such a lack of definition has led to the unsatisfactory decision to "level down" (or apply rights of the most disadvantaged group to/for all groups). Such a least common denominator approach can hardly work in an international system with as many "denominators" as states. *See* Deborah Brake, "When Equality Leaves Everyone Worse Off: The Problem of Leveling down in Equality Law," 46 *Wm. & Mary L. Rev.* 513 (2005).

92 This book only describes the problems inherent in working with various notions of equality in these international organizations' constitutions. It does not try to solve these problems. Such a problem worsens when one considers the changing understanding of equality over time. For a description of how this problem has affected constitutional law, *see* William Nelson, "The Changing Meaning of Equality in Twentieth-Century Constitutional Law," 52 *Wash. & Lee L. Rev.* 3 (1995).

93 *See* "ACS Convention," *supra* this chapter, note 76, preamb. The "friendly" in "friendly relations" probably presupposes enough equality to keep such relations friendly. Naturally, nothing in the jurisprudence of international organizations law even hints at a way of constructing a legal test or rights/obligations around the notion of "friendly relations."

94 Convention on International Civil Aviation preamb., Dec. 7, 1944, *available at* www.icao.int (last visited Mar. 25, 2020).

also connects equal opportunity and access to education with economic security, as "all human beings, irrespective of race, creed or sex, have the right to pursue both their material well-being and their spiritual development in conditions of freedom and dignity, of economic security and *equal opportunity*."[95] In addition, the ILO's programs aim to provide "the assurance of equality of educational and vocational opportunity."[96] The rest of the ILO Charter focuses on protecting workers' rights of equal pay for equal work.

Why should international organizations make such equality a primary principle? Most researchers view equality as an instrumental value for achieving greater justice. One argument holds that international organizations *owe* their effort to bring about such equality of opportunity in order to promote justice worldwide.[97] Another argument notes that equality of opportunity helps to right the wrongs concomitant with concentrated power, allowing just principles of the international organizations to form organically, rather than by *diktat*.[98] Equality of opportunity provides the capacity for citizens and their organized representations, like states and international organizations, to advocate for their desired "final" or most just principles and values. If international organizations hope to promote justice, and justice relies on just representation of all individuals affected by international organizations, these organizations must give active expression through voting, hiring and other policies aimed at promoting such equality of opportunity.[99]

Other constitutions place value on other types of equality. For example, the International Telecommunication Union affords equal opportunity protections to "youth(s), persons with disabilities [and those from] rural" areas, besides gender equality.[100] Some of these types of equality cover indigenous peoples, migrants, minorities, people with disabilities and women, as well as racial and religious discrimination, *inter alia*.[101] The Eurasian Economic

---

95 "ILO Constitution," *supra* Chapter 3, note 56, annex at (a) (emphasis added).
96 *Id.* at (j).
97 *See, e.g.*, Stephen Macedo, "What Self-Governing Peoples Owe to One Another: Universalism, Diversity, and the Law of Peoples," 72 *Fordham L. Rev.* 1721 (2004).
98 *See* Thomas Nagel, "The Problem of Global Justice," 33 *Philo. & Pub. Affairs* 113 (2005).
99 *See* Drude Dahlerup, "Electoral Gender Quotas: Between Equality of Opportunity and Equality of Result," 43 *Representation* 73 (2007).
100 Constitution of International Telecommunication Union preamb., May 17, 1865 (amended 1994, 1998, 2002, and 2006), *available at* www.itu.int (last visited Mar. 25, 2020) [hereinafter "ITU Constitution"].
101 For the complete list and the legal instruments referred to promising these types of equality, *see* Li Weiwei, "Equality and Non-Discrimination Under International Human Rights Law," Nor. Ctr. Human Rights Res. Notes 03/2004 (2004), *available at* www.corteidh.or.cr (last visited Mar. 25, 2020).

Jurisprudence of aspirational values 179

Community's mission statement refers to the creation of "equal conditions for production and entrepreneurial activities," "creating equal conditions for access by foreign investment," for business operations and citizens' rights to "education."[102] In some cases, equality complements related principles like equity. The Commonwealth Secretariat's constitution – expanding the UN's principles – affirms the value of equity, rather than equality.[103] While equity has firmer legal foundations from its ample application in common law legal systems, the role of international bodies in achieving such equity remains contentious.[104] Nevertheless, the most cited type of equality consists of gender equality.

Gender equality has remained an important value for international organizations since their modern formation in the twentieth century.[105] For example, the African Union places the "promotion of gender equality" as one of its defining principles.[106] The East African Community's constitution lists gender equality as a "fundamental principle of the community."[107] However, most organizations follow a tack similar to the UN's in defining gender equality as a condition or basic requirement for the achievement of other principles and goals. For example, UNESCO's constitution aims "to contribute to peace and security ... without distinction of race, *sex*, language or religion."[108] Including gender in a catch-phrase consisting of other potentially divisive characteristics defining the "peoples" the UN serves represents probably the most common, and least committal, approach to promoting such rights.[109]

---

102 Treaty on the Eurasian Economic Union preamb., May 29, 2014, *available at* www.un.org/en/ga/sixth/70/docs/treaty_on_eeu.pdf (last visited Mar. 25, 2020)
103 "Commonwealth Secretariat Memorandum," *supra* this chapter, note 32, preamb.
104 *See* S. Chattopadhyay, "Equity in International Law: Its Growth and Development," 5 *Ga. J. of Int'l & Comp. L.* 382 (1975).
105 Gender issues featured prominently in the League of Nations and the 1919 Paris Peace Conference. See Hilkka Pietila, *Engendering the Global Agenda: The Story of Women and the United Nations, UN Non-Government Liaison Service* (2002).
106 Constitutive Act of the African Union art. 4, July 11, 2001, *available at* www.au.int (last visited Mar. 25, 2020) [hereinafter "AU Constitution"].
107 Protocol on the Establishment of the East African Customs Union art. 6, Mar. 2, 2004, *available at* www.eac.int (last visited Mar. 25, 2020) [hereinafter "EAC Constitution"].
108 "UNESCO Constitution," *supra* this chapter, note 58, art. 1 (emphasis added).
109 Howland makes a persuasive case for including these ways of dividing people together in one list. For example, religious differences may exacerbate (or even define) gender-based discrimination. *See* Courtney Howland, "Challenge of Religious Fundamentalism to the Liberty and Equality Rights of Women: An Analysis under the United Nations Charter," 35 *Col. J. Transnat'l L.* 271 (1997).

At the other end of the spectrum, some international organizations' constitutions provide significant details related to the organization's duties to promote gender equality. The African-Asian Rural Development Organization's constitution notes that "by ensuring that gender equality principles get mainstreamed into the national development agenda and gender sensitization is carried out at all levels."[110] The East African Community's constitution gives the body a far more comprehensive, and detailed, competence to work towards gender equality than most other international organizations. In particular, the Community's member states vow to adopt legislation and similar measures that do the following:

(a) promote the empowerment and effective integration and participation of women at all levels of socioeconomic development especially in decision-making;
(b) abolish legislation and discourage customs that are discriminatory against women;
(c) promote effective education awareness programmes aimed at changing negative attitudes towards women;
(d) create or adopt technologies which will ensure the stability of employment and professional progress for women workers; and
(e) take such other measures that shall eliminate prejudices against women and promote the equality of the female gender with that of the male gender in every respect.[111]

Nevertheless, the proposal of gender equality laws and protocols for the Community clearly shows that these constitutional provisions remain unimplemented.[112] The actual results on the ground of such equality remain mixed.[113]

---

110 The 2012 amendment to its declaration added statements on women becoming "equal partners in development" and the broader goal of "ensur[ing] gender equality in all spheres of life." "AARDO Declaration," *supra* this chapter, note 59, preamb.
111 "EAC Constitution," *supra* this chapter, note 107, art. 121.
112 *See* The East African Community Gender Equality and Development Bill (2016), available at www.eala.org/documents/view/the-east-african-community-gender-equality-and-development-bill2016 (last visited Mar. 25, 2020); Protocol on the Establishment of the East African Community Protocol on Gender Equality, available at www.eassi.org/wp-content/uploads/2018/08/draft-eac-protocol-on-gender-equality.pdf (last visited Mar. 25, 2020).
113 See Nursel Aydiner-Avsar et al., "East African Community Regional Integration: Trade and Gender Implications," UNCTAD/DITC/2017/2 (2017) (providing statistics and results); Marren Akatsa-Bukach, "The EAC Gender Equality and Development Pilot Barometer" (2017), available at https://tgnp.org/wp-content/uploads/2017/09/The-East-Africa-Gender-Equality-and-Development-PILOT-BAROMETER.pdf (last visited Mar. 25, 2020).

Other international organizations' constitutions go into even more additional depth. As already explained, the African-Asian Rural Development Organization's Declaration stresses gender equality, but it sees equal access to resources as the way of achieving such equality. Therefore, the Organization and its members "pledge to take measures that would ensure that rural women are accorded *full and equal access to* and *control over* land and other productive resources including credit, technologies, market and other services."[114] However, for many international organizations, their support consists of unhelpful cheerleading guides, rather than resources or legal changes, which seem to point to a lack of genuine desire to give women legal or property rights.[115]

Researchers have noted organizations' lack of genuine engagement with the principle of gender equality as a justification for them to hold up such equality as a key principle. International organizations still treat gender as something to mainstream, or as just another attribute of project and human resource management, in the same way that environmental policy has been mainstreamed.[116] As Olga Avdeyeva finds for the EU, gender policy depends far more on local politics than on international organizations' admonitions.[117] Other authors question the line between norms promoted by international organizations and underlying deep values guiding the organization, and thus the rules comprising the firmament of international organizations law.[118]

Recent work also shows how such an approach to gender equality brings such change directly into conflict with other principles and values, such as sovereign self-determination. According to some commentators,

---

114 "AARDO Declaration," *supra* this chapter, note 59, preamb. (emphasis added). Highlighting its role in mitigating "the adverse impact of gender inequality on the economic growth of Afro-Asian region and the disproportionate burden of poverty on women," the AARDO sees its role as to "strive to adopt measures to reduce workload on women and drudgery, expand gainful employment opportunities for women and ensure equal pay for work of equal value." *Id.*, paras. 6–7.

115 *See* Elizabeth King & Andrew Mason, *Engendering Development: Through Gender Equality in Rights, Resources, and Voice* (2001).

116 *See* Maitrayee Mukhopadhyay, "Mainstreaming Gender or 'Streaming' Gender Away: Feminists Marooned in the Development Business," *in The Palgrave Handbook of Gender and Development* ch. 4 (Wendy Harcourt ed. 2016).

117 *See* Olga Avdeyeva, "States' Compliance with International Requirements Gender Equality in EU Enlargement Countries," 63 *Pol. Res. Q.* 203 (2008).

118 For example, Krook and True argue that norms of gender equality shifted and changed during the 1990s, representing values adopted by the organizations, rather than values making up a part of its DNA. *See* Krook & True, *supra* Chapter 1, note 121, at 103.

the Millennium Development Goals show just how the UN tries to impose standards, even when they are supposedly mutually agreed standards.[119] Views like these note that such standards, particularly in the Middle East, represent oft-unwanted values in many jurisdictions where international organizations try to encourage them.[120] International organizations trying to provide women with access to resources supposedly engage in something far more intrusive than mere bureaucratic action at a distance.[121] Such work influences politics of the most primordial (and hidden) kind.[122] No one would argue *against* such equality. Nevertheless, systems and people continue to uphold a status quo that denies women access to many resources and opportunities.[123] Even the mere term "gender equality" itself has become the subject of intense political disagreement and dispute.[124]

Equality as respect for sovereign autonomy

Behind every constitution's appeal for equality between states lies the principle of state sovereignty. According to the standard formula, state

---

119 *See* Gita Sen & Avanti Mukherjee, "No Empowerment without Rights, No Rights without Politics: Gender-Equality, MDGs and the Post-2015 Development Agenda," 15 *J. Human Dev. & Capabilities* 188 (2014).

120 *See* Beverly Metcalfe, "Women, Empowerment and Development in Arab Gulf States: A Critical Appraisal of Governance, Culture and National Human Resource Development (HRD) Frameworks," 14 *H.R. Dev. Int'l* 131 (2011).

121 *See* Valeria Esquivel, "Power and the Sustainable Development Goals: A Feminist Analysis," 24 *Gender & Dev.* 9 (2016).

122 Often these influences come from NGOs or other foreign entities. *See* Jutta Joachim, "Framing Issues and Seizing Opportunities: The UN, NGOs, and Women's Rights," 47 *Int'l Stud. Q.* 247 (2003).

123 Such gender biases have plagued international organizations for decades. For the history of political contestation around international organizations like the ILO, *see* Susan Zimmermann, "Equality of Women's Economic Status? A Major Bone of Contention in the International Gender Politics Emerging during the Interwar Period," *Int'l Hist. Rev.*, Nov. 15, 2017; Naila Kabeer, "Tracking the Gender Politics of the Millennium Development Goals: Struggles for Interpretive Power in the International Development Agenda," 36 *Third World Q.* 377 (2015).

124 In other words, the politics does not deal with the politics between women and men, or between institutions supporting each gender's interests. Instead, these politics deal with the interests that various groups have in defining the term "gender equality" and using it in popular discourse as well as in law. *See* Vlasta Jalusic, "Stretching and Bending the Meanings of Gender in Equality Policies," *in* The *Discursive Politics of Gender Equality: Stretching, Bending and Policymaking* 79 (Emanuela Lombardo et al. eds. 2009).

sovereignty plus autonomy (independence) equals equality.[125] As Michael Fowler and Julie Bunck note, "Sovereignty is a declaration of political responsibility for governing, defending, and promoting the welfare of a human community."[126] With this stylizing in mind, international organizations cannot be sovereign, and so they cannot legitimately represent or promulgate any values or principles. Nevertheless, they can promulgate ideas and adopt policies that aim to protect such sovereignty.

How do international organizations' constitutions view equality through the lens of equality between states? The Agency for the Prohibition of Nuclear Weapons in Latin America and the Caribbean (or OPANAL, taking the letters from its name in Spanish) bases its work "on the sovereign equality of States, mutual respect and good neighborliness."[127] Many authors see the protection of sovereignty underpinned by the OPANAL as the basis for achieving "utopian ideals."[128] Others view international organizations helping to protect sovereignty as "taking" part of that sovereignty for themselves.[129] If true, sovereignty would represent one of the only values enabling the autonomy of international organizations. Therefore, the autonomy described in this book derives from the delegation of sovereignty to international bodies with the ironic goal of protecting states' sovereignty.[130]

Other constitutions also directly reference equality between sovereign entities. The African Intellectual Property Organization, the African Union, the Association of Southeast Asian Nations and the Caribbean Community for Crime and Security's Implementation Agency for Crime and Security also reference "the principle of sovereign equality."[131] For organizations

---

125 While Kelsen's post-war cohort of researchers intensely debated such equality between sovereigns as the basis of international organizations law, few researchers consider the topic today. See Kelsen, *supra* Chapter 2, note 17, at 207. Since the end of the Cold War, most work on sovereignty has focused on power relations, rather than any prima facie right that states have to equal treatment, as they have nothing to be treated equally about.
126 Michael Ross Fowler & Julie Marie Bunck, *Law, Power, and the Sovereign State: The Evolution and Application of the Concept of Sovereignty* 12 (1995).
127 Good neighborliness is not defined in law.
128 Ryan Musto, "'A Desire so Close to the Hearts of all Latin Americans': Utopian Ideals and Imperfections behind Latin America's Nuclear Weapon Free Zone," 37 *Bull. Latin Amer. Res.* 160 (2017).
129 Geoffrey Cockerham, "The Delegation of Dispute Settlement Authority to Conventional International Governmental Organizations," 44 *Int'l Pol.* 732 (2007).
130 Clearly any discussion of an international organization's autonomy cannot exclude the autonomy of its member states, namely their sovereignty. See d'Aspremont, *supra* Chapter 3, note 123, at 63.
131 See, e.g., Agreement Revising the Bangui Agreement of March 2, 1977, on the Creation of an African Intellectual Property Organization art. 21(1), Feb. 24, 1999,

like the South Asian Association for Regional Cooperation, intermediary values like "peace, stability, amity and progress" serve to bring about the "principles of sovereign equality, territorial integrity, national independence, non-use of force and non-interference in the internal affairs of other States and peaceful settlement of all disputes."[132] Constitutions like these directly cite sovereign equality as a principal objective. On the other hand, for the UNIDO, such equality serves several instrumental purposes, as such equality seeks "to promote the common welfare of their peoples … on the basis of *sovereign equality, strengthening of the economic independence of the developing countries, securing their equitable share in total world industrial production and contributing to … the prosperity of all nations.*"[133]

Other constitutions tend to see such equality in more indirect terms. For the Economic Community of Central African States, such equality represents one of the "principles of international law governing relationships between States" and consists of "the principles of sovereignty, equality and independence of all States, non-interference in their internal affairs and the principle of the rule of law in their mutual relations."[134] Such a view of sovereign equality then translates roughly as autonomy, which is one of the values Chapter 2 analyzed closely. The Gambia River Basin Development Organization's constitution views sovereign equality as the "equal treatment of member states."[135] However, in the case of the UN, such equality consists of the "principle of equal rights and self-determination of peoples," with the plural "peoples" thus denoting equality between groups rather than individual members of those groups.[136]

Why do different constitutions view equality – and even sovereign equality – so differently? Studies like this one have only started to unpack the meanings behind the principles driving international organizations. In one study, the authors conclude the following:

---

available at www.oapi.wipo.net/doc/en/bangui_agreement.pdf (last visited Mar. 25, 2020).
132 "SAARC Charter," *supra* this chapter, note 15, art. 1.
133 "UNIDO Constitution," *supra* this chapter, note 30, preamb. (emphasis added). Notice how the other objectives in italics repeat, and clarify in some ways, the notion of equality originally mentioned at the start of the italicized list.
134 Economic Community of Central African States Charter preamb., Oct. 18, 1983, *available at* www.ceeac-eccas.org (last visited Mar. 25, 2020).
135 Gambia River Basin Development Organization Charter preamb., 1978, *available at* www.sec.gouv.sn/integration/omvg.html (last visited Mar. 25, 2020).
136 UN Charter, *supra* Chapter 1, note 7, art. 1(2) (the goal of such equality focusing on "friendly relations among nations" and "universal peace"). Article 55 further requires members to engage in development, based on "the principle of equal rights and self-determination of peoples." *Id.*, art. 55.

[E]conomic interdependence and the passage of time are important explanatory variables for predicting independence, implying that institutions are both functional and evolving. By contrast, the concentration of power within a region and the number and heterogeneity of member states do not provide much explanatory leverage, defying prominent theoretical arguments in the literature.[137]

In other words, structuralist explanations fail to explain these differences far more than one might expect. The subjective, *emic* view of these principles holds just as much explanatory power as the *etic* approach.[138]

Internal equality

What about equality within international organizations themselves? The UN's own hiring rules often set the stage for equality in staffing within the international organizations. Its Charter requires that "the United Nations shall place no restrictions on the eligibility of men and women to participate in any capacity and under conditions of equality in its principal and subsidiary organs."[139] Academic jurists highlight in almost every textbook on international organizations law the extent to which international organizations' constitutions and subsidiary rulemaking place great emphasis on gender equality.[140] However, as authors like Caroline Moser and Annalise Moser note, implementation of these lofty principles remains far from perfect.[141]

As with the UN, many international organizations try to apply the principle of equality within their own operating rules as much as they try to inspire such equality in their member states. The EU's constitution provides the most comprehensive example, by including provisions to combat gender discrimination, particularly in the area of equal pay for equal

---

137 Yoram Haftel & Alexander Thompson, "The Independence of International Organizations: Concept and Applications," 50 *J. Conflict Res.* 253 (2006).
138 *See* Michael W. Morris et al., "Views from Inside and Outside: Integrating EMIC and ETIC Insights about Culture and Justice Judgment," 24 *Acad. Man. Rev.* 781 (1999).
139 UN Charter, *supra* Chapter 1, note 7, art. 8.
140 To take one example, Schermers and Blokker describe rules to ensure equality of treatment of international organization staff. *See* Henry G. Schermers & Niels M. Blokker, *International Institutional Law: Unity Within Diversity* (5th rev. ed. 2011).
141 *See* Caroline Moser & Annalise Moser, "Gender Mainstreaming Since Beijing: A Review of Success and Limitations in International Institutions," 13 *Gender & Dev.* 11 (2005).

work.[142] In other areas, the Treaty of Lisbon requires that "in defining and implementing its policies and activities, the Union shall aim to combat discrimination based on sex, racial or ethnic origin, religion or belief, disability, age or sexual orientation."[143] The constitution also provides the legal basis for combating discrimination based on sex, racial or ethnic origin, religion or belief, disability, age or sexual orientation.[144] The constitution also gives effect to the Charter of Fundamental Rights of the European Union, which guarantees equal rights between the sexes.[145] These rules, while focusing outside of the Union's administrative bodies like the Council or Commission, nonetheless apply just as much inside the organization.[146]

The international judicial institutions provide one example of how rules around *representation* best seek to achieve member states' or other parties' equality. The Benelux Court of Justice requires equal numbers of appointments of deputy councilors, the judges, the deputy judges, the Advocates-General and Deputy Advocates-General from the three member countries.[147] The European Court of Human Rights' constitution includes similar strictures on the number of judges coming from member states – one per member state.[148] As for the ICC, each state may nominate judges, ensuring, at least in theory, at least nominal representation from each member state.[149] As such, provisions about representation serve the principle of equality.[150]

Nevertheless, the sheer variety of contexts in which equality crops up in these constitutions shows the wide margin for this principle's interpretation.

---

142 See "Treaty on the Functioning of the EU," *supra* Chapter 3, note 78, art. 157.
143 *Id.*, art. 10.
144 *See id.*, art. 19.
145 *See id.*, art. 6. *See also* Charter of Fundamental Rights of the European Union arts. 21 & 23, 2000 O.J. (C 364) 18.
146 Indeed, the internal adoption of such norms of equality serves as a role model for member states. For a wider discussion, *see* Fiona Beveridge, "'Going Soft'? Analysing the Contribution of Soft and Hard Measures in EU Gender Law and Policy," *in The Europeanization of Gender Equality Policies* 28 (Emanuela Lombardo & Maxime Forest eds. 2012).
147 *See* "Benelux Court of Justice," *supra* Chapter 3, note 64, art. 3(2).
148 *See* "ECHR," *supra* this chapter, note 65, art. 20 ("The Court shall consist of a number of judges equal to that of the High Contracting Parties.").
149 *See* "Rome Statute," *supra* Chapter 3, note 72, art. 36(3)–(4).
150 Analysis of the reliance of some principles (like equality) on others (like representation) has a long history. The "tracks" (or groups and networks) this book has found thus represent a later example of this thinking. For an early analysis of the joint appearance of these principles in international organizations' constitutions, *see* S.W. Armstrong, "The Doctrine of the Equality of Nations in International Law and the Relation of the Doctrine to the Treaty of Versailles," 14 *Am. J. Int'l L.* 540 (1920).

Jurisprudence of aspirational values

In the case of the African Intellectual Property Organization, the International Bureau of Weights and Measures, the Caribbean Community and the European Organisation for the Safety of Air Navigation, equality pertains to financial contributions as well as the equal distribution of budgets and surpluses. In translation, the Benelux Organization for Intellectual Property, the European Organisation for Astronomical Research in the Southern Hemisphere, the European Patent Office, the European Space Agency and the World Bank all refer to the *equal authenticity* of linguistic translations of their constitutions, which represents an attempt to treat each language equally. Finally, for organizations like the Benelux Court of Justice, the "Court's task is to promote equality in the application of legal rules that are common to the Benelux countries."[151] The ICC addresses equality in three ways – equality before the law (even for public officials), equality of suspects in investigations and equal rights for all accused persons (whether convicted or not).[152] The clearly different contexts for invoking the principle of equality show the importance of context and understanding the deeper "track" of other principles referenced alongside equality.

However, as this book has shown throughout, understanding principles like equality relies on seeing the term in context with other principles, like peace. For example, the UN Charter proposes to "maintain international peace and security."[153] Equality serves this higher end, as actions to "develop friendly relations among nations based on respect for the principle of equal rights and self-determination of peoples" represent "appropriate measures to strengthen universal peace."[154] Any interpretation of peace, like other principles, must take place in the highly specific context of other principles.

Mixing the principle of peace with other constitutional principles

Peace in the hierarchy of organizational principles

Many international organizations' *raison d'être* seems to revolve around ensuring peace. The UN was set up "to save succeeding generations from the scourge of war, which twice in our lifetime has brought untold sorrow to mankind."[155] UN members *must* make a commitment to peace.[156] The

---

151 "Benelux Court of Justice Charter," *supra* Chapter 3, note 64, art. 1(2).
152 *See* "Rome Statute," *supra* Chapter 3, note 72, arts. 27, 54 & 67.
153 UN Charter, *supra* Chapter 1, note 7, art. 1.1.
154 *Id.*, art. 1(2).
155 UN Charter, *supra* Chapter 1, note 7, preamb.
156 *Id.*, art. 4(1).

UN Charter also provides one of the first instances of universal values applicable to all states, such that "The Organization shall ensure that states which are not Members of the United Nations act in accordance with these Principles so far as may be necessary for the maintenance of international peace and security."[157] In particular, the "General Assembly may discuss any questions relating to the maintenance of international peace and security brought before it ... by a state which is not a Member of the United Nations ... and may make recommendations with regard to any such questions to the state or states concerned or to the Security Council or to both."[158] In line with the prevailing understanding of peace as security, the UN Charter lists seven instances where the General Assembly, the Secretary General or the Security Council deliberate or act for "the maintenance of international peace and security."[159]

Both the ASEAN and Commonwealth Secretariat explicitly refer to the UN Charter as defining the central role in both organizations for keeping peace.[160] The Organization of Central American States' constitution refers to principles that have changed over time. The Central American Court of Justice, a pre-First World War institution which preceded the Organization, adjudicated "all controversies or questions why may arise among them, of whatsoever nature and no matter their origin."[161] The Organization of Central American States replaced the now defunct court, taking over much of the previous Court's mandate to promote peace.[162] Its Tegucigalpa Protocol defines the Central American Integration System, which is a

---

157 *Id.*, art. 2.6.
158 *Id.*, art. 11(2).
159 These provisions include arts. 11(1), 12(2), 18, 24(1), 26, 73 and 99. Arts. 14, 52, 54, 84 and 106 all detail the procedures involved in the UN's goal of maintaining peace and security.
160 *See* Association of Southeast Asian Nations Charter art. 28, Nov. 20, 2007, available at www.asean.org (last visited Mar. 25, 2020) [hereinafter "ASEAN Charter"] ("Unless otherwise provided for in this Charter, Member States have the right of recourse to the modes of peaceful settlement contained in Article 33(1) of the Charter of the United Nations or any other international legal instruments to which the disputing Member States are parties."); "Commonwealth Secretariat Memorandum," *supra* this chapter, note 32, preamb. ("We believe that international peace and order are essential to the security and prosperity of mankind; we therefore support the United Nations and seek to strengthen its influence for peace in the world, and its efforts to remove the causes of tension between nations").
161 "Convention for the Establishment of a Central American Court of Justice," 2 *Am. J. Int'l L* 231, 231 (1908) (providing art. 1).
162 *See* Charles Ripley, "The Central American Court of Justice (1907–1918): Rethinking the World's First Court," 19 *Dialogues* 47 (2018).

Jurisprudence of aspirational values

scheme aimed at promoting integration by adherence to common values.[163] These common values consist of "peace, freedom, democracy and development."[164] These represent principles that constitutions like the UN Charter would immediately recognize and accept.

Some international organizations' constitutions refer to peace as one value among many. For the Commonwealth Secretariat, peace and the quality of life represent the final objects for the Secretariat, which are equal in value and dignity.[165] The ILO, another pre-First World War institution, affirms that "universal and lasting peace can be established only if is based upon social justice."[166] The preamble ends with a declaration underscoring that the Organization's objectives and its members' objectives serve "justice, humanity [and] the desire to secure the permanent peace of the world."[167] Such justice, humanity and democracy, inter alia, form the basis for understanding peace in context. As Armin von Bogdandy notes, "I see a future for general principles of international public authority, less as a source of law, but as condensed comparative legal argument."[168]

The constitutions of the international organizations set up in the early part of the twentieth century provide much of the context for that comparative argument. Another look at the UN Charter sets the scene for understanding peace in the context of other values. In being open to "peace-loving" states, the organization aims to encourage two ends.[169] These ends are "to practice tolerance and live together in peace with one another as good neighbours, and to unite our strength to maintain international peace

---

163 The Organization of Central American States' constitution refers only to technical matters concerning the organization of the body. See Charter of the Organization of Central American States (ODECA), 2 I.L.M. 235 (1963); "Tegucigalpa Protocol," *supra* this chapter, note 49.

164 *See also* "Tegucigalpa Protocol," *supra* this chapter, note 49, art 3. *See also id.*, art. 4 (providing that "peace, democracy, development and freedom constitute a harmonious and indivisible whole which shall guide the acts of the States Members of the Central American Integration System" and that "legal certainty with respect to relations between the Member States and the peaceful settlement of their disputes ...").

165 *See* "Commonwealth Secretariat Memorandum," *supra* this chapter, note 32, preamb.

166 "ILO Constitution," *supra* Chapter 3, note 56, preamb.

167 *Id.*

168 Bogdandy, *supra* Chapter 3, note 10, at 1909.

169 *See* UN Charter, *supra* Chapter 1, note 7, art. 4(1) ("Membership in the United Nations is open to all other peace-loving states which accept the obligations contained in the present Charter and, in the judgment of the Organization, are able and willing to carry out these obligations."). *See generally* Fry & Chong, *supra* Chapter 1, note 101, at 138 (analyzing his provision in the context of ICJ advisory opinions).

and security" and to "employ international machinery for the promotion of the economic and social advancement of all peoples."[170] In other words, peace and prosperity go together for this particular organization.[171] Similarly with a nineteenth-century international organization, the International Telecommunication Union, that Union seeks to "facilitate peaceful relations, [as well as] international cooperation among peoples and economic and social development."[172]

The Inter-Parliamentary Union's constitution provides another example of other principles that color the way an international organization's constitution understands peace. The 130-year-old organization has the explicit mandate to "work for peace."[173] Many of the Union's members helped to negotiate the 1899 Hague Conference establishing the precursor to the Permanent Court of Arbitration.[174] The first article of that court's constitution requires that signatories "use their best efforts to ensure the pacific settlement of international differences" and "work for peace."[175] The Court specifically provides a way to ensure peace by "entering into direct communication with the Power chosen on the other side, with the object of preventing the rupture of pacific relations."[176] In case that does not work, feuding countries "are charged with the joint task of taking advantage of any opportunity to restore peace."[177] In case they forget, the organization's treaty requires that "Contracting Powers consider it their duty, if a serious dispute threatens to break out between two or more of them, to remind these latter that the Permanent Court is open to them."[178] Therefore, for

---

170 UN Charter, *supra* Chapter 1, note 7, preamb.
171 Indeed, most constitutions refer to peace in the context of promoting economic development and social development. Works like Luard's, which miss this connection, obviously fail to tell the whole story behind the motivations for – and the reasons for – peace. *See* Evan Luard, *Conflict and Peace in the Modern International System: A Study of the Principles of International Order* (1988).
172 "ITU Constitution," *supra* this chapter, note 100, preamb.
173 Inter-Parliamentary Union Statute art. 1(2), Mar. 10, 1977 (as amended Oct. 2018), *available at* www.ipu.org (last visited Mar. 25, 2020) [hereinafter "IPU Statute"]. As the next section notes, the Union achieves this, in part, by promoting "the working of representative institutions." *Id.*
174 This served as the model of the still-existing Permanent Court of Arbitration. *See* Zlatko Sabic, "Building Democratic and Responsible Global Governance: The Role of International Parliamentary Institutions," 61 *Parl. Aff.* 267 (2008).
175 Convention for the Pacific Settlement of International Disputes art. 1, July 29, 1899, 32 Stat. 1799.
176 *Id.*, arts. 1 & 8(2).
177 *Id.*
178 *Id.*, art. 48 (1).

organizations like the Inter-Parliamentary Union, peace comes from dialogue and communication, which is a principle in its own right.[179]

The ASEAN constitution sketches out peace and security obligations most clearly, requiring that ASEAN members show the following:

(a) respect for the independence, sovereignty, equality, territorial integrity and national identity of all ASEAN Member States;
(b) shared commitment and collective responsibility in enhancing regional peace, security and prosperity;
(c) renunciation of aggression and of the threat or use of force or other actions in any manner inconsistent with international law;
(d) reliance on peaceful settlement of disputes;
(e) non-interference in the internal affairs of ASEAN Member States;
(f) respect for the right of every Member State to lead its national existence free from external interference, subversion and coercion;
(g) enhanced consultations on matters seriously affecting the common interest of ASEAN;
(h) adherence to the rule of law, good governance, the principles of democracy and constitutional government.[180]

Such provisions show how tied up peace remains with autonomy and sovereignty, and thus security. Indeed, since their inception, international organizations have balanced the principle of peace with member states' needs to maintain their own security with the threat or use of force.[181] If UN peacekeepers represent a means for ensuring "collective security," the power of the "General Assembly to recommend military action does provide a potential for abuse."[182] In most constitutions, such a carrot-and-stick (or peace and security) approach comes out as concomitant commitments to peace *and* security.

---

179 Walters, albeit looking at the UN Conference on Trade and Development (UNCTAD), represents an important first step in looking at how the principle of communication could help to foster peace. *See* Robert S. Walters, "International Organizations and Political Communication: The Use of UNCTAD by Less Developed Countries," 25 *Int'l Org* 818 (1971).
180 "ASEAN Charter," *supra* this chapter, note 160, art. 2(a)–(h).
181 Indeed, peace and security always have seemed like two opposing sides of the same issue, with security intimating future, potential violence. For a discussion of the seeming contradictory norms involved in peace and security, *see* Richard Betts, "Systems for Peace or Causes of War? Collective Security, Arms Control, and the New Europe" 17 *Int'l Sec.* 5 (1992).
182 *See* White, *supra* Chapter 1, note 19, at 103 (pointing out that the UN Charter restricts the General Assembly's ability to "recommend military measures to the most flagrant violations of international peace").

In the EU's case, its Treaty of Lisbon affirms the Union's objectives as "the Union's aim is to promote *peace*, its values and the well-being of its peoples."[183] However, again the Treaty "colors" such peace by requiring that "the Union shall uphold and promote its values and interests," clearly with a stress more on security than on peace. For the EU (and other bodies, as the following section shows), security brings about peace as "[the Union] shall contribute to peace, security ... ."[184]

Peace and security through/for prosperity

Several organizations' constitutions place peace and security in the wider discourse on progress, development and prosperity. For example, the African Union acknowledges that "the scourge of conflicts in Africa constitutes a major impediment to the socio-economic development of the continent," and thus the African Union's constitution incorporates "the need to promote peace, security and stability as a prerequisite for the implementation of the African Union's development and integration agenda."[185] The Union's constitution also refers to "peace, security and stability" as well as the "peaceful co-existence of Member States and their right to live in peace and security ... the right of Member States to request intervention from the Union in order to restore peace and security."[186] ASEAN represents another international organization to juxtapose peace and security in the same breath. In its preamble, it declares "a common desire and collective will to live in a region of lasting peace, security and stability," linking such a state with "sustained economic growth, shared prosperity and social progress."[187] The very purpose of ASEAN is "to maintain and enhance peace, security and stability and further strengthen peace-oriented values in the region" and "to ensure that the peoples and Member States of ASEAN live in peace with the world at large in a just, democratic and harmonious environment."[188] In both of these organizations' interpretations, peace and security aim to achieve development and other higher principles.[189]

183 "Treaty of Lisbon," *supra* this chapter, note 27, art. I-3(1).
184 *Id.*, art. 4.A (emphasis added).
185 "AU Constitution," *supra* this chapter, note 106, preamb.
186 *Id.*, arts. 3(f), 4(i) & (j).
187 "ASEAN Charter," *supra* this chapter, note 160, preamb. ¶ 6.
188 *Id.*, art. 1(1) & 1(4).
189 The "law and development" school emerged to try to explain how the development of legal principles associated with peace could relate to principles advocating development. This school has failed to attract much interest or influence in the wider literature. *See, e.g.*, Carol V. Rose, "The 'New' Law and Development Movement in the Post-Cold War Era: A Vietnam Case Study," 32 *L. & Soc. Rev.* 93 (1998).

Organizations may list peace and security together, albeit for progress and development. UNIDO strives towards "contributing to international peace and security."[190] There, peace and security serve for "*the prosperity of all nations*, in conformity with the purposes and principles of the Charter of the United Nations."[191] For the ITU, the Union has reaffirmed its commitment to peace, noting in a resolution about the Middle East peace process "that the fundamental principles of the Constitution and Convention of the International Telecommunication Union (Geneva, 1992) are designed to strengthen peace and security in the world for the development of international cooperation and better understanding among peoples."[192] Academic studies validate the role that such cooperation and better understanding plays in peace and security, as evidenced by membership in international organizations.[193]

Other organizations place the onus of development on peace and security together. The East African Community shows how a nexus of values depends on peace and security. The constitution starts out, "convinced that co-operation ... will raise the standards of living of African peoples, maintain and enhance the economic stability, [and] foster close and *peaceful* relations among African states."[194] The East African Community also demonstrates the importance of peace and security for development when it says the following: "The Partner States agree to foster and maintain an atmosphere that is conducive to peace and security through co-operation and consultations on issues pertaining to peace and security of the Partner States."[195] In order to achieve such an objective, "the Partner States agree to closely co-operate in defence affairs."[196] However, the whole point of these defense relationships serves the overarching goal of "social and economic development within the Community."[197] For the Arab League, security

---

190 "UNIDO Constitution," *supra* this chapter, note 30, preamb.
191 *Id.* (emphasis added).
192 *See* "ITU Constitution," *supra* this chapter, note 100, res. 32 (a)–(b). The annex to Resolution 34 (about South Sudan) also highlights the role of information technologies and connection in promoting peace. Resolution 130 reinforces the ITU's role "in building confidence and security" among its members. *Id.*, res. 130.
193 Russett and his co-authors find that shared memberships in these types of international organizations decreased the incidence of military disputes by about 23 percent (and 35 percent if both states are democratic). *See* Bruce Russett et al., "The Third Leg of the Kantian Tripod for Peace: International Organizations and Militarized Disputes," 52 *Int'l Org.* 441 (1998).
194 "EAC Constitution," *supra* this chapter, note 107, preamb. (emphasis added).
195 *Id.*, art. 124(1).
196 *Id.*, art. 125(1).
197 *Id.* (also providing that peace and security are "vital to the achievement of the objectives of the Community").

and peace seem like the League's main issue.[198] However, such prosperity appears as "economic and social relations."[199]

The wide range of values and principles appearing with peace and security show the ways that these values color the principle of peace. For ASEAN, the Association's objectives include "the promotion of peace, security, and stability within, and good neighbourliness among, the Partner States."[200] Such promotion shall occur by promoting "(a) mutual trust, political will and sovereign equality; (b) peaceful co-existence and good neighbourliness; (c) peaceful settlement of disputes."[201] Regarding summits, "The Summit shall review the state of peace, security and good governance within the Community and the progress achieved towards the establishment of a Political Federation of the Partner States."[202] As with the UN and ITU, the East African Community starts out linking peace and security to prosperity.[203]

The East African Community's constitution particularly shows how other principles color the way the constitution sees peace. The constitution cites five equally ranked objectives, namely "the promotion of peace, security, and stability within, and good neighbourliness among, the Partner States" and "mutual trust, political will and sovereign equality; peaceful co-existence and good neighbourliness; peaceful settlement of disputes."[204] Such a list highlights the role of trust and will as values, if not principles, and the peaceful settlement of disputes as a method of achieving peace and security. Indeed, the whole point of summits is to "review the state of peace, security and good governance within the Community."[205] In these summits, partner states must "preserve peace and strengthen international security."[206] However, for most researchers, international organizations'

---

198 As if to drive home the point, the constitution describes procedures for amendment "for the purpose of ... regulating the relations of the League with the international organizations that may be created in the future *to guarantee security and peace.*" Pact of the League of Arab States art. 19, Mar. 22, 1945, available at www.lasportal.org (last visited Mar. 25, 2020) (emphasis added).
199 *Id.*, art. 3 (requiring the Council to "collaborate with the international organizations which may be created in the future to guarantee peace and security and organize economic and social relations").
200 "ASEAN Charter," *supra* this chapter, note 160, art. 5(f).
201 *Id.*, art. 6.
202 *Id.*, art. 11(3).
203 "EAC Constitution," *supra* this chapter, note 107, preamb.
204 *Id.*, arts. 5(f) & 6(a)–(c).
205 *Id.*, art. 11(3) (with the other major point being identified in the sentence consisting of reviewing "the progress achieved towards the establishment of a Political Federation of the Partner States").
206 *Id.*, art. 123(d).

attempts to ensure peace smack of social engineering, and they try to make up for the lack of state building that member states should have done as a way of achieving security for themselves.[207]

Other organizations see progress by different names. UNESCO unsurprisingly places the value of culture at the fore, with other values stemming from such enculturation. As noted by its constitutional preamble:

> It is in the minds of men that the defences of peace must be constructed; That the wide diffusion of culture, and the education of humanity for justice and liberty and peace are indispensable to the dignity of man and constitute a sacred duty which all the nations must fulfil in a spirit of mutual assistance.[208]

Its constitution explicitly notes that "the purpose of the Organization is to contribute to peace and security by promoting collaboration among the nations through education, science and culture in order to further universal respect for justice, for the rule of law and for the human rights and fundamental freedoms which are affirmed for the peoples of the world, without distinction of race, sex, language or religion, by the Charter of the United Nations."[209] Such a formula places respect for justice, rule of law, and rights and freedoms at the head of the line, with peace and security *with equity* as the end, with collaboration as an instrumental principle in achieving such peace and security.

Settling disputes as the way to peace

Many international organizations' constitutions mentioning peace refer to dispute resolution as a means to peaceful ends. For example, ASEAN's constitution affirms the Association's adherence to the dispute resolution procedure detailed in the UN Charter, implying at least some basic agreement with the principles espoused by the UN.[210] Furthermore, the Charter states the following about dispute resolution: "Member States shall endeavour to resolve peacefully all disputes in a timely manner through dialogue, consultation and negotiation,"[211] and "[d]isputes which do not concern the interpretation or application of any ASEAN instrument shall be resolved peacefully in accordance with the Treaty of Amity and Cooperation in

---

207 *See* Keith Krause & Oliver Jutersonke, "Peace, Security and Development in Post-Conflict Environments," 36 *Sec. Dialogue* 447 (2005).
208 "UNESCO Constitution," *supra* this chapter, note 58, preamb.
209 *Id.*, art. 1(1).
210 "ASEAN Charter," *supra* this chapter, note 160, art. 28.
211 *Id.*, art. 22(1).

Southeast Asia and its rules of procedure."[212] The Charter, for its part, refers to several more principles, most notably cooperation.[213]

Several constitutions refer obliquely to war when talking about peace. The African Union's constitution gives its Assembly the right to "give directives to the Executive Council on the management of conflicts, war and other emergency situations and the restoration of peace."[214] The Caribbean Community, referring to war more subtly, seeks to ensure that "nothing ... prevent[s] any Member State from taking any action in pursuance of its obligations for the maintenance of international peace and security."[215] While commentators have sought to outline the principles behind a "just war," the nexus of principles guiding the way international organizations encourage or sanction wars remains almost completely unidentified.[216]

The UN also takes up the mantle of arbitrating and otherwise resolving conflicts, similarly to the Permanent Court of Arbitration, in that "the General Assembly may recommend measures for the peaceful adjustment of any situation, regardless of origin, which it deems likely to impair the general welfare or friendly relations among nations."[217] The UN Charter specifically proposes to "maintain international peace and security, and to that end: to take effective collective measures for the prevention and removal of threats to the peace, and for the suppression of acts of aggression or other breaches of the peace, and to bring about by peaceful means ... [the] adjustment or settlement of international disputes or situations which might lead to a breach of the peace."[218] If the UN has spearheaded the development of a *lex pacificatoria*, the constitutional principles reflecting such a law remain to be identified.[219]

212 *Id.*, art. 22(1) and 24(2).
213 This book does not analyze treaties and agreements that relate to the constitutions focused on in this study. Nevertheless, the Treaty of Amity shows that analyzing related conventions and agreements adds far more principles into the analysis. *See* Treaty of Amity and Cooperation in Southeast Asia Indonesia ch. I & III, Feb. 24, 1976, *available at* www.asean.org (last visited Mar. 25, 2020).
214 "AU Constitution," *supra* this chapter, note 106, art. 9(g).
215 Revised Treaty of Chaguaramas Establishing the Caribbean Community Including the Caricom Single Market art 225(c), May 7, 2001, *available at* www.caricom.org (last visited Mar. 25, 2020) [hereinafter "Caricom Treaty"].
216 Most legal researchers talk in circles around the issue of war in international organizations law. Chesterman provides one of the few detailed analyses of the principles driving international organizations to regulate war. *See* Simon Chesterman, *Just War or Just Peace?: Humanitarian Intervention and International Law* (2001).
217 UN Charter, *supra* Chapter 1, note 7, art. 14.
218 *Id.*, art. 1(1).
219 Bell's book reflects one of the most successful attempts to define a "law of peace" among international treaties and international organizations' principles. *See*

For the EU (and the other organizations identified below), security brings about peace as "[the Union] shall contribute to peace, security ..."[220] Like the UN, the EU seeks specifically to guarantee peace through its peacekeeping forces.[221] The EU's constitution highlights what member states may do in what accepted circumstances, and it requires member states to consult each other in order to protect the internal market from war, serious internal and international disturbances affecting the maintenance of law and order, and to maintain peace and international security.[222] These provisions reflect the broader principles in the EU treaties driving the Union to depoliticize armed conflict and treat such conflict as technical matters to resolve.[223]

The connection between representativeness and autonomy

Representation represents one of the core attributes of international organizations.[224] In the international organizations' constitutions, representation (or representativeness, as Chapter 2 referred to it) has three meanings.[225] First, representation arises in legislative (decision making) bodies, like a Board serves to protect and put forward member states' interests.[226] Second, representation arises with staff appointments, where diversity of

---

Christine Bell, *On the Law of Peace: Peace Agreements and the Lex Pacificatoria* (2008).
220 "Treaty of Lisbon," *supra* this chapter, note 27, art. 4.
221 *Id.*, arts. I-41, III-309, III-312.
222 *Id.*, art. III-131.
223 If true, such an approach would give international organizations far more power vis-à-vis states to resolve war. *See* Gezim Visoka & John Doyle, "Neo-Functional Peace: The European Union Way of Resolving Conflicts," 54 J. Comm. Mark. Stud. 862 (2016).
224 Behind representation stand authority, autonomy and the principles that sit at the core of an international order made up of national interests. *See* Cogan, *supra* Chapter 1, note 90, at 209.
225 The authors of this book do not wish to bog down the discussion in needless debates about the difference between representation and representativeness. These terms are used interchangeably in the book, but the purist jurist will object, as representation refers to the act of representing interests in an organization while representativeness refers to the basic quality or characteristic of the organization as allowing such representation. *See, e.g.*, Louis & Ruwet, *supra* Chapter 2, note 28, at 535.
226 Such representation does not exclude non-members like NGOs. For more on this topic (which this book admittedly ignores, other than to point to its existence), *see* Carole-Anne Senit et al., "The Representativeness of Global Deliberation: A Critical Assessment of Civil Society Consultations for Sustainable Development," 8 *Glob. Pol.* 62 (2017).

executive appointments may ensure impartial policy implementation.[227] Third, representation arises in judicial settings, where representatives may ensure the representation of particular disputants' interests and the interests of their member states if necessary.[228] However, even these different situational definitions belie the range of understandings about representation in international organizations. At their most optimistic, members seek representation in decision-making bodies as a governance mechanism aimed at promoting openness and thus effectiveness.[229] For the international organizations law textbooks that this book surveyed, general competence organizations fixed on particular aspirations strive for the representation that can ensure that their members hear and adopt their message. In other cases, some organizations view representation as a bulwark against a region's domination of a body.[230] Finally, for some, such representation seeks only to ensure a bare minimum of inclusion.[231] Representation in a body does

---

227 Such an approach assumes that the international organization serves as an agent to the principals represented in the representative organization. Having civil servants from these member states somehow thus aligns the agent's activity to its representatives' interests. For all the problems with this worldview, *see* Sabine Hassler, *Reforming the UN Security Council Membership: The Illusion of Representativeness* (2012).

228 Such a view of institutions holds on to atavistic notions of judges somehow bringing their state's interests into the court, a notion contrary to the entire international tribunal project. For a discussion of the problems of vesting these courts with national (or other parties') representativeness, *see* Daniel Terris et al., "Toward a Community of International Judges," 30 *Loy. L.A. Int'l & Comp. L. Rev.* 419 (2008).

229 As Tallberg and his co-authors note, international organization openness – namely representation of interests other than states – comes from governance problems, exposure to opposition, and increasing standards of openness worldwide at the national and local level. *See* Jonas Tallberg et al., *The Opening Up of International Organizations* (2013). For authors like Abbott and Snidal, responsive regulation results from representation in international organizations by businesses and others with an interest in effective regulation. *See* Kenneth W. Abbott & Duncan Snidal, "Taking Responsive Regulation Transnational: Strategies for International Organizations," 1 *Reg. & Governance* 96 (2013).

230 The Inter-Parliamentary Union's constitution gives one example of a constitution that fits into none of these categories. The organization's mandate to "work for peace" along with "cooperation among peoples and for the solid establishment of representative institutions" makes cooperation in representative institutions as a *sine qua non* for such representation itself. *See* "IPU Statute," *supra* this chapter, note 173, art. 1(2).

231 As such, operational constitutions (or constitutions that focus on procedures rather than heavily on substantive rights and issues) mistakenly seem like the least politicized way to ensure such a modicum of participation in an organization's governance. *See* Cogan, *supra* Chapter 1, note 90, at 209.

Jurisprudence of aspirational values

not ensure representativeness, and so there exist a variety of mechanisms aimed at closing this gap.[232]

Representation in voting, staff and judgment

Representation in voting schemes varies across international organizations, with many constitutions highlighting representation as a core principle.[233] Adopting the one-member-one-vote principle, the African Civil Aviation Commission (AFCAC) grants that "each AFCAC member state shall enjoy an equal right to be represented at AFCAC meetings."[234] The Commission's rules also grant that "all AFCAC member States shall be represented at the Plenary sessions."[235] The WHO requires that "Each Member shall be represented by not more than three delegates, one of whom shall be designated by the Member as chief delegate."[236] The WTO notes that "at each session of the Assembly each Full and Associate Member shall be represented by not more than five delegates, one of whom shall be designated by the Members as Chief Delegate."[237] The Organization for the Harmonization of Business Law in Africa's constitution refers to representation in that all decisions had to have at least two-thirds of representative members in agreement during voting.[238]

Most economic organizations ensure representation by having each member state represented, but applying weights to their votes. The African

---

232 *See* Schermers & Blokker, *supra* Chapter 1, note 5, at 550–53 (noting that one vote per member is not necessarily representative).
233 Posner and Sykes provide an interesting overview of these rules (and a less interesting idea for changing them). *See* Posner & Sykes, *supra* Chapter 1, note 80, at 195. Rapkin and his co-authors describe the different types of voting procedures in general and their implications on representation. *See* Rapkin et al., *supra* Chapter 1, note 120, at 77.
234 African Civil Aviation Commission Constitution art. 2, Jan. 17, 1969 (revised Aug. 16, 2016), *available at* https://au.int (last visited Mar. 25, 2020).
235 *Id.*, art. 9.
236 *See* Constitution of the World Health Organization art. 11, July 22, 1945, *available at* www.who.int (last visited Mar. 25, 2020) (stipulating that "these delegates should be chosen from among persons most qualified by their technical competence in the field of health, preferably representing the national health administration of the Member," with Rule 35 providing, "Each delegation shall be entitled to be represented on each main committee by one of its members. He may be accompanied at meetings of the committee by one or more other members, who may be accorded permission to speak but shall not vote").
237 "UNWTO Statute," *supra* this chapter, note 39, art. 9(2).
238 Treaty on the Harmonization of Business Law in Africa art. 8, Oct. 17, 1993, *available at* www.ohadalegis.com (last visited Mar. 25, 2020).

Development Bank requires that "each member shall be represented on the Board of Governors and board of directors."[239] Ensuring representation, the constitution also allows a representative to represent a member state on the board when "a matter particularly impacts a member."[240] The African Export Import Bank provides for shareholder representativeness and the votes they have to represent their interests. The Arab Bank for Economic Development in Africa has similar representation requirements for its Board, noting that "any Bank member not represented in the Board of Directors shall have the right to delegate a representative to attend meetings of the Board of Directors and participate in such meetings without being entitled to vote thereat."[241] Provisions allowing for representativeness in Board procedures also exist in the constitutions of the Asian Development Bank (in terms of its board of governors and in the description of voting procedures) and the Asian Infrastructure Investment Bank (applied to its board of governors).

The International Seabed Authority's constitution represents one of the more interesting cases of such representativeness, where it strives for *geographical* representativeness on its council in three ways. First, "land-locked and geographically disadvantaged States are *represented to a degree which is reasonably proportionate* to their representation in the Assembly."[242] Coastal states, especially those that are developing states, get the same treatment.[243] Such proportionality grants as many council seats as representatives in the Assembly, and representatives must be nominated by the group they are supposed to represent.[244] Unlike other constitutions that require rotation of council members among member states, the Seabed Authority's constitution requires "due regard" for such rotation only if a member seeks re-election.[245]

Several other international organizations use geographical notions of representation, in staff appointments as well as in assembly representation.

---

239 Agreement Establishing the African Development Bank, art. 30, *available at* www.afdb.org (last visited Mar. 25, 2020).
240 *Id.*, art. 34.
241 "BADEA Agreement," *supra* Chapter 3, note 128, art. 21(iii).
242 "UNCLOS," *supra* Chapter 3, note 90, art. 161(2)(2)(a) (emphasis added).
243 *Id.*, art. 161(2)(2)(b).
244 *See id.*, art. 161(2)(2(c) ("Each group of States Parties to be represented on the Council is represented by those members, if any, which are nominated by that group.").
245 *Id.*, art. 161(4)(4) ("Members of the Council shall be eligible for re-election, but due regard should be paid to the desirability of rotation of membership."). Article 5(2) uses the exact same language, though for Board members. *Id.*, art. 5(2).

Jurisprudence of aspirational values

For example, the UN Charter specifically requires "due regard shall be paid to the importance of recruiting the staff on as wide a geographical basis as possible."[246] The Charter also refers to having "equitable geographical distribution" among those the General Assembly elects for non-permanent members of the Security Council.[247] Similarly, the UNESCO constitution requires that "the Committee shall elect a Bureau consisting of a Chairperson, two Vice-Chairpersons, a Rapporteur and two members, with a view to having each geographical group represented."[248] Such representativeness also should be reflected in the observer institutions of UNESCO.[249] The UNIDO constitution references such geographical representation in its board.[250] Other subsidiary organs and technical committees established by the Conference or the Board also must "give due regard to the principle of equitable geographical representation."[251] To drive home the point, "the Board shall consist of 53 Members of the Organization elected by the Conference, which shall give due regard to the principle of equitable geographical distribution."[252]

The WHO's constitution also includes the "principle of rotation among geographical regions" for those elected to the boards and executive staff, noting that the selection of "the Chairman and officers" incorporates "respecting the principles of equitable geographical representation, gender balance and balanced representation of developing and developed countries and countries in transition."[253] The WHO's representation on the Board consists of the following:

> Its officers, viz. a Chairman, four Vice-Chairmen and one Rapporteur, from among its members each year at its first session after the Health Assembly, following a principle of rotation among geographical regions. These officers shall hold office until their successors are elected. The Chairman shall not become eligible for re-election until two years have elapsed since he ceased to hold office.[254]

---

246 UN Charter, *supra* Chapter 1, note 7, art. 101.
247 *Id.*, art. 23.
248 "UNESCO Constitution," *supra* this chapter, note 58, rule 39(2).
249 *Id.*, art. IV(2) & rule 41.
250 "UNIDO Constitution," *supra* this chapter, note 30, art. 7(3).
251 *Id.*
252 *Id.*, art. 9.I.
253 "WHO Constitution," *supra* this chapter, note 236, rule 16. Klabbers contends that rotating candidates by geography provides a compromise so "that different regions are adequately represented." Klabbers, *supra* Chapter 1, note 37, at 211. Klabbers goes on to rightly contend that this compromise aids in legitimizing an international organization. *See id.*
254 *See* "WHO Constitution," *supra* this chapter, note 236, rule 12.

Even regional and limited competence organizations reference such geographical notions of representation. The Caribbean Community's constitution mentions representation three times. In the first instance, such representation concerns member-state representation in voting.[255] The second instance concerns member-state representation in subcommittee meetings.[256] The third time defines the "secretariat as representative of the community."[257] Organizations of limited competence also generally reference representativeness three times: the assurance of each member having official representation, for executive staff representing the organization and in rules for voting.[258]

Nevertheless, many organizations do not have such geographical understanding of representation. The International Rubber Study Group includes representativeness in procedures defining how staff represent the international organization.[259] The organization's constitution does not mention geographical concerns. Indeed, one wonders why organizations even focus on geography.[260] Many researchers consider geographical representativeness as *dépassé*.[261] After controlling for a range of factors, geographical factors do not necessarily lead to similarity of interests in international organizations.[262] Such an approach has found its most advanced expression in international courts and tribunals.[263]

---

255 See "Caricom Treaty," *supra* this chapter, note 215, art. 27(1) ("Each Member State represented on Community Organs and Bodies shall have one vote.").
256 *Id.*, art. 70(3).
257 *Id.*, art. 228.
258 The EU's limited competence organizations provide an excellent example that proves the general point. For a discussion, *see* Stefan Talmon, "Responsibility of International Organizations: Does the European Community Require Special Treatment?" in *International Responsibility Today: Essays in Memory of Oscar Schachter Maurizio* 405 (Maurizio Ragazzi ed. 2005) (providing a discussion of this point).
259 Constitution of the International Rubber Study Group art. IX(5) & art. XII (5), July 1, 2011, *available at* www.rubberstudy.com (last visited Mar. 25, 2020).
260 *See, e.g.*, Daniel Bethlehem, "The End of Geography: The Changing Nature of the International System and the Challenge to International Law," 25 *Eur. J. Int'l L.* 9 (2014).
261 For a fuller explanation, *see* John Agnew, "The Territorial Trap: The Geographical Assumptions of International Relations Theory," 1 *Rev. Int'l Pol. Econ.* 53 (1994).
262 Recent datasets have provided new insights into which states join international organizations and the reasons why states join them. *See* Jon Pevchouse et al., "The Correlates of War 2 International Governmental Organizations Data Version 2.0," 21 *Conflict Mgmt. & Peace Sci.* 101 (2004).
263 For some, considerations of nationality and member states' interests could only undermine the legitimacy of these instances. For others, these tribunals represent

International judicial organizations also have (often complicated) representation requirements in their secretariat or main body. Many courts do not have specific nationality requirements for justices and employees.[264] The Benelux Court of Justice represents a judicial organization with such nationality requirements. The Court's executive staff may represent the Court, in that "the Court shall be represented by the President."[265] The Court's constitution also allows for the representation of each nationality among senior staff members and the same nationality to maintain its representation. However, these nationality rules are overly complex.[266] Such rules on the nationality of court officers illustrate the importance of representation, political legitimacy and even sovereignty.[267]

Another aspect of representation in these judicial organizations relates to the representation of the parties involved in a dispute. The ICC's constitution refers only to court representation, as in a criminal defendant has the right to be represented by counsel. The Permanent Court of Arbitration's constitution notes, "Each party is represented before the Tribunal by an agent, who serves as intermediary between the Tribunal and the

---

the most advanced expression of the end of the Westphalian order in international organizations. For a fuller discussion, *see* Claire Cutler, "Critical Reflections on the Westphalian Assumptions of International Law and Organization: A Crisis of Legitimacy," 27 *Rev. Int'l Stud.* 133 (2001).

264 For a useful, practical guide to which courts establish nationality requirements for staff and officials, *see* Yale Law School Career Development Office, Opportunities with International Tribunals and Foreign Courts, date unknown, *available at* https://law.yale.edu/system/files/area/department/cdo/document/cdo_international_tribunals_public.pdf (last visited Mar. 25, 2020).

265 "Benelux Court of Justice Treaty," *supra* Chapter 3, note 64, art. 4(a).

266 *See id.* ("The functions of President and First and Second Vice-President of the Court and also of the first-chamber is completed by rotation for a period of three years."). However, a commenced (but interrupted) three-year mandate must be completed by a councilor of the same nationality. *See id.*, art. 3(5) The Court's General Assembly elects the Court president, a first and second vice-president of several nationalities, by an absolute majority. *See id.* However, voting determines the order of nationality to chair the presidency and the vice-presidency. *See id.* This order then carries on for nine years, after which a new round of voting to establish this order commences. This mechanism does not seem particularly simple.

267 The principle of states' sovereignty probably most explains the need for national representation in many international courts' constitutions. If these courts reduce or otherwise affect a state's sovereignty, then national representation represents a possible means by which states exercise their delegated sovereignty. For this argument, *see* Karen J. Alter, "Delegating to International Courts: Self-Binding vs. Other-Binding Delegation," 71 *L. & Cont. Prob.* 37 (2008).

Government who appointed him."[268] As for the European Court of Human Rights, like the ICC, it allows for the representation that ensures the defendant's rights to be represented.[269]

These constitutions similarly allow for the representation of member states with disputes. The African Court of Human and People's Rights allows that "the Commission may ask the States concerned to provide it with all relevant information. When the Commission is considering the matter, States concerned may be represented before it and submit written or oral representation."[270] The Central American Court of Justice's constitution provides that "each one of the Governments or individuals directly concerned ... has the right to be represented before it by a trustworthy person or persons, who shall ... do everything that in their judgment shall be beneficial to the defense of the rights they represent."[271] However, many courts' constitutions prefer to sacrifice representation for autonomy – or the perception of autonomy – in provisions designed to create an independent judicial class, which is the topic of the following subsection.[272]

Non-representation as autonomy: independence of justices and judges

Many international organizations' constitutions, especially those of judicial organizations, refer extensively to the independence of the court and its justices and officials.[273] The UN Charter includes numerous mentions of independence and freedom.[274] Autonomy for staff means not favoring one member state over another, as well as the notion that national interests

---

268 "Convention for the Pacific Settlement of International Disputes," *supra* this chapter, note 175, art. 89.
269 "ECHR," *supra* this chapter, note 65, art 1(1)(c).
270 "ACHPR Protocol," *supra* this chapter, note 18, art. 51(1)–(2).
271 "Convention for the Establishment of a Central American Court of Justice," 2 *Am. J. Int'l L* 231 (1908) (providing art. XVII).
272 Such independence appears more prominently in new international tribunals' constitutions – reflecting the trend in this area of international law. For a description of these trends, *see* Ruth Mackenzie & Philippe Sands, "International Courts and Tribunals and the Independence of the International Judge," 44 *Harv. Int'l L.J.* 271 (2003).
273 Surprisingly, work on such independence did not start in earnest until the late twentieth century. For an overview of the legal research on such independence and autonomy, *see* Eric A. Posner & John Yoo, "Judicial Independence in International Tribunals," 93 *Cal. L. Rev.* 1 (2005).
274 *See* UN Charter, *supra* Chapter 1, note 7, arts. 1(3), 2(4), 13(b), 55(c), 62(2), 73(b), 76(b) and 105(2).

should not influence the carrying out of staff members' duties.[275] For example, to guarantee the independence of the World Bank Administrative Tribunal from the broader Bank Group, the Bank Group must guarantee and respect the Tribunal's independence.[276]

For many researchers, credibility and legitimacy derive from independence, especially for international judicial organizations.[277] For example, the Central American Court of Justice requires that the Secretary General "shall have a demonstrated commitment to the integration process, a high degree of impartiality, independent judgment and integrity."[278] The ICC requires its Deputy Registrar to swear "to exercise his or her respective functions impartially and conscientiously"[279] Regarding other court staff, "in the employment of staff, the Prosecutor and the Registrar shall ensure the highest standards of efficiency, competency and integrity."[280] The Organisation for Security and Co-operation in Europe (OSCE) Court of Conciliation and Arbitration requires the Registrar, conciliators and arbitrators to swear "that they will exercise their powers impartially and conscientiously … before taking their seats on the Commission, and perform their functions in full independence."[281]

Both the member states and the staff in these organizations themselves have the duty to protect such autonomy. The African Court of Human and People's Rights provides an example of such two-way obligations. The constitution affirms that "the independence of the judges shall be fully

---

[275] Most of the authors that this book analyzed to create its list of principles addressed this issue. *See* Amerasinghe, *supra* Chapter 1, note 9, at 158–59; White, *supra* Chapter 1, note 19, at 43; Sands & Klein, *supra* Chapter 1, note 39, at 308 & 314; Schermers & Blokker, *supra* Chapter 1, note 5, at 375.

[276] Statute of the World Bank Administrative Tribunal art. 1(2), Apr. 30, 1980. *See also* id., art. VI(3) (stating that the World Bank Administrative Tribunal "shall prepare and manage its budget independently").

[277] This book's dataset contained sixteen international judicial organizations. Most of the references to autonomy in the data refer to these international organizations' constitutions. Most of these constitutions included explicit statements on the judges' independence and freedom from influence. A handful of constitutions required officials possessing "high moral character." Others required fair and unbiased trial proceedings and judgments. Many also contained provisions requiring judge qualifications and impartiality.

[278] "Tegucigalpa Protocol," *supra* this chapter, note 49, art. 26.

[279] "Rome Statute," *supra* Chapter 3, note 72, art. 45.

[280] *Id.*, art. 44(2).

[281] Convention on Conciliation and Arbitration within the OSCE (Stockholm Convention) art. 5, Dec. 15, 1992, *available at* www.osce.org (last visited Mar. 25, 2020).

ensured in accordance with international law."[282] Nevertheless, the job of protecting such independence comes from member states as well as the Court itself. In the Court's constitution, member states "shall have the duty to guarantee the independence of the Courts and shall allow the establishment and improvement of appropriate national institutions entrusted with the promotion and protection of the rights and freedoms guaranteed by the present Charter."[283] On the other hand, judges must "make a solemn declaration to discharge their duties impartially and faithfully."[284] Indeed, judges must recuse themselves from involvement in "any activity that might interfere with the independence or impartiality of [the] judge or the demands of the office."[285]

Other institutions do not so explicitly spell out the two-way nature of such autonomy. The African Development Bank Administrative Tribunal, which is the administrative tribunal for the African Development Bank, requires that "in the exercise of their duties, the judges shall be completely independent from the Bank or any other authority. They shall not receive any instructions or be subject to any constraint."[286] Such an approach thus targets both the international organization (by imposing obligations on the institution and its judges) as well as member states (to avoid giving instructions to these judges).[287] The Central American Court of Justice's constitution seeks such autonomy through recruiting rules. In such an approach, rules focus on the character of the judges themselves, requiring that judges are "selected from among the jurists who possess the qualifications ... [for] high judicial office, and who enjoy the highest consideration, both because of their moral character and their professional ability."[288] Thus, the source

---

282 The second article also promotes such disinterestedness, in requiring judges with past knowledge or experience with aspects of the case or its parties recuse themselves. See Protocol on the Statute of the African Court of Justice and Human Rights art. 17.1, July 1, 2008, *available at* https://au.int/ (last visited Mar. 25, 2020).
283 *Id.*, art. 26.
284 *Id.*, art. 16.
285 *Id.*, art. 18.
286 Statute and Rules of Procedure of the Administrative Tribunal of the African Development Bank Administrative Tribunal art. VII(1), July 16, 1997, *available at* www.afdb.org (last visited Mar. 25, 2020).
287 Such an approach approximates domestic approaches to ensuring such autonomy, in the more problematic area of international law. For a discussion of such an approach in the EU context, *see* Jürgen Bast, "On the Grammar of EU law: Legal Instruments," Jean Monnet Working Paper 9/03 (2003).
288 "Tegucigalpa Protocol," *supra* this chapter, note 49, art. VI.

of such autonomy may vary, depending on the view of the constitution's framers of the source of such autonomy.[289]

Other constitutions define a doctrine of judicial autonomy based both in official admonitions of independence and in hiring rules. The Court of Justice of the Andean Community combines both approaches, including official independence and personal independence. Official independence comes from the provision that "the judges shall enjoy full independence in the exercise of their duties."[290] Some of the rules aimed at ensuring personal independence include requirements about their character and prohibitions against moonlighting. As for the judge's characteristics, judges must "enjoy a good moral reputation, and fulfill the necessary conditions for exercising the highest judicial functions in their respective countries or be highly competent jurists."[291] Regarding moonlighting, "they may not perform other professional activities, either paid or free of charge, except for teaching; they shall also refrain from any act that is incompatible with the nature of their position."[292] The ICJ seems to be going in this general direction.[293]

Other constitutions focus heavily on the character and recruitment side of the equation that has autonomy equaling contract restrictions and member-state prohibitions. For example, the ICC requires candidates of "high moral character, impartiality and integrity" in addition to "possess[ing] the qualifications."[294] The rules guaranteeing the "independence of the judges" also combine admonitions for judges' independence and prohibitions on moonlighting. In particular, ICC judges are required to be independent in fulfilling their functions: "Judges shall not engage in any activity which is likely to interfere with their judicial functions or to affect confidence in their independence [and] judges required to serve on a full-time basis at the seat of the Court shall not engage in any other occupation of a professional nature."[295] The ICC's constitution adds a fourth, recusal requirement, often

---

289 For example, Bravo argues that differing conceptions of sovereignty explain why Caribbean integration promoted by regional international organizations fell far short of the EU's efforts. *See* Karen Bravo, "CARICOM, the Myth of Sovereignty, and Aspirational Economic Integration," 31 *N.C. J. Int'l L. & Com. Reg.* 145 (2005). Such differences in basic constitutional principles help to explain why and how different organizations apply principles like autonomy differently.
290 "Cartegena Agreement," *supra* this chapter, note 10, art. 6.
291 *Id.*
292 *Id.*
293 *See* Abdulqawi Yusuf, ICJ President Speech to the UN General Assembly, Oct. 25, 2018, *available at* www.icj-cij.org/files/press-releases/0/000-20181025-PRE-02-00-EN.pdf (last visited Mar. 25, 2020).
294 "Rome Statute," *supra* Chapter 3, note 72, art. 36(3a).
295 *Id.*, art. 40(1), 40(2) and 40(3). As with the European Court of Human Rights, the fourth point notes that "any question regarding the application of paragraphs 2

omitted from other constitutions, requiring the disqualification of judges from participating on a case in situations that could cast *reasonable* doubt on the judge's ability to remain impartial in the case.[296]

The International Tribunal for the Law of the Sea's constitution includes the usual formula of personal characteristics and moonlighting, with an extra requirement to remain impartial.[297] Regarding personal characteristics, the Tribunal's constitution requires that members must have "recognized competence in the field of the law of the seas," having "the "highest reputation for fairness and integrity"[298] The Tribunal's constitution also forbids "incompatible activities."[299] These activities include the "exercise [of] any political or administrative function, or [associating] actively with or [being] financially interested in any of the operations of any enterprise concerned with the exploration for or exploitation of the resources of the sea or the seabed or other commercial use of the sea or the seabed."[300] Finally, "no member of the Tribunal may act as agent, counsel or advocate in any case."[301] In particular, Tribunal members must take a solemn vow "in open session" to "exercise [their] powers impartially and conscientiously."[302] These rules represent some of the most detailed and strict, likely due to the intersection of large commercial interests involved in the Tribunal's cases.[303]

and 3 shall be decided by an absolute majority of the judges. Where any such question concerns an individual judge, that judge shall not take part in the decision." *Id.* Thus, judges judge other judges' capacity to judge.

296 *Id.*, art. 41(2)(a).
297 The Tribunal's rules hold special interest for legal researchers. While the Tribunal must focus on upholding the provisions of the treaty that created the tribunal, the Tribunal must both consider the law of international organizations and contribute to that law. See Wood, *supra* Chapter 1, note 151, at 351.
298 "UNCLOS," *supra* Chapter 3, note 90, pt. XI, art. 2.
299 *Id.*, art. 7. As with most other judicial organizations, "Any doubt on these points shall be resolved by decision of the majority of the other members of the Tribunal present." *Id.*, art. 7(3).
300 *Id.*, art. 7(1). Such independence obviously does not represent an unqualified good. Many legal researchers argue that strengthening tribunals like this one would both reduce the scope for political action and result in excessive amounts of international regulation. For a full description, see John E. Noyes, "The International Tribunal for the Law of the Sea," 32 *Cornell Int'l L.J.* 109 (1999).
301 "UNCLOS," *supra* Chapter 3, note 90, art. 7(2).
302 *Id.*, art. 11.
303 Unlike many other tribunals, this Tribunal's decisions help to create an entire legal regime. See Vladimir Golitsyn, "The Role of the International Tribunal for the Law of the Sea in Global Ocean Governance," *in Stress Testing the Law of the Sea: Dispute Resolution, Disasters & Emerging Challenges* 9 (Stephen Minas & Jordan Diamond eds. 2018).

Freedom-limiting rules also help to protect the autonomy of other court officials, besides judges. Prosecutors, arbitrators and "members of the court" must take vows or follow rules that force them to act impartially, at the service of the institution's autonomy. For example, the Benelux Court of Justice requires all the members of the Court and the Public Prosecutor's office to "exercise their duties in all impartiality and independence."[304] The ICC requires all staff (legal and administrative) to swear an oath that "the judges, the Prosecutor, the Deputy Prosecutors, the Registrar and the Deputy Registrar" carry out their duties "impartially and conscientiously."[305] Impartiality serves the interests of autonomy.[306] The ICC's rules also define the prosecutor's office "as a separate organ of the Court."[307] In that vein, "A member of the Office shall not seek or act on instructions from any external source."[308]

Rules governing the behavior of court staff thus guarantee independence and autonomy by restricting the freedom of staff to engage in behavior undermining trust in the court.[309] For example, the Rome Statute of the ICC states, "Neither the Prosecutor nor a Deputy Prosecutor shall engage in any activity which is likely to interfere with his or her prosecutorial functions or to affect confidence in his or her independence. They shall not engage in any other occupation of a professional nature."[310] The presidency may excuse the prosecutor (or his or her deputy) from a case, with the following requirement:

> Neither the Prosecutor nor a Deputy Prosecutor shall participate in any matter in which their impartiality might reasonably be doubted on any ground. They shall be disqualified from a case ... if, *inter alia*, they have previously been involved in any capacity in that case before the Court.[311]

---

304 "Benelux Court of Justice Treaty," *supra* Chapter 3, note 64, art. 4(1).
305 "Rome Statute," *supra* Chapter 3, note 72, art. 45.
306 Indeed, these courts' decisions – as well as their constitutions – help to create the regime by which such impartiality helps to guarantee their autonomy. See Theodor Meron, "Judicial Independence and Impartiality in International Criminal Tribunals," 99 *Am. J. Int'l L.* 359 (2005).
307 "Rome Statute," *supra* Chapter 3, note 72, art. 42(1).
308 *Id.*
309 Only three of the sixteen judicial organizations' constitutions in this book's survey – the Advisory Centre on WTO Law, the International Institute for the Unification of Private Law, and the Iran–US Tribunal – *did not* refer to autonomy, particularly of their judges, or otherwise.
310 "Rome Statute," *supra* Chapter 3, note 72, art. 42(5).
311 *Id.*, art. 42(6) and 42(7) (for the text in quotes).

Conclusion

International organizations' constitutions refer to numerous principles. These references appear in "tracks," or groups and networks in a statistical setting. This chapter has analyzed how references to differing groups of principles in international organizations' constitutions take on different meanings, depending on the context. The chapter has looked at the many principles and values that international organizations law researchers have almost completely ignored: values and principles like progress, harmony, self-determination and respect. Human rights represent a particularly cherished value in most international organizations' constitutions. However, neither lawyers nor researchers can decide on the definition and applicability of these rights, much less their meaning for international organizations. Researchers will need to understand the "simple" principles discussed in this book before they can describe the ways in which human rights obligations interact with these principles.

The rest of the chapter attempted to describe the elements of various "tracks" or different meanings that groups of principles take on together in a constitution. Equality has a range of meanings, from equality between individuals to equality between states. Equality between states naturally complements a constitution seeking to promote the autonomy of a member. Equality promotes cooperation between individuals and genders, just as much as between organizations. For some constitutions, such equality forms the basis for representation in these organizations. In other constitutions, representation itself seeks to promote the equality targeted by the constitution's principles. For several universal international organizations, equality serves as a constitutional principle aimed at increasing the organization's authority, by seeming more legitimate. In other cases of these same types of organizations, like the UN, the constitution espouses the use of the organization's authority to help bring about equality.

---

312 The amount of deference according to these tribunals and attached bodies like prosecutors' offices clearly depends on the "track" of principles upheld in their constitutions. For a "deference" interpretation of the way these principles determine the competence of these tribunals, see Roger P. Alford, "Federal Courts, International Tribunals, and the Continuum of Deference," 43 *Va. J. Int'l L.* 675 (2003).

This chapter has illustrated the ways that these tracks or groupings of principles seek to advocate the principle of peace in international organizations' constitutions. While many constitutions seek peace, many rely on cooperation, authority and autonomy behind sometimes necessarily bellicose security arrangements and groupings. In other constitutions, mutual support and communication serve members to bring about peace, especially in cases where a security alliance must engage in war. However, for some constitutions, communication, cooperation and support serve as the principles required to de-escalate a crisis. Rather than serve the interests of security, these principles support the international organization's recommendations as honest broker between feuding states.

The final section illustrated the ways that representativeness helps to bolster an organization's autonomy and thus its efficiency. Especially for international judicial organizations, national representation still plays an important role in establishing these tribunals' authority and autonomy. In other cases, particularly with non-judicial organizations, constitutional principles of autonomy help the organization's representatives to cooperate, and they further bolster their authority. Without using statistics, this chapter has illustrated some of the legal doctrines used to pull these principles together into the tracks that this book has discussed throughout.

The next chapter puts these tracks of principles into perspective. It shows that, just as multiple tracks of principles appear in international organizations' constitutions, these tracks and groupings make up pluralistic *laws* governing international organizations. Researchers looking to find patterns and jurisprudential doctrines in these tracks should look for a classification scheme instead of a grand unified theory.

5

Towards a new jurisprudence of international organizations law

Introduction

Treaties form the basis for most, if not all, international organizations. These treaties provide principles that govern all aspects of an international organization and define its character and activities. Given each international organization's foundation on a separate "constitution," if one could view these treaties as constitutions, can one talk of a singular law of international organizations?[1] The first chapter of this book reviewed the various textbooks of international organizations law – by Bowett, Schermers, White, Amerasinghe, Klabbers, and Blokker – which paint international organizations' constitutions with a broad, generalizing brush. They assume that similarity in these organizations' constitutions means similarity in a *singular* law of international organizations. Chapter 2 showed extreme variation in these constitutions and the principles they contain. Even when they contain similar references to principles, Chapters 3 and 4 illustrated wildly different operational, jurisprudential interpretations of these principles. The authority and representativeness mentioned together in one constitution can give international civil servants greater autonomy. In another constitution, very similar wording can restrain the organization's activities, vesting such authority in member states. What does this mean for the law of international organizations? Do similarities, differences and even a taxonomy of principles in these constitutions provide clues for the

---

[1] Talk of international organizations' charters as constitutions between states has a long and ignoble history. Most modern legal researchers have rejected such a notion as a matter of law, although the analogue still remains useful to both international organizations' officials and legal researchers like. For some of this thinking, see Ernst-Ulrich Petersmann, "Constitutionalism and International Organizations," 17 *Nw. J. Int'l L. & Bus.* 398 (1997); Testsuo Sato, *Evolving Constitutions of International Organizations: A Critical Analysis of the Interpretative Framework of the Constituent Instruments of International Organizations* (1996).

development of international law, particularly as such law relates to these international organizations?

This chapter ties together some of the threads woven in the previous chapters. It discusses the history of thought in the field of international organizations law as it applies to a "common law" of international organizations' constitutions. It also discusses the case against such a common law. Legal researchers have seen the folly of trying to develop a unified law of international organizations, even if they did not have access to a database like the one at the heart of this book. This chapter reviews some of this thinking and shows how the analysis of these constitutions bolsters their case. The third section describes the developing jurisprudence, particularly in international tribunals, against the idea of a single unifying law of international organizations. As reflected in the diversity observed in the network analyses and legal analyses of constitutions provided in the preceding chapters, this chapter sees *laws* of international organizations, not a singular *law* of international organizations. Any attempt in the future to describe the law of international organizations must accept this variegated plurality, this differentiated heterogeneity, in the principles underpinning our international organizations' constitutions.

The similarity of constitutions as law in the making?

No one really knows whence the idea of international organizations law, as a discipline, emerged. Henry Schermers claimed to play a role in its creation in the 1950s.[2] His doctoral dissertation and later works supposedly benefited from his work in the Dutch Ministry of Foreign Affairs, where he helped his supervisors to deal with issues relating to international organizations' formation, structure and operation by referring to similar constitutional "law" found in already existing international organizations. Some of Schermers' students – most notably Niels Blokker – have continued in this tradition. Accordingly, they seek to find similarities between international organizations' constitutions in an attempt to create a singular *law* of international organizations.[3] Never mind that negotiators, politicians and diplomats negotiated each international organization's constitutions given that organization's own particular context. Why would any constitution drafter

---

2 *See* Henry G. Schermers, "The Birth and Development of International Institutional Law," 1 *Int'l Org. L. Rev.* 5, 5–6 (2004).
3 For example, Blokker asserts that from the Second World War to 1990, "IOs started to copy each other's rules widely." *See* Niels M. Blokker, "General Introduction," in *Evolutions in the Law of International Organizations* 8 (Roberto Virzo & Ivan Ingravallo eds. 2015).

just copy another, previous constitution? What legal (or even logical basis) would validate pinching provisions from one international organization's constitution, even if many organizations have something similar?[4]

The traditional approach to creating international law does not consist of copying constitutions, even when a constitution lacks a particular provision. Most legal researchers accept that these kinds of constitutions codify already existing customary international law.[5] For example, Wolfgang Friedmann would claim that these constitutions – as international law – reflect the relations between sovereign states.[6] Why would completely different states or similar states that are attempting to codify custom in a completely different area of international life resort to (or feel compelled to resort to) similar provisions governing that often tenuous relationship? Arthur Weisburd might claim that the meaning behind the words used may slip, and blackletter law may not exactly correspond to the content of that existing or desired future relationship.[7] Indeed, following Timothy Meyer's *Capture Thesis*, international organizations' member states may desire "the fragmentation of customary law that can result from codification [which] actually prevents a unified understanding of customary law from emerging – the exact opposite of codification's ostensible purpose."[8] Some researchers like Mark Villiger might even go so far as to note that some degree of separation exists between customary law and treaty law.[9] However, who could imagine that identical custom exists everywhere – enough so that similar constitutional provisions would make sense?

Some similarities must exist to create the custom that underpins the treaty in the first place. For example, Richard Baxter asserts that "the authorities are heard to say that treaties, whether bilateral or multilateral, are 'sources' of international law by reason of a 'widespread process of transformation of treaty law into international customary law.'"[10] In other words,

---

4 Alter, for example, highlights the copying of European-style international courts. *See* Karen J. Alter, "The Global Spread of European Style International Courts," 35 *W. Euro. Pol.* 135 (2012). However, even if other regions admittedly copied the idea, their own region's needs, negotiating tactics and even languages militated for significant variation in the model.
5 A litany of researchers have argued for decades that constitutions follow custom, rather than vice versa.
6 *See* Wolfgang Friedmann, *The Changing Structure of International Law* 122 (1964).
7 *See* Arthur Weisburd, "Customary International Law: The Problem of Treaties," 21 *Vand. J. Transnat'l L.* 1 (1988).
8 Timothy Meyer, "Codifying Custom," 160 *U. Pa. L. Rev.* 995 (2012).
9 *See* Mark Villiger, *Customary International Law and Treaties* 64–148 (1997).
10 *See* Richard Baxter, "Multilateral Treaties as Evidence of Customary International Law," 41 *Brit Y. B. Int'l L.* 275, 276 (1966).

constitutions – if they all read similarly enough – might create the basis of international law, but only if these provisions help to create the custom that underpins such law.[11] To be sure, a complex relationship exists between treaties and custom. However, who could believe that customs in different parts of the world converge enough to require or even allow similar constitutional language? Conventional thinking on the subject – as typified by Michael Akehurst – views that acts, not claims or exhortations in treaties, create international law.[12] Authors like Bin Cheng would recoil at the idea.[13]

By the late 2000s, Baxter's idea that international organizations' constitutions could provide the basis of a robust international law looked iffy. Baxter was quick to exclude, again without explaining why, "[t]he accretion of a body of customary international law about the constitutive instruments of international organizations."[14] Bowett allowed for the possibility of a common law of international organizations in 1963, when he analyzed their common institutional problems.[15] Later editions of his work made these assertions more explicit.[16] In 2008, Finn Seyersted's posthumous book *Common Law of International Organizations* tried to extend Baxter's project, claiming that the accretion of international organizations' constitutions could form the basis of a type of international law based on custom.[17] Unfortunately, Seyersted provided little evidence that the commonalities he saw between international organizations formed customary law or another type of binding law.[18] Seyersted did not develop any theory that could

---

11 *See* Wolfgang Friedmann, "The Changing Dimensions of International Law," 62 *Colum. L. Rev.* 1147, 1163 (1962).
12 Michael Akehurst, "Custom as a Source of International Law," 47 *Brit. YB Int'l L.* 1, 3 (1975). *See also* Karol Wolfe, *Custom in Present International Law* 42 (1993).
13 *See* Bin Cheng, "Custom: The Future of General State Practice in a Divided World," in *The Structure and Process of International Law: Essays in Legal Philosophy Doctrine and Theory* 532 (R. Macdonald & D. Johnston eds. 1983).
14 *See* Baxter, *supra* this chapter, note 10, at 277 (citing Rosalyn Higgins, *The Development of International Law through the Political Organs of the United States* (1963)). Perhaps Baxter excluded constitutions of international organizations as a mere delimitation, as opposed to a substantive comment on the nature of these treaties, and so his lack of an explanation would be excusable.
15 *See* D.W. Bowett, *The Law of International Institutions* 273–340 (1963).
16 *See* Sands & Klein, *supra* Chapter 1, note 39, at 16.
17 *See* Finn Seyersted, *Common Law of International Organizations* 4 (2008) ("hop[ing] that the book may help lecturers and text-book writers to reflect the *customary* law, common to all [intergovernmental organizations], which has developed in practice").
18 Klabbers in particular has commented publicly about Seyersted's lack of evidence in this regard. *See* Jan Klabbers, "On Seyersted and His Common Law of International Organizations," 5 *Int'l Org. L. Rev.* 381, 382–83 (2008).

explain how mere commonalities in international organizations' practice could transform into a law that then would bind an international organization and its members. After all, customary international law requires a close study of the practice of *states*, among other things, not the practice of international organizations.[19]

Instead of creating such a theory, Seyersted spent his time focusing on general notions of the legal personality of international organizations, the inherent powers that might flow from such personality, and their jurisdiction. Such work only marginally tried to show commonalities among international organizations.[20] Seyersted's book begins by bizarrely breaking down "common law" into its two components, merely excluding "extended jurisdiction" from the commonalities shared by international organizations.[21] For him, the "common law ... is *not* primarily laid down in constitutions or other conventions but ... has developed in practice as customary law."[22] Such law, instead, "includes the basic aspects of the internal law of the organizations (constitutional, administrative and procedural law) – as well as the entire law on their external relations of public and private international law (international personality and choice of law respectively), which are not at all dealt with in their respective constitutions."[23] Seyersted continues, noting that "this law is common to all IGOs [intergovernmental organizations] (unless they exceptionally have deviating provisions) and is thus 'common law,' both in the literal sense and in the Anglo-Saxon sense of customary law."[24]

Seytersted has a lot of explaining to do before we may accept his theory of a common law of international organizations. He does not explain how "this law" is common to all international organizations or "common law" at all. He does not provide examples of commonalities. Even a cursory

---

19 A bevy of commentators since have highlighted the point. *See, e.g.*, Jan Klabbers, International Law 26–28 (2013); Peter Malanczuk, Akehurst's *Modern Introduction to International Law* 39 (1997).
20 *See* Seyersted, *supra* this chapter, note 17, at 37–244.
21 He also spends his time, for some reason, tracing the roots of the words "law" and "loi." *Id.*, at 3.
22 *Id.*, at 4. Such customary law "covers the aspects not laid down in the constitutions and other conventions." *Id.*
23 *Id.* To belabor the point, he notes that "the common law of intergovernmental organizations is not normally found in the constitutional or other conventions between the member States, but in customary law developed in common by the numerous existing [intergovernmental organizations]." *Id.*, at 21. In other words, constitutions may not form such law in themselves. However, the customs they may engender do.
24 *Id.*, at 4. Later, he claims that "this law has been developed in common by the ever increasing number of IGOs." *Id.*, at 23.

review of international organizations' constitutions and practice fails to find such commonalities. Even organizational titles differ from organization to organization, with some having administrators, others specialists and yet others presidents and staff.

Other supporters of Seyersted's ideas have used similarly fuzzy explanations. In particular, Elihu Lauterpacht relies on common sense rather than customary law in noting the following:

> Each [individual international constituent instrument] is a separate treaty, legally distinct from every other. Yet common sense suggests that, where a similar problem arises in more than one organization, its solution in one context must have a bearing on its solution in another.[25]

Lauterpacht proposes more than just allowing "the meaning given to an expression in one treaty [being] applied to a comparable expression in another."[26] Instead, he assumes that "comparable expressions" already exist, rather than allowing for the transplanting (or "cross-fertilization") of a provision from one international organization's constitution into another.[27] Lauterpacht's approach differs from Seyersted's in relying on common sense rather than customary law, but their methods of using nebulous and unconvincing proof tie them well together.

Jurisprudence against constitutional similarity creating law

At least two international cases reject Seyersted's idea of a common law for international organizations based on supposed customary law. The first case involves an interwar-era case involving an attempt by a governor representing Lithuania to dismiss the president of Lithuania. At its heart, the case tested whether international officials and courts could accept the rummaging-through of treaties to find similarities that might hold up as customary law.

In 1932 the Permanent Court of International Justice issued a ruling in the *Interpretation of the Statute of the Memel Territory*.[28] The case

---

25 *See* Elihu Lauterpacht, "The Development of the Law of International Organizations by the Decisions of International Tribunals," 152 *Recueil des Cours*. 377, 396 (1976-IV).
26 *Id*.
27 Lauterpacht's examples do not support his case because he assumes such identity between the terms used in these constitutions, rather than the inspirational cross-borrowing often done with international treaties. See *id*., at 397–402.
28 Interpretation of Statute of Memel Territory (U.K. v. Lith.), 1932 P.C.I.J. (ser. A/B) No. 49, at 294, 300 (Aug. 11).

represents one of the first tests of whether treaty obligations arise when the instrument in question lacks the normal formality of a treaty.[29] This chapter's interest in this case extends to the following immediate question: does a power to appoint necessarily include an implied power to dismiss? The answer would raise a much deeper question: does typical wording in constitutions and treaties apply to all similar constitutions and treaties, even if they do not have such wording?

In *Memel*, the Four Powers – Great Britain, France, Italy and Japan – brought a claim against Lithuania relating to the powers of the governor. In that case, the Four Powers argued that the Memel Territory regional governor's dismissal of the President of the Directorate of Memel (the head of the executive branch in Lithuania's Memel Territory) contravened the Statute of the Memel Territory.[30] The Statute of the Memel Territory served as the constitution for that territory, following the signing of a convention in 1924 involving the Four Powers and Lithuania. In that Paris convention, the Four Powers had transferred sovereignty of the Memel Territory to Lithuania, subject to conditions. An annex to the convention, the Statute of Memel, allowed the territory to enjoy "legislative, judicial, administrative, and financial autonomy" – within certain limitations.[31] The case's key issue concerned whether the governor representing Lithuania had the ability to dismiss the president.[32] The Four Powers asserted that the governor had no right to dismiss.[33] The Four Powers interpreted the Statute's requirement that the president should stay in power as long as he had the Memel Chamber of Representatives' confidence as a prohibition on the governor's power to dismiss the president while he enjoyed such confidence.[34]

---

29 Many subsequent analyses called upon the Court's holdings in arguments. *See, e.g.*, Bruce Ackerman & David Golove, "Is NAFTA Constitutional?," 108 *Harv. L. Rev.* 799, 844 (1995); Peter Spiro, "Treaties, Executive Agreements, and Constitutional Method," 79 *Tex. L. Rev.* 961, 987 (2001). The case also deals with protecting minorities through autonomous regimes – a subject this section does not discuss. For more on these issues, *see* Hurst Hannum, "Rethinking Self-Determination," 34 *Va. J. Int'l L.* 1, 6 (1993); Hersch Lauterpacht, *The Development of International Law by the International Court* 324 (1958).
30 *See* Interpretation of Statute of Memel Territory (U.K. v. Lith.), 1932 PCIJ (ser. A/B) No. 49, at 295–96, 301.
31 *See id.*, at 299. *See also* Yoram Dinstein, "Autonomy Regimes and International Law," 56 *Vill. L. Rev.* 437, 448 (2011) (quoting Convention Concerning the Territory of Memel, May 8, 1924, 29 LNTS 85, 89).
32 *See* Interpretation of Statute of Memel Territory (U.K. v. Lith.), 1932 PCIJ at 301–3, 310–12.
33 *See id.* at 312.
34 *See id.*

Lithuania, for its part, asserted that the Statute implied such a power, which in any case did not explicitly prohibit such a dismissal.[35] Moreover – and most importantly for this chapter's purposes – Lithuania also argued that many other constitutions had provisions related to similar dismissals. Thus, as standard practice and custom, such dismissal powers could reasonably be inferred in the Charter's own provisions.

The Court found for the governor, although not for his approach to constitutional law. The Court reasoned that, when giving autonomy to the Memel Territory, the parties could not have intended to divide sovereignty over the territory.[36] At the same time, the Court determined that the Statute's purpose was not to give Lithuania rights, but to limit the Memel Territory's autonomy.[37] It concluded that "the right of the Governor to dismiss the President of the Directorate is not excluded" and that dismissal could even help Lithuania to protect its rights, where such rights were threatened and where no other options were available.[38] However, the Court was unwilling to extend this power to dismiss to non-exceptional circumstances, based merely as an implied power accompanying the power to appoint.[39] Lithuania had not even argued for such dismissal powers outside of these types of exceptional circumstances anyway.

The reasoning the Court used applies as much to this chapter's situation as to theirs. The Court refused to consider Lithuania's argument – that the Statute intended to grant the governor certain authorities, which included the ability to dismiss the president.[40] The Court found that Lithuania's argument consisted "almost entirely of deductions drawn from the contents of constitutions in force in other countries, from the constitutional practice of other countries and from the statements made in the works of authors who had studied those constitutions."[41] In other words, the Court refused to accept that rummaging through other constitutions for similar dismissal provisions represents a valid basis for making international law. Such law could not comfort any applicant seeking to apply that dismissal provision to a constitution that originally lacked such a dismissal provision. Just

---

35 See id.
36 Such autonomy "should not disturb the unity of the Lithuanian State and should operate within the framework of Lithuanian sovereignty." Id., at 313.
37 See id., at 314.
38 The rights of autonomous minorities represent an important part of this story, which this book has omitted for reasons of brevity. Therefore, the Court's holdings relate to this principle as much as, if not more than, the issue of the dismissal. See id., at 318–19.
39 See id., at 319–20.
40 See id., at 320.
41 Id.

because many constitutions contain a provision does not necessarily make that provision international law.

The UK Court of Appeal reached a similar decision in the *International Tin Council* case. In the late 1980s Maclaine Watson & Co. sued to win compensation from the International Tin Council's member states when the insolvent Council defaulted on loans and contracts after the 1985 tin price collapse.[42] The plaintiffs "contended that there is a rule of international law that where sovereign states by treaty bring into being an international organization which is intended to engage in commercial transactions, the member states are liable."[43] In the judgment, Lord Oliver of Aylmerton further explained how, "[i]n an endeavour to establish acceptance of the supposed rule, attention was drawn to some 16 treaties establishing international organisations which contained provisions expressly excluding liability on the part of the members, but there was a very large number of similar treaties which did not ... ."[44] To "prove" member states' secondary liability in international law, the plaintiffs pointed to sixteen of sixty-four constitutions of international organization that "exclu[ded] or limit[ed] the liability of members of international organisations in various ways ... [s]ome of [which] provided for express warnings to be given to persons dealing with the international organisation, to the effect that the members were not liable for the debts of the organisation."[45]

---

42 *See* Maclaine Watson & Co. v. Int'l Tin Council (1989) 3 All ER 523 (House of Lords); Maclaine Watson & Co. v. Int'l Tin Council (1988) 3 All ER 257 (Court of Appeal). *See also* Ilona Cheyne, "International Tin Council," 39 *Int'l & Comp. L.Q.* 945 (1990); Ilona Cheyne, "The International Tin Council," 38 *Int'l & Comp. L.Q.* 417 (1989); Nicola Dickens, "The Legacy of the Tin Council," 3 *Insolv. L. & Pol'y.* 104 (1987); Colin Warbrick & Ilona Cheyne, "The International Tin Council," 36 *Int'l & Comp. L.Q.* 931 (1987); Douglas Colliver, "Winding Up of International Organisation," 2 *J. Int'l Banking L.* 68 (1987); Geoffrey Marston, "The Personality of International Organisations in English Law," 2 *Hofstra L. & Pol'y Symp.* 75 (1997).
43 The plaintiff claimed that these member states were responsible "for the organisation's debts to third parties (whether states or individuals) unless (a) the treaty expressly excludes such liability and (b) the exclusion is brought to the notice of third parties." Maclaine Watson & Co. v. Int'l Tin Council (1989) 3 All ER 523, 554 (House of Lords).
44 *Id.*, at 554–55.
45 *Id.*, at 257, 276. These sixteen treaties were the foundational instruments for the International Atomic Energy Agency, the Asian Development Bank, the International Sugar Organisation, the Caribbean Development Bank, the African Development Fund, the International Cocoa Organisation, the African Development Bank, the International Natural Rubber Organisation, the Common Fund for Commodities, the International Bank for Reconstruction and Development, the International

Lord Justice Kerr, while sympathetic to these arguments, had to admit that such reasoning makes for poor lawmaking. Noting the "significance of the practice of states in relation to these treaties ... and the absence of any such provision in relation to the [Tin Council],"[46] Justice Kerr explained that "[f]or a long time [he] was persuaded, as [he thought they] all were, that this would provide the answer which justice require[d] in these deplorable cases[, b]ut in the end, with reluctance and regret, [he] was driven to the conclusion that the edifice will not stand up."[47] He further observed that international organizations' rights and obligations "are governed by the system of law under which it is incorporated," and then agreed with Lord Justice Ralph Gibson by saying the following:

> [O]ne cannot deduce an acceptance of liability in the Sixth International Tin Agreement [based on the sixteen "limited liability treaties"]. These treaties cannot in themselves provide sufficient evidence of the practice of states for that purpose.[48]

Lord Justice Ralph Gibson found little basis for assuming that, even if most or all international organizations' constitutions included (or excluded) a provision or financial liability, that such liability should extend as international law. Analyzing the sixteen treaties cited in the case, he noted, "I am unable to accept that the practice shown in these treaties can fairly be regarded as recognition by the states concerned of a rule of international law that absence of a non-liability clause results in direct liability.... Nothing is shown of any practice of states as to the acknowledgment or acceptance of direct liability by any states by reason of the absence of an exclusion clause."[49] Agreeing, Lord Justice Nourse stated the following about these sixteen treaties:

> [They] are not in the end of very great assistance.... There being no established practice of making provision in regard to the liability of member states,

---

Finance Corporation, the International Development Association, the East African Development Bank, the International Institute for Cotton, the Caribbean Food Corporation, and the International Sea-Bed Authority. See *id.*, at 321–23.

46 *Id.* at 257, 276.
47 *Id.* at 257, 301.
48 *Id.*, at 306.
49 *Id.*, at 354. He calls "the inclusion of these clauses in constituent treaties of a number of international organizations ... likely to engage in financial transactions ... impressive." *Id.* He further notes that "such terms are consistent with the acceptance by the states concerned that liability of members would arise if no such terms were included." *Id.*, at 355. However, he then notes "a state of uncertainty as to the rules of public international law" and thus the provisions tried to "warn those dealing with the organisation." *Id.*, at 354–55.

whether for or against, it cannot be assumed, in cases where no exclusion or limitation is found, that the liability exists.[50]

To summarize, these judges held that similarities in international organizations' constitutions do not apply to constitutions lacking similar provisions. Such a decision supports the Permanent Court of International Justice's decision in *Memel* that similar treaties and charters do not create ethereal international law binding on all organizations.[51]

Critics might point to the International Court of Justice's 1980 *Interpretation of the Agreement of 25 March 1951 between the WHO and Egypt* advisory opinion as evidence against the "few sparrows makes a spring" view of international organizations law.[52] The case involved the "legal rules and principles" that govern transfer of a regional office of the WHO out of Egypt, against the Egyptian government's wishes.[53] Commentators ostensibly never have referred to this advisory opinion when looking for similarities between international organizations' constitutions. In determining the legal rules and principles governing the departure, the Court looked at the contractual relationship existing between the WHO and Egypt for decades.[54] However, the Court looked at "a considerable

---

50 Firmly in the "it depends" camp of international jurisprudence, the Right Honorable Lord Justice Nourse finds the following: "What can be said is that it may exist; and further, that for those who intend to exclude or limit it there are precedents readily available for that purpose." *Id.*, at 330. This perhaps is not the best example of a judge taking a stand on a particular point.

51 As with the *Interpretation of the Statute of the Memel Territory* case, ostensibly no commentators until now have focused on this aspect of the *Maclaine Watson & Co. Ltd. v. International Tin Council* case in the context of the law of international organizations. Amerasinghe cites this case, but he does not discuss this aspect of the proceedings. See Chittharanjan Amerasinghe, "Liability to Third Parties of Member States of International Organizations: Practice, Principle and Judicial Precedent," 85 *Am. J. Int'l L.* 259 (1991).

52 *See* "Interpretation of the Agreement of 25 March 1951 Between the WHO and Egypt, Advisory Opinion," 1980 *I.C.J. Rep.* 73, 76, 95 (Dec. 20).

53 Much scholarly work has addressed this topic before. For example, *see* William Hein, "Interpretation of the Agreement of the 25 March 1951 Between The WHO and Egypt," in *International Court of Justice: Reports of Judgments, Advisory Opinions and Orders* 89–90 (1980); Jan Klabbers, "The Transformation of International Organizations Law," 26 *Eur. J. Int'l L.* 9, 59–63 (2015); Christine Gray, "The International Court's Advisory Opinion on the WHO–Egypt Agreement of 1951," 32 *Int'l & Comp. L.Q.* 534 (1983).

54 The relationship existed arguably since 1949, when Egypt "transferred the operation of the Alexandria Sanitary Bureau to the Organization," as well as the host agreements with other international organizations. "Interpretation of the Agreement of

number of host agreements of different kinds, concluded by States with various international organizations."[55]

The Court used those host agreements to conclude that host states and international organizations have mutual obligations to resolve problems that arise with regard to "revision, termination or denunciation of a host agreement."[56] It subsequently applied this rule to the facts and determined that Egypt and the WHO had the obligation "to co-operate in good faith with respect to the implications and effects of the transfer of the Regional Office from Egypt," which derived from "general international law, ... the Constitution of the Organization and ... the agreements in force between Egypt and the Organization."[57] At first glance, the advisory opinion seems to find for a unitary international law of international organizations, governed by the mass of existing treaties, even if in this narrow issue.

However, the Court failed to create law in this case. It failed to articulate a theory as to how the provisions of host agreements – that were unrelated to the question the Court was faced with – could be applied to the agreement before the Court. In other words, the Court took a decision on a host agreement and on privileges and immunities for an agreement that lacked those similar provisions. Commentators like Andrew Mitchell and Charles Brower have tried to help articulate such a theory for the Court.[58] Nevertheless, the Court's reliance on these unrelated host agreements to fill in the supposed gaps in the WHO–Egypt Agreement could be said to argue for a transcendent common law of international organizations existing above and beyond individual constitutions.

This advisory opinion does little to help advocates of such a position. For one thing, the Court completely changed the question. The imprecise WHO–Egypt Agreement could not address the applicability of the notice provision to the situation at hand or determine the legal responsibilities of

---

25 March 1951 Between the WHO and Egypt, Advisory Opinion," 1980 *I.C.J. Rep.* 73, 92–95 (Dec. 20).

55 *Id.*, at 94.
56 These relate to mutual obligations involving the need to "act in good faith," "co-operate in good faith," provide notice of "not less than twelve months" where the treaty in question has an implied right of denunciation and "have reasonable regard to the interests of the other party to the treaty." *Id.*, at 94–95.
57 *Id.*, at 95–96.
58 They discuss the mutual obligations the Court created, but they do not even acknowledge how the Court borrowed from other host agreements. *See* Andrew Mitchell, "Good Faith in WTO Dispute Settlement," 7 *Melb. J. Int'l L.* 339, 344 (2006); Charles H. Brower Jr., "International Immunities: Some Dissident Views on the Role of Municipal Courts," 41 *Va. J. Int'l L.* 1, 33, 54 (2000).

the disputants.[59] Therefore, the Court failed to directly answer the question posed by the WHO, presumably given the Court's unwillingness to admit a gap in the law and the supposedly hypothetical nature of the original question posed.[60] Regardless of the reason, such a change undermines the Court's advisory jurisdiction.[61] As so much *obiter dicta*, the Court's advice did not correspond to the question, thereby making relatively little – if any – contribution to international law.[62] Not that advisory opinions play a large role in establishing international law anyway.[63]

The difference in opinions in the Court comprises a second reason why the Opinion fails to help Seyersted's one-law-to-rule-them-all approach. The eight separate opinions delivered in the case show that the majority disagreed on how to answer the question the Court itself invented. Researchers such as Christine Gray have called opinions like this "judgment by lowest common denominator."[64] Such a diversity of opinions thus further undermines the seeming weight of this advisory opinion.

Other ICJ decisions also contradict the advisory opinion. In the ICJ's 1996 *Legality of the Use by a State of Nuclear Weapons in Armed Conflict* advisory opinion, the Court refused to answer the question posed by the World Health Assembly, as the question of the legality of nuclear weapons did not fall "within the scope of [the] activities" of the WHO.[65] Many

---

59 See "Interpretation of the Agreement of 25 March 1951 between the WHO and Egypt, Advisory Opinion," 1980 *I.C.J. Rep.* 73, 76, 91–93, 95 (Dec. 20). *See also* Gray, *supra* this chapter, note 53, at 536 (inferring that the majority thought the Agreement was not applicable to the situation at hand).
60 *See* Gray, *supra* this chapter, note 53, at 537.
61 The ICJ Statute requires that "[q]uestions upon which the advisory opinion of the Court is asked shall be laid before the Court." "ICJ Statute," *supra* Chapter 1, note 122, art. 65(2). The provision requires the Court to respond to the questions asked and to whatever question it likes.
62 Hudes and Schlemmer-Schulte find similarly, that such types of decisions serve as the equivalent of common law "obiter dicta." *See* Karen Hudes & Sabine Schlemmer-Schulte, "Accountability in Bretton Woods," 15 *ILSA J. Int'l & Comp. L.* 501, 511 (2009). Taft also finds that court decisions that do not address the question or issue before the court – namely "unnecessary to resolv[ing] the case" – also provide poor grounds for settling law. William Taft, IV, "Self-Defense and the Oil Platforms Decision," 29 *Yale J. Int'l L.* 295, 295 (2004).
63 As Frowein and Oellers-Frahm find, "It is clear that advisory opinions have no binding force as such." Jochen Frowein & Karin Oellers-Frahm, "Advisory Opinions," in *The Statute of the International Court of Justice: A Commentary* 1605, 1621 (Andreas Zimmermann et al. eds. 2012).
64 *See* Gray, *supra* this chapter, note 53, at 536.
65 *See* "Legality of the Use by a State of Nuclear Weapons in Armed Conflict," Advisory Opinion, 1996 *ICJ Rep.* 66, 74–77 (July 8).

commentators have analyzed the Court's judicious use of its own discretion in deciding (or not, as the case may be) to hear a case.[66] At least one commentator would agree that the "real question before the Court" was whether the WHO could ask it a non-health-related question.[67] The 1996 refusal to respond to the WHO's request for an advisory opinion – whatever its other virtues and vices – undermines the legitimacy of the 1980 request for an advisory opinion. Both had little to do with health, which was the basis for refusing the 1996 request. Both dealt with larger questions involving interstate relations. As such, the ICJ's 1980 *Interpretation of the Agreement of 25 March 1951 between the WHO and Egypt* advisory opinion remains a dead end on the road to creating international organizations law.

What do these cases teach us? Both the *Interpretation of the Statute of the Memel Territory* case and the *Maclaine Watson & Co. Ltd. v. International Tin Council* cases refuse to find for generalizing, overriding principles in international organizations' constitutions. If the 1980 *Interpretation of the Agreement of 25 March 1951 between the WHO and Egypt* advisory opinion remains valid law on the books, the case only muddies the waters of international jurisprudence. The Court's good sense in 1996 to refuse to opine on nuclear weapons both overrules any precedent that the flawed *Interpretation of the Agreement of 25 March 1951 between the WHO and Egypt* advisory opinion might make and shows a commitment to pluralistic principled international organizations law.

The laws of international organizations

Advocates of a single, encompassing *law* of international organizations have not adequately articulated a theory behind the unity they see in the field. Similarity between the constitutions of international organizations is

---

66 Klabbers has applauded the case of the Court's refusal to create a universal, global law. See Jan Klabbers, "Global Governance before the ICJ: Re-reading the WHA Opinion," 13 *Max Planck YB UN Law* 1 (2009). Rostow analyses the attempt of the WHO to overstep its bounds, grossly simplifying his otherwise detailed argument. See Nicholas Rostow, "The World Health Organization, the International Court of Justice, and Nuclear Weapons," 20 *Yale J. Int'l L.* 151 (1995). Strahan, for his part, fears that the WHO's attempt to legislate the issue of international politics and customs could lead to less support for the Court and the UN system in general. See Martin M. Strahan, "Nuclear Weapons, the World Health Organization, and the International Court of Justice: Should an Advisory Opinion Bring Them Together?," 2 *Tulsa J. Comp. & Int'l L.* 395 (1995).
67 See Gray, *supra* this chapter, note 53, at 535.

not enough to establish the existence of a unified law. International organizations' constitutions have very different language and provisions, as this book has shown. Even for provisions using similar language, like those relying on the "international character of international civil servants," their meaning differs greatly across these constitutions. Provisions related to the autonomy of an international organization change meaning radically when read in combination with other constitutional principles like representativeness, equality and authority.

Neither case law nor logic supports the unitarians' approach. As late as 2011, researchers like Tomer Broude and Yuval Shany have supported *Multi-Sourced Equivalent Norms in International Law* (to read the title of their book on the subject).[68] The book tries to describe "normative parallelism" and similar norms within different branches of international law. However, the book does not – and cannot – support unity within international law. Instead, the authors writing in support of "multi-sourced equivalent norms" point to regional agreements, different provisions that might have similar interpretations or impacts and a range of other examples that support the "multi-sourced" part of the story much more than the "equivalent" part.

The general consensus among academics remains: the constitutions, as well as relevant treaties and general international law, govern international organizations. Courts like the US's own Supreme Court have refused to use common provisions – like those related to immunity – in international organizations' constitutions as proof of some kind of general *binding* international law applicable to the Court and the US.[69] Much to the chagrin of many, courts' refusal to find universal principles in these treaties and charters costs the UN and the international community greatly in areas like peacekeeping.[70]

Other academics have noted – and in some cases lamented over – the extent to which common provisions in charters and treaties do not create

---

68 *See Multi-Sourced Equivalent Norms in International Law* (Tomer Broude & Yuval Shany eds. 2011).
69 Immunity represents one of the key areas analyzed by researchers in this area. If Young notes the Supreme Court's failure or refusal to deduce general principles in international organizations' constitutions, Hertz bemoans this as a blow to these organizations' transparency and accountability. *See* Aaron Young, "Deconstructing International Organization Immunity," 44 *Geo. J. Int'l L.* 311, 348 (2012); Steven Herz, "International Organizations in U.S. Courts: Reconsidering the Anachronism of Absolute Immunity," 31 *Suffolk Transnat'l L. Rev.* 471, 483–84 (2008).
70 *See* Devon Whittle, "Peacekeeping in Conflict: The Intervention Brigade, Monusco, and the Application of International Humanitarian Law to United Nations Forces," 46 *Geo. J. Int'l L.* 837, 849 (2015).

binding law. Many commentators, like Nigel White and Sorcha MacLeod for example, note that general treaty provisions governing institutional responsibility of EU institutions do not automatically extend to all international organizations through some kind of generalizing process in international law.[71] Indeed, as Luis Miguel Hinojosa Martinez notes, the UN Security Council has whipped up enormous controversy in attempts to dictate anti-terrorism law, contrary to international custom and often member states' own laws.[72]

Even the many commentators who address charters and treaties dealing with human rights do not claim – with limited exceptions – some kind of ethereal, unified law to rule international organizations' work or recommendations on human rights.[73] Such claims have particularly affected the international tribunals and courts, which themselves refuse to apply any notion of *jus gentium* or *jus cogens* in international organizations' constitutions to protect human rights.[74] The EU's own human rights obligations provide a stark illustration, showing how general principles enshrined in its own treaty as well as UN treaties defy (to the authors' chagrin) generalization as a single human rights law applicable to all international

---

71 In their article, White and MacLeod describe how, despite provisions in international conventions making private sector military contractors accountable for their actions, the widespread use of these provisions cannot generalize to create an obligation in all treaties applicable to all states. See Nigel D. White & Sorcha MacLeod, "EU Operations and Private Military Contractors: Issues of Corporate and Institutional Responsibility," 19 *Eur. J. Int'l L.* 965, 970–71 (2008).
72 See Luis Miguel Hinojosa Martinez, "The Legislative Role of the Security Council in its Fight Against Terrorism: Legal, Political and Practical Limits," 57 *Int'l & Comp. L.Q.* 333, 345 (2008). For a similar perspective, see also Andrea Bianchi, "Assessing the Effectiveness of the UN Security Council's Anti-Terrorism Measures: The Quest for Legitimacy and Cohesion," 17 *Eur. J. Int'l L.* 881, 886 (2006).
73 If Edwards notes the limits of trying to ascribe such rights to these constitutions when they do not appear, authors like Wahi's and MacKay's impassioned appeals for such overreaching strike a dissonant chord in the reader, bordering on activism by academics. See Alice Edwards, "The Optional Protocol to the Convention Against Torture and the Detention of Refugees," 57 *Int'l & Comp. L.Q.* 789, 815 (2008); Namita Wahi, "Human Rights Accountability of the IMF and the World Bank: A Critique of Existing Mechanisms and Articulation of a Theory of Horizontal Accountability," 12 *U.C. Davis J. Int'l L. & Pol'y* 331, 364 (2006); Fergus MacKay, "Universal Rights or a Universe Unto Itself?: Indigenous Peoples' Human Rights and the World Bank's Draft Operational Policy 4.10 on Indigenous Peoples," 17 *Am. U. Int'l L. Rev.* 527, 564 (2002).
74 For a fascinating description of how this plays out in the international criminal courts, see Göran Sluiter, "International Criminal Proceedings and the Protection of Human Rights," 37 *New Eng. L. Rev.* 935, 937 (2003).

organizations.[75] Indeed, despite the apparent desirability of policies like economic sanctions in support of human rights rules globally, authors like August Reinisch see limits in the UN's own constitution in trying to overgeneralize international organizations' constitutions.[76]

Instead, far more fruitful work by authors like Diane Desierto and Colin Gillespie attempts to understand the heterogeneity of interpretations and viewpoints, particularly relating to principles like those enshrined in the International Covenant on Civil and Political Rights and the economic, social and cultural principles the Covenant embodies.[77] Even in treatments like Christian Schliemann's analysis of the OECD's Multinationals' Guidelines, *de lege ferenda* (or future law as it should be) does not need to have any more consolidation or merging than *de lege lata* (or law as it is now).[78] Even pushers of common principles in international organizations' constitutions and international law more generally, such as Armin von Bogdandy, accept that the heterogeneity of principles in these documents prevents any attempt to create a singular meaning for principles in international law.[79] The field of international organizations law should understand this heterogeneity, instead of imposing a false order upon it.

---

75 *See* Tawhida Ahmed & Israel De Jesus Butler, "The European Union and Human Rights: An International Law Perspective," 17 *Eur. J. Int'l L.* 771, 776–77 (2006).
76 *See* August Reinisch, "Developing Human Rights and Humanitarian Law Accountability of the Security Council for the Imposition of Economic Sanctions," 95 *Am. J. Int'l L.* 851, 858 (2001).
77 *See* Diane Desierto & Colin Gillespie, "A Modern Integrated Paradigm for International Responsibility Arising from Violations of Economic, Social, and Cultural Rights," 3 *Cambridge J. Int'l & Comp. L.* 556, 590 (2014).
78 *See* Christian Schliemann, "Procedural Rules for the Implementation of the OECD Guidelines for Multinational Enterprises – A Public International Law Perspective," 13 *German L.J.* 51, 61 (2012).
79 *See* von Bogdandy, *supra* Chapter 3, note 10, at 1923.

6

Conclusion

To date, the prevailing view of international organizations has been that they provide a formal channel of interstate cooperation. Since the mid-nineteenth century, international organizations have focused mostly on particular regions or specialized purposes. At the same time, they enshrine several common principles and values, although not as many as the leading textbooks on international organizations law would have us believe. This book has put these principles and values to the test. Using a database of the founding constitutions of 191 international organizations, which represents the largest statistical census of these documents to date, this book has empirically assessed whether international organizations share the same values and principles, at least on paper. Unsurprisingly, the book found large differences between international organizations. The following are some of the main points that this empirical assessment has provided.

- Main principles and values from the leading international organizations law textbooks include aspiration, authority, communication, cooperation, efficiency, equality, peace, recommendation and representativeness.
- Other principles and values could include progress, harmony, humanity and human rights, among many others.
- Groups of principles work together to form some kind of semantic (if not legal) concept above and beyond the meaning of these principles individually.
- It is not possible to group international organizations by what they purportedly do or should do.
- Certain time periods coincide with the rising importance of certain networks of principles in international organizations' constitutions.
- It is unwise to confuse a pattern exhibited among the constitutions of international organizations from the latter part of the twentieth century with a general pattern for all international organizations.
- Particular principles play significant and quantifiable key and supporting roles in international organizations' constitutions, with executive

staffing principles serving as the key principle in the network of principles.
- No analysis of international organizations law can omit the principles driving executive staff and remain relevant.

With the map of international organizations' principles and values that this book provides, future researchers are now equipped to explore how the associations, groups and networks from the data translate into international organizations law. The latter chapters of this book illustrated the quantitative links from the first chapters by using the standard tools of legal analysis. Other researchers are hereby invited to use this book's raw data to find their own links to better understand international organizations law. However, perhaps the more interesting continuation from where this book leaves off would be an empirical study of how international organizations exhibit these principles and values in actual practice, not just on paper – such stuff as *magnum opi* are made of.

As for international organizations law, the drafters of international organizations' constitutions deliberately drafted them to meet the *sui generis* needs of those particular organizations. Over-reaching researchers looking to stitch together provisions from these constitutions – or some kind of *ratio decidendi* (to use a common-law term) in opinions and cases from international courts like the ICJ – have no theory to support these attempts.[1] Instead of finding a single, unitary law of international organizations, researchers should search for *laws* (plural) for these international organizations. The search for these laws naturally begins by understanding the multiple principles and multiple interpretations of even the same principle in the hundreds of international organizations' constitutions in existence. Researchers should focus their efforts on creating the theoretical foundations for such a *pluralistic* (common) law of international organizations.

The benefits of making actual, blackletter-law comparisons of constitutional provisions seem obvious. Such comparisons aid in the development of knowledge about the laws of international organizations. Such comparisons also can promote the reform of these international organizations' constitutions, once such analysis has clearly identified what each constitution provides to its organization. Moreover, such comparison can help lawyers to work within and between multiple international organizations, once they have become sufficiently familiar with the principles driving each

---

1 Nevertheless, each new generation of researchers tries to argue for such an approach to interpreting these constitutions. For a discussion from the post-war period of finding such *ratio*, see Hexner, *supra* Chapter 3, note 180, at 341.

organization's laws. Finally, *if* a unifying law of international organizations will one day exist, such comparisons may help in creating stronger unifying theories for such a law. However, such attempts ought to start with the data and the provisions in these constitutions.

This book has contributed to the development of such a theory. It has outlined the heterogeneous principles driving these constitutions' laws. It has shown how, simply by grouping words in these constitutions, several "tracks" (or groups and networks) exist among constitutional principles. Principles like authority and autonomy may combine in over seventy constitutions. Some doctrines like the principle of unity might lead to useful future theorizing. The book also has identified many constitutional principles like progress and human rights that defy even statistical analysis.

Alongside this statistical analysis, this book also empirically has shown the limits to developing such theories. The meanings of combinations of principles – like authority and autonomy, and thus their effects on concrete rights, obligations and work programs – differ significantly across constitutions. Moreover, this book has shown statistically how constitutions from different time periods, from different parts of the world and even from organizations of different sizes refer to different combinations of principles. Such data suggests that legal researchers should look for a classification of legal principles, rather than a grand unifying theory.

Bibliography

Books and treatises

Alvarez, José E., *International Organizations as Law-Makers* (2006).
Amerasinghe, C.F., *Principles of the Institutional Law of International Organizations* (2d ed. 2005).
Armstrong, David, et al., *International Organisation in World Politics* (3d ed. 2004).
Barnett, Michael, & Martha Finnemore, *Rules for the World: International Organizations in Global Politics* (2004).
Bell, Christine, *On the Law of Peace: Peace Agreements and the Lex Pacificatoria* (2008).
Ben-Ari, Rephael Harel, *The Legal Status of International Non-Governmental Organizations: Analysis of Past and Present Initiatives (1912–2012)* (2013).
Bennett, Alvin Le Roy, *International Organizations: Principles and Issues* (1995).
Benvenisti, Eyal, *The Law of Global Governance* (2014).
Bowett, D.W., *The Law of International Institutions* (1963).
Breyer, Stephen, *The Court and the World: American Law and the New Global Realities* (2015).
Brölmann, Catherine, *The Institutional Veil in Public International Law: International Organisations and The Law of Treaties* (2007).
Broude, Tomer, & Yuval Shany (eds.), *Multi-Sourced Equivalent Norms in International Law* (2011).
Buira, Ariel, *Reforming the Governance of the IMF and the World Bank* (2006).
Chesterman, Simon, *Just War Or Just Peace?: Humanitarian Intervention and International Law* (2001).
Coleman, Katharina, *International Organisations and Peace Enforcement: The Politics of International Legitimacy* (2007).
Conley, John, & William O'Barr, *Just Words: Law, Language, and Power* (2005).
Dai, Xin-yuan, *International Institutions and National Policies* (2007).
Duffield, Mark, *Development, Security and Unending War: Governing the World of Peoples* (2007).
Emadi-Coffin, Barbara, *Rethinking International Organisation: Deregulation and Global Governance* (2002).
Engstrom, Viljam, *Constructing the Powers of International Institutions* (2012).
Fayol, Henri, *General and Industrial Management* (1949).

Fowler, Michael Ross, & Julie Marie Bunck, *Law, Power, and the Sovereign State: The Evolution and Application of the Concept of Sovereignty* (1995).
Friedmann, Wolfgang, *The Changing Structure of International Law* (1964).
Geyer, Florian, *Security Versus Justice?: Police and Judicial Cooperation in the European Union* (2016).
Ginty, Roger Mac, *International Peacebuilding and Local Resistance: Hybrid Forms of Peace* (2011).
Goldstone, Richard, et al., *International Judicial Institutions: The Architecture of International Justice at Home and Abroad* (2015).
Haas, Ernst, *Beyond the Nation-State: Functionalism and International Organization* (1964).
Haas, Ernst, et al., *Scientists and World Order: The Uses of Technical Knowledge in International Organizations* (1977).
Hardt, Heidi, *Time to React: The Efficiency of International Organizations in Crisis Response* (2014).
Hartley, Trevor, *European Union Law in a Global Context: Text, Cases and Materials* (2004).
Hassler, Sabine, *Reforming the UN Security Council Membership: The Illusion of Representativeness* (2012).
Heupel, Monika, & Theresa Reinold (eds.), *The Rule of Law in Global Governance* (2016).
Higgins, Rosalyn, *The Development of International Law through the Political Organs of the United States* (1963).
Hirsch, Moshe, *The Responsibility of International Organizations Toward Third Parties: Some Basic Principles* (1995).
Hooghe, Liesbet, et al., *Measuring International Authority: A Postfunctionalist Theory of Governance* (2017).
Hurd, Ian, *International Organizations: Politics, Law, Practice* (2013).
Iriye, Akira, *Global Community: The Role of International Organizations in the Making of the Contemporary World* (2002).
Jørgensen, Knud Erik (ed.), *The European Union and International Organizations* (2009).
Kaddous, Christine, *The European Union in International Organisations and Global Governance: Recent Developments* (2015).
Kelsen, Hans, *Principles of International Law* (1952).
King, Elizabeth, & Andrew Mason, *Engendering Development: Through Gender Equality in Rights, Resources, and Voice* (2001).
Kissack, Robert, *Pursuing Effective Multilateralism: The European Union, International Organisations and the Politics of Decision Making* (2010).
Klabbers, Jan, *Advanced Introduction to the Law of International Organizations* (2015).
Klabbers, Jan, *An Introduction to International Organizations Law* (3d ed. 2015).
Klabbers, Jan, *International Law* (2013).
Kochenov, Dimitry, & Fabian Amtenbrink, *The European Union's Shaping of the International Legal Order* (2013).
Koskenniemi, Martti, *The Politics of International Law* (2011).
Kwiatkowska, Barbara, et al., *International Organizations and the Law of the Sea: Documentary Yearbook* (1997).

Lauterpacht, Hersch, *The Development of International Law by the International Court* (1958).
Lindblom, Anna-Karin, *Non-Governmental Organizations in International Law* (2005).
Luard, Evan, *Conflict and Peace in the Modern International System: A Study of the Principles of International Order* (1988).
Malanczuk, Peter, Akehurst's *Modern Introduction to International Law* (7th rev. ed. 1997).
Meron, Theodor, *Human Rights and Humanitarian Norms as Customary Law* (1989).
Mitrany, David, *A Working Peace System: An Argument for the Functional Development of International Organization* (1944).
Nedergaard, Peter, *European Union Administration: Legitimacy and Efficiency* (2006).
Pietila, Hilkka, *Engendering the Global Agenda: The Story of Women and the United Nations, UN Non-Government Liaison Service* (2002).
Reinalda, Bob, *Routledge History of International Organizations: From 1815 to the Present Day* (2009).
Richmond, Oliver P., *Peace in International Relations* (2008).
Sands, Philippe, & Pierre Klein, *Bowett's Law of International Institutions* (6th ed., 2009).
Sarooshi, Dan, *International Organizations and their Exercise of Sovereign Powers* (2007).
Sato, Tetsuo, *Evolving Constitutions of International Organizations: A Critical Analysis of the Interpretative Framework of the Constituent Instruments of International Organizations* (1996).
Schermers, Henry G., & Niels M. Blokker, *International Institutional Law* (5th rev. ed. 2011).
Schweigman, David, *The Authority of the Security Council Under Chapter VII of the UN Charter: Legal Limits and the Role of the International Court of Justice* (2001).
Seyersted, Finn, *Common Law of International Organizations* (2008).
Shelton, Dinah, *Commitment and Compliance: The Role of Non-binding Norms in the International Legal System* (2003).
Silander, Daniel, & Don Wallace (eds.), *International Organizations and the Implementation of the Responsibility to Protect* (2015).
Simmons, Beth, *Mobilizing for Human Rights: International Law in Domestic Politics* (2009).
Skogly, Sigrun, *Human Rights Obligations of the World Bank and the IMF* (2012).
Spijkers, Otto, *The United Nations, the Evolution of Global Values and International Law* (2011).
Steiner, Henry J., et al., *International Human Rights in Context: Law, Politics, Morals* (2008).
Tallberg, Jonas, et al., *The Opening Up of International Organizations* (2013).
Trondal, Jarle, et al., *Unpacking International Organisations: The Dynamics of Compound Bureaucracies* (2010).
Villiger, Mark, *Customary International Law and Treaties* (1997).
Wehrenfennig, Daniel, & Christopher Balding, *Theorizing International Organizations: An Organizational Theory of International Institutions* (2011).

Wessel, Ramses, & Steven Blockmans, *Between Autonomy and Dependence: The EU Legal Order Under the Influence of International Organisations* (2012).
White, Nigel D., *The Law of International Organisations* (2d ed. 2016).
Whitworth, Sandra, *Feminism and International Relations: Towards a Political Economy of Gender in Interstate and Non-Governmental Institutions* (1994).
Wolfe, Karol, *Custom in Present International Law* (1993).
Xu, Yi-Chong, & Patrick Weller, *The Working World of International Organizations: Authority, Capacity, Legitimacy* (2017).

Articles, book chapters and news reports

Abbott, Kenneth, W. & Duncan Snidal, "Taking Responsive Regulation Transnational: Strategies for International Organizations," 1 *Reg. & Governance.* 96 (2013).
Abbott, Kenneth W., & Duncan Snidal, "Why States Act Through Formal International Organizations," 42 *J. Conflict Res.* 3 (1998).
Ackerman, Bruce, & David Golove, "Is NAFTA Constitutional?," 108 *Harv. L. Rev.* 799 (1995).
Adams, Zoe, et al., "The CBR-LRI Dataset: Methods, Properties & Potential of Leximetric Coding of Labour Laws," Working Paper 489, Centre for Business Research, University of Cambridge, *available at* https://ideas.repec.org/p/cbr/cbrwps/wp489.html (last visited Mar. 25, 2020).
Agnew, John, "The Territorial Trap: The Geographical Assumptions of International Relations Theory," 1 *Rev. Int'l Pol. Econ.* 53 (1994).
Ahluwalia, Montek Singh, "The WTO: Is It All Over or Can Something be Done?," LiveMint, Oct. 29, 2018, *at* www.livemint.com (last visited Mar. 25, 2020).
Ahmed, Tawhida, & Israel De Jesus Butler, "The European Union and Human Rights: An International Law Perspective," 17 *Eur. J. Int'l L.* 771 (2006).
Ahrne, Göran, et al., "The Paradox of Organizing States: A Meta-Organization Perspective on International Organizations," 7 *J. Int'l Org. Stud.* 5 (2016).
Akatsa-Bukach, Marren, "The EAC Gender Equality and Development Pilot Barometer" (2017), *available at* https://tgnp.org/wp-content/uploads/2017/09/The-East-Africa-Gender-Equality-and-Development-PILOT-BAROMETER.pdf (last visited Mar. 25, 2020).
Akehurst, Michael, "Custom as a Source of International Law," 47 *Brit. YB Int'l L.* 1 (1975).
Aletras, Nikolaos, et al., "Predicting Judicial Decisions of the European Court of Human Rights: A Natural Language Processing Perspective," 2 *Peer J. Comp. Sci.* 93 (2016).
Alford, Roger P., "Federal Courts, International Tribunals, and the Continuum of Deference," 43 *Va. J. Int'l L.* 675 (2003).
Allee, Todd, & Manfred Elsig, "Are the Contents of International Treaties Copied-and-Pasted? Evidence from Preferential Trade Agreements," World Trade Institute Working Paper 8, Aug. 2016, *available at* https://boris.unibe.ch (last visited Mar. 25, 2020).
Alston, Philip, "Conjuring Up New Human Rights: A Proposal For Quality Control," 78 *Am. J. Int'l L.* 607 (1984).
Alter, Karen J., "Delegating to International Courts: Self-Binding vs. Other-Binding Delegation," 71 *L. & Cont. Prob.* 37 (2008).

Alter, Karen J., "The Global Spread of European Style International Courts," 35 *W. Euro. Pol.* 135 (2012).

Altwicker, Tilmann, & Oliver Diggelmann, "How is Progress Constructed in International Legal Scholarship?," 25 *Eur. J. Int'l L.* 425 (2014).

Amerasinghe, Chittharanjan, "Liability to Third Parties of Member States of International Organizations: Practice, Principle and Judicial Precedent," 85 *Am. J. Int'l L.* 259 (1991).

Anand, R., "The Formation of International Organizations and India: A Historical Study," 23 *Leiden J. Int'l Law.* 5 (2010).

Anawalt, Howard C., "The Right to Communicate," 13 *Denv. J. Int'l L. & Pol'y.* 219 (1984).

Anderfuhren-Biget, Simon, et al., "The Values of Staff in International Organizations," *in Routledge Handbook of International Organization* (Bob Reinalda ed. 2013).

Andoura, Sami, & Peter Timmerman, "Governance of the EU: The Reform Debate on European Agencies Reignited," European Policy Institutes Network Working Paper 19, Oct. 2008, *available at* www.files.ethz.ch/isn/92938/WP%20019.pdf (last visited Mar. 25, 2020).

Armstrong, S.W., "The Doctrine of the Equality of Nations in International Law and the Relation of the Doctrine to the Treaty of Versailles," 14 *Am. J. Int'l L.* 540 (1920).

Avdeyeva, Olga, "States' Compliance with International Requirements Gender Equality in EU Enlargement Countries," 63 *Pol. Res. Q.* 203 (2008).

Baber, Walter F., & Robert V. Bartlett, "The Role of International Law in Global Governance," *in The Oxford Handbook of Climate Change and Society.* 653 (John S. Dryzek et al. eds. 2011).

Baker, Andrew, "Restraining Regulatory Capture? Anglo-America, Crisis Politics and Trajectories of Change in Global Financial Governance," 86 *Int'l Aff.* 647 (2010).

Barabucci, Gioele, et al., "Managing Semantics in XML Vocabularies: An Experience in the Legal and Legislative Domain," Paper Presented at the Balisage Markup Conference in Montreal, Canada, Jan. 2010, *available at* www.researchgate.net/profile/Silvio_Peroni/publication/256766569_Managing_semantics_in_XML_vocabularies_an_experience_in_the_legal_and_legislative_domain/links/02bfe50d48d3b9543d000000.pdf (last visited Mar. 25, 2020).

Barnett, Michael, N., "The New United Nations Politics of Peace: From Juridical Sovereignty to Empirical Sovereignty," 1 *Global Gov.* 79 (1995).

Barnett, Michael N., & Martha Finnemore, "The Politics, Power, and Pathologies of International Organizations," 53 *Int'l Org.* 699 (1999).

Bassioni, Cherif, "A Functional Approach to General Principles of International Law," 11 *Mich. J. Int'l L.* 768 (1990).

Bauer, Michael, & Jorn Ege, "Bureaucratic Autonomy of International Organizations' Secretariats," 23 *J. Eur. Pub. Pol'y.* 1019 (2016).

Baxter, Richard, "Multilateral Treaties As Evidence Of Customary International Law," 41 *Brit Y. B. Int'l L.* 275 (1966).

Benoist, Bruno de, et al., "Conclusions of the Joint WHO/UNICEF/IAEA/IZiNCG Interagency Meeting on Zinc Status Indicators," 28 *Food & Nutrition Bull.* S480 (2007).

Benvenisti, Eyal, & Alon Harel, "Embracing the Tension between National and

International Human Rights Law: The Case for Discordant Parity," 15 *Int'l J. of Constit. L.* 36 (2017).
Benvenisti, Eyal, & George Downs, "The Empire's New Clothes: Political Economy and the Fragmentation of International Law," 60 *Stan. L. Rev.* 595 (2008).
Berner, Katharina, "Authentic Interpretation in Public International Law," 76 *Heidelberg J. Int'l L.* 845 (2016).
Bethlehem, Daniel, "The End of Geography: The Changing Nature of the International System and the Challenge to International Law," 25 *Eur. J. Int'l L.* 9 (2014).
Betts, Richard, "Systems for Peace or Causes of War? Collective Security, Arms Control, and the New Europe," 17 *Int'l Sec.* 5 (1992).
Beveridge, Fiona, "'Going Soft'? Analysing the Contribution of Soft and Hard Measures in EU Gender Law and Policy," *in The Europeanization of Gender Equality Policies.* 28 (Emanuela Lombardo & Maxime Forest eds. 2012).
Bezuijen, Jeanine, "Governance Above the State: Explaining Variation in International Authority," Ph.D. Thesis at Vrije Universiteit Amsterdam (2015), *available at* https://research.vu.nl/ws/portalfiles/portal/42152383 (last visited Mar. 25, 2020).
Bianchi, Andrea, "Assessing the Effectiveness of the UN Security Council's Anti-Terrorism Measures: The Quest for Legitimacy and Cohesion," 17 *Eur. J. Int'l L.* 881 (2006).
Biasiotti, Mariangela, et al., "Legal Informatics and Management of Legislative Documents," Global Centre for ICT in Parliament Working Paper No. 2, Jan. 2008, *available at* pdfs.semanticscholar.org (last visited Mar. 25, 2020).
Blokker, Niels M., "General Introduction," *in Evolutions in the Law of International Organizations.* 8 (Roberto Virzo & Ivan Ingravallo eds. 2015).
Blokker, Niels M., & Ramses A. Wessel, "Editorial: Updating International Organizations," 2 *Int'l Org. L. Rev.* 1 (2005).
Bohloulzadehl, Ghassem, "The Nature of Peace Agreement in International Law," 10 *J. Pol. & L.* 208 (2017).
Bohman, James, "International Regimes and Democratic Governance: Political Equality and Influence in Global Institutions," 75 *Int'l Aff.* 499 (1999).
Boli, John, & George M. Thomas, "World Culture in the World Polity: A Century of International Non-Governmental Organization," 62 *Amer. Soc. Rev.* 171 (1997).
Borlini, Leonardo, "Soft Law, Soft Organizations e Regolamentazione 'Tecnica' di Problemi di Sicurezza Pubblica e Integrità Finanziaria," 27 *Rivista di Diritto Internazionale.* 356 (2017).
Bradford, Anu, "How International Institutions Evolve," 15 *Chic. J. Int'l L.* 47 (2014).
Bradlow, Daniel D., & Claudio Grossman, "Limited Mandates and Intertwined Problems: A New Challenge for the World Bank and the IMF," 17 *Human Rights Q.* 411 (1995).
Brake, Deborah, "When Equality Leaves Everyone Worse Off: The Problem of Leveling down in Equality Law," 46 *Wm. & Mary L. Rev.* 513 (2005).
Bravo, Karen, "CARICOM, the Myth of Sovereignty, and Aspirational Economic Integration," 31 *N.C. J. Int'l L. & Com. Reg.* 145 (2005).
Briggs, Herbert, "Power Politics and International Organization," 39 *Am. J. Int'l L.* 664 (1945).

Brosig, Malte, "Overlap and Interplay Between International Organisations: Theories and Approaches," 8 *S. Af. J. Int'l Aff.* 147 (2011).
Brower, Charles H., Jr., "International Immunities: Some Dissident Views on the Role of Municipal Courts," 41 *Va. J. Int'l L.* 1 (2000).
Brown, Chester, "The Cross-Fertilization of Principles Relating to Procedure and Remedies in the Jurisprudence of International Court and Tribunals," 30 *Loy. L.A. Int'l & Comp. L. Rev.* 219 (2008).
Bryant, Katherine, "Agency and Autonomy in International Organizations: Political Control and the Effectiveness of Multilateral Aid," Paper Presented at the 8th Annual Conference on The Political Economy of International Organization, Sept. 30, 2015, *available at* http://wp.peio.me/wp-content/uploads/PEIO9/102_80_1443656227537_KatherineBryant30092015.pdf (last visited Mar. 25, 2020).
Burns, Kylie, & Terry Hutchinson, "The Impact of 'Empirical Facts' on Legal Scholarship and Legal Research Training," 43 *Law Teacher.* 153 (2009).
Campbell, A.I.L., "The Limits of the Powers of International Organisations," 32 *Int'l & Comp. L.Q.* 523 (1983).
Caserta, Salvatore, & Pola Cebulak, "The Limits of International Adjudication: Authority and Resistance of Regional Economic Courts in Times of Crisis," 14 *Int'l J. L. in Context.* 275 (2018).
Casey, Lee A., "The Case Against the International Criminal Court," 25 *Fordham Int'l L.J.* 840 (2001).
Castañeda, Fabián Augusto Cárdenas, "A Call for Rethinking the Sources of International Law: Soft law and the Other Side of the Coin," 13 *Mex. Ybk Int'l L.* 355 (2013).
Charney, Jonathan I., "Universal International Law," 87 *Am. J. Int'l L.* 529 (1993).
Chattopadhyay, S., "Equity in International Law: Its Growth and Development," 5 *Ga. J. of Int'l & Comp. L.* 382 (1975).
Cheng, Bin, "Custom: The Future of General State Practice in a Divided World," in *The Structure and Process of International Law: Essays in Legal Philosophy Doctrine and Theory.* 532 (R. Macdonald & D. Johnston eds. 1983).
Cheyne, Ilona, "International Tin Council," 39 *Int'l & Comp. L.Q.* 945 (1990).
Cheyne, Ilona, "The International Tin Council," 38 *Int'l & Comp. L.Q.* 417 (1989).
Chilton, Adam S., & Eric A. Posner, "Treaties and Human Rights: The Role of Long-Term Trends," 81 *L. & Contemp. Prob.* 1 (2008).
Ciorciari, John, "The Lawful Scope of Human Rights Criteria in World Bank Credit Decisions: An Interpretive Analysis of the IBRD and IDA Articles of Agreement," 33 *Cornell Int'l L.J.* 331 (2000).
Cockerham, Geoffrey, "The Delegation of Dispute Settlement Authority to Conventional International Governmental Organizations," 44 *Int'l Pol.* 732 (2007).
Cogan, Jacob Katz, "Representation and Power in International Organization: The Operational Constitution and Its Critics," 103 *Am. J. Int'l L.* 209 (2009).
Coicaud, Jean-Marc, "Evaluation, International Organizations, and Global Policy: An Introduction," 7 *Global Pol.* 420 (2016).
Colliver, Douglas, "Winding Up of International Organisation," 2 *J. Int'l Banking L.* 68 (1987).
Cooper, Scott, et al., "Yielding Sovereignty to International Institutions: Bringing System Structure Back In," 10 *Int'l Stud. Rev.* 501 (2008).

Cutler, Claire, "Critical Reflections on the Westphalian Assumptions of International Law and Organization: A Crisis of Legitimacy," 27 *Rev. Int'l Stud.* 133 (2001).
d'Aspremont, Jean, "The Multifaceted Concept of the Autonomy of International Organizations and International Legal Discourse," *in International Organizations and the Idea of Autonomy.* 63 (Richard Collins & Nigel D. White eds. 2011).
d'Aspremont, Jean, & Eric De Brabandere, "The Complementary Faces of Legitimacy In International Law: The Legitimacy of Origin and the Legitimacy of Exercise," 34 *Fordham Int'l L.J.* 190 (2011).
Dahl, Robert A., "Can International Organizations Be Democratic? A Skeptic's View," *in Democracy's Edges.* 19 (Ian Shapiro et al. eds. 1999).
Dahlerup, Drude, "Electoral Gender Quotas: Between Equality of Opportunity and Equality of Result," 43 R*epresentation.* 73 (2007).
Dakhlallah, Farah, "The League of Arab States and Regional Security: Towards an Arab Security Community?," 39 *Brit. J. Middle Eastern Stud.* 393 (2012).
Daugirdas, Kristina, "How and Why International Law Binds International Organizations," 57 *Harv. Int' L.J.* 325 (2016).
de la Rasilla del Moral, Ignacio, "The Unsolved Riddle of International Constitutionalism," 12 *Int'l Comm. L. Rev.* 81 (2010).
de la Serna Galván, Mónica Lourdes, "The Security Council's Interpretation of UN Charter Article 39 (Threat To The Peace): Is the Security Council a legislator For The Entire International Community?" 11 *Mex. Y.B. Int'l L.* 147 (2011).
De Mulder, Richard, et al., "Jurimetrics Please," 1 *Eur. J. L. & Tech.* 135 (2010).
De Schutter, Olivier, "Human Rights and the Rise of International Organizations: The Logic of Sliding Scales in the Law of International Responsibility," *in Accountability for Human Rights Violations by International Organizations.* 55 (Jan Wouters & Eva Brems eds. 2011).
Debevoise, Whitney, "International Financial Institution Governance: The Role of Shareholders," *AIIB Y.B. Int'l L.* 29 (2018).
Dehousse, Renaud, "Delegation of Powers in the European Union: The Need for a Multi-Principals Model," 31 *W. Euro. Pol.* 789 (2008).
Dekker, Ige F., & Ramses A. Wessel, "Governance by International Organizations: Rethinking the Normative Force of International Decisions," *Governance and International Legal Theory.* 215 (Ige F. Dekker & Wouter G. Werner eds. 2004).
Delbrück, Jost, "Prospects for a 'World (Internal) Law'?: Legal Development in a Changing International System," 9 *J. Glob. Leg. Stud.* 401 (2002).
Delbrück, Jost, "The International Obligation to Cooperate–An Empty Shell or a Hard Law Principle of International Law?," *in Coexistence, Cooperation and Solidarity in International Law.* 3 (Holger P. Hestermeyer ed. 2011).
Desierto, Diane, & Colin Gillespie, "A Modern Integrated Paradigm for International Responsibility Arising from Violations of Economic, Social, and Cultural Rights," 3 *Cambridge J. Int'l & Comp. L.* 556 (2014).
Dickens, Nicola, "The Legacy of the Tin Council," 3 *Insolv. L. & Pol'y.* 104 (1987).
Dijkstra, Hylke, "Collusion in International Organizations: How States Benefit from the Authority of Secretariats," 23 *Glob. Gov.* 601 (2017).
Dinstein, Yoram, "Autonomy Regimes and International Law," 56 *Vill. L. Rev.* 437 (2011).
Dixon, William J., "Democracy and the Management of International Conflict," 37 *J. Conflict Res.* 42 (1993).

Douglas-Scott, Sionaidh, "The European Union and Human Rights after the Treaty of Lisbon," 11 *Human Rights L. Review*. 645 (2011).
Dreher, Axel, & Stefan Voigt, "Does Membership in International Organizations Increase Governments' Credibility?: Testing the Effects of Delegating Powers," 39 *J. Comp. Econ*. 326 (2011).
Dupuy, Pierre-Marie, "International Law: Torn Between Coexistence, Cooperation and Globalization," *Eur. J. Int'l L*. 278 (1998).
Durkee, Melissa, "Industry Lobbying and 'Interest Blind' Access Norms at International Organizations," 111 *Am. J. Int'l L*. 119 (2017).
Edwards, Alice, "The Optional Protocol to the Convention Against Torture and the Detention of Refugees," 57 *Int'l & Comp. L.Q*. 789 (2008).
Ege, Jörn, & Michael W. Bauer, "How Financial Resources Affect the Autonomy of International Public Administrations," 8 *Glob. Pol'y*. 75 (2017).
Ellis, David C., "Theorizing International Organizations: The Organizational Turn in International Organization Theory," 1 *J. Int'l Org. Stud*. 11 (2010).
Epstein, David, & Sharyn O'Halloran, "Sovereignty and Delegation in International Organizations," 71 *L & Contemp. Prob. Winter*. 77 (2008).
Esquivel, Valeria, "Power and the Sustainable Development Goals: A Feminist Analysis," 24 *Gender & Dev*. 9 (2016).
Fassbender, Bardo, "The United Nations Charter as Constitution of the International Community," 36 *Colum. J. Transnat'l L*. 529 (1998).
Feaver, Donald, "Fiduciary Principles and International Organizations," *in Fiduciary Duty and the Atmospheric Trust*. 165 (Charles Sampford et al. eds. 2011).
Ferraro, Tristan, "International Humanitarian Law's Applicability to International Organisations Involved in Peace Operations," *in Proceedings of the Bruges Colloquium*. 42 (College of Europe ed., 2012).
Footer, Mary E., "The (Re)Turn to 'Soft Law' in Reconciling the Antinomies in WTO Law," 11 *Melb. J. Int'l Law*. 241 (2010).
Fossum, John-Erik, & Agustin Menendez, "Still Adrift in the Rubicon? The Constitutional Treaty Assessed," *in The European Constitution: The Rubicon Crossed?*. 97 (Erik-Oddvar Eriksen et al. eds. 2005).
Franck, Thomas M., "Legitimacy in the International System," 82 *Am. J. Int'l L*. 705 (1988).
Franck, Thomas M., "The 'Powers of Appreciation': Who Is the Ultimate Guardian of UN Legality?," 86 *Am. J. Int'l L*. 519 (1992).
Fratianni, Michele U., & John C. Pattison, "International Organisations in a World of Regional Trade Agreements: Lessons from Club Theory," 24 *World Econ*. 333 (2001).
Friedmann, Wolfgang, "The Changing Dimensions of International Law," 62 *Colum. L. Rev*. 1147 (1962).
Frowein, Jochen Abr., "The Internal and External Effects of Resolutions by International Organizations," 49 *J. For. Pub. L. & Int'l L*. 778 (1989).
Frowein, Jochen Abr., & Karin Oellers-Frahm, "Advisory Opinions," *in The Statute of the International Court of Justice: A Commentary*. 1605 (Andreas Zimmermann et al. eds. 2012).
Fry, James D., "*Early Security Council Efforts at Nuclear Non-Proliferation Law and Policy: Cooperation Forgotten*," 21 *Transnat'l L. & Contemp. Probs*. 337 (2012).

Fry, James D., "Pluralism, Religion, and the Moral Fairness of International Law," 3 *Oxford J. L & Rel.* 393 (2014).
Fry, James D., "Rights, Functions, and International Legal Personality of International Organizations," 36 *B.U. Int'l L.J.* 221 (2018).
Fry, James D., *Termination of Secretaries General* (forthcoming 2022).
Fry, James D., & Agnes Chong, "Membership in the United Nations," *in Leading Judicial Decisions of the Law of International Organizations.* 138 (Ramses A. Wessel et al. eds. 2015).
Fuentes, Carlos Iván, "The Interpretative Principles of the Vienna Convention on the Law of Treaties and the Pact of San Jose in the Jurisprudence of Inter-American Court of Human Rights," Oct. 1, 2008, *available at* https://ssrn.com/abstract=1276479 (last visited Mar. 25, 2020).
Garcia, David, & Paolo Vacca, "Improving the Efficiency, Democracy and Legitimacy of the EU Institutions Within the Current Treaties: Possibilities and Limits," Union of European Federalists Policy Brief, Feb. 2016, *available at* www.federalists.eu/fileadmin/files_uef/POLICY/Policy_Briefs/2016/Policy_Brief_Improving_efficiency_democracy_and_legitimacy_of_the_EU_institutions_within_the_current_Treaties_20_proposals.pdf (last visited Mar. 25, 2020).
Gartzke, Erik, & Christina Schneider, "Data Sets and Quantitative Research in the Study of Intergovernmental Organizations," *in The Routledge Handbook of International Organization.* 41 (Bob Reinalda ed. 2013).
Gibney, Elizabeth, "Charity Begins at CERN," *Nature*, July, 15, 2014, *available at* www.nature.com/news/charity-begins-at-cern-1.15558 (last visited Mar. 25, 2020).
Gilligan, Michael, "Is There a Broader-Deeper Trade-off in International Multilateral Agreements?," 58 *Int'l Org.* 459 (2004).
Goldenziel, Jill I., "Regulating Human Rights: International Organizations, Flexible Standards, and International Refugee Law," 12 *Chi. J. Int'l L.* 453 (2014).
Golitsyn, Vladimir, "The Role of the International Tribunal for the Law of the Sea in Global Ocean Governance," *in Stress Testing the Law of the Sea: Dispute Resolution, Disasters & Emerging Challenges.* 9 (Stephen Minas & Jordan Diamond eds. 2018).
Goodman, Ryan, & Derek Jinks, "How to Influence States: Socialization and International Human Rights Law," 54 *Duke L.J.* 621 (2005).
Graham, Erin R., "International Organizations as Collective Agents: Fragmentation and the Limits of Principal Control at the World Health Organization," 20 *Eur. J. Int'l Rel.* 366 (2013).
Gray, Christine, "The International Court's Advisory Opinion on the WHO-Egypt Agreement of 1951," 32 *Int'l & Comp. L.Q.* 534 (1983).
Grek, Sotiria, "International Organisations and the Shared Construction of Policy 'Problems': Problematisation and Change in Education Governance in Europe," 9 *Eur. Edu. Res. J.* 396 (2010).
Gruenberg, Justin S., "An Analysis of United Nations Security Council Resolutions: Are All Countries Treated Equally?," 41 *Case W. Res. J. Int'l L.* 513 (2009).
Gutner, Tamar, & Alexander Thompson, "The Politics of IO Performance: A Framework," 5 *Rev. Int'l Org.* 227 (2010).
Guzman, Andrew T., "International Organizations and the Frankenstein Problem," 24 *Eur. J. Int'l L.* 999 (2013).

Guzman, Andrew T., & Jennifer Landsidle, "The Myth of International Delegation," 96 *Cal. L. Rev.* 1693 (2008).

Guzman, Andrew T., & Timothy Meyer, "International Soft Law," 2 *J. Legal Analysis*. 171 (2010).

Hafner-Burton, Emilie M., "Sticks and Stones: Naming and Shaming the Human Rights Enforcement Problem," 62 *Int'l Org.* 689 (2008).

Hafner-Burton, Emilie M., & Alexander H. Montgomery, "Power Positions: International Organizations, Social Networks, and Conflict," 50 *J. Conflict Res.* 3 (2006).

Hafner-Burton, Emilie M., & Kiyoteru Tsutsui, "Human Rights in a Globalizing World: The Paradox of Empty Promises," 110 *Am. J. Socio.* 1373 (2005).

Haftel, Yoram, & Alexander Thompson, "The Independence of International Organizations: Concept and Applications," 50 *J. Conflict Res.* 253 (2006).

Hannum, Hurst, "Rethinking Self-Determination," 34 *Va. J. Int'l L.* 1 (1993).

Harlow, Carol, "Global Administrative Law: The Quest for Principles and Values," 17 *Eur. J. Int'l L.* 187 (2006).

Held, David, "The Changing Structure of International Law: Sovereignty Transformed?," *in The Global Transformations Reader: An Introduction to the Globalization Debate*. 161 (David Held & Anthony McGrew eds. 2003).

Heldt, Eugénia, & Henning Schmidtke, "Measuring the Empowerment of International Organizations: The Evolution of Financial and Staff Capabilities," 8 *Glob. Pol.* 51 (2017).

Helfer, Laurence, "Understanding Change in International Organizations: Globalization and Innovation in the ILO," 59 *Vanderbilt L. Rev.* 649 (2006).

Herren, Madeleine, "Towards a Global History of International Organization," *in Networking the International System: Global Histories of International Organizations*. 1 (Madeleine Herren ed. 2014).

Herz, Steven, "International Organizations in U.S. Courts: Reconsidering the Anachronism of Absolute Immunity," 31 *Suffolk Transnat'l L. Rev.* 471 (2008).

Hexner, Ervin, "Interpretation by Public International Organizations of their Basic Instruments," 53 *Am. J. Int'l L.* 341 (1959).

Hickey, James E., Jr., "The Source of International Legal Personality in the 21st Century," 2 *Hofstra L. & Pol'y*. 1 (1997).

Hill, Jonathon, "Comparative Law, Law Reform and Legal Theory," 9 *Ox. J. Legal Stud.* 101 (1989).

Hoffman, Steven J., & John-Arne Røttingen, "Assessing the Expected Impact of Global Health Treaties: Evidence From 90 Quantitative Evaluations," 105 *Am. J. Pub. Health*. 26 (2014).

Hooghe, Liesbet, & Gary Marks, "The Authority of International Organizations: The Effects of Scope and Scale," UNC Chapel Hill Working Paper, 2013, *available at* www.unc.edu (last visited Mar. 25, 2020).

Hoole, Francis W., "The Appointment of Executive Heads in UN Treaty-Based Organizations," 30 *Int'l Org.* 91 (1976).

Hossain, Kamrul, "The Concept of *Jus Cogens* and the Obligation Under The U.N. Charter," 3 *St. Clara J. Int'l L.* 372 (2005).

Howland, Courtney, "Challenge of Religious Fundamentalism to the Liberty and Equality Rights of Women: An Analysis under the United Nations Charter," 35 *Col. J. Transnat'l L.* 271 (1997).

Hudes, Karen, & Sabine Schlemmer-Schulte, "Accountability in Bretton Woods," 15 *ILSA J. Int'l & Comp. L.* 501 (2009).
Hung, Melissa, "Obstacles to Self-Actualization in Chinese Legal Practice," 48 *Santa Clara L. Rev.* 213 (2008).
Jalusic, Vlasta, "Stretching and Bending the Meanings of Gender in Equality Policies," *in The Discursive Politics of Gender Equality: Stretching, Bending and Policymaking.* 79 (Emanuela Lombardo et al. eds. 2009).
Joachim, Jutta, "Framing Issues and Seizing Opportunities: The UN, NGOs, and Women's Rights," 47 *Int'l Stud. Q.* 247 (2003).
Johnstone, Ian, "Law-Making through the Operational Activities of International Organizations," 40 *Geo. Wash. Int'l L. Rev.* 87 (2009).
Joseph, Jonathan, "Governmentality of What? Populations, States and International Organisations," 23 *Global Soc.* 413 (2009).
Judge, Anthony, "International Organization Networks: A Complementary Perspective," *in International Organizations: A Conceptual Approach.* 381 (Paul Taylor & A.J.R. Groom eds. 1977).
Kabeer, Naila, "Tracking the Gender Politics of the Millennium Development Goals: Struggles for Interpretive Power in the International Development Agenda," 36 *Third World Q.* 377 (2015).
Kammerhofer, Jörg, "International Legal Positivism," *in The Oxford Handbook of the Theory of International Law.* 407 (Anne Orford & Florian Hoffmann eds. 2016).
Kapur, Devesh, & Richard Webb, "Governance-Related Conditionalities of the International Financial Institutions," *G-24 Disc. Paper 6*, United Nations Conference on Trade and Development, Aug. 2000, *available at* www.pdfs.semanticscholar.org (last visited Mar. 25, 2020).
Kauffmann, Celine, "International Regulatory Co-operation: The Role of International Organisations in Fostering Better Rules of Globalisation," OECD, 2016, *available at* www.oecd.org (last visited Mar. 25, 2020).
Keith, Linda Camp, "Constitutional Provisions for Individual Human Rights (1977–1996): Are They More than Mere 'Window Dressing?'," 55 *Pol. Res. Q.* 111 (2002).
Kelsen, Hans, "The Principle of Sovereign Equality of States as a Basis for International Organization," 53 *Yale L.J.* 207 (1944).
Keohane, Robert O., "The Demand for International Regimes," 36 *Int'l Org.* 325 (1982).
Keohane, Robert O., & Joseph S. Nye, Jr., "Transgovernmental Relations and International Organizations," 27 *World Pol.* 39 (1974).
Klabbers, Jan, "Global Governance before the ICJ: Re-reading the *WHA Opinion*," 13 *Max Planck YB UN Law.* 1 (2009).
Klabbers, Jan, "Institutional Ambivalence by Design: Soft Organizations in International Law," 70 *Nordic J. Int'l L.* 403 (2001).
Klabbers, Jan, "On Seyersted and his Common Law of International Organizations," 5 *Int'l Org. L. Rev.* 381 (2008).
Klabbers, Jan, "*Sui Generis?* The European Union as an International Organization," *A Companion to European Union Law and International Law.* 1 (Dennis Patterson & Anna Södersten eds. 2016).
Klabbers, Jan, "The Emergence of Functionalism in International Institutional Law: Colonial Inspirations," 25 *Eur. J. Int'l L.* 645 (2014).

Klabbers, Jan, "The Paradox of International Institutional Law," 5 *Int'l Org. L. Rev.* 151 (2008).
Klabbers, Jan, "The Transformation of International Organizations Law," 26 *Eur. J. Int'l L.* 9 (2015).
Kobbah, Joshua, "African Values and the Human Rights Debate: An African Perspective," 9 *Hum. Rts. Q.* 309 (1987).
Koh, Kyon-Gun, "Reservations to Multilateral Treaties: How International Legal Doctrine Reflects World Vision," 23 *Harv. Int'l. L.J.* 71 (1983).
Koremenos, Barbara, et al., "The Rational Design of International Institutions," 55 *Int'l Org.* 761 (2001).
Koskenniemi, Martti, "The Fate of Public International Law: Between Technique and Politics," 70 *Modern L. Rev.* 1 (2007).
Koskenniemi, Martti, "The Place of Law in Collective Security," 17 *Mich. J. Int'l Law.* 455 (1996).
Koskenniemi, Martti, "The Police in the Temple: Order, Justice and the UN," 6 *Eur. J. Int'l L.* 325 (1995).
Kostakos, Georgios, "Division of Labor Among International Organizations: The Bosnian Experience," 5 *Global Gov.* 461 (1998).
Kratochwil, Friedrich, & John Ruggie, "International Organization: A State of the Art on an Art of the State," 40 *Int'l Org.* 753 (1986).
Krause, Keith, & Oliver Jutersonke, "Peace, Security and Development in Post-Conflict Environments," 36 *Sec. Dialogue.* 447 (2005).
Krook, Mona-Lena, & Jacqui True, "Rethinking the Life Cycles of International Norms: The United Nations and the Global Promotion of Gender Equality," 18 *Eur. J. Int'l Rel.* 103 (2010).
La Porta, Rafael, et al., "Investor Protection and Corporate Valuation," 57 *J. Fin.* 1147 (2002).
La Porta, Rafael, et al., "Law and Finance," 106 *J. Pol. Econ.* 1113 (1998).
Lake, David A., "Authority, Coercion and Power in International Relations," *in Back to Basics: State Power in a Contemporary World.* 55 (Martha Finnemore & Judith Goldstein eds. 2013).
Lall, Ranjit, "Beyond Institutional Design: Explaining the Performance of International Organizations," 71 *Int'l Org.* 245 (2017).
Lauterpacht, Elihu, "The Development of the Law of International Organizations by the Decisions of International Tribunals," 152 *Recueil des Cours.* 377 (1976-IV).
Leiter, Brian, "The Demarcation Problem in Jurisprudence: A New Case for Skepticism," 31 *Oxford J. Leg. Stud.* 663 (2011).
Lempert, David H., "A Dependency in Development Indicator for NGOs and International Organizations," 9 *Glob. Jur.* 1 (2009).
Lenz, Tobias, et al., "Patterns of International Organization: Task Specific vs. General Purpose," RSCAS 2014/128, 2014, *available at* https://papers.ssrn.com/sol3/papers.cfm?abstract_id=2554275 (last visited Mar. 25, 2020).
Li, Weiwei, "Equality and Non-Discrimination Under International Human Rights Law," Nor. Ctr. Human Rights Res. Notes 03/2004 (2004), *available at* www.corteidh.or.cr (last visited Mar. 25, 2020).
Linarelli, John, "The European Bank for Reconstruction and Development: Legal and Policy Issues," 18 *B.C. Int'l & Comp. L. Rev.* 361 (1995).
Lindoso, Vinicius, & Nina Hall, "Assessing the Effectiveness of Multilateral Organizations," Oxford University Blavatnik Sch. of Gov't Working Paper BSG-

WP-2016/013, Apr. 2016, *available at* www.bsg.ox.ac.uk (last visited Mar. 25, 2020).
Lixinski, Lucas, "Treaty Interpretation by the Inter-American Court of Human Rights: Expansionism at the Service of the Unity of International Law," 21 *Eur. J. of Int'l L.* 585 (2010).
Loevinger, Lee, "Jurimetrics: The Methodology of Legal Inquiry," 28 *L. & Contemp. Prob.* 5 (1963).
Loevinger, Lee, "Jurimetrics: The Next Step Forward," 12 *Jurimetrics J.* 3 (1971).
Logano, Wendy, "New World's Producers Set to Announce Trade Group to Rival International Olive Council," *Olive Oil Times*, 2016, *at* www.oilolivetimes.com (last visited Mar. 25, 2020).
Long, David, & Lucian Ashworth, "Working for Peace: The Functional Approach, Functionalism and Beyond," *in New Perspectives on International Functionalism.* 1 (Lucian Ashworth & David Long eds. 1999).
Lough, Benjamin, et al., "Measuring Volunteer Outcomes: Development of the International Volunteer Impacts Survey," Center for Social Development Working Paper No. 09–31 (2009), *available at* https://openscholarship.wustl.edu (last visited Mar. 25, 2020).
Louis, Marieke, & Coline Ruwet, "Representativeness from Within: A Comparison between the ILO and the ISO," 14 *Globalizations.* 535 (2017).
Macedo, Stephen, "What Self-Governing Peoples Owe to One Another: Universalism, Diversity, and the Law of Peoples," 72 *Fordham L. Rev.* 1721 (2004).
MacKay, Fergus, "Universal Rights or a Universe Unto Itself?: Indigenous Peoples' Human Rights and the World Bank's Draft Operational Policy 4.10 on Indigenous Peoples," 17 *Am. U. Int'l L. Rev.* 527 (2002).
Manger, Mark S., & Clint Peinhardt, "Learning and the Precision of International Investment Agreements," 43 *Int'l Interactions.* 920 (2017).
Mansfield, Edward, & Jon Pevehouse, "Democratization and International Organizations," 60 *Int'l Org.* 137 (2006).
Marks, Gary, "International Authority," *at* http://garymarks.web.unc.edu/data/international-authority/ (last visited Mar. 25, 2020).
Marmorstein, Victorial, "World Bank Power to Consider Human Rights Factors in Loan Decisions," 13 *J. Int'l L. & Econ.* 113 (1979).
Marston, Geoffrey, "The Personality of International Organisations in English Law," 2 *Hofstra L. & Pol'y Symp.* 75 (1997).
Martin, Lisa L., & Beth A. Simmons, "International Organizations and Institutions," *in Handbook of International Relations.* 192 (Walter Carlsnaes et al. eds. 2002).
Martinez, Luis Miguel Hinojosa, "The Legislative Role of the Security Council in its Fight Against Terrorism: Legal, Political and Practical Limits," 57 *Int'l & Comp. L.Q.* 333 (2008).
Martinez-Diaz, Leonardo, "Boards of Directors in International Organizations: A Framework for Understanding the Dilemmas of Institutional Design," 4 *Rev. Int'l Orgs.* 383 (2009).
McArthur, John W., & Eric Werker, "Developing Countries and International Organizations," 11 *Rev. Int'l Org.* 155 (2016).
Mearsheimer, John, "The False Promise of International Institutions," 19 *Int'l Sec.* 5 (1995).
Merle, Marcel, "International Non-Governmental Organizations and their Legal Status," 1 *International Associations Statutes Series* appendix 3.5 (1988).

Meron, Theodor, "Judicial Independence and Impartiality in International Criminal Tribunals," 99 *Am. J. Int'l L.* 359 (2005).
Meron, Theodor, "On a Hierarchy of International Human Rights," 80 *Am. J. Int'l Law.* 1 (1986).
Metcalfe, Beverly, "Women, Empowerment and Development in Arab Gulf States: A Critical Appraisal of Governance, Culture and National Human Resource Development (HRD) Frameworks," 14 *H.R. Dev. Int'l.* 131 (2011).
Meuwese, Anne, & Mila Versteeg, "Quantitative Methods for Comparative Constitutional Law?," *in Practice and Theory in Comparative Law.* 230 (Maurice Adams & Jacco Bomhoff eds. 2012).
Meyer, Timothy, "Codifying Custom," 160 *U. Pa. L. Rev.* 995 (2012).
Mitchell, Andrew, "Good Faith in WTO Dispute Settlement," 7 *Melb. J. Int'l L.* 339 (2006).
Mitchell, Sara, "Cooperation in World Politics: The Constraining and Constitutive Effects of International Organizations," Paper Presented at the Conference Intergovernmental Organizations in Action, Mar. 26–27, 2006, *available at* ir.uiowa.edu (last visited Mar. 25, 2020).
Möldner, Mirka, "Responsibility of International Organizations – Introducing the ILC's DARIO," 16 *Max Planck YB UN L.* 281 (2012).
Molos, Dimitrios, "Turning Self-Determination on Its Head," 4 *Phil. & Pub. Iss.* 75 (2014).
Morris, Michael W., et al., "Views From Inside and Outside: Integrating EMIC and ETIC Insights About Culture and Justice Judgment," 24 *Acad. Man. Rev.* 781 (1999).
Moser, Caroline, & Annalise Moser, "Gender Mainstreaming Since Beijing: A Review of Success and Limitations in International Institutions," 13 *Gender & Dev.* 11 (2005).
Mukhopadhyay, Maitrayee, "Mainstreaming Gender or 'Streaming' Gender Away: Feminists Marooned in the Development Business," *in The Palgrave Handbook of Gender and Development* ch. 4 (Wendy Harcourt ed. 2016).
Musto, Ryan, "'A Desire so Close to the Hearts of all Latin Americans': Utopian Ideals and Imperfections Behind Latin America's Nuclear Weapon Free Zone," 37 *Bull. Latin Amer. Res.* 160 (2017).
Nafaa, Hassan, "The Study of Relationships Between the International Organizations and the Member States: A System Approach," 7 *Int'l Interactions.* 337 (2008).
Nagel, Thomas, "The Problem of Global Justice," 33 *Philo. & Pub. Affairs.* 113 (2005).
Nelson, William, "The Changing Meaning of Equality in Twentieth-Century Constitutional Law," 52 *Wash. & Lee L. Rev.* 3 (1995).
Ness, Gayl, & Steven Brechin, "Bridging the Gap: International Organizations as Organizations," 42 *Int'l Org.* 245 (1998).
Neuman, Gerald, "Human Rights and Constitutional Rights: Harmony and Dissonance," 55 *Stan. L. Rev.* 1863 (2003).
Neumayer, Eric, "Do International Human Rights Treaties Improve Respect for Human Rights?" 49 *J. Conflict Prev.* 925 (2005).
Nielson, Daniel L., & Michael J. Tierney, "Delegation to International Organizations: Agency Theory and World Bank Environmental Reform," 57 *Int'l Org.* 241 (2003).

Nielson, Daniel, & Michael Tierney, "Principals and Interests: Common Agency and Multilateral Development Bank Lending," Working Paper, Nov. 2006.

Norris, Pippa, "Confidence in the United Nations: Cosmopolitan and Nationalistic Attitudes," *in The International System, Democracy and Values*. 17 (Yilmaz Esmer & Thorleif Pettersson eds. 2009).

Noyes, John E., "The International Tribunal for the Law of the Sea," 32 *Cornell Int'l L.J.* 109 (1999).

Oberg, Marko, "The Legal Effects of Resolutions of the UN Security Council and General Assembly in the Jurisprudence of the ICJ," 16 *Eur. J. Int'l L.* 879 (2005).

Odermatt, Jed, "The Development of Customary International Law by International Organizations," 66 *Int'l & Comp. L.Q.* 491 (2017).

O'Donoghue, Aoife, "International Constitutionalism and the State," 11 *Int'l J. Const. L.* 1021 (2013).

Olsson, Ilhami Alkan, "Four Competing Approaches to International Soft Law," 58 *Scand. Stud. L.* 177 (2013).

Oosthuizen, Gabriël H., "Playing the Devil's Advocate: The United Nations Security Council Is Unbound by Law," 12 *Leiden J. Int'l L.* 549 (1999).

Palmetear, David, & Petros Mavroidis, "The WTO Legal System: Sources of Law," 92 *Am. J. Int'l L.* 398 (1998).

Parish, Matthew, "An Essay on the Accountability of International Organizations," 7 *Int'l Org. L. Rev.* 277 (2010).

Park, Ki-Gab, & Kyong-Wha Chung, "Responsibility of International Organizations," 2 *Kor. U. L. Rev.* 1 (2007).

Payton, Autumn, "Building a Consensus (Rule) for International Organizations," Paper Prepared for the Annual Conference on The Political Economy of International Organization (2014), *available at* wp.peio.me (last visited Mar. 25, 2020).

Petersmann, Ernst-Ulrich, "Constitutionalism and International Organizations," 17 *Nw. J. Int'l L. & Bus.* 398 (1997).

Petersmann, Ernst-Ulrich, "Time for a United Nations 'Global Compact' for Integrating Human Rights into the Law of Worldwide Organizations: Lessons from European Integration," 13 *Eur. J. Int'l L.* 621 (2002).

Pevehouse, Jon, "Democracy from the Outside-In? International Organizations and Democratization," 56 *Int'l Org.* 515 (2002).

Pevehouse, Jon, et al., "The Correlates of War 2 International Governmental Organizations Data Version 2.0," 21 *Conflict Mgmt. & Peace Sci.* 101 (2004).

Pollack, Mark, "Principal-Agent Analysis and International Delegation: Red Herrings, Theoretical Clarifications and Empirical Disputes," Bruges Political Research Papers No. 2, Feb. 2007, *available at* http://aei.pitt.edu/7344/ (last visited Mar. 25, 2020).

Posner, Eric A., & Alan O. Sykes, "Voting Rules in International Organizations," 15 *Chicago J. Int'l L.* 195 (2014).

Posner, Eric A., & John Yoo, "Judicial Independence in International Tribunals," 93 *Cal. L. Rev.* 1 (2005).

Prosser, Tony, "Constitutions as Communication," 15 *Int'l J. Const. L.* 1039 (2017).

Qin, Julia-Ya, "Judicial Authority in WTO Law: A Commentary on the Appellate Body's Decision in China-Rare Earths," 13 *Chin. J. Int'l L.* 639 (2014).

Rama-Montaldo, Manuel, "International Legal Personality and Implied Powers of International Organizations," 44 *Brit. Y.B. Int'l L.* 111 (1970).

Rapkin, David, et al., "Representation and Governance in International Organizations," 4 *Pol. & Gov.* 77 (2016).

Reinisch, August, "Developing Human Rights and Humanitarian Law Accountability of the Security Council for the Imposition of Economic Sanctions," 95 *Am. J. Int'l L.* 851 (2001).

Ripley, Charles, "The Central American Court of Justice (1907–1918): Rethinking the World's First Court," 19 *Dialogues.* 47 (2018).

Röben, Volker, "The Enforcement Authority of International Institutions," 9 Germ. L. Rev. 1965 (2008); Matthias Ecker-Ehrhardt, "Why Parties Politicise International Institutions: on Globalisation Backlash and Authority Contestation," 21 *Rev. Int'l Pol. Econ.* 1275 (2014).

Rocabert, Jofre, et al., "The Rise of International Parliamentary Institutions? Conceptualization and First Empirical Illustrations," Presentation at the European Consortium for Political Research Joint Sessions in Salamanca, Apr. 10–15, 2014, *available at* www.polsoz.fu-berlin.de (last visited Mar. 25, 2020).

Rockmore, Daniel N., et al., "The Cultural Evolution of National Constitutions," 69 *J. Assoc. Info. Sci. & Tech.* 483 (2017).

Romano, Cesare, "The Proliferation of International Judicial Bodies: The Pieces of the Puzzle," 31 *N.Y.U. J. Int'l L. & Pol.* 709 (1999).

Rose, Carol V., "The 'New' Law and Development Movement in the Post–Cold War Era: A Vietnam Case Study," 32 *L. & Soc. Rev.* 93 (1998).

Rostow, Nicholas, "The World Health Organization, the International Court of Justice, and Nuclear Weapons," 20 *Yale J. Int'l L.* 151 (1995).

Runavot, Marie-Clotilde, "The Intergovernmental Organization and the Institutionalization of International Relations: The Modelling of International Organization at Stake," *in Evolutions in the Law of International Organizations.* 17 (Roberto Virzo & Ivan Ingravallo eds. 2015).

Russett, Bruce, et al., "The Third Leg of the Kantian Tripod for Peace: International Organizations and Militarized Disputes," 52 *Int'l Org.* 441 (1998).

Sabic, Zlatko, "Building Democratic and Responsible Global Governance: The Role of International Parliamentary Institutions," 61 *Parl. Aff.* 267 (2008).

Sambanis, Nicholas, "Short-Term and Long-Term Effects of United Nations Peace Operations," 22 *World Bank Econ. Rev.* 9 (2008).

Sarooshi, Dan, "Some Preliminary Remarks on the Conferral by States of Powers on International Organizations," Jean Monnet Working Paper 4/03 (2003).

Sberro, Stephan, "Culture and International Law," 20 *Eur. J. Int'l L.* 463 (2009).

Schachter, Oscar, "Human Dignity as a Normative Concept," 77 *Am. J. Int'l Law.* 848 (1983).

Schafer, Armin, "Resolving Deadlock: Why International Organizations Introduce Soft Law," 12 *Eur. L.J.* 194 (2006).

Schermers, Henry G., "The Birth and Development of International Institutional Law," 1 *Int'l Org. L. Rev.* 5 (2004).

Schifano, Adrien, "Distribution of Power within International Organizations," 14 *Int'l Org. L. Rev.* 346 (2017).

Schiff, Maurice, & L. Alan Winters, "Regional Cooperation, and the Role of International Organizations and Regional Integration," World Bank Pol. Res.

Working Paper 2872, July 2002, *available at* http://documents.worldbank.org (last visited Mar. 25, 2020).

Schlesinger, Rudolf, "Research on the General Principles of Law Recognized by Civilized Nations," 51 *Am. J. Int'l L.* 734 (1957).

Schliemann, Christian, "Procedural Rules for the Implementation of the OECD Guidelines for Multinational Enterprises – A Public International Law Perspective," 13 *German L.J.* 51 (2012).

Schneider, Christina J., "Weak States and Institutionalized Bargaining Power in International Organizations," 55 *Int'l Stud. Q.* 331 (2011).

Schreuer, Christoph, "Regionalism v. Universalism," 6 *Eur. J. Int'l Law.* 477 (1995).

Schwabach, Aaron, & Arthur Cockfield, "The Role of International Law and Institutions," *in* UNESCO *Encyclopedia of Life Support Systems* (2016), *available at* www.eolss.net (last visited Mar. 25, 2020).

Schwartz, Bryan, & Elliot Leven, "International Organizations: What Makes Them Work?," 30 *Can. Y.B. Int'l L.* 165 (1992).

Schwebel, Stephen, "The International Character of the Secretariat of the United Nations," 30 *Brit. Y.B. Int'l L.* 71 (1953).

Scott, Joanne, & David Trubek, "Mind the Gap: Law and New Approaches to Governance in the European Union," 8 *Eur. L.J.* 1 (2002).

Shaffer, Gregory, et al., "The Extensive (But Fragile) Authority of the WTO Appellate Body," 79 *L & Contemp. Prob.* 237 (2016).

Shaffer, Gregory, & Tom Ginsburg, "The Empirical Turn in International Legal Scholarship," 106 *Am. J. Int'l L.* 1 (2012).

Shaffer, Gregory, & Mark Pollack, "Hard vs. Soft Law: Alternatives, Complements, and Antagonists in International Governance," 94 *Minn. L. Rev.* 706 (2010).

Sen, Gita, & Avanti Mukherjee, "No Empowerment without Rights, No Rights without Politics: Gender-equality, MDGs and thePpost-2015 Development Agenda," 15 *J. Human Dev. & Capabilities.* 188 (2014).

Senit, Carole Anne, et al., "The Representativeness of Global Deliberation: A Critical Assessment of Civil Society Consultations for Sustainable Development," 8 *Glob. Pol.* 62 (2017).

Sihvo, Olena, "Global Constitutionalism and the Idea of Progress," 2018 *Helsinki L. Rev.* 10 (2018).

Simmons, Beth, & Lisa Martin, "International Organizations and Institutions," *in Handbook of International Relations.* 192 (Walter Carlsnaes et al. eds. 2002).

Simoncini, Marta, "Paradigms for EU Law and the Limits of Delegation: The Case of EU Agencies," 9 *Persp. Federalism.* 47 (2017).

Sluiter, Göran, "International Criminal Proceedings and the Protection of Human Rights," 37 *New Eng. L. Rev.* 935 (2003).

Sohn, Louis B., "The Human Rights Law of the Charter," 12 *Tex. Int'l L.J.* 129 (1977).

Spiro, Peter, "Treaties, Executive Agreements, and Constitutional Method," 79 *Tex. L. Rev.* 961 (2001).

Stone, Randall W., "Informal Governance in International Organizations," 8 *Rev. Int'l Org.* 121 (2013).

Strahan, Martin M., "Nuclear Weapons, the World Health Organization, and the International Court of Justice: Should an Advisory Opinion Bring Them Together?," 2 *Tulsa J. Comp. & Int'l L.* 395 (1995).

Symons, Jonathan, "The Legitimation of International Organisations: Examining

the Identity of the Communities that Grant Legitimacy," 37 *Rev. Int'l Stud.* 2557 (2011).
Taft, William, IV, "Self-Defense and the Oil Platforms Decision," 29 *Yale J. Int'l L.* 295 (2004).
Tallberg, Jonas, et al., "The Performance of International Organizations: A Policy Output Approach," 23 *J. Eur. Pub. Pol'y.* 1077 (2016).
Talmon, Stefan, "Responsibility of International Organizations: Does the European Community Require Special Treatment?," *in International Responsibility Today: Essays in Memory of Oscar Schachter Maurizio.* 45 (Maurizio Ragazzi ed. 2005).
Talmon, Stefan, "The Security Council as World Legislature," 99 *Am. J. Int'l L.* 175 (2005).
Terris, Daniel, et al., "Toward a Community of International Judges," 30 *Loy. L.A. Int'l & Comp. L. Rev.* 419 (2008).
Tosato, Gian Luigi, "How to Pursue a More Efficient and Legitimate European Economic Governance," Institute for International Affairs Working Paper 16/03 (2016), *available at* www.iai.it/sites/default/files/iaiwp1603.pdf (last visited Mar. 25, 2020).
Union of International Associations, Types of International Organizations, *at* https://uia.org/archive/types-organization/cc (last visited Mar. 25, 2020).
Union of International Associations, Yearbook of International Organizations, *at* https://uia.org/yearbook (last visited Mar. 25, 2020).
Visoka, Gezim, & John Doyle, "Neo-Functional Peace: The European Union Way of Resolving Conflicts," 54 J. *Comm. Mark. Stud.* 862 (2016).
Voeten, Erik, "International Judicial Independence," *in Interdisciplinary Perspectives on International Law and International Relations: The State of the Art.* 421 (Jeffrey L. Dunoff and Mark A. Pollack eds. 2013).
von Bernstorff, Jochen, "Procedures of Decision-Making and the Role of Law in International Organizations," *in The Exercise of Public Authority by International Institutions.* 777 (Armin von Bogdandy et al. eds. 2010).
von Bogdandy, Armin, "General Principles of International Public Authority: Sketching a Research Field," 9 *German L.J.* 1909 (2008).
von Bogdandy, Armin, "General Principles of International Public Authority: Sketching a Research Field," 9 *Germ. L.J.* 1909 (2008).
von Bogdandy, Armin, & Ingo Venzke, "Beyond Dispute: International Judicial Institutions as Lawmakers," 12 *German L.J.* 979 (2011).
Wahi, Namita, "Human Rights Accountability of the IMF and the World Bank: A Critique of Existing Mechanisms and Articulation of a Theory of Horizontal Accountability," 12 *U.C. Davis J. Int'l L. & Pol'y.* 331 (2006).
Walters, Robert S., "International Organizations and Political Communication: The Use of UNCTAD by Less Developed Countries," 25 *Int'l Org.* 818 (1971).
Waltl, Bernhard, & Florian Matthes, "Towards Measures of Complexity: Applying Structural and Linguistic Metrics to German Laws," Jurix: International Conference on Legal Knowledge and Information Systems in Krakow (2014), *available at* pdfs.semanticscholar.org (last visited Mar. 25, 2020).
Warbrick, Colin, & Ilona Cheyne, "The International Tin Council," 36 *Int'l & Comp. L.Q.* 931 (1987).
Weisburd, Arthur, "Customary International Law: The Problem of Treaties," 21 *Vand. J. Transnat'l L.* 1 (1988).

Weiss, Edith Brown, "The Rise or the Fall of International Law," 69 *Fordham L. Rev.* 345 (2001).
Weissbrodt, David, & Matthew Mason, "Compliance of the United States with International Labor Law," 98 *Minn. L. Rev.* 1842 (2014).
Wessel, Ramses A., "Towards World Legislation? The Exercise of Public Authority by International Institutions," Paper Presented at the Conference World Legislation: Perspectives from International Law, Legal Theory and Political Philosophy, Vrije Universiteit Amsterdam, Nov. 12, 2010, *available at* www.utwente.nl/en/bms/pa/research/wessel/wesselconf6.pdf (last visited Mar. 25, 2020).
Wessel, Ramses A., & Steven Blockmans, "The Legal Status and Influence of Decisions of International Organizations and other Bodies in the European Union," *in The European Union's External Action in Times of Crisis* ch. 7 (Piet Eeckhout & Manuel Lopez-Escudero eds. 2016).
White, Nigel D., "Separate but Connected: Inter-Governmental Organizations and International Law," 5 *Int'l Org. L. Rev.* 175 (2008).
White, Nigel D., & Sorcha MacLeod, "EU Operations and Private Military Contractors: Issues of Corporate and Institutional Responsibility," 19 *Eur. J. Int'l L.* 965 (2008).
Whittle, Devon, "Peacekeeping in Conflict: The Intervention Brigade, Monusco, and the Application of International Humanitarian Law to United Nations Forces," 46 *Geo. J. Int'l L.* 837 (2015).
Wood, Michael, "The International Tribunal for the Law of the Sea and General International Law," 22 *Int'l J. Marine & Coastal L.* 351 (2007).
Woods, Ngaire, et al., "Effective Leadership in International Organizations," World Economic Forum Global Agenda Council on International Governance Systems, Ref. No. 211014, Apr. 2014, *available at* www3.weforum.org/docs/WEF_Effective_Leadership_International_Organizations_report.pdf (last visited Mar. 25, 2020).
Woods, Ngaire, "The Challenge of Good Governance for the IMF and the World Bank Themselves," 28 *World Dev.* 823 (2000).
Woods, Ngaire, & Amrita Narlikar, "Governance and the Limits of Accountability: The WTO, the IMF, and the World Bank," 53 *Int'l Soc. Sci. J.* 170 (2001).
Wouters, Jan, et al., "Managerial Accountability: What Impact on International Organisations' Autonomy?," *Leuven Ctr. for Glob. Gov. Stud.* 43 (2010), *available at* https://ghum.kuleuven.be (last visited Mar. 25, 2020).
Young, Aaron, "Deconstructing International Organization Immunity," 44 *Geo. J. Int'l L.* 311 (2012).
Young, Corey Rayburn, "Constitutional Communication," 96 *B.U. L. Rev.* 303 (2016).
Zamora, Stephen, "Voting in International Economic Organizations," 74 *Am. J. Int'l L.* 566 (1980).
Zimmermann, Susan, "Equality of Women's Economic Status? A Major Bone of Contention in the International Gender Politics Emerging During the Interwar Period," *Int'l Hist. Rev.*, Nov. 15, 2017.
Zurn, Michael, et al., "International Authority and its Politicization," 4 *Int'l Theory.* 69 (2012).

Speeches and reports of international organizations

Abdulqawi Yusuf, ICJ President Speech to the UN General Assembly, Oct. 25, 2018, *available at* www.icj-cij.org/files/press-releases/0/000-20181025-PRE-02-00-EN.pdf (last visited Mar. 25, 2020).

Aydiner-Avsar, Nursel, et al., "East African Community Regional Integration: Trade and Gender Implications," UNCTAD/DITC/2017/2 (2017).

Brownlie, Ian, & Guy S. Goodwin-Gill, Joint Opinion Prepared on the Instruction of Mr. Anders B. Johnsson Secretary General Inter-Parliamentary Union, May 31, 1999, *available at* www.ipu.org (last visited Mar. 25, 2020).

European Commission, "College Sets Out Options for an Efficient EU and its Future Budget," *Weekly Meeting Comm.*, Feb. 14, 2018, *available at* https://ec.europa.eu/commission/news/college-sets-out-options-efficient-eu-and-its-future-budget-2018-feb-14_en (last visited Mar. 25, 2020).

Gaja, Giorgio, "International Law Commission: First Report on the Responsibility of International Organizations of the Special Rapporteur," UN Doc. A/CN.4/532, 2003.

International Law Commission, "Report on the Work of its Fifty-Fifth session: The Responsibility of International Organisations," UN Doc. A/58/10, 2003.

International Law Commission, "Responsibility of International Organizations: Comments and Observations Received from International Organizations," Doc. A/CN.4/545, June 25, 2004.

OECD, "International Regulatory Co-Operation: The Role of International Organizations," GOV/RPC(2016)5/REV1 (2016), *available at* www.oecd.org (last visited Mar. 25, 2020).

United Nations, "International Character of Secretariat," 13 *Dig. Int'l L.* 858 (1968).

Index

Advisory Centre on World Trade Organization Law 25, 92, 174
African Civil Aviation Commission 92, 174, 199
African Court of Human and People's Rights 163–64, 204–6
African Development Bank 174, 206
African Export Import Bank 58, 120–21, 136–37, 147, 149, 174, 200
African Intellectual Property Organization 174, 183, 187
African Telecommunications Union 161, 166, 168–69, 174
African Union 179, 183, 192, 196
African-Asian Rural Development Organization 171, 180–81
Africa Rice Centre 95, 174
Agency for the Prohibition of Nuclear Weapons in Latin America and the Caribbean (OPANAL) 162, 183
American Arbitration Association 157
Andean Community 161, 163, 207
Arab Bank for Economic Development 74, 95, 137–38, 146, 151, 200
Arab League 20, 27, 193
arbitration 143
Asia Pacific Association of Agricultural Research Institutions 55
Asian Development Bank 55, 200
Asian Infrastructure Investment Bank 125–26, 137, 139, 143–50, 200
aspirations 12–13, 77, 92
 aspirational values 81–82, 158, 165
 legitimate aspirations 164

Association of Caribbean States 60, 174, 177
Association of Southeast Asian Nations (ASEAN) 183, 188, 191–96
authority 13, 17–18, 20, 25, 28, 32–40, 58, 74, 81, 92, 106
 external 143, 155
 to recommend 114, 135, 151–56
 unity-of-authority 133–35, 156
Authority of the Common Market 131
autonomy 59, 62–64, 92, 109, 136, 182, 191, 204
 perceived 141

Bank of Central African States 129, 150
Benelux Court of Justice 126, 149, 186–87, 203, 209
Benelux Organization for Intellectual Property 187

Caribbean Community 187, 196, 202
Caribbean Community for Crime and Security 183
Caribbean Development Bank 138–39, 144, 147–48, 150, 153
Caribbean Postal Union 60
Caribbean Telecommunication Union 60
categorization of international organizations 25–29, 32, 87–88, 104
 economic 199
 judicial and non-judicial 28, 69–70, 78, 186, 203, 205

categorization of international
  organizations (*cont.*)
  large and small 122
  limited and general competence 70,
    75–78, 118, 202
  regional and universal 25–27, 67–69,
    101, 118, 169–72, 210
  sectoral 168–69
  technocratic 32, 90, 101
Central American Court of Justice 188,
  205–6
Central American Integration System
  170, 188
change 80, 96, 166
classification
  of international organizations 88,
    101, 156
  of provisions 43
cluster analysis 31, 86
common law of international
  organizations 52, 156, 170,
  213–17, 230
Commonwealth Secretariat 166, 175,
  179, 188–89
communication 13–14, 29–37, 64, 81,
  92, 97, 114–15, 120, 144
  statistical analysis 65
competence 27, 70, 75–77, 198
cooperation 14, 36, 50, 62, 70, 77–78,
  95, 103
  statistical analysis 65
correlation 34, 62–67, 83–85, 120
custom 156, 213

design of constitution 125
dispute resolution 195
diversity of principles 55
division 65, 101

East African Community 179–80,
  193–94
East African Development Bank 116
Eastern and Southern African Trade
  and Development Bank 59, 126,
  147–48, 151, 153
Economic Community of West African
  States 20, 116

effects of constitution 46–48
efficiency 15, 29, 36, 79, 88–89, 95,
  118
eigencentrality 92, 95–96
equality 6, 39, 44, 57, 60, 70–75, 84,
  90, 95, 97, 158–63, 174
  definition 175
  gender equality 179–82, 185
equity 12, 179, 195
Eurasian Economic Community 179
European Bank for Reconstruction and
  Development 59, 131, 135, 139,
  145–47, 153–55
European Chemicals Agency 129,
  148–49
European Court of Human Rights 78,
  172, 186, 204
European Investment Bank 176
European Organisation for
  Astronomical Research in the
  Southern Hemisphere 187
European Organisation for the Safety
  of Air Navigation 187
European Organization for Nuclear
  Research (CERN) 45, 126, 129,
  135, 138, 142, 153–54
European Patent Office 187
European Space Agency 187
European Union (EU) 14, 28–29, 68,
  79–80, 128–29, 165, 171–72, 175,
  181, 185, 192, 197, 227
  Charter of Fundamental Rights of the
    European Union 186
  Treaty on the Functioning of the
    European Union 128, 152

factor analysis 88
funding 40, 45, 51, 138, 169

Gambia River Basin Development
  Organization 184
geographical representation 200–1
Gulf Cooperation Council 27, 160,
  165

harmony 90
human rights 161, 171–74, 227

Index

implied powers 39, 218–19
Indian Ocean Rim Association 60
influence 11, 141–43
Inter-American Development Bank 126, 140, 155
Intergovernmental Committee for the Coordination of Rio de la Plata Basin 20
Intergovernmental Organisation for International Carriage by Rail 124, 174
International Bank for Reconstruction and Development 114
International Bureau of Weights and Measures 174, 187
international character 74, 138
International Civil Aviation Organisation 177
International Court of Justice (ICJ) 39, 143–44, 152, 207, 222–25
  Statute of the International Court of Justice 39
International Criminal Court (ICC) 78, 127, 131, 149, 152–54, 186–87, 203–9
International Development Association 133–34, 166
International Finance Corporation (IFC) 133, 142, 145–46, 153, 174
International Fund for Agricultural Development 174
International Fusion Energy Organization 140
International Investment Bank 130, 154
International Labour Organization (ILO) 124–25, 178, 189
  Charter 141, 148, 151
International Law Commission 19
International Monetary Fund (IMF) 15, 27, 75, 114, 120–21, 130–31, 146, 155, 172, 174
International Organization of Vine and Wine 168
International Rubber Study Group 202
International Seabed Authority 130–31, 200
International Telecommunication Union 49–50, 178, 190, 193
International Tribunal for the Law of the Sea 208
International Union for Protection of New Varieties of Plants 125
Inter-Parliamentary Union 116, 171, 190
Islamic Development Bank 118, 140

joining tree analysis 85
judges 155, 205–9
judicial authority 28
jus cogens 5, 50, 108, 136, 172, 227

Klabbers, Jan 8–9, 76, 88, 176
Kruskal-Wallis test 80–81

Mann-Whitney U test 25, 67, 119
membership 119
methodological criticisms 39

network analysis 35–36, 92, 101
NGOs 142

objectives 27, 131, 164
Organisation for Economic Co-operation and Development (OECD) 2–3, 77, 228
Organisation for Islamic Cooperation 60, 163, 175
  Parliamentary Union 161, 169
Organisation for Security and Cooperation in Europe (OSCE) 205
Organization for the Harmonization of Business Law in Africa 199
Organization of Central American States 169–70, 188

patterns 29, 34
peace 16–17, 35, 59, 96, 187
Permanent Court of Arbitration 203
Permanent Court of International Justice 217–19
politics 140, 153, 167, 181

principles 20, 35, 57, 61, 162
  groups of principles 32, 58, 65, 92, 95, 104–5, 158–60, 210
progress 165–67

recommendation 17–18, 34, 59, 107–9, 113–14, 137, 150
representativeness 18, 54, 64, 77, 96, 197
rule of law 164, 195

scope 26
social science 53
soft law 17, 41, 109, 113, 122, 157
South Asian Association for Regional Cooperation 163, 184
Southern African Development Community 134, 137, 164, 172
sovereignty 59, 183, 191
staff
  appointment 109, 114, 134, 137, 150
  executive staff 25, 36, 61, 69, 78, 82, 95, 97, 101–4, 105, 201, 203
  members 74, 79
  principles 58, 64–65
statistical analysis 20, 77, 80, 118, 231
statistical procedure 25, 31
statistically significant 25, 29, 64–74, 81–84, 118

technocratic 32, 90, 96, 107
time periods 97, 104

United Kingdom Court of Appeal 220
United Nations 2, 20, 27, 52, 59, 64, 173–74, 179, 182, 184–85
  Charter 75, 111–13, 127, 150–51, 163–66, 171, 176, 185, 187–90, 195–96, 201, 204
  Economic and Social Council 110, 149–51
  Educational, Scientific and Cultural Organization (UNESCO) 114, 171, 179, 195, 201
  General Assembly 110–13, 152, 188, 191, 196, 201
  Industrial Development Organization (UNIDO) 166, 184, 193, 201

Vienna Convention on the Law of Treaties 19, 50, 113
voting 39, 130, 199–202

war 97, 187, 196
World Bank 15, 27, 114, 142, 172, 187
World Intellectual Property Organization 45
World Health Organization (WHO) 110, 199, 201, 223–25
World Tourism Organization 168, 172
World Trade Organization (WTO) 50, 74, 114, 123–24, 141, 199

Printed in the USA
CPSIA information can be obtained
at www.ICGtesting.com
JSHW011731231024
72258JS00023B/370

9 781526 182425